EXPLORING THE BOUNDARIES OF INTERNATIONAL CRIMINAL JUSTICE

INTERNATIONAL AND COMPARATIVE CRIMINAL JUSTICE

Series Editors:

Mark Findlay, *Institute of Criminology, University of Sydney, Australia*
Ralph Henham, *Nottingham Law School, Nottingham Trent University, UK*

This series explores the new and rapidly developing field of international and comparative criminal justice and engages with its most important emerging themes and debates. It focuses on three interrelated aspects of scholarship which go to the root of understanding the nature and significance of international criminal justice in the broader context of globalization and global governance. These include: the theoretical and methodological problems posed by the development of international and comparative criminal justice; comparative contextual analysis; the reciprocal relationship between comparative and international criminal justice and contributions which endeavor to build understandings of global justice on foundations of comparative contextual analysis.

Other titles in the series:

The International Criminal Court and National Courts
A Contentious Relationship
Nidal Nabil Jurdi
ISBN 978 1 4094 0916 8

The Limits of Criminal Law
A Comparative Analysis of Approaches to Legal Theorizing
Carl Constantin Lauterwein
ISBN 978 0 7546 7946 2

Domestic Deployment of the Armed Forces
Military Powers, Law and Human Rights
Michael Head and Scott Mann
ISBN 978 0 7546 7346 0

Democracy in the Courts
Lay Participation in European Criminal Justice Systems
Marijke Malsch
ISBN 978 0 7546 7405 4

Exploring the Boundaries of International Criminal Justice

Edited by

RALPH HENHAM
Nottingham Trent University, UK

and

MARK FINDLAY
University of Sydney, Australia

Routledge
Taylor & Francis Group
LONDON AND NEW YORK

First published 2011 by Ashgate Publishing

2 Park Square, Milton Park, Abingdon, Oxon OX14 4RN
711 Third Avenue, New York, NY 10017, USA

Routledge is an imprint of the Taylor & Francis Group, an informa business

First issued in paperback 2016

British Library Cataloguing in Publication Data
Exploring the boundaries of international criminal justice. – (International and comparative criminal justice)
1. Trials. 2. Criminal procedure (International law) 3. Criminal justice, Administration of. 4. Sentences (Criminal procedure)
I. Series II. Henham, Ralph J., 1949– III. Findlay, Mark.
345'.07-dc22

Library of Congress Cataloging-in-Publication Data
Exploring the boundaries of international criminal justice / [edited] by Ralph Henham and Mark Findlay.
p. cm. – (International and comparative criminal justice)
Includes bibliographical references and index.
ISBN 978-0-7546-4979-3 (hardback : alk. paper) – ISBN 978-0-7546-8931-7 (ebook)
1. International criminal courts. I. Henham, Ralph J., 1949– II. Findlay, Mark.
KZ6304.E99 2011
345'.01–dc22

2010048105

ISBN 13: 978-0-7546-4979-3 (hbk)
ISBN 13: 978-1-138-25402-2 (pbk)

Contents

List of Tables

Notes on Contributors

Edwin Bikundo is a Lecturer at the School of Criminology and Criminal Justice at Griffith University in Brisbane, Australia. He has teaching and research interests in International and Comparative Law, International Criminal Law, International Humanitarian Law, the Law of Evidence, Law and State Security, Sociological Jurisprudence and Critical Theory. Before joining the School of Criminology and Criminal Justice at Griffith University he was a member of the Law Faculty at the University of Sydney prior to which he studied at the University of Pune in India, Utrecht University in the Netherlands and at the Kenya School of Law. Edwin also practised law as an Advocate of the High Court of Kenya and taught at the Faculty of Law at the University of Nairobi and the Faculty of Arts at Egerton University both in Kenya. His PhD research was titled: Criminal Aggression: Using or Abusing Legality? It explored the ramifications of criminalising aggression in international law as implying a global monopoly on the legitimate use for force.

Nicholas Dorn is Professor of International Safety and Governance in the School of Law, Erasmus University, Rotterdam. During the preparation of the work published herein he was also Research Fellow in the School of Social Sciences, Cardiff University, which received research coordination funding from the European Commission in connection with the work. His overarching research interest is the (im)balance between public and private interests. His 2008–2009 work covers regulation of licit markets including financial markets, private–public security, strategic intelligence, and cosmopolitan currents. Publications home page: ssrn.com/author=821888.

Mark Findlay holds research chairs in the UK, Singapore and Australia, at the Law schools of the University of Sydney, Singapore Management University and Leeds University. He is an Associate Senior Research Fellow at the Institute of Advanced Legal Studies, University of London. Recently he was instrumental in the establishment of the Worldwide Universities Network International and Comparative Criminal Justice Research Network. Professor Findlay currently publishes on transforming international criminal justice, the globalisation of crime, and crime and global governance.

Caroline Fournet (LLM Lund, DEA Strasbourg, PhD Leicester) is a Senior Lecturer in Law at the University of Exeter (United Kingdom). Her research interests are Public International Law, Human Rights Law, International Humanitarian Law and International Criminal Law, with a particular emphasis on the law of genocide. Her publications include two monographs: *International*

Crimes – Theories, Practice and Evolution, with a foreword by Professor Malcolm N. Shaw QC (London: Cameron May, 2006) and *The Crime of Destruction and The Law of Genocide: Their Impact on Collective Memory* (Ashgate Publishing, 2007).

Ralph Henham is Professor of Criminal Justice at Nottingham Law School, Nottingham Trent University. He has researched and published extensively on the theoretical, comparative and policy-related aspects of sentencing. His current research interests are in the fields of international sentencing, international penal theory, comparative sentencing and penology, and the relationship between sentencing and the legitimacy of trial justice. Recent publications include *Punishment and Process in International Criminal Trials* (2005), *Transforming International Criminal Justice: retributive and restorative justice in the trial process* (2005) and *Beyond Punishment: Achieving International Criminal Justice* (2010) (both with Mark Findlay). He has held visiting positions at the universities of Cambridge, Oxford, Sydney and the European University Institute, Florence.

Ernesto Kiza has worked as project coordinator and consultant on diverse transitional justice projects for the Max Planck Society, the ICTY, and the OSCE. He holds a PhD in economy and social science (Dr. rer. pol.). His major research interests are in mass-victimisation, the criminology of international crimes, irregular migration, contemporary security theorems and practices, and international relations theory. Currently he works as as Project Manager at Haufe Akademie, Germany.

Sylvia Ngane is a doctoral candidate and Graduate Teaching Assistant at the School of Law, University of Leeds, UK. Before her PhD she worked as assistant to the Special Rapporteur on Human Rights Defenders in Africa at the African Commission on Human and Peoples' Rights (Banjul, The Gambia). She also worked as a law clerk at the International Criminal Court and International Criminal Tribunal for the Former Yugoslavia respectively. Sylvia is currently acting as Rapporteur on an international research workshop on the role of the Special Rapporteurs of the Human Rights Council in the development and promotion of international human rights norms. Recent publications include 'Witnesses before the International Criminal Court', *Law and Practice of International Courts and Tribunals* 8 (2009) 431–57.

Holger-C. Rohne graduated in law from the University of Freiburg (Germany) in 2001 and subsequently became a Researcher at the Max Planck Institute for Foreign and International Criminal Law (Freiburg). He has received training in Restorative Justice and mediation and researched and published on mass-victimisation and the interrelation between traditional and modern approaches to conflict resolution. He is particularly interested in identifying the impact of cultural influences on victims' attitudes in war-torn regions and contrasting them with existing domestic and international responsive instruments. Dr. Rohne co-authored the first international comparative survey among war-victims in Asia, Africa and Europe: 'Victims of War' (2006). Following his interest in the Middle East, he conducted an in-depth study on second intifada victims: 'Opferperspektiven im interkulturellen Vergleich', trans. *Victims' perspectives in intercultural comparison* (2007). Further, Dr. Rohne co-edited the volumes *Conflicts and Conflict Resolution in Middle Eastern Societies* (2006) and *Restoring Justice after Large-scale Violent Conflicts* (2008).

Richard Vogler teaches Criminal Law, Comparative Criminal Procedure and Criminology at the University of Sussex. He has worked as a defence advocate in England and in 2005 published his 'World View of Criminal Procedure' and in 2008 'Criminal Procedures in Europe' with Barbara Huber. He has also advised the governments of Ukraine, Georgia, Azerbeijan and Kyrgzstan on criminal justice reform and served as Criminal Justice Assessor for the Council of Europe and Visiting Expert for the US Department of Justice's Rule of Law Program in Eastern Europe and Eurasia.

Clive Walker is Professor of Criminal Justice Studies at the School of Law, University of Leeds. He was Director of the Criminal Justice Studies from 1987 until 2000, and was head of the School between 2000 and 2005. He has written extensively on emergency issues, with many published papers not only in the UK but also in several other countries, especially the USA, where he has been a visiting professor at George Washington University and Stanford University. His books have focused upon terrorism and the law, including *The Anti-Terrorism Legislation*, the second of edition of which was published by Oxford University Press in 2009. In 2003, he was a special adviser to the UK Parliamentary Select Committee which was considering what became the Civil Contingencies Act 2004. A further book commentating upon that legislation, *The Civil Contingencies Act 2004: Risk, Resilience and the Law in the United Kingdom*, was published by Oxford University Press in 2006. He has also been called upon to provide advice to UK and overseas Parliamentary and governmental agencies on terrorism.

Chapter 1
Introduction: Rethinking International Criminal Justice?[1]

International criminal justice is in transition. Fifteen years after the emergence of the modern institutions of international criminal justice through the creation of the International Criminal Tribunal for the former Yugoslavia (ICTY), the 'idea' of international criminal justice has become normalised to an extent that few imagined possible at its inception. Experimentation with international investigation and adjudication techniques and processes during this period has also helped normalise the use of criminal justice tools in international conflict resolution interventions. Yet the system that has been 'normalised' remains a specific and contested vision of what shape international criminal justice (ICJ) can and should take, the nature of its operation and institutions, the impacts it has and interests it should serve – and the direction in which it should evolve.

The formalised dimensions of international criminal justice, especially with the advent of the permanent International Criminal Court (ICC), now predominate as the exemplary if not prevailing face of global justice. With its emphasis on complementarity between international prosecution and domestic process, the ICC has offered out recognition of international criminal justice as a peace and justice paradigm of last resort. In this shadow of complementarity – and growing international donor *fatigue* – we are seeing increasing resort to variations and adaptations in the fact-finding, truth-seeking, norm-enforcing and liability-apportioning processes that implement international criminal norms, especially at the national level. Traditional and localised forms of justice[2] and victim voices[3] are beginning to find a tentative place in the unfurling system of international criminal justice. And there is increasing cross-fertilisation between international and domestic criminal trial processes, other types of fact-finding bodies, expeditionary policing and other international control mechanisms (such as sanctions and peacekeeping). All this is further evidence of the incorporation of international criminal justice into efforts at global governance beyond political hegemony and international agency. New

---

1 Some of the thoughts and reflections in the early and later part of this Introduction are assisted by the work of James Cockayne and the *Re-imagining International Criminal Justice Project* Team of the International and Comparative Criminal Justice Network.

2 See for example the issue of the *International Journal of Transitional Justice* (November 2009) on 'Global and Local Approaches to Transitional Justice'.

3 See for example Mark Findlay, 'Activating a Victim Constituency in International Criminal Justice' (2009) *International Journal of Transitional Justice*, 3: 183–206.

ideologies of international justice are being advanced by NG0s as well as regional state alignments keen to employ justice in peace-making and reconstruction. The ambit of international criminal justice, and its fluid mandate, has exploded well beyond the intentions of the Nuremberg and Tokyo tribunals.

But the mixed evaluations of the International Criminal Court after half a decade of operation and its first prosecutions have challenged the sense of inevitability that had begun to develop around the progressive 'criminalisation' of international security and control strategies. The 'success' of the 'project' of international criminal justice is increasingly doubted, opening up new opportunities and obligations to re-imagine international criminal justice,[4] and to question if there might be other – perhaps even better – ways of achieving some of the objectives that international criminal justice seeks to achieve.[5] An increasing number of courts, practitioners and commentators are questioning whether and how the autonomous development of this 'system' can be justified. They want its understanding limited instrumentally, as part of a broader set of related regulatory tools and strategies for effective global governance, including UN sanctions, peacemaking and peacekeeping, diplomatic fact-finding, international police cooperation and international human rights mechanisms.[6] Some even argue that absolutist notions of 'justice' should consequently give way to larger regulatory objectives – such as the pursuit of peace, or the protection of human rights. Other commentators embrace the widest aspirations for international criminal justice and argue for new conceptions and forms of trial (and alternative) justice to take global governance into a new and exciting age of pluralist regulation opportunity.[7] How are these two divergent positions to be reconciled in any cohesive or consistent development for international criminal justice?

Not co-incidentally in international relations literature and policy commentary, there are strident criticisms of the selective and apparently symbolic nature of the system as it actually operates. Attention is increasingly drawn to the gap between the rhetoric of its most ardent backers and the lived-experience of victims of injustice. The growth in victim opinion survey research in recent times gives

4 See Mirjan Damaška, 'What is the Point of International Criminal Justice?' (2008) *Chicago Kent Law Review*, 83(1): 329.

5 Mark Findlay and Ralph Henham, *Transforming International Criminal Justice: Retributive and Restorative Justice in the Trial Process* (Cullompton: Willan Publishing, 2005); Mark Findlay and Ralph Henham, *Beyond Punishment: Achieving International Criminal Justice* (Basingstoke: Palgrave MacMillan, 2010).

6 See for example James Cockayne, 'Unintended Justice: The UN Security Council and International Criminal Governance', in Adam Crawford, ed., *International and Comparative Criminal Justice and Urban Governance: Convergence and Divergence in Global, National and Local Settings* (Cambridge University Press, forthcoming); and Mark Findlay, *Governing through Globalised Crime: Futures for International Criminal Justice* (Cullompton: Willan Publishing, 2008).

7 See Mark Findlay, *Crisis What Crisis: Legal Regulation in New Visions of Global Risk and Security* (London: Taylor & Francis, forthcoming).

empirical substance to our worries for legitimacy that the absence of any true victim constituency plaguing international criminal justice will present. This gap fuels arguments that there are incompatibilities between the pursuit of 'peace' and the rendering of 'justice'. There are associated reservations about the expanding divide between the massive investment of political, human and financial capital in adversarial trial processes and the lack of attention to other aspects that one might expect of a true 'system' of international criminal justice: effective and rights-respecting policing and enforcement systems, effective detention arrangements, and alternative remedial avenues for those to whom the system of 'high' international criminal justice is not accessible.

As a result, there is developing interest among policy-makers and academic commentators alike in generating credible concepts of 'effectiveness' in transitional and international criminal justice.[8] This evaluation requires an associated reflection on a more appropriate framework for international criminal justice service delivery particularly in its trial forms so essential for declaratory influence and due process advancement.[9] But that trend, which has so far tended to focus on efforts to developing empirical methodologies for measuring the impacts of justice on local perceptions and broader justice outcomes, has not yet been accompanied by a critical examination of what *kind* of outcomes we do, can and should expect international criminal justice to deliver. How should we assess the adequacy of international criminal justice? What contribution do we expect it to make to larger projects of global governance and the maintenance of public order? What have been the strengths and weaknesses of the system of international criminal justice, as it has developed recently?

Why the Need to Re-imagine International Criminal Justice

After a decade and a half of the latest phase of international criminal justice, scholars are no closer to a multi-disciplined appreciation of this regulatory frame. There are many reasons for this. We have identified:

- competition over what analytical form predominates as the authorised language of commentary and critique;
- an unhealthy attachment of research and scholarship to the political mission of international criminal justice; as a result
- the failing of scholars and researchers to dig deep into some of the metaphors and symbols on which international criminal justice is based;
- a western-centric approach to the analysis of aims and functions, particularly where connections such as rights and justice are asserted;

8 See for example the forthcoming issue of the *International Journal of Transitional Justice* on measuring effectiveness in transitional justice.

9 Findlay and Henham (2010), chaps 5, 6 and 7.

- assumptions about the constitutional legality informing international criminal justice which are self-serving particularly to international customary law;
- fundamental disjunctures over what international criminal justice should be doing and for whom it operates;
- an essential incapacity to question the relevance of international criminal justice for global governance.

This is to name but a few.

Against these realisations is the reality that the legal, operational, policy, political and normative ramifications of whatever international criminal justice might be are moving along paths of discourse and development that rarely intersect. Lawyers, politicians, diplomats, policy analysts, NGO officials and scholarly commentators are not talking the same language, and seem little concerned by the divergence.

That could be said to be so until the ICC became an active (if a somewhat dysfunctional) institution, and its first trial revealed just how endangered is the global legitimacy of international criminal justice for victim communities in particular. If truth and reconciliation commissions, war crimes tribunals, transnational crime conventions, mutual assistance policing and victim reparation and state reconstruction are somehow to come together into a credible global justice form then much more needs to be done in analysing the expectations and responses to the aims of ICJ. This challenge is more relevant when international criminal justice misses out on the 'givens' that underpin most credible domestic criminal justice traditions:

- established constitutional authority
- resilient legislative frameworks
- well-developed legal jurisprudence
- coherent procedural entity
- profitable and independent professionals
- robust institutions and agencies
- complementary collateral regulatory paradigms

The question that therefore presents itself is 'where-to International Criminal Justice?'

A precondition for any coalescence of understanding between 'those who do' and 'those who critique' in justice circles is the development of compatible language and a resultant conversation between the stakeholders in each sector which values the other, and respects different forms of analysis. This collection, we hope, will advance the relevance of research-based policy and broaden the common discourse around crucial theoretical and operational challenges for international criminal justice

Scholarly Imaginings?

In an essay[10] some years back which looked at the foundations of international criminal justice we identified two motivating paradigms:

- human rights concerns
- political pragmatism

These influences are not mutually exclusive or even distinct. In fact, to suggest them as separate motivations was itself a little misleading. Dialectic analysis of justice forms is common in socio-legal studies. However, it tends to distract the understanding of justice complexities by over-emphasising either their normative representations or their political utility. In addition, this type of analysis alienates practitioners and professionals by divesting justice of its potentialities as well as recognising its limitations.

Simplistic as the distinction may be it does suggest two of the primary directions of scholarship concerning international criminal justice in the last decade. The *human rights school* grows from a mix of international humanitarian law and restorative justice foundations and has spawned much of the commentary on international criminal law and on transitional justice. So it could be said that the human rights commentators and analysts have serviced major NGO peace and conflict resolution initiatives. The influence of this perspective in arguing a jurisprudence of international criminal law could be seen as no less influential than the judicial narrative emerging from the war crimes tribunals and associated legal commentary. Rights discourse has offered much more than procedural technologies as arguing international criminal law.

The *political pragmatists* are the expertise behind the institutional explosion in ICJ. It would be wrong to see this influence as limited to formal institutionalisation. Obviously the expert panels that supported the international law commission and helped draft and ground the UN internatinal criminal justice entities were critical to their legitimacy. But also, parallel justice processes like truth commissions and juridical hybrids required the legitimation of supportive scholarship.

Whatever path taken, those scholars with 'clout' in a policy and operational sense were closely aligned with the mechanisms and emerging traditions which they reviewed. It is not surprising then that those of us who were critical of this synergy challenged the analytical independence and integrity of much of the resultant literature. Influence came at a price.

10 Mark Findlay and Clare Mclean, 'Emerging International Criminal Justice', (2007) *Current Issues in Criminal Justice* 18/3: 457–80.

International Criminal Justice – All Things to All Men?

For those researchers and scholars on the inside, or those throwing rocks at the window, it was rare to see an essential reflection on the nature and form of international criminal justice as a problematic entity of global governance. What is international criminal justice? Like international criminal law, does it yet merit investigation as a discreet regulatory system or does it remain not much more than an off-shoot of other legal or administrative systems, themselves exhibiting suspect independence from bi-lateral or state-accorded authority?

To start with what is *international* about it? Just because the institutions of global justice exercise jurisdiction beyond the state or the region, and claim to deal with mass victimisation through new laws or merged traditions, internationalism evades many of the features of ICJ. The initial activity of the ICC, for instance, has branded it more an African criminal court rather than being concerned in any proportionate or incremental way with the most significant global harms. It is logical that the internationalism of the formal institutions of ICJ in particular will be easily impugned as they rely so essentially on the constitutional authority of a deeply sectarian Security Council.

Are the major global crimes the primary concerns of ICJ? The general public would no doubt be amazed that the ICC and the international tribunals do not prosecute terrorism, drug-trafficking, money-laundering, transnational organised crime or international corruption. Even if we incorporate the principal international conventions against transnational crime within the remit of ICJ, economic and environmental crimes most likely to harm most of us don't get much attention.

And what of its justice? The victors in post-military conflict are never before the international criminal tribunals. At best the ICC can only deal selectively with a dozen or so perpetrators annually. Truth and reconciliation does not give retribution to the victim. Mass localised justice endangers the rights of victim witnesses left behind after their testimony is heard. Where is the justice in any of that?

Managing Unhelpful Dichotomies

The distinction between formal and informal international criminal justice which is at the heart of the transitional justice movement presents a danger not only for justice service delivery. If most media and political interest is focused on the international criminal justice symbolic *top end*, while the majority of justice that victim communities access, remains informal, under-resourced and unreported, accountability and procedural fairness are the first to be sacrificed.

Second-class justice for the masses, without the benefit of professional intervention or legal regulation, is the reality of international criminal justice on the ground. This is a consequence of legal separatism, the suspicions of the restorative movement, profound misunderstandings of victim expectations, the politicisation of the international criminal trial and the failure to recognise humanity rather than hegemony as the natural constituency of international criminal justice. We have argued in several contexts that transformation of global justice and the international criminal trial in particular holds out much to bridge the two tiers of justice and thereby enhance victim-based legitimacy.

But for legal purists like Damaška the fault is not with justice dichotomies but unrealistic and expansive aims for international criminal justice which should embrace the frameworks of adversarial retributivism, and eschew peace and conflict resolution. What this argument fails to understand is that the eventual legitimacy of international criminal justice rests on much more than show trials. Victims worlds-away from The Hague will not for long accept the declaratory dimension of the ICC as enough to merit their confidence and commitment.

Dichotomies plague policy and operational discourse in similar measure. The criminal justice tools of the UN are wedged by an artificial but irreconcilable peace and justice divide. It is here that scholarly critique and applied research can reveal pathways to reconciliation and a more effective regulatory pluralism.

Need for Dialogue – Talking the Same Language?

To achieve the type of regulatory pluralism wherein the potential of international criminal justice and its relevance are maximised sectoral stakeholders need to start talking the same language. We predict that as the risk/security focus of globalisation moves away from the allegory of global terror and toward risks we will all suffer (global warming, health pandemics and economic collapse) real and resounding questions will be asked of regulatory and control mechanisms such as criminal justice. The answers will be tested against a cost benefit critique which crime control has never faced in past neo-liberal neo-conservative decades. It will be then that those who make their living from planning, authorising, practising or modelling and evaluating criminal justice will be of necessity forced to seek similar languages of justification and relevance.

Adding a Critical Dimension

Criminal justice, international even more than domestic, in the wake of the recent global economic collapse is being called to account as an independent regulatory strategy. Against most regulatory process and outcome measures the formal justice institutions in particular, have been exposed as failures in terms of cost/benefit, and even their own limited control or prevention aspirations. Policing will not be justified in terms of perception management. Courts and trials will need to achieve more than symbolic presence. Punishment will no longer benefit from an untested confidence in deterrence. Disillusionment with retribution as reason enough to punish is already upon us. Politicians who have relied on governing through crime will as quickly turn on criminal justice when its regulatory potency is called into account by constituencies more universally exposed to risk and requiring security. Policy makers and practitioners will be forced to incorporate rather than ignore critical scholarship if they are to weather the disenchantment of political hegemony and civil society.

The challenge for scholars and researchers will be to avoid the compromise caused from panic as research funding dries up, or the rejection of irrelevance if they cannot provide new models and not just old critiques of the justice processes in decline. For this outcome to be minimised, practitioners as well as researchers face the prospect of letting go their traditional trappings of status, and to re-skill and reinvent in a new age of regulatory pluralism and disciplinary cross-over. Old enemies and old allies will need to be engaged with in a context where critical scholarship is repositioned and policy promotion is far more scrutinised.

Resolving Conflicts of Interest

The Lubanga trial has exposed conflicts of interest for practitioners and policy makers which scholars and practitioners should have seen coming. A very few critics with an eye on the need to transform international criminal justice to meet its expansive aims have been forewarning these outcomes from the inception of the court and the growing prominence of the show trial as the declaration of global justice. But practitioners were convinced that their conventional ways of doing business, without the benefit of academic augmentation would see them through. They were wrong. And now lawyers, judges, administrators and policy-makers are scratching their heads and looking for answers, many contained in the literature with which they are totally unfamiliar. A distinct challenge for scholars and researchers is to make accessible that literature and to enrich it with the practical outcomes and applications of critical theorising.

An example of these solutions lies in our arguments for trial transformation. Put simply, we say that victim communities are the rightful constituency for international criminal justice. That being the case legitimate victim expectations should inform the procedures and outcomes of international criminal trials, remaining central as they are to the political imagining of global justice. Surveys show that these interests expect retributive and restorative justice and that there is no acceptance of two separate tiers of justice to service these needs. In fact, the due process considerations of trial procedure should not be left to those very few victims attaining witness status. Having argued that there is nothing normatively and procedurally intractable about the international criminal trial which bars inclusion of restorative perspectives, the challenge was then to show how it would work. How would fact and evidence sit with truth and history? How would the role of the juridical professional change to accommodate and facilitate this transition? How would competing victim expectations be reconciled? Could responsibility replace liability as a legitimate trial outcome?

In Lubanga the independent prosecutor clashed with his NGO and Security Council allies, as well as his judicial masters and his victim witness 'clients'. More than this, the prosecutor misconceived the role and representation of victim interests in the international criminal trial. Answers to this misconception and the conflicts of interest which generated them will not be found in conventional domestic trial practice. Scholars and researchers need to devise and communicate some new options for justice delivery to meet these challenges within the parameters of the Rome statute expanded.

Moving from Metaphor

Formal international criminal justice is largely metaphoric. As suggested above there will never be enough investigations, prosecutions, trials and sanctions to achieve even a legalist interpretation of the practical aims for ICJ. Scholars and researchers need to reveal the nature and capacity of metaphor and not simply critique its impotence or limited reach. Further than this, legal scholars need to break away from the normative and procedural hermeneutics of their discipline and question conventions such as an individual liability model, or the possibility of a homogeneous world criminal procedure.

Metaphor has an important place in justice models of any form. The didactic mission of criminal justice has important governance credentials. But metaphor must not mask morphology. International criminal justice is in the business of changing the world for the better and not just making it look and sound that way.

An important capacity of the scholar and researcher is to reveal the utility of metaphor as an instrument for change rather than as a technique for representing change in the face of regression.

Offering Cross-Over

As a consequence of being paid to be critical most scholars and researchers can provide the grease which oils the different cogs in the justice process, international or otherwise. It is difficult to distance one's approach to an institution, agency or process when it is your daily occupation. This is never more so than when issues like professional reputation or operational impact depend on a narrow range of internally constructed and evaluated outcomes (for example, prosecution and conviction rates). The particular frames of reference governing stakeholder positioning also constrain the capacity for cross-over sector to sector, and makes unlikely any truly multi-disciplinary engagement.

Scholars and researchers are pressured for just such engagement on a daily basis. Even academic lawyers, who have not been known for their adaptability or inter-disciplinary tolerance, are now defined in the better law schools as comparativists. Academic environments like this must more regularly and routinely provide a safe haven for justice stakeholders to mix and talk beyond their comfort zones. In the academic environment where controversy and critique are healthy and not heretic, policy should converge with practice and be ready to see how it is done in foreign contexts.

Facing the Challenges of Relevance and Legitimacy

Stakeholders working in otherwise self-contained institutional and process worlds, readily believe that relevance and consequent legitimacy can only be effectively determined within the normative and applied contexts of their worlds. Victim dissatisfaction and disillusionment with international criminal justice critically confound that confidence.

For the purposes of future debate we propose this contestable relationship between legitimacy and relevance:

- the constituency rather than the constitution of international criminal justice needs to determine measures of relevance and resultant legitimacy;
- victims are that constituency for global justice and as such legitimate victim interests become the yardstick of relevance. Satisfaction of those interests will generate victim-centred legitimacy;
- the satisfaction of victim interests is best achieved cross-sectorally.

International criminal justice will grow as its relevance and legitimacy grow. ICJ will expand as a governance tool and will do so in order to ensure the other regulatory components within global governance are accountable to legitimate victim interests. This accountability function will become more important than any particular sectoral aspirations that exist for it.

This Collection

In the spirit of *rethink*, the aim of this collection is to identify some critical themes for developing our understanding of international criminal justice, and appreciating its significance for governance and peace-making in post-conflict and transitional societies. Both theory and research in international criminal justice have moved on at a rapid pace and, particularly with the emergence of the ICC, academics and practitioners has been forced to confront difficult issues of legitimacy in relation to international criminal justice and its future role. The urgency of this work has recently been re-enforced by the procedural difficulties which the ICC has encountered as it struggles to establish its credentials as an effective force for governance in international criminal justice and the protection of human rights.

One thing is clear: international criminal justice can no longer be analysed in any meaningful sense from a purely 'rule of law' perspective, more particularly since the weakening of state sovereignty has increased exponentially during the later modern period. The globalisation of crime and questions of justice are now irrevocably inter-twinned with those of international politics and western hegemony.[11] This is sharply evidenced by the disproportionate focus on certain forms of 'criminality' that is said to challenge western civilisation, and is thereby almost inevitably is associated with ideological confrontation and the need for regime change. An underlying critique is that the pre-occupation of western liberal democracies with the so-called risk/security nexus following 9/11 is driven by the need to defend economic as much as ideological interests.[12]

In truth, moral pluralism and the relativity of justice mean that the claims of international criminal justice to enforce the foundational universal values of international humanitarian law through international trial justice ring hollow. Instead, international criminal justice stands apart from effective forms of accountability and is in danger of becoming the tool of ideological imperialism, driven by the partisan need to secure economic advantage and supremacy in a world of increasing population and diminishing resources.[13] In this new penal environment, international criminal justice is secularised and presented as an impartial framework for delivering outcomes with universal legitimacy.

We profoundly reject the negative implications of this vision for the future of international criminal justice. As the title of this volume suggests, we believe there is scope for developing a more positive role for international criminal justice in global governance. In *Transforming International Criminal Justice* (2005), we argued that discretionary decision-making in international trials should be seen as the appropriate context for developing more integrated and inclusive forms of international criminal justice. We suggested that the perceived legitimacy of international punishment will be enhanced by making trial justice more inclusive to victims and the relative demands for justice in post-conflict societies. We gave substance to these aspirations in *Beyond Punishment: Achieving International Criminal Justice* (2010), focusing on how international trials can engage more effectively with dialogues and representations of justice from within victim communities. We argued that the integration of restorative forms of justice within the international criminal trial requires structures which engage, resolve and produce strategies for particular communities of justice.

Rather than reflecting the hegemony of retributive justice, international trial process should adopt a problem-solving approach aimed at producing what is collectively accepted as a morally legitimate and therefore just outcome that will contribute to peace and reconciliation. Accordingly, we also see a clear role for international trial justice as a crucial element of transitional justice, capable of infusing its structures with humanitarian values linked firmly to communities of interest rather than those of hegemony. In this, we envisage international

11 Mark Findlay, *The Globalisation of Crime: Understanding transitional relationships in context* (Cambridge University Press, 1999).

12 Findlay, (2008).

13 Findlay, (forthcoming).

trial justice as capable of making a substantial contribution towards developing criminal justice as a form of international governance.

The interrelationship of international trial outcomes with elements for achieving transitional justice will depend on the relevant context and its transitional needs. It cannot be assumed that these will correspond to any pre-conceived notions of governance, or the role and structures needed to deliver criminal justice (Teitel: 2000). These require deconstruction within the contexts which inform the reasons for conflict and the phenomenology of justice. Such an imperative is reflected in our initial focus on addressing problems of theory and methodology in international criminal justice.

Specific Research Challenges for International Criminal Justice

What are the central issues with which our contributors grapple? Some of the following research questions provide a common frame of reference for discussion amongst a broad academic, policy research and practitioner community, that are addressed in the chapters we offer. These questions seek to provide detailed answers to the questions 'Where has international criminal justice come from? And where is it going?'

1. *Historical development*: How has international criminal justice emerged over the last decade and a half in the forms it currently takes? What schools of thought, institutional interests or influential actors have given it its current shape? How have these stakeholders and influences steered, strengthened and on the other-hand limited the evolution of international criminal justice?
2. *Balancing interests*: Whose interests does contemporary international criminal justice serve? Victims? Perpetrators? Defendants? Lawyers? States? Corporations? Which institutional, industrial and disciplinary interests does it currently serve, and how? What conflicts of interest have plagued recent international criminal justice processes and how should these be addressed? Is there a particular balance struck at different levels, and if so, is it a just balance? Who decides what that balance will be?
3. *Different regulatory faces*: Is there a 'system' there at all? Or is international criminal justice a historically contingent collection of overlapping but largely autonomous policing, trial, investigation and control instruments and regulatory enterprises? Is that 'autonomy' a problem – and if so, for whom – or is it inherent in the nature of criminal investigation and trial process? Should these various tools and strategies be better connected? If so, how will that come to pass? To what extent is 'independence' a two-edged sword for the formal institutions of international criminal justice?
4. *Authority, legitimacy and accountability*: What are the main determinants of the forms that international criminal justice is currently

delivered through? How have they developed, and why have they developed that way? Are there particular conceptual, structural – or even personal – blockages (for example, sovereignty, judicial independence, legal pluralism, punishment vs prevention) that have prevented them developing in other directions? Is the separation of adversarial and restorative justice processes necessary or helpful? In attempting to achieve 'trial based' justice has there developed a problematic association between prosecutorial agencies and NGOs in the field? How have victim witnesses been affected as a result? How is the ongoing legitimacy of international criminal justice influenced by the legitimate interests, expectations and opinions of victim communities?

5. *Global governance and regulatory pluralism*: How do the various existing manifestations of international criminal cooperation and justice connect to other existing regulatory strategies designed to deal with security and public order – at the local, national, regional and international level? Are there disconnects or blockages, and if so, what are their sources (personal, institutional, historical, political, doctrinal ...)? Are there alternative strategies emerging – for example, through domestication and hybridisation of international criminal justice, adaptation of international criminal norms into private law (for example, through the US Alien Tort Claims Act), blending of restorative and retributive justice models, or accommodation of 'traditional' justice norms and institutions)?
6. *Conceptual and institutional dichotomies*: Why have certain critical dichotomies emerged around the aims of international criminal justice and the institutions and processes of its delivery, pitting 'peace' against 'justice', 'formal' against 'informal' justice, 'modern' against 'traditional', 'global' against 'local', 'fact' against 'truth', and 'criminal trial' against 'reconciliation' processes? Do these dichotomies demonstrate essential divisions in the political authority, cultural constituencies, and stakeholders of international criminal justice and other regulatory processes? Or are these divisions constructed, and if so, to what purpose?
7. *New challenges*: How will existing international criminal justice delivery models be reshaped and retooled to deal with new risks, threats and transgressions that international actors may consider worthy of regulation through international criminal justice strategies, specifically: (1) lower-level violations of international humanitarian law and human rights (that is, those not rising to the levels now prosecuted before international and internationalised courts and tribunals); (2) transnational organised crime; (3) environmental crimes; and (4) white-collar, financial and corporate crime? To what extent can criminal justice models – with their focus on (1) independent determinations of 'facts' based on 'evidence', (2) characterisations of that fact-base as compliant or non-compliant with legal standards, and (3) apportionment of liability (individual and collective) – accommodate the 'risk prevention' and/or 'collective responsibility' models of governance that may be used to deal with some of these security and public-order threats?

Contributions

This collection therefore highlights the potential for transforming international criminal justice and emphasises the importance of utilising appropriate methodologies for its understanding and evaluation. The contributions are divided into two parts.

The first part begins by addressing the critical problem of accountability in international criminal justice, especially through exploring the implicit tensions that exist between the positivistic nature of its universal legal norms and the social contexts of international trial justice delivery. The section also confronts the paradox of individual and collective accountability in international trials and explores the underlying hegemonic forces which help to shape the contours of liability. It also addresses problems of theory and method in the comparative analysis of international criminal justice, particularly in terms of establishing victims' expectations, and situating this debate in the broader context of promoting legitimate outcomes for international criminal justice. This discourse includes some reflections on particular strategies for achieving post-conflict justice, including truth and reconciliation and hybridised approaches, focusing particularly on questions of victimisation and collective accountability. The section concludes by analysing the configuration of procedural norms in international criminal trials and the rationality and forces that determine it.

Caroline Fournet's contribution draws attention to the apparent paradox of reconciling legal and social concepts of accountability in the context of international criminal trials. In acknowledging that international criminal justice has struggled to come to terms with the idea of delivering trial outcomes that engage with the aspirations and expectations of victim communities, Fournet argues that the preventative potential of legal accountability remains dangerously underdeveloped and that non-legal goals such as healing, restoration and reconciliation need to be more effectively combined to provide contextualised forms of legal accountability. She suggests that the already fragile universal force of legal accountability could be fatally undermined if international criminal justice fails to move accountability beyond the purely legal sphere.

Fournet observes how the extinction of offences through the granting of amnesties, and the obfuscation of the 'truth' they perpetuate, generates a general mistrust towards international trials and sentencing and sustains an ideology of revenge and vengeance. These negative effects are compounded by the questionable morality of granting amnesty for international crimes and massive human rights violations.

However, Fournet's most telling observation concerns the role of trial justice in the so-called judicialisation of history and her assertion that the interpretative monopoly of historians over such events appears to be over. The failure of alternative mechanisms, such as TRCs, to assert a definitive version of the 'truth', even if it is flawed, is a significant omission, given its undoubted therapeutic and cathartic effects for victims in post-conflict states. She argues that the kind of 'truth' manufactured by TRCs really acts to complement the individualised truth of international trials, so corresponding to a vision of justice based on national reconciliation, rather than penalisation. The important point is the notion that the judicialisation of history ultimately reinvents the concept of justice by proclaiming 'truth' as a new form of justice. It is the legitimacy of this 'truth' which lies at the crux of achieving international criminal justice (Findlay and Henham: 2009/10).

Fournet correctly asserts that forms of accountability falling short of prosecution and legal accountability have all so far failed the universal goals of prevention and deterrence because they have effectively ignored the justice needs of victims and communities in post-conflict states. She argues that this potentially catastrophic state of affairs must be countered by asserting the expressive capacity of international punishment to reach beyond retributive justice to engage with the universal commitment towards achieving international peace and security.

Fournet also draws attention to the vital contribution international trial justice can make in establishing the collective memory of international crimes and their prevention, in addition to their individual cathartic and therapeutic effects. She rightly lauds the advances made by the ICC 'towards a formal recognition of the dignity and the rights of victims', especially their rights of participation, although critics suggest that the relevant provisions of the ICC Statute are more rhetorical than real, since the decision-making power of victims is limited by its ideological and normative framework (Findlay and Henham: 2010). Consequently, although the integrative capacity of legal accountability is currently constrained by the moral parameters of its penal ideology, it is argued that the potential exists to change the current individualised and particularised 'truth' manufactured by international trials and expand its ability to contribute to post and transitional forms of justice.

Chapter 2 picks up on the wider goals of the ICC and international criminal justice but suggests it will only be through a focus on truth and responsibility rather than fact and liability that these will satisfy the victim constituency which Chapter 1 explores. The ICC is presently constrained to prosecuting the juridical individual and this does not even extend to corporate liability. Vicarious responsibility can be tortuously assigned through limited notions of command responsibility and superior orders. The unconvincing ICTY jurisprudence on common purpose and joint criminal enterprise is in no way sufficient, Findlay argues, to include corporate and collective perpetration so common in the suffering of victim communities. The reality of this limitation is not simply rooted in the proof constraints of individual liability. This chapter calls for both changes in the Court's approach to liability, but also a more long-standing and far reaching engagement with responsibility as the focus for deliberation and outcome. Findlay and Henham have recently proposed (2010) that only with the international criminal trial seizing the capacity to manage truth as much as fact, and to apportion responsibility rather than liability as a consequence, will the greater 'criminals' be drawn into 'communities of justice'. Ngane's discussion (Chapter 5) of the importance for the Court's truth-telling function, of *truthful* oral testimony, resonates with Findlay's assertion that trial transformation will ensure better victim-centred outcomes and consequent legitimacy.

The 'rights protection paradigm' characterising what we see as the transformed trial is reintroduced in this chapter. This then is linked to a developed notion of 'communitarian integrity' which not only offers a frame for fairness in international criminal justice, but also a measure for distilling competing victim interests (further explored in the chapter to follow).

Findlay offers an impression that the didactic and retributive functions of the ICC (referred to by critics of the wider aims of the court, as its true purpose) are in fact the constraints on its impact and legitimacy. One way of institutionally ensuring this constraint is through an over-emphasis on the truth/fact divide. The chapter continues Ngane's interpretation that truth as much as fact has a vital place in the discourse and narrative of international criminal justice. From here the harmonising possibilities for trial justice emerge. If responsibility stands at least equal with the quest for liability, then restorative and retributive decision processes and outcomes are possible. From here, and depending on the context of collective perpetration, more than individual responsibility for collective victimisation, even within the present procedures of the ICC, might be on offer. The procedural impediments to this achievement are then interrogated as challenges in current legal thinking and contemporary theorising of victim interests. Imagining collective and organisational liability in the wider responsibility frame is a centre of this discussion. The already-existing international humanitarian approaches to agency for protecting human rights abuses, Findlay asserts as insufficient for the satisfaction of legitimate victim interests. And as Fournet suggests, the historiography of international justice through truth-telling assumes a greater appropriateness where responsibility is at issue.

The chapter concludes with a brief interest in the languages of liability, justification and excuse, and culpability, all staples of criminal law discourse. Much more can and should be said about developing these languages of knowledge in the 'telling' of international criminal justice. This discussion leads to general considerations of victim-driven truth and fact deliberations, which lead naturally into the following chapter's concerns for victim expectations in post-conflict societies.

Providing contextual understandings of socio-legal phenomena like victimisation within different cultures and jurisdictional boundaries is problematic. These difficulties are multiplied when we seek to develop understandings both within and across jurisdictional boundaries. The balance between phenomenology and social reality (that is, what counts as an epistemologically valid explanation) lies in the extent to which there is agreement as to what constitutes 'objective fact' or 'objectivity'. Although the reality of victimisation is epistemologically conjectural, we can nevertheless postulate (depending on our theoretical persuasion) some a priori principles by which to measure/evaluate whether such a phenomenon 'objectively' exists. The subjectivity of the phenomenon, on the other hand, is concerned with such issues as the perceived legitimacy of the causes and consequences of 'war'; what it subjectively 'feels' like to be a victim, rather than simply having been ascribed that status; and how these intimate influences have shaped the individual attitudes of those claiming victimisation.

Any social theory which seeks to address the nature and significance of victimisation must necessarily address its legal, socio-historical, economic and political dimensions. For comparative analysis this involves appreciating the multi-layered nature of the relationships between the values and actions which produce victimisation within particular cultures and being able to make epistemologically acceptable generalisations about them.

The notion of victimisation as a social phenomenon has both objective and subjective dimensions. Kiza and Rohne's contribution focuses on both dimensions because it is examines the relationship between the attitudes and perceptions of victims and a range of post-conflict justice issues. Consequently, the study deals with what 'ought' to be and what 'is' through analysing the subjective accounts which describe the experiences and feelings of victims. It is not a conventional empirical study in the sense that that it seeks to hypothesise about observed and quantifiable 'facts' such as sentencing patterns. Rather it applies quantitative techniques to the analysis of what is essentially an account of the subjective perception of 'facts' describing what it is like to be a victim in a particular post-conflict society and how this impacts on the perception of what constitutes justice for war crimes. The 'objectivity' of these accounts can only really be evaluated to the extent that we are able to understand their meaning within particular contexts.

The repercussions of this are considerable because, both theoretically and methodologically, there is a clear distinction to be drawn between exploring the aspirational and empirical dimensions of social experience. The objectivity of any social phenomenon mirrors its subjectivity (and vice versa); the relationship is reciprocal. We can attempt to 'explain' how definitions of 'objectivity' are produced through the analysis of subjective experience, which is a recursive and constantly changing process. Hence, this approach tries to fix the meaning or contextualise social life by deconstructing the subjectivity of individual experience and making generalisations about the extent to which such experiences and understandings are held collectively. The translation of these collective aspirations into satisfying and legitimate justice outcomes is a challenge we argue, for trial transformation (Findlay and Henham: 2005, 2010).

Self-evidently, such methodologies will be culturally contextual in suggesting ways in which the objectivity of process is constructed subjectively. In this sense, Kiza and Rohne's chapter demonstrates why war victimisation should be conceived as a social construct involving the interplay between the causes and effects of war and the perceived appropriateness of particular forms of legal and institutional redress. Hence, the reciprocal relationship between ideology and context is crucial to understanding how the interplay between social structure and human agency becomes characterised as war victimisation. From a transitional perspective, their research confirms the urgent need for international trial justice to engage with the aspirations of victims and communities in a meaningful way if its outcomes are to make a significant contribution to ideological reconciliation and structural renewal.

As Vogler's chapter suggests, the extent to which the normative framework of international courts and tribunals has become more 'inquisitorial', hybridised, or is *sui generis* remains a topic of a considerable academic debate. The rules governing the admissibility of evidence in the ICC, for example, reflect an uneasy hybridisation of adversarial and inquisitorial approaches. The approach remains adversarial in the sense that the procedural norms are chiefly concerned with establishing a version of the facts that will either vindicate or negate the prosecution's allegations of guilt made in the indictment. In other words, the trial as a context for determining guilt or innocence ensures that the norms which control how factual information is admitted to the record are selectively perceived to conform to this overriding need to establish individual criminal responsibility for what is alleged.

Significantly, Vogler notes that ICC trial judges may use their wide discretionary powers to call evidence of their own volition in the interests of discovering the 'truth', yet the nature of the 'truth' that the process is capable of producing remains firmly circumscribed by norms which demand a predominantly confrontational approach. Similarly, the assessment of procedural fairness and the ambit of rights are made against norms which effectively exclude the participation of victims and communities of interest beyond existing parameters for delivering justice.

However, the perception of such 'filtered' information is not simply a matter dictated by the nature of the legal process as a juridical form. Social context and social norms influence how trial information is selectively perceived both within the trial and also within the wider 'community', howsoever defined. Vogler's insights illustrate why it is so important for establishing the legitimacy of trial justice that procedural norms and their evaluation are set against a deep appreciation of their social context and the relative significance of different forms of criminal justice intervention.

Elsewhere we have argued that international trial justice more generally requires a normative structure that allows connections between individual and collective forms of responsibility to be explored within a broader framework of penal objectives which includes restorative justice (Findlay and Henham: 2005, 2010). In order to facilitate this key decision sites or points within the criminal process where evidence crucial to enable the trial to contribute to the achievement of these objectives should be identified, and the relevant normative framework modified (Findlay: 2001: 33). Moves in the right direction have already been made by adopting a more 'inquisitorial' approach to the development of international criminal procedure by the ad hoc tribunals and the ICC. There is now much greater emphasis on judicial case management and status conferences, as well as a growing trend towards reliance on written rather than oral testimony. However, this falls far short of engaging with one of the fundamental problem of ICJ. This involves a realignment in the rationality for intervention on the part of hegemonic powers towards a greater engagement with the social contexts of war and conflict. A more principled and inclusive procedural framework will surely follow such a change of ideological direction. Nowhere better is the fragility of such a framework exposed than in the standing of victim witnesses and aspirations for their oral testimony.

On the surface, Ngane's chapter appears to be about jurisdictional responsibility. However, within that question lies consideration of 'responsible for what?' Oral testimony before the international criminal tribunals, and the ICC in particular, has become the cornerstone of a truth-evaluating function. In this context the judge's decision is captive to the integrity of witness testimony. If such testimony is false then the standing of the tribunal as a 'moral court' remains at risk. Surely in order to protect that integrity the harshest penalties and the most certain prosecutions must face the perjured witness. Or is it so simple?

The chapter describes the duties of witnesses before the ICC in their role as truth-tellers. What underlies this discussion are implicit considerations of how such witnesses come to be before the court and what expectations they carry with them resulting from their testimony. As the first trial before the ICC clearly revealed, victim witnesses in particular were looking for more than simply a forum to tell their story. The trauma of confronting the accused induced confusion and retraction. What does this say about the prosecution relationship with such witnesses and the negotiation of interests that must accompany witness proofing? And what does this mean for the 'truth' to emerge through testimony, and motivations to distort?

Much of the recent criticism of the ICC has focused on conflict of interests. Witnesses are introduced to the Office of the Prosecutor through NGOs or UN operatives on the ground, and such pathways suggest possibility for enticement and inducement likely to confuse and compromise the witnesses understanding of why they are to testify and what they are to say. Bearing this in mind, where lies and fabrication are revealed does it truly endorse the 'moral court' concept to hold the witness individually liable and to prosecute and punish as a result, by the citizen/state (or less likely, the international tribunal)? Ngane explores the reasons for this individualised approach against the reality of so few contempt prosecutions eventuating. Maybe it is the different 'types' of witnesses, their different journeys to the trial, their differential relationships with the prosecutor, and their diffuse engagement with what truth can be that better explains prosecutorial reluctance than jurisdictional preciousness or circumspection about deterrent value.

Ngane indicates the problem also might deeply locate in the authority of the court. Again, we suggest this is more than an issue of jurisdiction. This drives the legalist consideration of why state responsibility over international intervention. Should state coercion be an automatic consequence of citizenship? Then if so where does the 'moral court' and its unique intentions for witness testimony take on its own responsibility to witnesses and victims? We are left to consider the state of the law, but much more.

For the second part of the collection, these themes of achieving justice beyond form and procedure are developed within the broader hegemonic discourse of international criminal justice and its viability as a force for promoting governance and peace-making at both the global and local level. In elaborating this context, contributions examine the impact of globalised crime on international criminal justice and the ways in which international trial outcomes might be evaluated from a governance perspective within international criminal justice. Each analysis is further developed against broader considerations of the strategic role of international regulatory frameworks for achieving post-conflict and transitional justice.

An important place to intersect justice with governance is with themes of inclusion and exclusion (again taken up by Findlay in Chapter 8). Bikundo presents his theorising to 'illuminate some obscure connections between international crime and global governance'. These connections are contextualised within the nascent concerns of aggression, and the abuse of power. Bikundo employs the device of 'bio-politics' and the regulatory links offered through 'bio-legality' to fuse law with life, essentially preceding the understanding of violence as the precursor to law.

Global governance, it is suggested in the chapter, is achieved through monopolising force by criminalising rival violence through the law. Extracted from local concerns and globalised, the links between law, life and death are revealed as drivers for a sectarian and aggressive violence, where abuse of power receives the sanctity of legality.

The savage reality of governing through globalised crime (Findlay: 1999, 2008) is recorded in the torture case-study. The manner in which total prohibition through convention law has been debased and 'justified' by the war on terror echoes the impotence of legality and at the same time its necessity in validating abuse of process. Sovereignty defending security gives aggression against the body and the state its governance potential, above fear of brutality alone. War is waged against the body, aggression is sanctified through securitisation.

Law, life and death is the essential theoretical nexus for the chapter. Explaining law's relationship with violence in the context of criminalising (or not) acts of aggression, presents a larger critique of the partiality of international law in exclusion and inclusion projects. Law and legality, it is argued, are grounded to simultaneously protect and expose life as a consequence of inclusion and exclusion. The marginalised are deserving of aggression and legally sanctioned violence. More than this, the biology of politics is created through the biology of legality, both seeing their definition in discriminatory and aggressive violence. International criminal justice as global governance supplies the machinery and motive to abandon people and places to the ravages of authorised (if abusive) violence. Consequential patterns of governance (and spaces for governability) reflect, produce and destroy resistance to the distorted relationship between law and violence.

Dorn expands the consideration of governance beyond governing through crime. The chapter declares an interest in 'two inter-twined international aspects of governance engaging with administrative and criminal law in terms of the dynamics between states, international bodies and cosmopolitan actors'. Dorn sees the global policy space as multi-layered and multi-sourced. As such, the challenge of the chapter is to understand, within an international/administrative regulatory frame along with the criminal courts and tribunals, elements of 'contingency and surprise' more than predictability in global governance.

Dorn prefers a concept of 'multi-source governance' which acknowledges for global governance the influence of sovereign states and their federal incarnations, multi-lateral systems for implementing the two regulatory streams on which the chapter is interested, and the cosmopolitan control influences of the private sector and civil society. His is a recognition of pluralist regulatory strategies at work (or at war) in global governance.

The international administrative strategies which Dorn sees as preceding militarist intervention and criminal justice adjudication are either disciplinary (trade sanctions) or supportive (capacity building). The chapter lays out recent examples of both forms and critiques their regulatory reality in a cosmopolitan governance model. It is a 'push me – pull you' story. States and alliances aspire to administratively regulate and align their intentions for legitimacy goals. Cosmopolitan challenges for commercial advantage contest the political imperatives as producing outcomes which are unfair, ineffective and negative against a wider governance frame.

Dorn sees, however, that in the case of the international courts and tribunals, the historical dynamics seemed to be reversed. He puts this down to the positive role of cosmopolitan networks arguing for and supporting the internationalisation of justice institutions. This supportive atmosphere he considers to be complemented by organisational solidarity and capabilities, which gains the support of a majority of states, despite the selective attempts at neutralisation from a powerful few.

The chapter concludes with a modelling exercise. State bargaining, multilateral management and cosmopolitan challenge are the causal dynamic destabilising the regulatory impact of administrative sanctions internationally. Reverse the order and direction of the stages and one has the explanation for the success of international criminal justice trial institutions and processes in advancing global governance.

Chapter 8 takes considerations of governance back to crime, and addresses the transition in the global risk/security nexus from terror to more pervasive, collectivised and incipient harms. Unlike Dorn, Findlay sees benefit in the analytical device of globalisation to search for meaning in the progress from risk to governance, using global crime as a bridge. It is argues that risk and security discourse (epitomised in the 'war on terror') have become the sectarian tools of global governance which Bikundo earlier identified as essential for inclusion and exclusion. Findlay would have it that global governance is reliant on risk and security in both identifying and prioritising challenges to global order and preferring international criminal justice responses for legitimating militarist control.

The chapter advances our earlier considerations of governing through globalised crime (Findlay: 2008). While retaining the importance of crime as a construct for governance, and control resting on the relationship between risk and security, the chapter moves more specifically away from metaphor and governance symbolism.

Speculation is directed to the consequences of governing through crime in an era where crime harms are more actual, widespread and universally experienced. It is suggested that this will redirect the risk/security nexus away from hegemonic and sectarian prioritisation of harm inevitably towards real risk and clearer actual security challenges. This in turn may lessen the importance of international criminal justice on its own as a global governance tool.

Why so? Well, as is becoming more the case with economic rationalist pressures for cost benefit analysis of domestic criminal justice impacts on social order, global politics will not have the benefit of a criminal justice smokescreen or para-justice excess justified by the presumed impediments of a rights-based justice delivery. If the victim-base of global crime expands massively as global risks become more everyday and less responsive to political reassurance, global governance will collapse into the risk society. Findlay predicts that demands for a more accountable international criminal justice will come on the tail of a more localised and universalist approach to global governance. Communitarian victim interests will replace cosmopolitan commercial expediency. The repositioning of global risk towards the reality of pervasive harm will eventuate in civil society becoming more engaged in governance deliberations and less satisfied by sectarian and politicised symbolism. This then leads on to a consideration of law and criminal justice in more pluralist regulatory strategies. In particular, as the penultimate chapter ruminates, what will be the relevance of retributive logic and penality in a new age of global governance?

The idea that international sentencing might have a role to play in promoting reconciliation and peace in societies ravaged by social conflict is superficially attractive. However, beyond the political rhetoric of international relations it is difficult to visualise exactly what this might mean, except in purely abstract terms. The problem stems from the fact that our perceptions of 'international criminal justice' are relative so that it appears futile to argue that it has some kind of instrumental force having significance at both the international and domestic level. However, this is exactly what we, as individuals and citizens, are led to believe. The trial structures purporting to deliver 'international criminal justice' and the values it represents are depicted as universally relevant and its outcomes applicable wherever international crimes are alleged to have been committed.

Henham's chapter seeks to deconstruct this myth by highlighting some of the problems inherent in understanding the role of sentencing in international criminal trials. He also considers those arguments which question the capacity of international trial justice to act as an instrumental force for achieving 'justice' and assesses its role as a major contributor to the broader objectives of international criminal justice. He concludes that international sentencing could provide an appropriate context for developing more integrated and inclusive forms of international criminal justice, envisaging trial justice as a more effective and constructive partner for other structures and practices.

The most striking thing to emerge from Walker's contribution is that the true paradox between global terrorism and security-based policing lies in the Weberian tendency for regulatory frameworks of terrorist control and security to recursively reproduce themselves, so extending the reach of their bureaucratic tentacles to ultimately frustrate the very purposes for which they have been created. Such a tendency is evident from the way in which Walker describes the need for a more localised police response to global terrorism in the face of the apparent impotence of international regulatory control.

Despite a political recognition that policing strategies need to engage more with the social contexts of terrorism, the covert and preventative nature of the objective appears at odds with conventional notions of community-based policing. This reality may frustrate the achievement of either objective. Intelligence-led, militarised forms of policing of the kind that polarised the communities of Northern Ireland clearly subvert the governance objective, yet even the greater familiarity of individuals and communities with covert and other intrusive surveillance regimes does not validate such approaches beyond their utility in maintaining repressive forms of hegemonic control.

Again the theme of civil society engagement in global governance emerges as a key concern. As Walker describes, the processes of community engagement have become more subtle in the post-modern era, yet the so-called struggle for 'hearts and minds' remains problematic where the disjunction between moral values and the reality of social life is deeply rooted in basic ideological differences and fundamental disagreement about how to achieve social change. Overcoming extremism requires police engagement at a new and altogether different level: 'To be tough on terrorism and on the causes of terrorism is a much more ambitious undertaking and has inevitably embroiled security policing bodies in community work'.

Perhaps the expansion of community involvement to include conventional policing arrangements including multi-agency and public assurance is the way forward, as Walker concludes. One thing is certain: as with the delivery of international trial justice and other globalised forms of procedural and regulatory justice, such a transformation requires structural shifts in governance ideology which extend beyond acceptance of the need for greater police-community engagement. It requires a coordinated governance project for criminal justice for which the delivery of localised justice is the central concern of all its structures and agents.

PART I
Achieving Justice in Post-Conflict Societies

Chapter 2

Mass Atrocity: Theories and Concepts of Accountability – On the Schizophrenia of Accountability

Caroline Fournet

In the aftermath of mass atrocities, an insurmountable challenge arises, that of healing the victims and the nation while simultaneously reconstructing – through restoration and reconciliation – the destroyed society and ensuring the non-repetition of the atrocities. Processes for achieving this seemingly impossible goal could be regrouped under one single term: accountability.

From the outset, and by a simple glance at the vocabulary, the complexity raised by the issue of accountability is obvious. And indeed, accountability – traditionally understood as a legal term – aims not only at preventing new occurrences of the atrocities but also at achieving non-legal goals: healing, restoration and reconstruction. As Minow explains, '[t]he very vocabularies of healing and restoration are foreign to the legal language underpinning prosecutions',[1] and thus to the legal language used in order to ensure the accountability of massive human rights violators. The admitted and official purpose of legal accountability – through prosecution and punishment – is to try individuals, and nothing else. Justice, it is generally argued, has an objective and impartial duty and must not engage neither with historical events nor sociological considerations. Trials are held to express the rule of law, not to heal victimised nations and peoples. Yet, such an assertion must be expressly moderated and, as the present study will attempt at demonstrating, the notion of accountability, faced with all the developments on the international criminal law scene, has evolved. This evolution, it is here submitted, has indeed altered the traditional role of trials and of justice and, consequently, the face of the concept of accountability has dramatically changed. Far from strictly remaining at a purely legal level, accountability processes now 'include a wide range of measures – truth-telling, judicial reform, prosecutions, exhumations and reburials, memorialisation, reparations (including rehabilitation, restitution and compensation), lustration of police and security forces, and other guarantees of non-repetition'.[2]

1 Minow, M. (1998), *Between Vengeance and Forgiveness* (Boston: Beacon Press) 63.

2 Roht-Arriaza, N. (2002), 'Civil Society in Processes of Accountability', in Bassiouni, M.C. (ed.) (2002), *Post-Conflict Justice* (Ardsley, New York: Transnational

In this new context, accountability transcends the legal sphere and covers all measures – legal or not – intended at preventing any repetition of the crimes and atrocities while attempting to give a primary role to victims, both as victims and as witnesses. Still, notwithstanding the conceptual transformation of the notion, accountability has yet to fulfil its ultimate preventive goal. The ill-respect of the 'Never Again' promise made over and over again since the end of the Second World War serves as a poignant reminder of the failure of accountability mechanisms to prevent mass atrocities from happening again, and again … and it is precisely the reason behind such failure that the present chapter proposes to address, namely the schizophrenic nature of the concept of accountability. As previously mentioned, accountability covers a wide array of different theories and mechanisms and has developed outside the legal world. While this evolution has to be celebrated as a reinforcement of the willingness to prevent mass atrocities from occurring or recurring, it is here argued that legal accountability should still be given precedence in the sense that it has much to offer in terms of prevention if, and only if, it also accepts to encapsulate the non-legal goals of healing, restoration and reconciliation.

Notwithstanding the evolution on the international scene, legal accountability – prosecutorial forms of accountability – remains at the core of the concept: lack of legal accountability means impunity, which inevitably ensures the recurrence of the atrocities. As Zolo rightly observes,

> It can hardly be denied that widespread impunity is a fact and there is an important link – though not decisive or exclusive – between the political-judicial restoration of social equilibrium and the start of a process of peace-making. However, international criminal justice has not yet proven to be capable of remedying widespread impunity, except to a minor degree and with normative ambiguities.[3]

And indeed, legal accountability is not deprived of serious shortcomings and has in fact much to learn from non-prosecutorial forms of accountability, and notably from Truth and Reconciliation Commissions. This is not, however, to say that such non-prosecutorial forms of accountability do not have their own inherent defects but rather that the best of both forms of accountability must be gathered to create a new hybrid form of accountability, located at a cross-roads between prosecutorial and non-prosecutorial accountability. Ultimately, if accountability is going to achieve its goals and fulfil its aims, legal and non-legal considerations must be reconciled, legal and non-legal elements must be combined.

Publishers, Inc.) 97–114 at 97.

3 Zolo, D. (2004), 'Peace through Criminal Law?', *Journal of International Criminal Justice* 2, 727–34 at 730.

Non-Prosecutorial Forms of Accountability: Truth and Reconciliation Commissions (TRCs)

The international criminal law scene is currently confronting profound disruptions and undergoing a deep conceptual change. Due to the schizophrenia of the notion of accountability, international criminal justice is now faced with a plurality of options. To resist this disease, which could undermine the universality of international criminal justice and thus be lethal to the whole system, it is here argued that international criminal justice needs to adapt and go beyond the purely legal sphere to cover other forms of accountability.

The most obvious symptom of this schizophrenic diversification of the concept of accountability is the proliferation of Truth and Reconciliation Commissions (TRCs), which have been established in the aftermath of mass atrocities around the globe, generally as an alternative or as a supplement to prosecutorial forms of accountability. One of the most famous examples of TRCs is probably the Truth and Reconciliation Commission for South Africa but it is worth noting that, far from being an isolated instance, other such Commissions have been set up elsewhere, including Argentina, Bolivia, Chad, Chile, East Timor, Ecuador, El Salvador, Ghana, Guatemala, Haiti, Liberia, Morocco, Nepal, Nigeria, Panama, Peru, Philippines, Sierra Leone, Sri Lanka, Uganda, Uruguay and Zimbabwe.[4] As argued by Garapon, faced with this new challenge, international criminal justice, to be truly universal, must reinvent tradition:

> Another universalization test for international criminal justice is its capacity to imagine forms of justice other than those of Western trials. In this regards, we may note that the most original forms of transitional justice were invented outside of Europe (think of South America and South Africa). If inspiration came from the European twentieth century, the most imaginative applications came from elsewhere.[5]

International criminal justice, arguably born as a distinct legal corpus at Nuremberg and Tokyo, must now adjust to different cultures and must resist the temptation of being the vehicle of Western traditions and morals. In this respect, TRCs – as a reflection of a more popular justice – seem to be a more favourable option. Not only do they provide for a more flexible approach to accountability, ensuring easy access to justice and avoiding onerous and lengthy legal proceedings, but they also allow for a greater proximity with the culture and traditions of the people directly concerned by the mass atrocities. In the context of TRCs, victims are often offered

---

4 For a schematic overview of TRCs, see Hayner, P.B. (2006), 'Truth Commissions: a schematic overview', *International Review of the Red Cross* 88: 862, 295–310.

5 Garapon, A. (2004), 'Three Challenges for International Criminal Justice', *Journal of International Criminal Justice* 2, 716–26 at 722.

a primary role while perpetrators are encouraged to face their criminal past.[6] Unlike international criminal justice which might be remote from the concerns and preoccupations of the nation and the people destroyed by the occurrence of mass atrocities and which might be seen as a new form of Western colonialism, TRCs present the indisputable advantage of resisting Western intrusion and of responding to the needs of the recovering society by respecting its culture and traditions.

Still, and notwithstanding the advantages of TRCs, these should probably remain an accessory form of accountability and should not replace prosecutorial mechanisms designed to avoid impunity. It is here submitted that TRCs are a less desirable accountability mechanism compared to prosecutions, but only insofar as the latter draws upon the former to dramatically improve and to, at long last, become efficient. It is true that this issue might be automatically solved by the fact that prosecutorial forms of accountability are, now more than ever, here to stay. As Schabas notes, 'given the presence of the ICC, the coexistence of the two bodies [a court and a truth commission] will no longer be an option, but simply a fact',[7] but this should not in any case stop legal accountability from changing, evolving and, ultimately, improving.

A Questionable Trade-Off: The Issue of Amnesties

Although TRCs do not need to act as an exclusive accountability mechanism and can act as a complement to judicial proceedings,[8] it may be observed that, even when TRCs have transmitted their information to judicial authorities for possible prosecution of massive human rights violators, 'the fragility of the political or judicial system' has more often than not meant than such prosecutions never happened in reality.[9] Interestingly, as noted by Garapon, '[w]e must not overlook a very important dimension of the concept of international criminal justice – pressure to act, to negotiate, to yield, to change one's behaviour or to adopt a new

6 Notwithstanding the proximity to victims offered by TRCs, it is worth noting that one of the main criticisms raised with respect to the South African TRC was the absence, or the low amounts, of damages awarded, prompting victims to use the American Alien Tort Claims Act 1789: see *South African Apartheid Litigation* case, Federal Court of New York (Southern District) 29 November 2004. See Garapon, A. (2008), *Peut-on réparer l'histoire? Colonisation, esclavage, Shoah*, Paris: Editions Odile Jacob, 228.

7 Schabas, W.A. (2004), 'Conjoined Twins of Transitional Justice? The Sierra Leone Truth and Reconciliation Commission and the Special Court', *Journal of International Criminal Justice* 2, 1082–99 at 1098.

8 Ibid.

9 Ratner, S.R. and Abrams, J.S. (2001), *Accountability for Human Rights Atrocities in International Law – Beyond the Nuremberg Legacy*, Second Edition (Oxford University Press) 234.

policy', pressure which seems to be absent following Truth and Reconciliation Commission's reports.[10]

Even further, in many instances, amnesties and pardons have been granted as a means to promote reconciliation and in exchange of perpetrators' testimonies and acknowledgement of their crimes. While recognition by perpetrators is an extremely important way of trying to heal the wounds of the victims and while such recognition can scarcely be achieved by judicial proceedings, for obvious fear of sentencing, it is nonetheless doubtful that amnesties or pardons are beneficial in the long run. More problematically from a theoretical standpoint, the trend towards granting amnesties against (pseudo?) truth-telling has generated general mistrust towards trials and sentencing and has ignored the fundamental idea that justice is not revenge. When international criminal tribunals are set up, it is to judge and condemn massive violations of human rights in the name of the international community, it is certainly not to exercise revenge or victor's justice. Ignoring the requirements of justice by granting amnesties for massive violations of human rights contains more risks than advantages. Specifically as regards South Africa, Ratner and Abrams have explained that the granting of amnesties 'has elicited some dramatic admissions concerning the apartheid's regime abuses, but has also ignited a wrenching national debate over whether such confessions are worth the price of individual impunity for some unbearably awful deed'.[11]

There were certainly some very convincing reasons to adopt the amnesty plan in the South African context and, as Minow explains,

> Imprisoned for twenty-seven years for his political work, the freed Nelson Mandela then helped to negotiate the peaceful end of South Africa's apartheid. A crucial item in the negotiation was how the new government should deal with the events and consequences of the apartheid period. The outgoing leaders made some form of amnesty for those responsible for the regime a condition for the peaceful transfer to a fully democratic society. The interim constitution, a remarkable document of negotiated political transformation, called for a process for freeing participants in apartheid from prosecution. It gave explicit reference to the African concept, *ubuntu*, meaning humaneness, or an inclusive sense of community valuing everyone.[12]

Notwithstanding these reasons and the commitment to *ubuntu*, the fact remains that amnesties operate an extinction of the offence itself. As Scharf recalls,

10 Garapon, A. (2004), op. cit. note 5, at 718. As an illustration, Garapon cites the example of the arrest of General Augusto Pinochet which appeared to have had a greater impact on the prosecution of Chilean criminals under the Pinochet regime than the report of the Comisión Nacional de Verdad y Reconciliación. Ibid.

11 Ratner, S.R. and Abrams, J.S. (2001), op. cit. note 9, at 235. Footnote omitted.

12 Minow, M. (1998), op. cit. note 1, at 52.

> the term 'amnesty' is derived from the Greek word 'amnestia' – meaning forgetfulness or oblivion. In the present context, amnesty is an act of sovereign power immunizing persons from criminal prosecution for past offenses.[13]

The questionable validity of amnesties for the perpetration of mass atrocities has been recognised by law and, as Roht-Arriaza rightly observes, '[t]here is an increasing trend in international human rights bodies explicitly to condemn amnesties for certain particularly grave offenses, even those granted by successor regimes'.[14] Whether the granting of amnesty is totally prohibited where universal jurisdiction is mandatory, or whether it is considered as inappropriate where there is a customary international law duty to prosecute or extradite, amnesty for international crimes and thus for massive human rights violations is, in any event, not a recommended measure. Despite inconsistent state practice, there are strong legal reasons suggesting its incompatibility with international law. In fact, amnesty for international crimes would arguably be contrary to the principles of individual criminal responsibility recognised in the Nuremberg Charter and Judgment. According to Cassese,

> the validity of such amnesty [to persons responsible of grave breaches of international humanitarian law and mass violations of human rights] is doubtful. Arguably, the prohibition of such crimes and the consequent obligation of states to prosecute and punish their authors should be considered a peremptory norm of international law (*jus cogens*): hence, states should not be allowed to enter into international agreements or pass national legislation foregoing punishment of those crimes.[15]

In the same vein, the Human Rights Committee held that:

> Amnesties are generally incompatible with the duty of States to investigate such acts; to guarantee freedom from such acts within their jurisdiction; and to ensure that they do not occur in the future. States may not deprive individuals of the right to an effective remedy including compensation and such full rehabilitation as may be possible.[16]

---

13 Cited in Paust, J.J. et al. (2000), *International Criminal Law, Cases and Materials*, Second Edition (Carolina Academic Press) 21.

14 Roht-Arriaza, N. (2001), 'Special Problems of a Duty to Prosecute: Derogation, Amnesties, Statutes of Limitation, and Superior Orders', in Roht-Arriaza, N. (2001), *Impunity and Human Rights in International Law and Practice* (Oxford University Press) 59.

15 Cassese, A. (1998), 'On the Current Trends towards Criminal Prosecution and Punishment of Breaches of International Humanitarian Law', *EJIL* 9, 6.

16 UN Human Rights Committee General Comment No. 20 in relation to Article 7 of the International Covenant on Civil and Political Rights.

It is also worth recalling here that, during the signature of the Lomé Peace Agreement for Sierra Leone,[17] the UN Secretary-General had formulated a reservation to the general amnesty provided for in the Agreement, recalling that amnesty was not applicable to international crimes, crimes against humanity, war crimes or serious violations of the laws and customs of war. As a result, the Statute of the Special Court for Sierra Leone[18] provides that amnesty will not impede legal action as regards such crimes,[19] and the Appeals Chamber of this Special Court has ruled that the amnesties enshrined in the Agreement did not constitute legal impediments for the Court to exercise its jurisdiction over the persons and acts covered by these amnesties.[20] More specifically, while linking the concept of amnesties with that of universal jurisdiction, the Appeals Chamber found that the latter implied that amnesties granted by one state could not prevent another state from exercising its jurisdiction over perpetrators of international crimes and eloquently expressed this idea in the following terms: 'A State cannot bring into oblivion and forgetfulness a crime, such as a crime against international law, which other States are entitled to keep alive and remember.'[21]

Finally, and probably more universally, the Preamble of the Rome Statute also implies that deferring prosecution because of the existence of a national amnesty would be incompatible with the purpose of the Court, which is to ensure criminal prosecution of persons who commit serious international crimes. Thus, the Preamble

> Affirm[s] that the most serious crimes of concern to the international community as a whole must not go unpunished and that their *effective prosecution* must be ensured [...]

---

17 Peace Agreement Between the Government of Sierra Leone and the Revolutionary United Front of Sierra Leone, 7 July 1999.

18 Statute of the Special Court, annexed to the Agreement between the United Nations and the Government of Sierra Leone on the Establishment of the Special Court for Sierra Leone, signed on 16 January 2002.

19 Article 10 of the Statute entitled 'Amnesty' reads as follows: 'An amnesty granted to any person falling within the jurisdiction of the Special Court in respect of the crimes referred to in articles 2 to 4 [crimes against humanity; violations of Article 3 common to the Geneva Conventions and of Additional Protocol II; other serious violations of international humanitarian law] of the present Statute shall not be a bar to prosecution.' See generally Cissé, C. (2002), 'Le Tribunal Spécial pour la Sierra Leone', *International Law FORUM du droit international* 4, 7–11.

20 *The Prosecutor* v. *Morris Kallon and Brima Buzzy Kamara*, Special Court for Sierra Leone, SCSL–2004–15–AR72(E) and SCSL2004–16–AR72(E), Decision on Challenge to Jurisdiction: Lomé Accord Amnesty (Appeals Chamber, 13 March 2004). See generally Meisenberg, S.M. (2004), 'Legality of amnesties in international humanitarian law – The Lomé Amnesty Decision of the Special Court for Sierra Leone', *International Review of the Red Cross* 86: 856, 837–51.

21 Ibid., at para 67.

> Recall[s] that it is the *duty of every State to exercise its criminal jurisdiction* over those responsible for international crimes.
> Emphasize[s] that the International Criminal Court established under this Statute shall be complementary to *national criminal jurisdiction.*[22]

Notwithstanding the importance of the Preamble,[23] it must nonetheless be admitted here that some provisions of the Statute seem to allow the Court to recognise amnesty in certain given circumstances. According to Scharf,

> the preambular language and the procedural provisions were negotiated by entirely different drafting groups, and in the rush of the closing days of the Rome Conference, the Drafting Committee never fully integrated and reconciled the separate portions of the Statute.[24]

And indeed, Article 16 of the Statute provides that the Court would be required to defer to a national amnesty if the Security Council has requested that it respects an amnesty-for-peace deal and thereby to refrain from prosecution. Such provision seems however to be the product of political compromise – leaving the door open for the Security Council to decide of the opportunity of prosecuting massive violators of human rights – and is arguably incompatible with the aims of the ICC themselves. Perhaps more convincingly, such provision is definitely contrary to the compulsory duty to exercise jurisdiction which exists with respect to violations of the 1949 Geneva Conventions,[25] and of the Genocide Convention.[26] In any event, the reach of Article 16 may be limited by Article 17(1) of the same Statute, which does not list amnesty as a cause of inadmissibility of a particular case.

Ultimately, and beyond all legal considerations, there are significant moral arguments as to the total inadequacy of amnesty for international crimes and massive human rights violations. As Neier explains,

---

22 See Preamble of the ICC Statute. Emphasis added.

23 See Article 31(1) of the Vienna Convention on the Law of Treaties. The Preamble may be a source of interpretation of the treaty as it indicates both its context and its object and purpose. See generally Stahn, C. (2005), 'Complementarity, Amnesties and Alternative Forms of Justice: Some Interpretative Guidelines for the International Criminal Court', *Journal of International Criminal Justice* 3, 695–720.

24 Scharf, M.P. (1999), 'The Amnesty Exception to the Jurisdiction of the International Criminal Court', *Cornell International Law Journal* 32, 522.

25 See Article 49 of Geneva Convention I. As Scharf however notes, '[a] counter argument can be made [...] that the Rome Statute codifies only the substantive provisions of the 1949 Geneva Conventions and the Genocide Convention, and does not incorporate those procedural aspects of the Conventions that require prosecution. Accordingly, the nature of the charges might constitute a significant factor to be considered, but would not necessarily be a bar to recognizing an amnesty'. Scharf, M.P. (1999), op. cit. note 24, at 524.

26 See Article VI of the Genocide Convention.

> the state, acting on behalf of all, should demonstrate respect for sufferers from crime, and its seriousness about its own proscriptions against criminality, by punishing the transgressors. The victims count on the state not to overlook or forgive their victimization. They reserve this right to themselves.[27]

And as Bassiouni further stresses,

> Accountability is the antithesis of impunity, which occurs either de facto or through amnesties. But amnesty is essentially a form of forgiveness, granted by governments, for crimes committed against a public interest. How, though, can governments forgive themselves for crimes they committed against others? And how can governments forgive crimes committed by some against others? The power to forgive, forget or overlook in the cases of genocide, crimes against humanity, war crimes and torture, is not that of the governments, but of the victims.[28]

An Incomparable Benefit? Truth-telling

It is certainly an understatement to assert that truth is a complex concept and truth-telling is thus a data very difficult to measure and to recognise as such. As Todorov notes, justice 'is better equipped to contribute towards the establishment of [factual] truth', but it 'is ill suited for establishing … the meaning of events'.[29] Yet, notwithstanding the restricted role justice should play as to the establishment of the truth, it seems that, through the self-empowerment of both courts and TRCs to know of past events, we are entering an era of judicialisation of history in which historians have lost their monopoly over the interpretation of such events. As Abrams and Hayer observe,

> emerging principles of international law have recognised a right of victims and their families to be apprised of the truth concerning human rights abuses and a corresponding duty upon States to investigate and disseminate the truth. These principles proceed from the dual notions that the truth is essential both to respecting and restoring the individual victim's human dignity and to the community's collective interest in understanding its history so that it may achieve reconciliation and prevent recurrence of the abuses.[30]

---

27 Neier, A. (1998), *War Crimes – Brutality, Genocide, Terror, and the Struggle for Justice* (New York: Times Books) 61.

28 Bassiouni, M.C. (1999), 'The Need for International Accountability', in Bassiouni, M.C. (ed.) (1999), *International Criminal Law, Volume III: Enforcement*, Second Edition (New York: Transnational Publishers, Inc.) 22.

29 Todorov, T. (2004), 'The Limitations of Justice', *Journal of International Criminal Justice* 2, 711–15 at 712.

30 Abrams, J.S. and Hayner, P. (2002), 'Documenting, Akcnowledging and Publicizing the Truth', in Bassiouni, M.C. (ed.) (2002), op. cit. note 2, 283–93, at 283.

In fact, as expressly specified in their very title, Truth and Reconciliation Commissions are set up to 'tell the truth'. Their task is to make a full account of what has happened and to draw a record for history of unprecedented educational value for generations to come. As specified in section 6(1) of the Truth and Reconciliation Commission Act 2000, the TRC for Sierra Leone was set up 'to create an impartial historical record of violations and abuses of human rights and international humanitarian law related to the armed conflict in Sierra Leone, from the beginning of the Conflict in 1991 to the signing of the *Lomé Peace Agreement*, to address impunity, to respond to the needs of the victims, to promote healing and reconciliation and to prevent a repetition of the violations and abuses suffered'.[31]

Perhaps surprisingly, the truth-telling mission of TRCs seems to have escaped criticism and to have been widely accepted. In contrast the role of judges on the international criminal law scene came under strict scrutiny and severe criticism when courts have taken the opportunity of trials to simultaneously create a historical record and establish the truth. From an objective viewpoint, however, it appears that trials can acquire great historical value and fulfil an incomparable educational role, even if these are – as they should be – merely consequences of the trials rather than their primary aims. For instance, as Douglas observes with respect to the Nuremberg trials,

> Robert M.W. Kempner, a junior prosecutor at Nuremberg, called the Nuremberg trials the 'greatest history seminar ever held in the history of the world,'[32] [while] Sir Hartley Shawcross, the British chief prosecutor, echoed this idea, declaring that the Nuremberg tribunal would 'provide … an authoritative and impartial record to which future historians may turn for the truth.'[33] Many important histories of the Holocaust, such as Raoul Hilberg's *The Destruction of the European Jews*, could not have been written without the massive archive of documentary material assembled through Nuremberg's act of legal discovery.[34]

This is of course not to say that judges should reinvent themselves as historians and be entitled to become a type of mythmakers empowered to shape a sanctified and sacred vision of the past. This is also not to say that courts are entitled to dictate history and to impose a certain vision of the truth, which would be absolute and universal. There can indeed be very clear conflicts between what is being said in the course of a trial and the historical truth, if only because trials deal with

31 Truth and Reconciliation Commission Act 2000, Supplement to the Sierra Leone Gazette vol. CXXXI, No. 9. See generally Schabas, W.A. (2004), op. cit. note 7.

32 Quoted in Buruma, *The Wages of Guilt*, pp. 144–5. Kempner was referring to both the trial of the major war criminals and the subsequent trials of Nazi criminals before American courts. Footnote in original.

33 *Nuremberg Judgment*, vol. 3, p. 92. Footnote in original.

34 Douglas, Lawrence (2001), *The Memory of Judgment – Making Law and History in the Trials of the Holocaust* (New Haven: Yale University Press) 2.

the individual criminal responsibility of one perpetrator and thus focus on some clearly restricted elements rather than on the whole event. In this respect, a harsh criticism was expressed by Arendt who, in *Eichmann in Jerusalem*, argued – and rightly so – that 'the purpose of a trial is to render justice, and nothing else; even the noblest of ulterior purposes – 'the making of a record of the Hitler regime which would withstand the test of history' … – can only detract from the law's main business: to weigh the charges brought against the accused, to render judgment, and to mete out due punishment'.[35] While this sharp criticism is not to be ignored, while it constitutes a clear warning sign as to the dangers of moving away from the primary goal of trials, an analysis of international criminal justice shows that most of the trials and their judicial documents actually constitute priceless and unprecedented historical archives.

In any event, courts seem to be absolutely conscious of their restricted role and, as the District Court of Jerusalem expressly and unequivocally affirmed in the *Eichmann* case, the primary purpose of this trial was to try a man, and its educational impact was to be considered only as a 'by-product':

> the path of the court was and remains clear. It cannot allow itself to be enticed into provinces which are outside its sphere. The judicial process has ways of its own, laid down by law and these do not change, whatever the subject of the trial may be. … These … remarks do not mean that we are unaware of the great educational value implicit in the very holding of this trial … to the extent that this result has been achieved in the course of proceedings it is to be welcomed … but as far as this court is concerned, they are to be regarded as by-products of the trial.[36]

Yet, even if it is merely a consequence, a 'by-product' of legal proceedings, the record of – and for – history can be achieved by trials, which, through the establishment of individual criminal responsibility and the simultaneous construction of an individualised, a particularised truth, thus complement the work of TRCs and their express ambition to 'tell the truth'. This is not, however, to omit the failures of some trials to correctly identify the factual truth and one may here recall the dramatic episode of the trial of John Demjanjuk, in the course of which the heavy reliance on testimonies led to an incorrect identification of the accused and thus to an erroneous conviction.[37] The misidentification was, however, not a total mistake in the sense that John Demjanjuk had been identified as Ivan the

---

35 Arendt, Hannah (1963), *Eichmann in Jerusalem – A Report on the Banality of Evil*, (New York: Penguin Books) 253.

36 *Attorney-General of the Government of Israel* v. *Eichmann*, 36 ILR 5 (Israel District Court – Jerusalem, 1961), at para 2.

37 Douglas, L. (2001), *The Memory of Judgment – Making Law and History in the Trials of the Holocaust* (New Haven: Yale University Press) 96–7.

Terrible who served at Treblinka while he was in reality Ivan the Terrible from Sobibor. As Douglas explains,

> The process of appeal concomitant with the collapse of the Soviet Union and the new emerging information suggested that there had been two Ukrainian Ivans, one at Sobibor and one at Treblinka. Ivan the Terrible had been one Ivan Marchenko. This new information did not exculpate Demjanjuk as it strengthened the conviction that he had served at Sobibor, it still casted doubt on whether Israeli justice was about to execute the right man as Ivan the Terrible. Consequently, in July 1993, the Israeli Supreme Court overturned Demjanjuk's conviction.[38]

Notwithstanding this judicial mistake and the questions it raised as to the reliability of witnesses and of judges, it still remains that the trial documents constitute fantastic historical archives, of great educational value, on Treblinka. As the Supreme Court rightly noted, 'the district court's verdict is not only a legal document, but also an historical and educational document of great significance'.[39]

Detractors of this admittedly extensive vision of international criminal justice will protest at the heresy and sacrilege contained in the idea that courts can dictate history and will thus invoke the unprecedented truth-telling significance of TRCs. This vision seems however to be too restrictive to be correct, if only because, ultimately, it appears to give the truth as expressed by massive human rights violators precedence over the truth as expressed by judicial authorities respecting the rule of law and offering the guarantees of a fair trial. It may also be opportune to recall here that, in most democratic states, the concept of justice is based on the ancestral principle *Res judicata pro veritate habetur* – what is tried must be considered as the truth – and the authority of judicial rulings thus has a normative value and an important symbolic power. Conversely, the absence of judicial rulings has the exact same symbolic force and bears with it the idea that the crimes never occurred in the first place. In this context, and notwithstanding their advantages, TRCs might well be too limited an option.

Still, even if TRCs are not seen as necessary and if they seem to be a pale compensation in cases where judicial proceedings remain absent, they nonetheless offer another vision of the truth, which may act as a complement to the individualised truth as established by judicial proceedings and which arguably corresponds to another vision of justice, based on national reconciliation rather than on penalisation.[40] Ultimately, the judicialisation of history, as illustrated by the roles played by trials and by TRCs, reinvents the concept of justice and

---

38 Ibid.

39 Criminal Appeal 377/88. *The State of Israel* v. *Ivan (John) Demjanjuk*: Judgment of the Supreme Court of Israel (Jerusalem: Supreme Court, 1993) p. 7 in Douglas, L. (2001), op. cit. note 36, at 210.

40 See Garapon, A. (2008), op. cit. note 6, at 10–11.

establishes truth as a new form of justice. Rather than being radically confronted, these two visions of justice should be compared and it is beyond doubt that judicial proceedings have a lot to learn and should in fact draw upon the functioning of TRCs if they are to ensure full accountability, in terms of prosecutions of course, but also in terms of healing, of restoration, of reconstruction and ultimately of prevention.

Prosecutions as the Main Form of Accountability: Suggestions for Improvement

> By its dramaturgy, justice has the power, in the course of the debates, to intensely arise consciousness of what has happened, of the horror of the crime itself.
>
> Robert Badinter[41]

As previously mentioned, truth commissions have the immense benefit of offering a flexible option particularly 'suited to achieving [accountability, reconciliation and the transition from an authoritarian past] in countries where limited resources, the absence of a strong and impartial legal system, and other circumstances make a judicial approach infeasible'.[42] Furthermore, as Havel observes, 'truth commissions (as they are now evolving) have the markedly superior characteristic, rarely apparent in criminal trials, of systematic consideration of the victims of the investigated oppression.'[43]

Still, notwithstanding the advantages offered by TRCs, accountability short of prosecutions is bound to fail in achieving its universal goals of prevention and of guarantee of non-repetition. It must nonetheless be simultaneously admitted that, so far, legal accountability has failed dramatically to succeed in its deterrent and preventive roles. In other words, short of truth-telling and of 'systematic consideration of the victims', legal forms of accountability are also bound to fail. Faced with this dismemberment, this schizophrenia of accountability mechanisms, international criminal justice must evolve.

International criminal justice has yet to acknowledge the importance of victims-witnesses as actors of the trials. From its very conception, international criminal justice has indeed been incapable of fully considering the role of victims both as victims and as witnesses and this failure probably explains the current

---

41 In Chalandon, S. and Nivelle, P. (1998), *Crimes Contre l'Humanité – Barbie, Touvier, Bousquet, Papon* (Paris: Plon/Libération) VII. Translation by the author. The original version reads as follows: 'Par sa dramaturgie même, la justice a le pouvoir, au cours des débats, de faire prendre intensément conscience de ce qui est advenu, de l'horreur même du crime.'

42 Abrams, J.S. and Hayner, P. (2002), op. cit. note 30, at 291.

43 Havel, B.F. (2002), 'Public Law and the Construction of Collective Memory', in Bassiouni, M. Cherif (ed.) (2002), op. cit. note 2, at 389. Footnote omitted.

schizophrenia of accountability. It is beyond any doubt that, although very few victims were called to testify at Nuremberg,[44] these trials still carved into history the crimes perpetrated in the course of the Nazi reign over Europe and constituted a crucial landmark in both the memorialisation and the promise of non-repetition of the crimes. It is nonetheless submitted here that the exceptional circumstances in which these trials took place, putting a symbolic end to years of persecution and of oppression, perhaps eluded the importance of the role victims as victims and as witnesses should have on the international criminal justice scene.

More significant in terms of memorialisation of the Nazi crimes was the *Eichmann* trial, which clearly put the emphasis on victims and witnesses, giving them a predominant role to play. The purposes of this trial were to generate interest among the Israeli population as a whole, and among the Israeli youth in particular, for the crimes perpetrated during the Second World War and, to this end, to trigger a process of identification with the victims.[45] In fact, the *Eichmann* trial was the first ever trial to be broadcasted live on the radio in Israel and on television in other countries.[46] According to Wieviorka,

> The Eichmann trial marks a pivotal moment in the history of the memory of the genocide, in France and the United States as well as in Israel. It opens a new era, in which the memory of the genocide becomes central to the way many define Jewish identity, even as the Holocaust demands to be admitted to the public sphere. Scholars from various countries who have studied the evolution of the construction of memory have all noticed this shift.[47]

Adopting a similar view, Douglas also stresses that the *Eichmann* trial was understood, notably by Segev,

> 'principally as "national group therapy", a ritual of national catharsis in which a collective public space was made available in which to grieve for traumatic private memory.'[48] Until the trial, Segev observes, the survivor experience was very much a suppressed fact of Israeli social and cultural life, one that conjured the despised history of the Jew as hapless victim and thus conflicted with the

44 Wieviorka, A. (2006), *The Era of the Witness* (Ithaca: Cornell University Press) 67.

45 See generally Wieviorka, A. (2003), 'La Mémoire du Génocide', *Le Monde* (14 April 2003).

46 The trial was not broadcast live on the Israeli television due to a lack of infrastructure. Later on, the *Demjanjuk trial* was broadcast live on Israeli television.

47 Wieviorka, A. (2006), op. cit. note 44, at 56. To cite only a few examples: Tom Seguev for Israel in *The Seventh Million*; Rochelle G. Saidel for the United States in *Never Too Late To Remember*; Annette Wieviorka for France, 'Autour d'Auschwitz', in *Allemagne France, Lieux de mémoire d'une histoire commune*, ed. Jacques Moritz and Horst Müller (Paris: Albin Michel, 1995), 187–205. Footnote in original.

48 Segev, T., *The Seventh Million*, p. 351 in Douglas, Lawrence (2001), op. cit. note 37, at 109.

> emerging national identity of the Israeli as a self-sufficient warrior. Survivors' memories, often enveloped in pain and shame, were secreted away, denied public or even private expression.[49]

The *Eichmann* trial was indeed the first ever instance in which the indictment was based on factual evidentiary tools and on testimonies. In the course of this trial, and in the words of Haïm Gouri, the witnesses *were* the facts:

> Nor did the numerous witnesses come to add to the accumulation of suffering and rage. They testified in order to illuminate the destruction in all its detail. … They were the very center of the trial, because they served as faithful proxies of the Holocaust. They were the facts.[50]

It is here argued that, if the *Eichmann* trial has been widely qualified as pivotal and crucial in the emergence and construction of the memory of the crimes perpetrated by the Nazis, this was not purely coincidental: it was because victims were offered a primary role to play as victims and as witnesses. In this context, trials were able to fulfil, just like TRCs aim at fulfilling, a therapeutic function.

The fact that contemporaneous international criminal justice seems to ignore victims as real parties to the trials and merely considers them as potential witnesses probably explains why the trials held in these arenas fail to attract general interest worldwide. For instance, the perpetrators of the Rwandan genocide remain unknown to the general public. Opponents of this vision of international criminal justice will probably argue that victim participation to the proceedings would impede courts from establishing coherent and principled forms of sentencing and from fulfilling their initial aims of international penalisation and retribution through appropriate punishment. In their eyes, victim participation would thus undermine the workability and credibility of the whole system. By reducing international criminal justice to a purely retributive justice, such argument seems, however, ill-founded and too restrictive. While there is little doubt that one of the functions of international criminal justice is punishment, its very existence also expresses the attachment of the international community to the prevention of crimes[51] as well as its willingness to maintain or restore international peace and security, in accordance with the express aims of the United Nations and as evidenced by the creation of the two ad hoc International Criminal Tribunals for the Former Yugoslavia and for Rwanda. Detractors might also contend that the courtroom is not the appropriate forum to hear victims' testimonies and that trials

---

49 Douglas, L. (2001), op. cit. note 37, at 109.

50 Wieviorka, A. (2006), op. cit. note 44, at 85.

51 See e.g. Preamble of the ICC Statute in which the States Parties re-affirm their determination 'to put an end to impunity for the perpetrators of these crimes and thus to contribute to the prevention of such crimes'.

risk becoming legal farces in which 'witnesses have the right to be irrelevant'.[52] Such criticism must, however, be expressly rejected, for the simple reason that there cannot be an 'irrelevant testimony' from victims of mass atrocities. Furthermore, it is precisely these testimonies, expressed in the solemnity of the courtroom, which will ultimately cure accountability of its schizophrenia and give back to international criminal justice as a prosecutorial form of accountability the preponderance it once had.

The impact and significance of the legal qualification of a crime as such by a court of law should not be underestimated. And indeed, by legally qualifying an act as criminal, trials simultaneously acknowledge not only the status of victims as victims and as witnesses, but also the status of the accused as criminal. The judicial criminal qualification indeed emphasises the implication of both law and trial proceedings in the determination of human behaviour and in the definition of a form of truth, which arguably reinforces the sense of justice for individual victims and victim communities. Victims want justice not only to see their tormentors punished but also to be recognised as victims through the official public recognition of the perpetration of the crime.[53] In the course of such trials, it is essential for those victims who wish to do so to be able to testify whether for individual purposes – testifying might somehow help them to exorcise their pain and to heal their wounds – or for collective reasons – they might feel that their testimonies will ultimately reinforce, if not ensure, the collective memory of the crime and thus guarantee its non-repetition.

The importance of trials in the recognition of the crime and of its victims is further enhanced by the highly symbolic places in which they take place and in which testimonies are told and – probably for the first time – actually heard and listened to. In the words of Wieviorka,

> The witnesses told their own stories and that is what gave weight to their words. The extraordinary force their words acquired can also be attributed to the place where they were pronounced, which gave them a political and social significance no book could confer. Their political dimension lay in the fact that the state, represented by the prosecutor, underwrote their testimony and thus lent it all the weight of the state's legitimacy and institutional and symbolic power. The witnesses' words attained a social dimension because they were uttered before judges whose responsibility it was to acknowledge the truth they contained and because they were relayed to the world media as a whole. For the first time since the end of the war, the witnesses had the feeling that they were being heard.[54]

---

52 This quote refers to *Yad Vashem Bulletin*, as quoted in Arendt, H. (1963), *Eichmann in Jerusalem – A Report on the Banality of Evil*, (New York: Penguin Books) 225.

53 See Garapon, A. (2002), *Des Crimes qu'on ne peut ni Punir ni Pardonner – Pour une Justice Internationale* (Paris: Editions Odile Jacob) 205.

54 Wieviorka, A. (2006), op. cit. note 44, at 84.

The importance of being able to testify in the course of a trial most certainly explains the huge number of voluntary witnesses who wished to testify at the *Eichmann* trial, in the course of which 111 witnesses were called.[55] As Wieviorka further explains, with the *Eichmann* trial, witnessing victims, survivors, were enabled to acquire their social identity as survivors and to be recognised as such by society as a whole:

> In contrast, with the Eichmann trial the survivors acquired the social identity of survivors because society now recognized them as such. Before the Eichmann trial, the survivors, at least those who so desired, maintained this identity in and for the organizations they themselves had formed. These organizations created a communal life closed in on itself, serving both to honor the memory of the dead and to maintain social ties among people who had lived through the same experiences … .[56]

And, even further, not only does testimony re-establish the identity of the survivors, it also re-establishes 'the identities of the descendants of those who died without graves, by allowing them to imagine the circumstances of their relatives' deaths and thus to begin the work of mourning'.[57] It is here submitted that only trials, and testimonies given in the course of such trials, can actually reintegrate the victims – survivors or not – into the post-conflict society and collective memory. Without trials, without a condemnation from a judicial – and somehow moral – instance representing society as a political entity, the social recognition of victims as victims will be, if not impossible, at least greatly impeded.[58] If the victims of Klaus Barbie, including the 44 children of Izieu arrested on 6 April 1944, have not fallen into oblivion, it is thanks to the trial of Barbie, largely initiated by Me Serge Klarsfeld, in the course of which survivors were called to testify and victims were remembered:

> Me Serge Klarsfeld does not plead. He does not throw his sleeves towards the ceiling's mouldings, he does not use any vocal effect, he talks with sadness, he does not even seem to be a lawyer. No, Me Klarsfeld reads. And this reading, certainly more than everything which is to be said during eight days by the thirty-nine lawyers of the partie civile, distresses. Klarsfeld, who escaped from the raid, hidden by the thin rampart of a partitioned wardrobe. Klarsfeld the historian, the militant, the Nazi hunter, the auxiliary of justice haunted since

55 Ibid., at 73–86.

56 Ibid., at 88.

57 Ibid., at 128.

58 See Garapon, A. (1999), 'La justice et l'inversion morale du temps', in Académie Universelle des Cultures (1999), *Pourquoi se souvenir? Forum International Mémoire et Histoire, UNESCO, 25 March 1998, La Sorbonne, 26 March 1998* (Paris: Editions Grasset and Fasquelle) 113–24 at 120.

> 1971 by the memory of the forty-four Jewish children of Izieu. Klarsfeld, who only pronounces the name of these children, like if he was on the verge of beginning a teaching class. Forty-four names, one after the other, recited in a deathly silence.[59]

It is precisely when trials give a predominant role to victims as victims and as witnesses that international criminal justice reaches its full dimension. In the words of Garapon,

> The judgment does not evacuate facts which belong to the past but it fixes them into collective memory by giving an official and definitive version of these facts. It limits the story, it symbolically puts an end to the course of evil.[60]

By 'symbolically putting an end to the course of evil', trials may fulfil their therapeutic and cathartic role and bring a sense of closure to victims. In this context, there thus should be no need for extra-legal or para-legal forms of accountability: the proliferation of Truth and Reconciliation Commissions might thus only be a healthy reaction to the inability of trials – and arguably unwillingness of judges– to acknowledge the importance of victims in the legal proceedings and to engage with healing, restoration and reconstruction after mass atrocities. In this context, the move taken by the ICC Statute towards a formal recognition of the dignity and the rights of victims, and notably of their right to participate actively in the proceedings, has to be greatly celebrated. And indeed, by cathartically trying those responsible for the most atrocious acts, by therefore determining their behaviour as criminal while simultaneously recognising the status of victims, international trials will establish an individualised and particularised truth, which will reinforce the sense of justice for victims and victim communities and which will ultimately transform truth into justice. It is thus to be hoped that such recognition will not remain dead letter as when victims are given a central role in the courtroom, when their testimonies are heard, listened to and taken into account and when their

59 Chalandon, S. and Nivelle, P. (1998), op. cit. note 41, at 111–12. The original version reads as follows: 'Me Serge Klarsfeld ne plaide pas. Il ne jette pas ses manches vers les moulures du plafond, n'use d'aucun effet de voix, parle avec tristesse, ne semble pas même être avocat. Non. Me Klarsfeld lit. Et cette lecture, plus que, certainement, tout ce qui doit être dit durant huit jours par les trente-neuf avocats de la partie civile, bouleverse. Klarsfeld, qui a échappé à la rafle, masqué par le mince rempart d'une armoire à double fond. Klarsfeld l'historien, le militant, le chasseur de nazis, l'auxiliaire de justice hanté depuis 1971 par le souvenir des quarante-quatre enfants juifs d'Izieu. Klarsfeld, qui se contente de prononcer le nom de ces enfants, à la manière d'un appel de début de classe. Quarante-quatre noms, l'un après l'autre, récités dans un silence de mort'.

60 Garapon, A. (1999), op. cit. note 58, at 118. Translation by the author. The original version reads as follows: 'Le jugement n'évacue pas des faits passés mais il les fixe dans la mémoire collective en en donnant une version officielle et définitive. Il borne le récit, stoppe symboliquement le cours du mal'.

tormentor is punished and sentenced, international criminal justice might well be the best option the concept of accountability has to offer, an option which goes beyond the law and into the truth … and maybe, just maybe, into reconciliation.

Chapter 3

Collective Responsibility for Global Crime: Limitations with the Liability Paradigm

Mark Findlay

Introduction

It is not just the communitarian constituency which is unique and therefore demanding in the development of international criminal justice (ICJ).[1] As the collective reality of global crime victimisation suggests, the jurisprudence of international criminal law needs to better confront and confer new notions and determinations of collective liability and responsibility.[2] Identifying generic crimes for prosecution is not enough. Liability itself needs to be creatively collectivised. And as this chapter suggests, if criminal liability is an insufficient determination in resolving the legitimate interests of victim communities, should international criminal justice look to responsibility and 'truth' as more effective measures for victim community satisfaction where collective perpetration is involved?

The treatment of joint criminal enterprise, command responsibility and superior orders by the war crimes tribunals and by the legal scholarship which supports their deliberations[3] has been distinctly unimaginative in addressing this tall order. The chapter argues that an inability to escape the confines of individual liability, when exercising even the retributive arm of international criminal justice, stands in the way of a more victim-centred and thereby restorative international criminal justice.

---

1 For a discussion of victim constituency see Findlay, M. (2009) 'Activating Victim Constituency in International Criminal Justice', *International Journal of Transformative Justice* 3: 183–286.

2 In this chapter the distinction is drawn between criminal liability determined as it is through investigation, prosecution and trial, and responsibility for harm established in a wider sense of truth-telling. As can be seen from the *Inquiries Act* (UK) section 2, even formal justice mechanisms can be charged with exposing responsibility for matters of public concern, while being expressly removed from findings of liability, civil or criminal.

3 For a critique of the judicial and academic analysis see Ambos, K. (2007) 'Joint Criminal Enterprise and Command Responsibility' *Journal of International Criminal Justice* 5: 159–74. Electronic copy available at: http://ssrn.com/abstract=1392063.

The same will be said for restrictive interpretations of individualised rights as a responsibility for international criminal law.[4] The Rome Statute[5] when determining *individual responsibility* states that the court shall have jurisdiction 'over *natural persons*[6] pursuant to this Statute'.[7] In the Rome Conference debates extending that liability to corporations was specifically considered and denied. The counter-argument was based on the recognition that many domestic law systems do not recognise the criminal liability of corporate entities. As such, the complementarity regime of the court could be compromised.

Alternatively, where corporate liability is a feature of domestic criminal law, there should be no reason to exclude the applicability of general notions to international crimes.

However, during an address to the fifth assembly of State Parties[8] the first Chief Prosecutor of the ICC, Louis Moreno-Ocampo, declared the intention to locate responsibility for crimes of genocide, war crimes and crimes against humanity in Ituri (Democratic Republic of Congo) in a wider arc.

> Different armed groups have taken advantage of the situation of generalised violence and have engaged in the illegal exploitation of key mineral resources … according to information received crimes reportedly committed in Ituri appear to be directly linked to the control of resource extraction sites. Those who direct mining operations, sell diamonds or gold extracted in these conditions, launder

4 Damgaard, C. (ed.) (2008) *Individual Criminal Responsibility for Core International Crimes*, Heidelberg: Springer Berlin.

5 Article 25:1, Rome Statute for the International Criminal Court (The Rome Statute). This is the empowering legislation for the International Criminal Court (ICC) settled by the UN Diplomatic Conference of Plenipotentiaries on the Establishment of an International Criminal Court (17 July 1998).

6 If it is possible to consider the corporation as a 'legal personality' then this might be a step towards aligning it with the concept of 'natural person'. Certainly if the prosecution for international crimes is carried out at a state jurisdictional level then the individuals with responsibility within the corporation would face possible prosecution.

7 In commenting on this Article, Albin Eser observes that '… there can be no doubt that by limiting criminal responsibility to individual natural persons, the Rome Statute implicitly negates – at least for its own jurisdiction – the punishability of corporations and other legal entities' (Eser, A. (2002) 'Individual Criminal Responsibility' in A. Cassese, P. Gaeta and J. Jones (eds) *The Rome Statute of the International Criminal Court: A commentary*, Oxford University Press, 778). The same is the case for the International Criminal Tribunal for the Former Yugoslavia (ICTY) and the International Tribunal for Rwanda (ICTR) – (Article 6, ICTY Statute; Articles 1 and 5, ICTR Statute).

8 Ocampo, L.M. (2006) 'Opening Remarks', *Fifth Session of the Assembly of State Parties*, Hague: ICC.

> the dirty money, or provide weapons, could be authors of the crime, even if they are based in other countries.[9]

No indictments have yet been laid by the ICC against corporations. Indeed, it has been argued[10] that both due to the significant evidentiary difficulties involved and on the principle of complementarity (if corporate criminal liability is not recognised in many national legal orders), it would be then inappropriate for the ICC to claim this jurisdiction.[11] Even as a mechanism for state reconstruction, the propensity to blame many for the crimes that are now sheeted back to the few, may not simply or incrementally produce wider reconciliation and satisfaction among the affected populace. The causal bi-products of individual and collective liability are as problematic at an international level as they are for state-based criminal justice.

The conflict resolution and peacemaking aims of the ICC, criticised by some as adventurous and inappropriate,[12] pressure for a transformed consideration of liability and responsibility within international criminal justice (ICJ). The ICC Prosecutor has signalled an interest to investigate beyond the immediate territory of local and regional armed conflict, and to extend narrower notions of criminal responsibility which have been accepted by the ad hoc tribunals. These courts have preferred to debate the nature of joint criminal enterprise,[13] common purpose and accessorial liability in international criminal law rather than embracing more collective concepts of responsibility which are at the heart of vicarious and corporate liability.[14]

The UN Special Court for Sierra Leone (SCSL) has also identified the unlawful international trade in diamonds as central to the funding and motivation for conflict. In response, the UN Security Council[15] expressed 'its concern at the role played by the illicit trade in diamonds in fuelling the conflict in Sierra Leone', and directed that steps be taken by certain states towards controlling the trade.

---

9 It should also be noted that the liability here could still be individualised, directed to human actors within the corporation in a manner not dissimilar to the treatment of individuals within military agencies by the Nuremberg military tribunal.

10 Eser (2002) 77.

11 The success rate for prosecutions at the Nuremberg Tribunal (and cases following) of persons playing an economic role in crime, was poor (Eser: 2002: 307–10).

12 See the detailed critique of expansive aims advanced in Damaška, M. (2008) 'What is the Point of International Criminal Justice?' *Chicago Kent Law Review* 83/1: 329.

13 For instance before the ICTY see, *Prosecutor v Tadic* Case No. IT-94-1-T, TC Judgement 7.5.97; *Prosecutor v Tadic* Case No. IT-94-1-A, Appeal Court Judgement 17 July 1999.

14 Exploring the problems with this approach see Danner, A. and Martinez, J. (2005) 'Guilty Associations: Joint criminal enterprise, command responsibility, and the development of international criminal law', *California Law Review* 93/75: 77–169.

15 UN Security Council Resolution 1306, 2000.

Even so, the SCSL has not indicted any individual or organisation for trading in diamonds which then exacerbated military conflict.[16]

The nature of liability is just one challenge for international criminal trial transformation in practice. The recognition of collective liability for communitarian victimisation is central in redirecting the constituency of international criminal justice which underpins the need and reality of trial transformation. In this regard, the necessity is, rather than adapting and straining pre-existing concepts of liability and sanction, to develop a new jurisprudence for international criminal justice which recognises responsibility for shared perpetration.[17] Shadowing this is the need to allow for a notion of shared victimisation which recognises the problematic and deeply contextual possibilities of overlap between criminal perpetration and victimisation. A new normative framework for ICJ, leading to a reconceptualisation of victimisation as the appropriate international justice constituency and a consequential engagement with truth and responsibility, are at the heart of the applied exploration of justice transformation referred to later in this chapter.

Against the limitations of individual and collective liability the transformed international criminal trial is designed to approach dynamics for change from two directions. Initially it is concerned with victim-centred restoration accepting the problem of demarcating victim communities which also may engage in criminal perpetration as retaliation or armed struggle. Second is the consideration of collective perpetration, either in the organisational sense with corporate criminality, or where crimes are exacerbated by the involvement of the many against the many. Terrorism is a case in point. From the internal dynamics of the international trial transformation is a mix of substantive and procedural re-ordering.[18] In a practical sense these changes will locate on concerns for standing, and for the origins of decision-making source narrative.

The confines of the analysis to follow do not allow for a full exploration of the needs for, and outcomes of international criminal trial transformation. Rather, the chapter narrows down consideration of collective responsibility as a vehicle for advancing the cause of communitarian international criminal justice, suggesting a more effective way to engage the legitimate interests of victim communities. On the way to this we need to consider:

- imagining new notions of liability for international criminal prosecutions, in the context of truth and responsibility
- identifying victim communities as a proper focus for international trial

16 The Special Court is analysed in Cockayne, J. (2004) 'Special Court for Sierra Leone', *Journal of International Criminal Justice* 2: 1154–62.

17 The normative framework which will underpin this new jurisprudence is explained in Findlay and Henham (2010).

18 It is suggested that for the ICC at least this can be achieved within the flexible intentions and applications of the Rome Statute while the secondary rules of procedure may need significant adjustment to incorporate restorative dimensions.

justice, with all the problems this may pose

- constructing new roles for the juridical professional[19] in international criminal trials, to manage and monitor trial transformation and justice synthesis
- suggesting how enhanced discretion and accountability in trial decision-making will achieve transformation, despite the trend in domestic justice environments to limit and diminish judicial discretion in particular
- ensuring that the victim's voice is a significant influence over the selection and activation of trial resolution options
- reconstructing the adversarial trial environment and wresting truth from fact and responsibility from liability in certain process formats, thereby
- ensuring the place of international criminal justice in a regime of global governance which works for the restoration of victim communities as much as the reconstruction of state and political hegemony.

As the location for international criminal trial justice the ICC (actually or symbolically) provides the institutional context for critically analysing the

future intersection between collective liability and communitarian responsibility.[20]

Institutional Ordering and Trial Transformation

The International Criminal Court (ICC) has advanced its role as incorporating the prosecution and punishment of select and significant offenders who endanger humanity, and thereby promoting the peace and security of mankind. It is also important to consider the court's institutional role in characterising selected victim communities, discriminating victims from collaborators and providing some degree of victim 'agency' through the victim support unit.

The court's mandate emerges from the UN Security Council and its standing from the laws and authority of member states. The ICC Statute claims for the court a 'distinct nature'[21] determined by its expansive aims and its differentiation from

---

19 The juridical professional – judges, prosecutors and defence lawyers – in transformed justice have the responsibility to inject fidelity into the accountability framework of ICJ. For a detailed examination of the importance of fidelity; see Ashworth, A. (2000) 'Testing Fidelity to Legal Values: Official involvement and criminal justice', *Modern Law Review* 63/5: 633.

20 For a discussion of the ICC as the institutional foundation of ICJ in the context of individual criminal liability, when compared to the ad hoc tribunals, and to domestic justice paradigms see Megret, F. (2009) 'In Search of the Vertical: An exploration of what makes international criminal tribunals different and why' http://SSRN.com/abstract=1281546.

21 Rome Statute of the International Criminal Court, 37 ILM 1002 (1998) (herein after *the Rome Statute*).

national courts. Aligned with this distinction, the constituencies of international criminal law, as symbolically ensured through the ICC, are victim communities in the most vulnerable states of genocide, war crimes, crimes against humanity and aggression. Despite the retributive focus and traditions of international trial justice, the ICC is being challenged through victim interests to:

- impugn the relevance of retribution as the sole or even primary focus for international criminal justice;
- realistically interpret the capacity to achieve general deterrence through trial outcomes;
- transform the trial process in a way which would recognise and ensure restorative justice paradigms with at least equal commitment;[22]
- require international criminal justice to focus its attention on legitimate victim interests by enhancing access, inclusivity and integration of these interests within the protective framework of the trial process;
- seek the reconciliation of victim community interests which are restorative and retributive as a responsibility of the juridical professionals who run international criminal trials; and thereby
- reposition the role of international criminal justice away from sectarian political dominion, towards accountable and pluralist order maintenance and justice delivery.[23]

While being forced to consider the liability of the 'legal individual' and at the same time aspiring to secure communitarian safety, the court from its first trial has faced pressures for procedural transformation fuelled through conflicts of interests and problematic indemnity.

Deriving the moral justifications for interfering in the lives of others from the notion that that conflict is essentially destructive of humanity, ICJ comprises processes seeking to resolve conflict by peaceful means which are intrinsically good. The ICC declares these essential purposes. Peace-making through trial justice suggests an engagement with competing 'truths' in ways similar to conventional trial fact-finding through adversarial argument.

The search for truth within the trial need not be some unattainable aspiration or distracted normative commitment. Nor should it be consigned to non-trial

---

22 For a detailed argument justifying this direction of trial transformation see Findlay, M. and Henham, R. (2005) *Transforming International Criminal Justice: Retributive and restorative justice in the trial process*, Collumpton: Willan Publishing, esp. chaps 7 and 8. For an elaboration of the mechanics of trial transformation see Findlay and Henham (2010).

23 For a discussion of the problematic nexus between crime and global governance see Findlay, M. (2008) *Governing through Globalised Crime: Futures for international criminal justice*, Collumpton: Willan publishing, especially chaps 7 and 9.

restorative resolutions.[24] It can take on, through trial transformation, as much of the operational reality and procedural appropriateness as verdict delivery within the trial process. Truth, thereby, will give a more legitimate and viable foundation for state reconstruction, than retribution and deterrence as didactic and unproven consequences of penality. Truth-telling becomes a purpose as well as an outcome of the transformed trial process.

In particular, the conflict resolution and victim restoration roles for the court rely on the fullest understanding of contextual historiography. However, trials are trials and the considerations for the court may seem bound by the indictment before it, and the construction of the prosecution case. How then will truth-telling insinuate itself where fact and evidence are the restricted trial discourse? Trial transformation intends that when, through prosecutorial initiative, defence application, victim representation or judicial intervention, the incapacity of the adversarial mode to satisfy key legitimate interests is identified, then diversion to 'truth-telling' and restorative resolutions will be an option. Whether this comes about through suspension of prosecution and conciliatory diversion, or transfer to a formal truth telling mode within the trial is a matter to be determined by the judge. The Rome Statute may not require amendment to achieve such procedural alternatives.[25]

As with the developing jurisprudence of the international criminal tribunals, trial transformation will be evolutionary and not instantaneous. Legal professionals within the court would need to approach transformation with good will for it to operationalise. The member states will have to accept that transformation better enhances the expressed purposes of the court, and thereby increases its legitimacy in the eyes of essential stake-holders, so that the original authority of the court is not withdrawn or challenged by disgruntled signatories.

Some say that to attach conflict resolution to the central aims[26] of the international criminal trial is asking too much, and doomed to frustration.[27] These criticisms have merit if the trial model under review is some narrow and constrained reflection of adversarial decision-making.[28] Even without the trial transformation we envisage, the ICC pre-trial and trial models have already moved away from an unreconstructed adversarial frame. For better or worse, the juridical professionals in the ICC re-iterate the court's exemplary function motivated by wide peace-making aspirations. These are beyond individual deterrence and concerns about impunity. They represent a fundamental belief that through strategic prosecution the ICC may have a much more extensive conflict resolution function than

24 As discussed later, Damaška (2008) opposes this view.

25 The rules of evidence and procedure prevailing in pre-trial and trial proceedings would have to be adjusted to enable this discretion.

26 Remembering that the ICC has clearly claimed this purpose for the court and not left it as a prosecutorial aspiration – See LRA indictment.

27 For instance, Damaška (2008).

28 This could not be said of the procedural hybrid form of the ICC.

the consequences of prosecuting individual liability in domestic courts might anticipate.

However, exemplary prosecutions and penalties cannot of themselves claim restorative potential. To maximise the restorative dimension of formal ICJ the normative foundations of the trial transformation process[29] must reflect a number of humanitarian principles. The most fundamental of these involves equal treatment and tolerance of human difference and frailty. The justice system and the trial in particular, must not be used as a form of oppression where the law and its execution evoke a theory of social control by force and violence. Further, the humanitarian normative foundation advances the legitimate interests of victim communities over the sectarian priorities of a limited cultural and political hegemony.[30]

It could be argued that the diversionary pathway to trial litigation and the deductive process of evidence accumulation and presentation favours justice through institutional and social exclusion. Added on to a trial context where access is much constrained and inclusivity formalised, the conventional criminal trial is a discriminatory regime (NB the processes of fact finding, confidentiality arrangements and awarding punishment). That explains why the normative repositioning of ICJ which respects restorative as well as retributive paradigms requires humanitarian foundations confirmed through improved procedural access, inclusivity and integration.[31]

Retributive international criminal justice now administered through a largely adversarial process is rationalised by substantive norms of law and procedure that conventionally ignore essential qualities of humanity at large, even though presumptions of equality before the law overlay trial fairness. This rationalisation is itself justified by a notion of due process where the accused person is protected against the vengeance of victim communities, and the domination of the state.[32] In this 'rights' paradigm we have argued[33] a strong justification for locating even limited restorative determinations within the international criminal trial is to benefit from measures of procedural fairness.

The selective 'rights focus' of the trial should also be an important expectation for victim interests seeking restoration, whether these rights take second place to accused's protections or not. It is the recognition of procedural fairness (in a more *balanced* setting than conventional adversarial trial fairness) and juridical accountability over humanity's interests which can be didactically asserted and valued through the transformed international criminal trial. The balance is provided the wider recognition of victim community interests through the exercise of juridical discretion over retributive or restorative procedures and outcomes.

29 As discussed in Findlay and Henham (2005).

30 For a discussion of the connection between humanity and hegemony see Findlay (2008), chap. 3.

31 This is discussed in greater detail in Findlay and Henham (2010), chap. 1.

32 See for example Article 6 of the European Convention on Human Rights.

33 Findlay and Henham (2005), chaps 7 and 8.

Once so enunciated in trial transformation, procedural fairness and the rights it recognises may act as a comparative normative framework for the processes of alternative institutions which will continue to have a much wider restorative remit in ICJ.

The retort to this wider declaratory mission to inject rights from the trial to alternative modes might be, 'Why not simply require these rights of international criminal justice generally?' The nexus between the increased satisfaction of victim interests and enhanced rights protection within the formal trial setting is ripe for empirical testing during the progression to trial transformation. Once set then this understanding should be offered by example rather than compulsion to other justice modes concerned to maximise legitimacy and governance influence (Findlay: 2008: chap. 7).

The 'rights protection' paradigm characterising the transformed trial is:

- Committed to communitarian rather than individual rights recognition.
- Respecting the preferred rights of accused persons in the adversarial trial mode, while victim voice will be given significance in pre-trial and trial fact determinations as well as in sentence.
- Where the restorative/mediatory role of victim voice will be given equal standing as any other key truth-teller (and contesting victim voices will be free to dispute the stories told).
- Where the sanctity of the trial and the pre-trial context as it protects witnesses and values evidence will prevail in both the retributive and restorative modes, and will value and protect the process of truth telling in the same way it validates and protects witness evidence.
- Injecting into restorative 'truth-telling' within and beyond the transformed trial expectation for the recognition and delivery of communitarian rights in which the juridical professional ensures agency.

Transformed trial process will also produce a new justice ordering where real institutional involvement will be accorded the victim voice. Integrating victim interests in a more sophisticated, even if only practically didactic fashion within the transformed international criminal trial will open up the prospects for 'fairness' as a measure of the humanity of justice processes. Communitarian integrity and, more importantly, an awareness of the contexts that give rise to cultural differences based as these may be in:

- alternative world views of fairness
- competing conceptualisations of primary knowledge
- valuable normative traditions
- community virtues

These are picked up by the 'truth-telling' opportunities in a transformed trial framework. In this regard, trial fairness will not simply be secured through the concern for the accused in the adversarial context, but more widely balanced in restorative opportunities for the victim and the offender.

The new institutional manifestation of transformative *trial* justice offers the possibility for reconciling differences of approach exemplified in the dialect of retributive and restorative justice. This dialectic is resolved through trial transformation, where in a common due process procedural context the juridical professionals are able to activate either or both justice options to satisfy legitimate victim expectations through conciliation rather than contest. The transformed trial, as a centre-piece within this transition transcends the debate about punishment before restoration by recognising much more than adversarial differences, thereby resolving conflict by using rules of law and procedure to facilitate flexible and conciliatory outcomes.

Having said this, as with the international criminal trial at present limited to retributive considerations, prosecutions are very selective and as such the interests covered are as symbolic as they are significant. To open up the trial to restorative possibilities will not invite a flood of victims to enjoy this new atmosphere of procedural fairness and retributive/restorative resolve. The vast majority of victim interests will still await recognition and resolution in the alternative justice domain. The limited resources of the juridical professional and the progressive politicisation of the prosecution process will confirm this inevitability.

If a limited didactic or expressive role for the international trial prevails, why do we justify, or even require, trial transformation embracing new restorative possibilities, and the 'truths' on which these are founded? Is this not expecting a radical repositioning of the trial without adequate victim coverage? Perhaps this is a sound criticism in the context of contemporary trial practice. But as Damaška[34] concedes even for the retributive adversarial trial, it is a dominant and valuable didactic rather than a reconstructive enterprise. In this sense trial transformation may not always or necessarily change this exemplary purpose into more practical outcomes. Truth-telling and historicising may necessarily replace guilt and penalty without essentially enhancing the possibility of individual responsibility. That is why collective perpetration and victimisation suggests a more vital arena for trial histories as a means to identify and apportion moral responsibility.

In light of the practical limitations of the international criminal trial ongoing (transformed or not) as a general context for examining the interests of humanity how can we re-argue access, inclusivity and integration in a more didactic sense? The answer lies in the representative inclusion of 'interests' rather than armies of victims. In that, a transformed trial recognises the needs of humanity as central 'pathways of influence'[35] in a decision site model, even if the trial outcomes could only ever (as is the case with retribution) satisfy these interests at the most symbolic level. In this expressive and truth-telling form, victim communities are championed in a small number of transformed trials for the wider restorative

34 Damaška (2008).

35 Findlay and Henham (2005), chap. 3.

impact in associated alternative (and fairer?) justice paradigms. In addition, if collective responsibility is better enforced within the transformed trial setting then victim community interests are more likely to be achieved.

The transformed trial, selective as its resolutions will remain, gives exciting new possibilities to the victim interests identified for access, inclusivity and integration. To achieve this, liability and responsibility will be on offer as possible resolutions within the trial process, enunciated through fact and or truth sources. In light of negotiation through judicial discretion the dichotomy of truth and liability vs fact and responsibility (discussed later) can be viewed as false at the level of both ideology and process if the transformed trial breaks free of its adversarial strait-jacket and recognises and values cultural plurality. A more central place for victim communities within the transformed trial will necessarily promote this harmonisation.

As Tamanaha[36] suggests, both fact and value are essentially cultural entities, through which they receive real social location. In this respect a new approach to fact and value as co-existing non-problematically (or at least outside adversarial discrimination) opens up the opportunity for transformative justice in a holistic sense, focusing on humanity and its protection. If there is a paradox between fact and value within international criminal justice it may lie in the recognition that transformed trial processes must integrate retributive and restorative justice to provide a wide normative context which is capable of satisfying different and sometimes contesting demands for justice.

In suggesting the transformative path we accept the following reservations:

- Limitations in victim access, inclusivity and integration depending on the political and prosecutorial dynamics of case selection and management.
- The significance of 'humanity' over partiality and sectarianism in focusing trial constituency and the interests it should reflect.
- The continuing need to grow alternative, transformative and restorative justice processes and resolutions to satisfy victim interests outside the didactic and conciliatory capacities of trial decision-making.

Trial transformation envisages adversarial and mediatory phases of the trial where fact and/or truth will be established for transformative purposes. However, it would be wrong to suppose that retributive or restorative objectives will predominate in either mode because the transformative rationale depends on negotiating, recognising and managing legitimate victim interests at any stage pre-trial and trial. These may or may not approximate retributive or restorative concerns. What transformation does mean is that conventional adversarial concepts of liability, the nature of the evidence required for liability attribution, and how much truth and

---

36 Tamanaha, B. (1979) *Realistic Social Theory: Pragmatism and social theory of law*, Oxford: Clarendon Press.

fact comes to be admitted for any purpose, need to be detached from their primary association with retributive outcomes.

It is through reconciling potential outcome modes through different styles of negotiation that a wider range of harm and a larger field of perpetrators can be brought within the justice net. The logical consequence of this is that more legitimate victim community interests are satisfied. However, to achieve this it is necessary to augment the search for individual responsibility with options for truth-telling and ascription of responsibility which may not meet evidentiary proof or adversarial predominance. Even so responsibility can draw in collective perpetration and communal suffering when criminal liability fails to technically achieve the limits of the law.

Truth/Fact Divide? – Much Ado about Nothing?

Before embarking on a brief interrogation of the separation between truth and fact, an observation on the place of truth within the trial is merited. In his illuminating essay on 'The Jury and Reality' Zen Bankowski[37] explores the search for truth within the trial. He suggests that any such search is based on epistemological premises requiring further testing. Bankowski challenges any assumption that the trial is about 'finding' truth in the manner that an explorer finds a new land. In his view the context of the adversarial trial not only restricts this, but was never essentially designed for any such eventuality. As a purposive exercise, fact-finding is not finding facts (or for that matter truth) in the trial at all. Rather than an epistemological exercise of uncovering what 'is', the trial suggests to the jury what 'ought' to be in a normative sense. Allan Norrie confirms this view in his critique of the subjective interpretation of the 'guilty mind'.[38] It is an inductive rather than empirical process of psychopathology. In this regard Norrie reminds us that historiographic as well as legal methodologies need to be employed in understanding the rise of individualised criminal liability.

Bankowski next suggests that there is a 'sociology' (or social interaction) that is the adversarial trial which gives a particular impetus to truth in the trial. In discussing the 'coherence of the case', Bankowski identifies fact as the outcome of decisions about persuasion and the minimising of doubt. Can the product be truth? From here the trial of fact becomes at the very least a 'truth certifying' process; a game adjudicated by the rules of evidence where one side wins the contest over guilt or innocence by overcoming pre-determined hurdles of proof, or countering these with justification or excuse. Is the product necessarily truth? Bankowski concludes that fact finding mechanisms within the conventional adversarial

37 Bankowski, Z. (1988) 'The Jury in Reality', in M. Findlay and P. Duff (eds) *The Jury under Attack*, London and Sydney: Butterworths, chap. 2.

38 Norrie, A. (2006) *Crime History and Reason*, London: Butterworths, chap. 1.

system say more about our aspirations for society and its governance than it does the achievement of epistemological truths.

Truth, as much as fact, has a vital place in the discourse and narrative of international trial justice. Under this recognition, the adversarial model of trial fact finding can co-exist at least in the pre-trial phase with mediation processes more common in the truth and reconciliation environment.[39] The conditions under which mediation may be the preferred approach in trial deliberations will obviously depend on where truth in place of contested fact is deemed through judicial discretion to best determine prevailing victim interests at any particular time in the process. The shift from fact to truth, and adversarial to mediation styles will evidence the dynamic process of transformed trial justice. So saying, it is the conventional trial format, and the self-interested investment of trial professionals in the status quo that will stand in the way of the transformation project. The achievement of wider court goals and the quest for legitimacy will counter structural resistance.

If judicial discretion is to be mobilised to orchestrate the shift between fact and truth, adversarial contest and mediation, it will need to become familiar with techniques for encouraging compromise and truth-telling to promote healing, as well as proportioning individual blame on the basis of legally defined harm. This choice will be pre-determined by whatever the revelation of truth or the determination of fact predominates at any decision-making stage[40] leading on to alternative concerns for responsibility and reconciliation or liability and retribution.

The essence of the trial as it currently stands is fact. Value needs inclusion for contested fact to assume the status of truth. The role of the judge in any such transition is crucial if the trial is to provide its context. These imperatives envisage a decision paradigm where the attribution of value to fact through the exercise of discretion provides the power for change. So the judge will have a pivotal role in deciding whether truth supports a determination of responsibility or liability, and their appropriate outcomes, and how fact and value should merge for these purposes. Judicial discretion will also negotiate how the choice and selection of outcomes may be derived from what is accepted as definitive truth and the ways in which legitimate victim and community interests will be recognised to drive the choice of alternative resolutions and their outcomes.

Harmonisation Possibilities – Liability vs Responsibility

Trial transformation is as much about diversifying trial decision-making processes as it is about opening up alternative outcomes. A crucial indicator of trial transformation is the radical and applied 'harmonisation' of two crucial decision-

39 Trankle, S. (2007) 'In the Shadow of Penal Law: Victim offender mediation in Germany and France', *Punishment and Society* 9: 395–416.

40 See for example Findlay and Henham (2005), chap. 3.

making paradigms. The first is the nexus between fact and liability around which the adversarial trial conventionally revolves. Next is the more broad concern for truth and responsibility which have featured in alternative international criminal justice resolution frameworks such as truth and reconciliation commissions.

The merging of these two paradigms is the natural, if not challenging, consequence of introducing restorative justice possibilities into a retributive trial process.[41] At the very least this means a reconceptualisation of the foundations of trial decision-making such as 'fact' and 'evidence' against wider interpretations of 'truth'. We have indicated in *Transforming International Criminal Justice* that evidence as both a facilitator of and an outcome from trial decision-making will through transformation be re-envisaged so that it may be employed for retributive and then where appropriate restorative deliberations.[42]

Well-known themes germane to fact/value debates have long fuelled socio-legal critique.[43] With this as a background the discussion of the purposes of 'evidence' within the transformed trial structure where the normative constituency is 'humanity' and the deliberative outcomes can be either retributive or restorative, can critically proceed.

The current divide in international criminal justice is between liability-focused trials and restorative truth-centred commissions. UN discourse narrows this down somewhat misleadingly as a tension between justice and peace-making. As an unproductive institutional and process divide, it fails at least to encapsulate and broadly satisfy the diverse and legitimate interests of victim communities.

Building on the case for integrating restorative and retributive justice within the international criminal trial, it is logical to open up the manner in which facts and truth can be established and applied for different but not inconsistent trial purposes. The widening application of what up until now, in the adversarial context, might be viewed as incompatible sources, necessitates unlocking the trial from narrow notions of liability and its retributive outcomes, without diminishing or dismissing these as they represent legitimate victim interests.

Juridical discretion is proposed as a constructive and creative context where evidence and truth can co-exist for enhanced trial objectives. The transformed trial can explore the stories which need to be told by victims and the truth to be negotiated for community reconciliation in a similar manner as conventionally the trial objective has focused on liability in preference to broader determinations of responsibility.

The challenge is to introduce a more active victim voice along with the establishment of truth and the responsibility which follows, not at the expense of retributive punishment where liability may also be up for grabs. Up until now, these

41 Argued for more fully in Findlay and Henham (2005), chaps 7 and 8.

42 There will be particular difficulties, however, in the status of evidence once applied to restorative contexts such as mediation, if it is then to return to its procedurally recognised standing in adversarial argument.

43 Tamanaha (1997), chap 2.

objectives have remained corralled in international criminal justice to distinctly separate contexts of legal determination and regulation.[44]

Depending on the context of collective perpetration and communal harm in particular, truth and responsibility may be the appropriate negotiation at the expense of liability through adversarial contest, within a new decision-making trial format. Hence, notions of individual criminal responsibility need to be broadened beyond individual culpability, recognising that conventional concepts of individual and collective fault must be argued against the communitarian understandings of what this means for legitimate victim interests. There are several important procedural and substantive hurdles to achieving this within current international trial models.

The First Hurdle – Jurisdictional Challenges

Particularly in Western Europe victim/offender mediation (VOM) is common as a precursor to the adversarial trial. In a detailed qualitative study of victim/offender mediation in Germany and in France, Stefani Trankle[45] presents problems which contradict the aims and working principles of VOM as well as the legal rights of participants even if an agreement between the parties has been reached. Trankle puts down the essence of the problem as being that VOM is not able to secure in practice its specific modus operandi in the framework of penal procedure. She argues that the informal and pedagogical logic of mediation is constrained by the penal framework, namely its power to impose its formal and bureaucratic logic on the mediation process. In her study it was the penal law that dominates the procedure of VOM and impedes the interaction process.

Trankle's research highlights the conceptual and procedural impossibility of successfully incorporating even early stage victim/offender mediation in a trial process not subject to transformation. The integration essential for mediation to work in any true sense of parity will be thwarted by the functional and structural imperatives of adversarial trial justice where prosecutorial dominance and victim marginalisation undermine the conciliatory nature of mediation. Trankle concludes that victim/offender mediation in the two jurisdictions targeted in her research does not work well within a system of penal law. Victim/offender mediation is based on ideals that are not easily compatible with the structural conditions laid down by the judicial framework in an adversarial and retributive model.

> From my point of view the main problem is the structural link between mediation and the penal system. The empirical problems described (in the study) add up to the question of whether victim/offender mediation ought to be institutionalised within,

44 Roche, D. (2005) 'Truth Commission Amnesties and the International Criminal Court', *British Journal of Criminology* 45: 565–81.

45 Trankle (2007).

> or outside, the penal system. The question is how much 'shadow of leviathan', that is how much formality and power control is necessary to guarantee procedural rights and how much mediation can endure without losing its specific character.[46]

The issue of destructive tension between mediation paradigms and penal decision-making frameworks has been widely discussed in the literature of legal sociology.[47] It is recognised that the more informal mediation is the more elements that do not belong to the penal procedure are introduced as such, and the less it can be controlled.

If the judiciary is to keep control over VOM and in so doing retain the conciliatory integrity of a restorative mode, then both the nature and framework for exercising judicial discretion needs to transform. The judiciary, in a conventional trial model, has at its disposal sufficient power to exert control on mediation officers and the progress of the mediation they deliver. On the other hand, too much control on formalism by the judiciary or trial professionals will so adulterate the restorative context of mediation as to make the essentials of parity between the non-professional parties impossible to obtain.

Trankle discusses the possibilities to improve the practice of victim/offender mediation within a penal system of trial justice. However, she does so within a very limited reform framework, not one which envisages the possibility or achievement of wholesale trial transformation. She warns against confusing a penal and psychological procedure which will tend to confuse participants regarding what it includes and excludes. In this sense the extension of the study is to:

- identify the impracticality of restorative justice within a conventional penal model;
- highlight the significance of judicial discretion in the management of restorative trial opportunities (conventional or transformed); and
- identify the particular relationships in a restorative enterprise which would need to transform if its decision-making pathways were to avoid the constrictions of retributive penality, and at the same time embrace restorative possibilities within a rights-protection trial framework. The essential consideration here is the management of otherwise alternative trial sources by a reconstituted judicial discretion.

Once jurisdiction for whatever intervention is preferred, has been settled, the issue of attributing liability or responsibility presents itself. For collective liability in particular, the legal individual remains the unrealistic focus of conventional international criminal trials. Crimes by groups against groups necessitate a broader engagement either for liability and punishment to follow or at least for truth and responsibility to be attributed.

46 Trankle (2007), 411.

47 Amongst others by Spittler, 1980; Von Trotha, 1982; Jung, 1998, 1999; and Trenzek, 2002, 2003; referred to in Trankle (2007).

The Second Hurdle – Collectivising Liability

International victim/offender interaction in the context of crimes against humanity or genocide realistically demands collective rather than individual engagement. Despite the reluctance of international criminal legislation and its instrumental processes to venture outside the crimes of the individual (and tortuous interpretations of liability through association), collectivised responsibility has been a major consideration in truth and reconciliation settings.

The ICTY in a number of decisions wrestled with the scope of 'joint criminal enterprise'.[48] This intention behind the doctrine is to construct through the commission of similar or collaborative acts, agreed to or contemplated, a culpable association with the perpetrator. In this way it is a doctrine to impute individual liability through association across a group. From an evidentiary standpoint the doctrine saves the prosecutor the necessity to prove communicated agreement or a causal link to the perpetration of the criminal act.

As Damaška concedes of the doctrine:

> … its animating idea – that of reaching the criminal masterminds – is sound. It responds to the fact that most international crimes are committed in an organizational context, so that looking for principal culprits beyond hands-on perpetrators makes eminent sense. It is the elaboration of that idea that causes concern. Under the presently prevailing understanding, the scope of membership in the enterprise, as well as its spatial and temporal range, are uncertain and liable to arbitrary extension.[49]

The sharpest criticism of 'common purpose' or joint criminal enterprise approaches to collective liability has been in circumstances where agreement is inferred from foresight of consequences, or as being within the accused's contemplation.[50]The slippage between judicial hindsight and actual foresight (or not) within the pressures and confusions of conflict and armed struggle can tend to dislocate evidentiary construction from truth.[51]

The difficulties facing courts in being satisfied that degrees of involvement equate with perpetration and individual liability, highlight the tensions when forcing inclination, impression and predisposition into a form of evidence equating

48 For a discussion of this see Haan, V. (2005) 'The Development of the Concept of Joint Criminal Enterprise at the International criminal Tribunal for the Former Yugoslavia', *Int. Crm. L R* 5: 167 at 169–94. Recent judicial discussion can be found in the *Prosecutor v Brdjanin*, Case No. IT-99-36-A, Judgement, 357–450 (ICTY Ap. ch. 3, April 2007).

49 Damaška (2008) 352.

50 Cassese, A. (2007) 'The Proper Limits of Individual Responsibility under the Doctrine of Joint Criminal Enterprise', *J Intl Crm J* 5: 109.

51 Rachlinski, J. (2007) 'A Positive Psychological Theory of Judging in Hindsight', *U Chi L R* 65: 571.

with the guilty mind of the individual. The legal wrangling over the interpretation of superior orders,[52] command responsibility[53] and equal culpability[54] emphasises the incapacity for collective liability to be viewed outside the constraints of the individual and his 'mind'.

Amann looks at the problem of collective liability with particular reference to genocide.[55]The state of mind required for the crime is the intent to destroy in whole or in part, a national, ethical, racial or religious group as such',[56] much more than mass killings. Conviction requires that the victim belongs to one of four designated protected groups. Evidence of the intent to destroy can take other crime forms but it must be directed against the designated protected group. Therefore, liability is essentially dependent on harming a specific victim community. Here, the group mentality in question is not merely that of certain perpetrators. It is the collective mentality which binds the protected group that also gives purchase to the prosecution and punishment endeavour. The question is asked with respect to genocide as against other forms of collective harm; so what? Does naming an act genocide bring it any added significance. Amann holds it does because international and domestic laws against collectivised harm and victimisation, 'operates as a means for articulation and nourishment of social values'.[57] To this extent the declaratory purpose of criminalising (or even holding responsibility for) genocide is as important as the punishment of the individual or the group.

This expressive function has special force in international criminal law, only now entering an era in which ongoing international criminal tribunals reinforce pronouncements of norms, such as the proscription against genocide in the 1948 Convention.[58] Even so, it is recognised that for genocide as a unique form of criminal liability, the limited range of protected groups affected by the collective harm so as to substantiate genocide resists upsetting the singular status of the proscription. For groups falling outside the protected range, with individual liability not sufficiently answering other heinous forms of collective victimisation, responsibility may await truth telling and restorative interventions beyond failed punishment. If collective liability remains a narrow legal construct in international criminal law then the argument to include considerations of truth and responsibility within the transformed international trial become a clearer aspiration. The attribution of

52 Ambos (2007).

53 Marston Danner, A. and Martinez, J. (2005) 'Guilty Associations: Joint Criminal Enterprise, Command Responsibility and the Development of International Criminal Law', *Cal L R* 93: 75.

54 Ohlin, D. (2007) 'Three Conceptual Problems with the Doctrine of Joint Criminal Enterprise', *J Intl Crm J* 5: 69.

55 Amann, D. (2002) 'Group Mentality, Expressivism and Genocide', *Int. Crm. L R* 2: 93.

56 Convention on the Prevention and Punishment of the Crime of Genocide Art II.

57 Amann (2002) 95.

58 Ibid.

responsibility depends on truth-telling beyond adversarial argument. The tensions inherent in adversarial contest are exacerbated when victimisation and perpetration are collectivised and cases are multiple. Contrary accounts are difficult enough to resolve as truth when there are two self-interested individuals in the frame. Multiply that through collective liability, and even legal fictions such as reasonable contemplation will not produce a credible truth-telling environment. As Haack suggests truth is not a consequence of the 'clash of bias and counter-bias' because, as with collective liability determinations, the more complex the investigated question, the more partisan polarisation becomes the straitjacket to historians.[59]

The Third Hurdle – Criminalising Organisations

In Australian domestic jurisdictions there are several recent models for the criminalising of organisations within which collective liability can be constructed. Kyriakakis[60] suggests that the integration of ICC crimes within the Commonwealth Criminal Code, aligned with the Code's approach to corporate liability, has created an opportunity to prosecute corporations for global crime, even under the universal jurisdiction principle.[61] The possible reach of the Code when testing Australian international crimes provisions against its framework of corporate liability might, it is argued, fill the void left by the ICC's restriction to the individual legal personality. The Code (at Part 2.5 section 12.1) makes it clear that all offences contained therein apply equally to bodies corporate as to natural persons.

The possibilities under the Commonwealth Code for making corporations responsible for the harm they cause may be wider than what is offered through the civil reparations route of the US *Alien Tort Claims Act 1789*,[62] provided the Code is extended off-shore reach. The Code would not need to rely on the authority of the law of nations or customary international law[63] in order to move corporate responsibility to a determination of criminal liability.

In the Code drafting conventional notions of the mind of the company are relied upon to establish liability through identification and transference. Constructing the mind of the company for the purposes of criminal liability is not possible,

59 Haack, S. (2004) 'Epistimology Legalised: Or truth, justice and the American way', *American Journal of Jurisprudence* 49: 43.

60 Kyriakakis, J. (2007) 'Australian Prosecution of Corporations for International Crimes: The potential of the Commonwealth Criminal Code', *Journal of International Criminal Justice* 5: 809–26.

61 Kyriakakis refers to the investigation by the Australian Federal Police into the possible role of Anvil Mining Limited in facilitating a military offensive in the Democratic Republic of Congo. This investigation, she alleges, indicates that Australia, like many other nations, is grappling locally with the possibility of corporate involvement in International crime.

62 28 USC 1350.

63 Joseph, S. (2004) *Corporations and Transnational Human Rights Litigation*, Oxford: Hart.

however, through aggregating individual 'culpabilities' exhibited by groups of individuals in the company. The unique feature of determining liability which would particularly lend itself to global crime, is the notion of 'criminal corporate cultures'.[64] Part 2.5 section 12.3 of the Code provides two routes for proving fault where culture is concerned. A company can be liable where:

- a corporate culture existed within the body corporate that directed, encouraged, tolerated or led to non-compliance with the relevant provision, or
- proving that the body corporate failed to create and maintain a corporate culture that required compliance with the relevant provision.

It cannot be said that the Code criminalises organisations per se. Rather, it identifies either the mind of the company or a criminal culture that influences that mind. In jurisdictions such as China, criminal liability and sanctions can attack organisational structures and entities, as well as their membership (Findlay: 2008: pp.205–6). In Hong Kong the *Societies Ordinance* advances the proscription model for the control of outlawed organisations and their membership. Interestingly, the criminalisation of the organisation was not the stated purpose of the recently enacted *Crimes (Criminal Organisations Control) Act (NSW) 2009*. This legislation was a criminal justice response to an outbreak of bikie gang violence in NSW. The Act claims extraterritorial operation to in part, have organisations 'declared' which will have criminal consequences for membership and association. A judge making a declaration needs to be satisfied that members associate 'for the purpose of organising, planning, facilitating, supporting or engaging in serious criminal activity, or the organisation represents a risk to public safety and order (section 9). Proof is only required on the balance of probabilities. Associated with declaration is the facility for the court to make control orders against individuals who associate with the organisation.

This is not the place to analyse the many problems associated with proving and prosecuting membership or association as determined in the Act. For the purpose of a concern with collective liability and the transferability to international criminal law, the issue of *association* is crucial. The Act views association as being in company with, or communicating with a member. Association becomes a criminal offence. It would appear under section 23 of the Act that association is a status offence; that is where criminal conduct is confirmed through the act of association. It is not clear whether an accused is also required:

- to share the objectives of the organisation regarding serious criminal activity
- to agree with others to share these objectives, or to have this agreement implied

64 'Corporate culture' means an attitude, policy, rule, course of conduct or practice existing within the body corporate generally or in the part of the body corporate in which the relevant activities takes place.

- to have agreement or shared objectives inferred as a natural consequence of association, or
- to intend to associate for any serious criminal purpose, or otherwise.[65]

It would seem, however, that some mental state is required for liability. This assumption can be drawn from the construction of defences to a charge of association. On the one hand, section 26(5) lists certain types of association (like close family membership, or in the course of lawful occupation) which might be disregarded for the purposes of the offence. While it can be assumed that the onus shifts to the accused to raise these issues in justification of association, the motive or intention for association outside the charge on the part of the accused is an essential proof. Beyond denying association, or that an associate was a member of a declared organisation the other defence against association would be that the accused knew that the organisation had been otherwise authorised to conduct activities which would in ordinary circumstance be considered seriously criminal or a challenge to order.[66]

If little else these two legislative approaches to collective liability identify the challenges in redirecting international criminal law away from approaches dealing with joint criminal enterprise, command responsibility or common purpose. Is it then best for the ICC to move more towards considerations of the collective challenge to human rights? In answering this question we continue to address corporations as criminal organisations, rather than say political resistance groups in transitional state conflict. Despite the obvious and documented impact of multinational corporations in fomenting civil unrest, corporations represent a legal fiction as individual legal entities, but resist criminal liability because of their collective and incorporated form. This increases the challenge for conventional criminalisation through prosecution and trial processes.

The Fourth Hurdle – Agency against Collective Human Rights Abuses

Schabas considers general principles of international individual criminal responsibility (accomplice liability in particular) and how they could be employed to prosecute 'economic actors' who participate in international crimes.[67] In the context of corporate crime these principles might be applied to the prosecution of individuals within the body corporate. As Schabas argues, Article 25 of the Rome

65 Section 26(6) relieves the prosecutor of the necessity to prove that the defendant associated with any particular purpose or that the association would have led to the commission of any offence.

66 See section 27(6) for the circumstances of authorisation.

67 Schabas, W.A. (2001) 'International Humanitarian Law: Catching the accomplices', *International Review of the Red Cross* 83: 439–56.

Statute has at least two potentials for linking accessorial liability to the nexus between business and international crime:

- Article 25 does not stipulate that the assistance provided (economically or through business) should be substantial in order to constitute aiding and abetting;
- the wording of the Article entitles the prosecution of an individual on the basis of having acted through a corporate entity to commit an international crime.[68]

The problems associated with working from the liability of the individual to that of the corporation in the economic sphere challenges a broader consideration of morality and good global citizenship. As Braithwaite and Fisse suggest for punishing corporations[69] the complexity of collective responsibility requires a rethink of conventional responses which might be appropriate for individuals, but not corporations. How can it be right that corporations profit from what would be considered as criminal for individuals simply because the law of global liability cannot find the technology to encompass the company perpetrator? Legal incapacity could never be equated with innocence, or to a lesser extent, moral probity and hence impunity.

McCorquodale and Simons[70] argue that states routinely support and assist their corporate nationals in prosecuting and advancing global trading interests. Even though states may not advocate human rights violations as a consequence of these extraterritorial adventures, through acts or omissions states may unwittingly contribute to corporations violating rights off-shore. Therefore, is there a case for home state responsibility in such situations of rights violations?

Corporations do carry human rights obligations. The nature of transnational corporations and their impact on the international legal system in a commercial sense at least is prefaced on good corporate citizenship. Where states carry human rights obligations for the actions of all corporations within the state's territory, global governance requires that international human rights law (IHL) has purchase over human rights violations by corporations advantaging themselves extraterritorially.[71]

---

68 For an expansion of this position see Chapman, A. (2004) 'The Complexity of International Criminal Law: Looking beyond individual responsibility to the responsibility of organisations, corporations and states', in R. Thakur and P. Malcontent (eds) *From Sovereign Impunity to International Accountability: The search for justice in a world of states*, Tokyo: United Nations Press.

69 Braithwaite, J. and Fisse, B. (1993) *Corporations, Crime and Accountability*, Cambridge: Cambridge University Press.

70 McCorquodale, R. and Simons, P. (2007) 'Responsibility Beyond Borders: State responsibility for extraterritorial violations by corporations of international human rights law', *Modern Law Review* 70/4: 598–625.

71 It should be remembered that IHL is often more seen as legitimating rights violations through armed conflict rather than presenting a framework of rights protections.

It could be argued that states become internationally responsible for rights violations[72] by their corporate citizens where:

- a corporation is exercising government authority, including where it has exceeded that authority;
- a corporation is acting under the instruction, direction or control of the state, including where it has ignored or contravened instruction;
- a state aids and assists the corporation with its activities, in the knowledge of circumstances of unlawful activity;
- a state may have international responsibility for a foreign subsidiary of a corporate national, where
- state practice shows that the state's relationship with transnational corporations is not territorially limited, and
- a duty of due diligence to protect from harm applies to the state, whether knowledge is actual or constructive, and the state facilitates that duty.

International organisations such as the OECD recognise the need for states to shoulder responsibility through their domestic jurisdictions (state responsibility), for rights violations by corporations where international law alone may not have clear purchase.

> (States should encourage corporate nationals) to respect human rights of those affected by their activities consistent with the host government's international obligations and commitments.[73]

In this guideline may lie the seeds of its own impotence. If international customary law fails to regulate corporate rights violators, why should we believe domestic regulations will be any more effective if the domestic jurisdiction has a chequered rights record through a reluctance to act on international rights obligations? Isn't this a more fundamental challenge to the state as the holder of both rights and obligations? Perhaps the notion of state responsibility in international law needs to give way, where global crime is concerned, to considerations of collective liability or responsibility effectively determined through a transformed ICJ. Once again the call for corporate responsibility may rely on histories of truth and costly revelations against corporate reputation.

---

72 In methods similar to states responsibility in international law, rather than through the domestic enactment of international criminal law.

73 OECD (2000) *Guidelines for Multinational Enterprises*, para 11.

Imperatives for Truth: The Historiography of Justice

Recording history as an aim of ICJ is closely connected to wider concerns for conflict resolution. Cassese[74] identifies the enunciation of an accurate historical record so that 'future generations can remember and be made fully cognizant of what happened' as a worthy purpose of ICJ.

This is no simple task. Contested histories proliferate as much in the experience of truth and reconciliation commissions, as alternate facts fuel adversarial examination. Even so, the didactic purpose of justice is undeniable in the widest presentation of the story at issue. The question remains as to whether the trial is the place for this 'truth-telling' and if so, how is it to be managed. Damaška denies the validity and possibility of judicial historiography because 'judges cannot sufficiently disentangle themselves from the web of legal relevancy'.[75] Even if this is so, it acts not so much as a denial of historical record for the achievement of ICJ, but rather the need for trial narrative to break free from the procedural strictures of fact-finding.

We assert that trial transformation makes truth-telling possible and appropriate. Why so?

- It acts as a precursor to restorative outcomes which address significant victim interests.
- It may produce justice understandings that adversarial evidence rules can conspire to restrict or conceal.
- It gives an expanded victim-voice which if not leading on to liability determinations will not necessarily compromise the rights of the accused.
- It opens up possibilities for judge-led mediation and conciliation where retributive outcomes are unlikely or inappropriate.

The effect of the 'truthful' recording of history which promotes reconciliation was referred to in the ICTY case of *Plavsic*. On this issue the tribunal stated:

> The Trial Chamber accepts that acknowledgement and full disclosure of serious crimes are very important when establishing the truth in relation to such crimes. This, together with acceptance of responsibility for the committed wrongs, will promote reconciliation. In this respect, the Trial Chamber concludes that the guilty pleas of Mrs Plavsic and her acknowledgement of responsibility, particularly in the light of her former position as President of the Republika Srpska, should promote reconciliation in Bosnia and Herzegovina and the region as a whole.[76]

---

74 Cassese, A (1998) 'Reflections on International Criminal Justice', *Modern Law Review* 61/1: 1–10 at 6–7.

75 Damaška (2008) 336.

76 *The Prosecutor v Plavsic* ICTY Ch III 27.2.2008, para 80.

The *Plavsic* declaration of responsibility is all the more remarkable in an adversarial context, even if rewarded with sentencing concessions for contrition. It was a concession which allowed on to the record a wealth of 'story' which would otherwise have been excluded in a contested trial.[77]

In the appeal from the trial of *Drazen Erdemovich* the tragic case turned on a soldier's responsibility when forced by threats of his own death to kill innocent victims under superior orders.[78] The accused's conviction was as much due to the legal/moral convention that it is better to sacrifice your own life rather than the lives of others rather than any glaring determination of a criminal mind.

Generally, on the purposes of the criminalisation in this instance the majority judgement observed:

> one of the purposes of international criminal law is to protect the weak and vulnerable in armed conflict situations. Judges McDonald and Vohrah, therefore, seek to facilitate the development and effectiveness of international humanitarian law and not to impede it. Thus, they 'give[s] notice in no uncertain terms that those who kill innocent persons will not be able to take advantage of duress as a defence and thus get away with impunity for their criminal acts in the taking of innocent lives.'[79]

On the issue of responsibility, in dissenting with the majority view Judge Sir Ninian Stephen emphasised the contextual relevance of responsibility in the face of immutable, if harsh legal principle.

> Whatever (the appellant) chose, the lives of the innocent would be lost and he had no power to avert that consequence. Hence, since the common law authorities – but for which one could say that the general principles of law favoured duress as a defence to all crimes – did not address the issue at stake, and since their underlying rationale did not justify excluding duress as a defence to unlawful killing in circumstances such as those facing the Appellant, the general principles of law would allow duress to be raised as a defence even to a charge of unlawful killing.

Moral responsibility, and pragmatic rationality, in this judge's view argued against the unqualified application which imposed liability no matter at what cost. Interestingly, the accused initially pleaded guilty even though he believed he was neither liable nor culpable, on the advice that duress didn't apply. This was the only appeal point that succeeded.

---

77 This should be put against an expectation of full disclosure which in turn might have increased sentence.

78 *The Prosecutor v. Drazen Erdemovic*, Case No. IT-96-22-A, A.C., 5 May 1997.

79 http://www.icty.org/sid/7463.

The experience of corporate criminal liability has been that stories of responsibility against histories of reputation may have far greater punitive impact than conventional sentencing options. Imprisoning corporate executives when they can be replaced, fining companies when the cost is passed on to the consumer, restricting the capacity to trade when it hurts shareholders each problematise the liability/punishment nexus transferred without creative adjustment from individual to collective liability. Braithwaite and Fisse[80] suggest that corporate compliance is best ensured by challenging and negotiating otherwise marketable reputations and respected organisational and trading histories in order to ensure responsibility. Responsibility flowing from the revelation of truth, contested or otherwise, surely represents an aspiration for more inclusive trial justice and not simply its denial within the context of evidence and fact trial 'languages'. If so, how does one represent a more balanced consideration of responsibility when the discourse of individual liability dominates international criminal justice? Part of the pathway to a more inclusive discourse on truth and responsibility is to touch on the failed 'language' of individual liability as the restrictive 'narrative' of international criminal law.

Languages of Capacity, Liability, Justification and Excuse, and Culpability

There is no time here to adequately interrogate the language of the law as it relates to fact-finding, evidence testing and liability attribution. We will restrict our consideration of language to the way it binds and ties fact (while at the same time denying the primacy of truth) to the importance of judicial narrative. The reason for this is the re-iteration of juridical discretion in the achievement of trial transformation, and the essential place of judicial narrative in holding the exercise of such discretion, accountable to victim interests. Through the process of accountability, we argue, the legitimacy of ICJ will be more significantly ensured.[81]

Trial transformation enables an engagement with truth at stages where the juridical professional determines that adversarial justice (and its fact fascination) are inappropriate for the achievement of significant victim interests. In talking away from evidence to truth, the judicial narrative will chart an exercise of discretion no longer essentially concerned with factors determining or denying liability. In fact, by admitting the wider histories of truth, judicial narrative will breach essential rules of evidence and compromise the search for liability in a sufficiently probative sense.

Capacity will take on new meaning. No longer will it be communicated in terms of volition to commit the criminal act. Instead it will carry more moral meaning, referring to responsibility rather than liability. The consequence of this will be that justifications or excuses will be crafted not to deny the evidence of the

80 Braithwaite and Fisse (1993) chap. 6.

81 Findlay (2008), chap. 9.

prosecution but to qualify or mitigate responsibility, particularly where contested histories are on offer.

Culpability will give way to responsibility. Guilt will not be the essential outcome of liability proven. Culpability can take on contributory and conditional forms. This will certainly enable a language of collective responsibility more compatible with restorative outcomes which up until trial transformation remained the province of alternative justice discourse.

In the context of a discourse on the 'right to truth' for victims of international armed conflict, Naqvi discusses the significance of 'legal truth'.[82] She holds that legal truth is merely a bi-product of a dispute settlement mechanism. We agree and as such argue that trial transformation must precede the more convincing approximation of legal truth.

> In trials dealing with international crimes, however, the significance of this bi-product of legal truth has taken on a new dimension owing no doubt to the unique objectives that international criminal law is supposed to fulfill and that go way above and beyond merely finding guilt or innocence of particular individuals. … this legal concept intersects with international criminal processes in various ways, at times strengthening the intended purpose to prosecute persons accused of international crimes and at times overriding the focus on the individual defendant and instead turning the attention of the case to the broader implications of international criminal trials. The desire for truth may even be used to justify non prosecution of certain alleged offenders in an 'amnesty-for-truth or 'use immunity' situations.[83]

Conclusion? – Victim-Driven Truth and Fact

Damaška represents the adversarial trial as progressing sometimes dysfunctionally 'when fact finding is organised as a sequence of two partisan cases'.[84]

If international criminal trials remain contained within a substantially adversarial model, the suggestion that fact and truth should co-exist in the evidentiary and proof project is dangerous indeed. One casualty likely is independent and impartial juridical decision-making, and there-from the potential to transform the trial into a more efficient deliberative environment:

> Judicial interference with partisan management of cases (for the purpose of historiography) deflates partisan incentives to develop more effective trial

82 Naqvi, Y (2006) 'The Right to Truth in International Law: fact or fiction', *International Review of the Red Cross* 88/862: 245–273.

83 Ibid: 246.

84 Damaška (2008) 337.

> strategies, and may also appear to help one side, compromising the court's neutrality *inter partes*.[85]

In an ideal world, as Damaška denies such possibilities;

> … there would be no reason to balance (accused's rights and victim interests) – they would co-exist in harmony. But in the real world, painful tradeoffs between them must be made.[86]

It is here our analysis parts company. Those who suggest, despite its ennobling humanitarian foundations, that telling victim-centred truths beyond the confines of evidence in the trial format is misconceived, do not go the next step to ask, why not. To exclude an essential humanitarian focus under the guise of coherence with procedural conventions is to ignore the potential through trial transformation of attaining the unattainable. It is more than an inevitable tension between wide communitarian and victim-centred rights aspirations and the definitive trial focus on the rights of the accused (which are today constantly compromised for far less noble intentions), that makes trial transformation heretic.[87]

In this chapter we have used the imperative of collective perpetration and the legitimate interests of victim communities, which define global crime, as the imperatives for trial transformation. In so doing we have shown how conventional exceptions to individual liability are not creating a novel and effective international criminal jurisprudence. Further, the commendable attempts of the nation state through extra-territoriality are not effectively requiring responsibility from corporate and collective violators even through the exercise of state responsibility required by international law.

We return to the simple potential of trial transformation, and its engagement with truth and responsibility as a pathway to satisfying victim communities collectively violated. This may not produce retributive declarations or the gaoling of otherwise-criminal corporate executives but the wide vista of restorative outcomes will be available within the due process protections of the transformed international trial to satisfy more victims collectively harmed.

---

85 Damaška (2008) 333.

86 Ibid.

87 L. Zedner and Carolyn Hoyle, 'Victims, Victimization, and the Criminal Process' in M. Maguire, R. Morgan and R. Reiner (eds), *The Oxford Handbook of Criminology*, (Oxford University Press 2007).

Chapter 4
Victims' Expectations towards Justice in Post-Conflict Societies: A Bottom-Up Perspective

Ernesto Kiza and Holger-C. Rohne

Introduction

The quest for achieving justice in the aftermath of mass violence is not a new challenge posed by the political and sociological aftermath stemming from large-scale violent conflicts. But only in recent years have we faced a decisive commitment by the states of the Westphalian International System to establish common norms and institutions in order to curb war-crimes, crimes against humanity and genocide. We can attribute this development to a number of historical factors. Furthermost, the development of something like a 'global' morality regarding the conduct and behaviour of state-actors towards each other in armed conflicts (humanitarian law) and towards their subjects (human rights) has contributed to a shift of perspectives within the understanding of how far-reaching the concept of state sovereignty shall be applied (Neubacher: 2005: 415ff.).

Unsurprisingly, the attempt to construct institutions designed to prosecute perpetrators of the worst crimes known to humanity was successful only after many years had passed since the first such modern proceedings – then as military tribunals – were held in Nuremberg (1945) and Tokyo (1946). Frozen by a total systemic antagonism, the beginning of an international jurisdiction over crimes against peace left barely room for the development of supranational institutions tasked with the prosecution of war-criminals. Although the world witnessed further horrible excrescent of gross human rights violations in the decades to come other issues were dominating the international agenda. When the Soviet Empire collapsed the dissolution of the Block Conflict gave birth to a new – probably more volatile – era of international politics (for an unfulfilled prophecy see Fukuyama: 1992; for a self-fulfilling prophesy see Huntington: 1996). Shaped by newly dealt cards, we have witnessed the rise of an economic project termed *Globalisation* (McMichael: 2004: 152ff.), the successful involvement of non-governmental organisations in world politics (Spiro: 1995: 251ff.), the expansion of state interventionism justified by *ius cogens* and *norms erga omnes* (Luedtke and Strutynski: 2007; Kiza: 2001; Chomsky: 2000), unilateral actions by the remaining superpower (Weiss et al.: 2004), and newly awoken powers grasping for hegemony (Olson: 1982;

Kegley and Wittkopf: 2006). Within this atmosphere of a new global anarchy (for example, Mearsheimer: 2003) or disorder (Ruf: 1994) new forms of regimes were constructed attempting to reign in the volatile structure of the international system after the Cold War – with yet questionable success. Hence, the efforts to put an end to impunity to war crimes, crimes against humanity, genocide and of course the crime of aggression – which remains suspiciously undebated in times of 'war on terror' – are part of the attempt to keep or to regain control in the wake of the destructive effects of mass violence and the related loss of morality.

These efforts, however, are to a large extent attributable to past and contemporary power politics (Teitelbaum: 2002). Although war crimes are nowadays predominantly perpetrated within the boundaries of less powerful states and non-western contexts, justice initiatives are shaped through the lens of exercising justice via a westernised criminal justice system. At the same time, the establishment of an effective international or universalised criminal justice is threatened by the unwillingness of the great powers to access the Rome Statute.[1] Among the population of war-torn regions this development fosters a sense of being subjected to double standards and an 'externalised' justice (Drumbl: 2003: 170ff. and 2007: 127) enforced by foreign powers and their hidden power agendas.

However, we can observe an increasing utilisation of criminal justice institutions, tasked to prosecute gross human rights abuses on the national level, within mixed institutions and also on the international level. It is beyond doubt that enormous implications are related to the exercise of International Criminal Justice (ICrimJ) as a path to peace[2] and – taking into account the contemporary international system – it seems only consequent that the implementation of related institutions is a top-down approach. For instance Meernik states that:

> We often hear the refrain 'no justice, no peace' from advocates, academics, and practitioners, which is supposed to convey the idea that there is a fundamental and appropriate level of fairness, equality, correctness, balance – pick your own

1 Decisive refers to the major players in the international quest for hegemony, namely the United States, China and Russia. As of October 2010, 114 countries are States Parties to the Rome Statute of the International Criminal Court. Out of them, 31 are African states, 15 are Asian states, 18 are from Eastern Europe, 25 are from Latin America and the Caribbean, and 25 are from Western Europe and other states. Updates on the status of the Rome Statute can be obtained from the World Wide Web at the ICC-site: http://www.icc-cpi.int/statesparties.html.

2 Note that with regard to the ICTY the Security Council was pointing out that it was 'Remaining convinced that the prosecution of persons responsible for serious violations of international humanitarian law committed in the territory of the former Yugoslavia contributes to the restoration and maintenance of peace in the former Yugoslavia' (S/RES/1166 1998), while the Rome Statute of the ICC is comparatively careful stating its purpose as to '[…] put an end to impunity for the perpetrators of these crimes and thus to contribute to the prevention of such crimes' but still aims to '[…] guarantee lasting respect for and the enforcement of international justice' (Rome Statute 1998, Preamble).

> noun – in the way a society, particularly its public institutions, treats its people. (Meernik: 2005: 272)

Nevertheless, the view of those directly affected by the respective atrocities remains largely unexplored and has to be anticipated on the basis of theoretical and generalising assumptions. The empirical inquiry into the victims' perspectives is still completely underdeveloped. Thus, the call for the integration and development of an international victimology and criminology in the field of transitional justice grows (for some cursory insights see Albrecht: 2002: 88; more in-depth arguments are developed by Roberts and McMillan: 2003; Drumbl: 2003; Hagan et al.: 2005; Sebba: 2006: 39; Kiza et al.: 2006: 47; Rohne: 2007: 2). Until today, however, the few empirical results that could have been a valuable source to improve instruments of achieving peace through justice are basically ignored – presumably for political reasons. We are particularly referring to a recent study done by the Afghan Independent Human Rights Commission (AIHRC: 2005) officially mandated to 'explore whether the people of Afghanistan want this [human rights abuses] to be addressed, and if so, how'. Shedding light on the population's view on essential facets of effectively dealing with the violent past, the study did not affect the political course of action in the country.

While the majority of the contributions in this volume are scrutinising the developments in the area of international criminal justice from a theoretical and/or a top-down perspective, this chapter will undertake the attempt to take a glimpse into another crucial perspective of ICrimJ, namely the exploration of some aspects of ICrimJ and transitional justice issues from a bottom-up perspective. Based on a pilot study we conducted among war victims in Africa, Asia and Europe, we are focusing on the perspective of victims but contrast them with results from population based studies in (post-) conflict and war-torn regions. We are terming this kind of research a bottom-up approach because it is designed to inspect the needs, opinions and attitudes of those who have suffered most from armed conflicts.[3]

In the following paragraphs, we explore how victims think past atrocities should be addressed and what measures should be taken in response. There is a vivid ongoing scholarly and (law-) professional debate about the best practices in transitional justice as well as the different means and approaches to be applied, about their impact, efficiency and effectiveness. As indicated above, this debate is strongly influenced by political factors. We aim to contribute to it by providing for some empirical data regarding the attitudes and perceptions of war-victims, hopefully enriching the discussion by the introduction of a crucial issue.

3 Yet, we are well aware that most opinions, beliefs and attitudes are formed by external circumstances that are developed in a top-down manner through dominant discourse.

Top-Down Normative Frameworks from a Bottom-Up Perspective

As argued before, in the past 10 to 15 years we have witnessed the rise of transversal and international attempts to curb impunity of culprits of gross human rights violations, among them perpetrators of war-crimes, crimes-against humanity and genocide. Several approaches exist to prosecute these persons including formal and traditional proceedings[4] as well as national, international or mixed tribunals; since 2002, the International Criminal Court as a permanent judicial institution took up its work to deal with large scale violence. These institutions and their respective normative frameworks have been largely constructed by politicians in a sphere dominated by *realpolitk*, seconded by law professionals (and sometimes by other stakeholders such as specific NGOs). Hence, institution-building and policy-making are implemented top-down, basically outside the scope of the affected populations (Drumbl: 2007). This is particularly problematic since the success of a certain procedure designed to deal with a violent past largely depends on the legitimacy it is given by the local population. The same is true for the implementation of ICrimJ. Furthermore, in order to foster peace and stability transitional justice measures need to positively affect the local attitudes on coexistence and reconciliation. Otherwise, they are likely to result in expensive and dysfunctional international protectorates (for example, BiH, Kosovo, Afghanistan), only suppressing ongoing societal conflicts that are likely to re-emerge in the future.[5] It is on these grounds, that we would like to contribute from a bottom-up perspective to the discussion on how to deal with mass victimisation by giving a voice to those who were personally harmed by such violence.

The lively debate and development of the field of ICrimJ attracts numerous scientists and practitioners from various disciplines. Curiously, criminology and victimology absconded from solid involvement, apart from a few exceptions (for example, Ewald: 2008; Coupland: 2007; Hagan: 2004; Hagan and Kutnjak Ivković: 2006; Meernik: 2005; Kiza et al.: 2006; Rohne: 2007), keeping to their conventional scope rather than facing the challenge posed by the phenomenon of mass violence. Until now, little empirical data is available on people's opinions about mechanisms of transitional justice, including ICrimJ. This is true for the populations in war-torn regions but even more so for attitudes of war-victims: Until recently, no survey among war victims had been conducted, neither on a national level nor on an international comparative basis. This fact is not only surprising because of the unchanged need to effectively deal with mass atrocities in numerous regions in the world but even more so in light of the attempts to systematically meet the horrific intra- and inter-societal challenges of mass violence by judicial means. Especially, the latter gave reason for the conduction of a pilot study to explore

4 For instance the Gacaca proceedings in Rwanda.

5 Notice at this point that most of the conflicts we have faced since the 1990s were of the internal type (Kiza: 2006). These are particularly hard to resolve and tend to be protracted or to re-emerge (e.g. Licklider: 1995).

the attitudes of war victims on how to rightfully respond to their victimisation.[6] In the following, we discuss some major findings of the study putting them in context with empirical evidence from existing population based studies in (post-) conflict regions.[7] It would be beyond the scope of this contribution to elaborate on regional peculiarities that were revealed in the study. Instead, we concentrate on an inclusive (macro) perspective in favour of developing some general trends among those victims surveyed.[8]

Amnesty Denied: War-Victims' Perspectives on Procedures and Punishment

At the heart of the search for appropriate ways to deal with the aftermath of mass victimisation is the choice of the responsive means. Among these means criminal prosecution seems to enjoy a universal popularity in reaction to disproportionate violence, violations of humanitarian law, and human rights. While the chapter headline already suggests a universal support for the retributive variant of transitional justice among those affected by mass violence, it is nevertheless worthwhile to examine the specifics of post-conflict justice as perceived from the bottom-up perspective. Thus are first elaborating on the desirability of prosecution from the victims' perspective. We then examine the legal foundations that the participants favoured regarding reactions to war-crimes as well as the interrelation between international/national approaches and formal/informal approaches. Correspondingly, the victims' expressed their favour for a related judicial setting, including national and/or international responsibilities as well as a differentiation between judicial and non-judicial instances.

In respect to the crucial importance of the victim's participation (FIDH: 2006; Sebba: 1996 and 2006; Fletcher: 2000) we also examined the related attitudes found among the victims surveyed, about their needs from a participatory perspective, and their perceived utility of participation or non-participation in proceedings.

Another vital question when dealing with the prosecution of crimes – especially international crimes[9] – is the application of different means of punishment. Outside the scope of theoretical discussions about retributive or utilitarian models

6 See Kiza et al. (2006) – the full report is available online at http://www.his-online.de/Download/Forschungsberichte/978-3-936096-73-6.pdf .The study included about 1,000 war victims in eleven (post-) war regions in Africa, Asia, and Europe.

7 Although such surveys are rare, the scarce data is basically corroborating each other with regard to major trends in peoples' opinions.

8 For regional perspectives see the specific studies mentioned in the text.

9 This is indeed a very specific field touching upon many fragile questions. For example one could rightfully argue that it is quite peculiar that someone who committed genocide in Rwanda is imprisoned somewhere where he is living under more luxurious conditions than his victims/the relatives of his victims. Furthermore, we are only just beginning to grasp the mechanics of sentencing in international courts, since the status do not provide us with a clear and functional normative basis of sentencing.

of punishment, the victims were asked to provide their view on how perpetrators should be punished in order to meet their particular needs.[10]

Finally, we turn to the question of attributing guilt in very complex situations of mass-violence and human rights abuses. This question incorporates very difficult concepts of attributing guilt in settings that are practically involving whole populations and where virtually everyone might become a perpetrator, a victim or both (Drumbl: 2007: 1–5; Young: 2006: 103ff.).

Prosecution

Starting with the most common notion of dealing with offenders, namely prosecution, the participants of our study were asked to express their attitude towards this topic.

Table 4.1 The Desire to Prosecute (in %)

Response	Total
Yes	79
No	7
No comment	7
Do not know	4
Missing	3

The question was: Should the person(s) that have done these things to you be prosecuted?[11]

The results contained in Table 4.1 were straightforward. An overwhelming majority of the respondents stated they were in favour of prosecution. Deducing from this outcome the support for an institutionalised approach – as the term prosecution suggested formal authorities being involved in the process – was indeed important for the majority of the participants, indicating that a well-organised approach to deal with the atrocities and crimes of the past is of high importance. These findings were also corroborated by the findings of other studies on desired reactions to war atrocities: The available data supports the assumption that affected populations want the respective offenders to be held responsible within a formalised proceeding.

10 Note that we are not elaborating on the purposes of punishment in this chapter. For further elaborations on this topic see Kiza et al.: 2006: 122ff.

11 Note that our study first evaluated the victimisation experiences of the participants (Kiza et al.: 2006: 80–95).

For instance, the ICRC found that 76% of all respondents wanted the perpetrators of international crimes to be put on trial, while only a small minority (7%) would grant them amnesty (ICRC: 1999).[12]

A similar result was found in a representative study on transitional justice issues in Afghanistan.[13] In general 61% of the participants stated they would be against granting amnesty to offenders even if they confessed their wrongdoings, while only a minority favoured such an amnesty. Being asked about possible stabilising or destabilising effects of criminal trials, the majority of all participants (76%) stated that bringing war criminals to justice would positively affect the security situation by increasing stability. However, only 27% held the opinion that *all* war criminals should be prosecuted. The majority of respondents (55%) indicated that it would be sufficient to prosecute those who have committed the most serious crimes and the architects of the atrocities, namely the commanders (AIHRC: 2005).

Taking a look at the opinions of the population in Uganda, the ICTJ found that with regard to the implementation of (further) transitional justice mechanisms there was a generally strong demand to hold perpetrators accountable (76%) (ICTJ: 2005: 4–5).[14] Persons exposed to at least one traumatic event that was listed in the research design of the study were more likely to stress the importance of accountability than those who were not. A little more than one-half of all respondents (53%) supported the pursuit of peace concomitant with trials and punishment; others opted for pursuing peace while granting amnesty (ICTJ: 2005: 33–5).

Judging from the available data, the tenor seems to be clear: personal accountability for international crimes is supported on a wide basis. However, this finding has to be put in perspective. While in all aforementioned studies a majority of respondents favoured prosecution in an institutionalised setting (note that this finding was corroborated at different points in time and throughout different cultural backgrounds) the number of respondents who did not opt for any formalised prosecution, that is, criminal justice, was also remarkably high. In terms of a 'democratic' decision, we may nevertheless speak of a common agreement of people to prosecute offenders.

The Legal Foundations of Prosecution

Having noticed a strong support for prosecution of perpetrators in different (post-) war regions, the question arises on which legal foundation such

12 The ICRC Study included about 13,000 people in 12 different countries. For each country a sample representative of the whole population was taken.

13 The AIHRC Sample included 4,151 respondents from 32 of 34 Afghan provinces. The sample was representative of the whole population. In addition 2,000 respondents participated in 200 focus groups.

14 The ICTJ included 2,585 respondents in its study. The sample was representative of the whole population in four districts in Northern Uganda.

procedures should be based on. This aspect is of vital importance when dealing with large scale violence that typically exceeds national dimensions or is even internationalised by external interventions. Taking into account national and international approaches on one hand as well as formal and informal concepts on the other, the participants of our study were asked to provide their opinion towards different options of legal foundations.

Overall, 66% of all participants clearly supported international law in the process of prosecution. Still strong but to a lesser extent was the support for domestic law as a basis for prosecuting the offenders of mass atrocities (41%). These results indicate a comparatively stronger trust in universal principles and international law than in the application of domestic criminal law. However, the strong support in international law is probably not based on the knowledge of the content of international law. Instead, the ICRC found that support of international law is often independent from the actual knowledge of its rules (ICRC 1999). Domestic law might be viewed with certain scepticism due to its normative framework that is typically not explicitly designed to deal with mass atrocities.[15] Furthermore, international law is likely to appear favourable in times when people cannot trust – or identify with – their own legal system which is often the case in times following mass violence and/or abusive regimes. Correspondingly, we found an outstanding support for domestic law when being embedded in a functioning legal framework.[16] It is, however, noteworthy, that international law seems to receive a general trust among the affected populations providing for a promising basis to build upon.[17]

This finding was corroborated by the ICRC study, where 46% of all respondents pointed towards international law as a main legal source – opposed to 22% opting for domestic law –, confirming the process of universalisation of law based on shared human values and principles. However, the role of religious principles (9%) as well as the – rather abstract – referral to common values, namely 'peoples' beliefs' (13%) were of significant importance for about one tenth of those surveyed by the ICRC.

Additionally, in our victim survey we found 19% of all respondents stating that the prosecution of offenders should be based on religious principles. Another 15% indicated that general values people hold are of vital importance for prosecuting the offenders, while only 3% of all participants favoured other options.

15 Although in many cases there are norms covering this particular aspect of crime, especially with regard to the expansion of such norms within the scope of a subsidiary approach of the ICC/Rome Statute (see e.g. Sieber: 2004).

16 This could be observed among the Israeli respondents (Rohne: 2007: 123; and 2008: 285). Notwithstanding, the overall support for international law dominated over the support of domestic law but was mostly combined with it.

17 This is not only true in terms of international jurisdiction but also with regard to a sense of an international community. Of course, this trust can be easily frustrated when being subject to double standards and political manoeuvres.

Many participants opted for a combination of the provided items.[18] Hence, an analysis of the answer profiles promised a further understanding of victims' statements.[19] The case-wise analysis revealed that the isolated mentioning of international law received the highest support among those surveyed (28%). The support for international law as the only basis to prosecute offenders was followed by the combination of international and domestic law with 16%. Another 11% were in favour of applying domestic law only. The items representing informal approaches ('religious principles' and 'values people hold') did not appear in the case-wise analysis as they were not mentioned frequently enough.

Deducing from these findings, we found the majority of the victims supporting formal legal approaches as a basis for prosecution, especially the application of international law. Nevertheless, the observed reference to informal legal principles or systems cannot be neglected. This is especially true from a regional perspective. In some regions the application of religious principles received an outstanding support, and sometimes even exceeded the support of formal domestic law. This was the case for Afghanistan (49% vs 29), the Philippines (38% vs 36%), (Southern) Sudan (29% vs 20%) and for the Palestinian sample (27% vs 15%). At the same time, in all of these samples the majority of participants still favoured the application of international law.

In contrast to our study, a population-based research in Afghanistan found that most participants favoured domestic law, Islamic law or a combination of both for the prosecution of the offenders, while only a small minority favoured prosecution based on international law (AIHRC: 2005). Whether this finding results from the international intervention and the desolate local security situation or if it rather roots in the wider scope of the survey including also non-victims (or a combination of both) we are not able to determine.

On the other hand, in the largely internationalised conflict in Bosnia-Herzegovina, the majority of the respondents (69%) focus on international law (ICRC: 1999: 44).

Due to the heterogeneous findings from different studies we cannot deduce with absolute certainty that there is a widespread support of universalised/international norms of prosecution. And while we are convinced of the fact that there is a set of common values amongst peoples in different world regions, there is still a large need for further inquiry in this particular problem, based on very carefully constructed research designs.

18 The aggregated percentages of total answers ranged from 134% to 170%.

19 A statistical method called configuration frequency analysis (CFA) (Krauth and Lienert: 1975) was utilised to extrapolate important answering profiles indicating typical answer profiles. Using a threshold of at least 10% of combined categories resulted in a coverage of 55% of all participants that could be included in typical groups therefore providing for typical answer profiles – whereas 44% did not provide for any coherent profile.

Responsibility for Prosecution

In the past we witnessed multiple forms of judicial institutions that were designed to prosecute offenders of war crimes. These institutions have ranged from domestic trials to special courts, and mixed tribunals to international ad-hoc tribunals with the first ones held in Nuremberg (1945–1949) and Tokyo (1946–1948) after WWII and about 50 years later in The Hague (International Criminal Tribunal for the former Yugoslavia (ICTY), 1993) and Arusha (International Criminal Tribunal for Rwanda (ICTR), 1994).[20] The efforts to end impunity with regard to war-related crimes culminated in the establishment of the permanent International Criminal Court (ICC) by the Rome Statute in 1998 which entered into force on 1July 2002. The morphology of mechanisms is complex, providing for a wide – yet restricted – range of possible settings of criminal justice institutions dealing with mass violence.

In order to find out about the victims' perspectives on these different settings, the participants of our study were asked about their view of who should be responsible for prosecution. Given the choice, more than a half of the participants (53%) indicated that an international court should be responsible for prosecution. In general, this finding confirms the decision of the international community to establish the ICC. Apparently, the fight against impunity for the most serious crimes on the basis of international law is not primarily perceived as an intra-societal matter but as falling into the sphere of the international community. However, there are limitations to this deduction: the support for international courts did not prevail in all of the surveyed regions: a rather low support became apparent among the respondents from Afghanistan (35%), the Philippines (35%) and the DRC (20%).

Moreover, 26% of all participants opted for a domestic solution favouring 'own courts' to be responsible for prosecuting war criminals while another 26% wanted their 'own government' to deal with the perpetrators. The 'mixed court' variant was represented with 24% of all participants; 8% of the participants wanted the military forces to deal with the offenders, possibly expecting harsher pursuance of punishment than from civilian courts; 13% of the respondents agreed that the 'civilian population' should prosecute the offenders. In context with other questions it became clear that only few of these respondents referred to self-justice measures; instead, most of them were pointing to the involvement of civilians in a truth-finding process rather than to punishment.[21] The case-wise analysis[22] provides for only little additional information. Corresponding to the support of

---

20 Both were military tribunals while the ICTY and ICTR were civil tribunals under the UN system.

21 For further details, see Kiza et al. 2006: 101; in total, 7% of the participants were indecisive, did not comment or refused to answer this question altogether.

22 Using a threshold of 5% allowed for the extraction of six different profiles representing 58% of all participants – with 42% not providing for a coherent profile.

legal foundations, the most frequent answer profile was the exclusive reference to an international responsibility to prosecute war criminals (24%). Further answer profiles were of rather marginal importance.[23]

Other available data suggests a trend to internationalise dealing with the past. For instance, among the Afghan population, the AIHRC study revealed that mixed jurisdiction – involving Afghan and international judges – seem to attract the highest support (50%), followed by the support for international judges (28%) (AIHRC: 2005: 24). Collapsing these categories confirms the noticeable acknowledgement of international involvement observed in our study. This acknowledgement, however, is seemingly limited by the wish of keeping a certain amount of sovereignty over ways to deal with the violent past and is opposed to the wish to apply sharia in war-crimes proceedings (see above).

The findings of the ICRC indicate a similar ambivalence between the internationalisation on one hand and the wish to keep domestic control over the process. The ICRC found 36% of the respondents favouring the jurisdiction of an 'international criminal court' while 24% preferred their 'own government' for such a task (ICRC: 1999: 47). Unfortunately, the ICRC did not take into account the possibility of mixed-courts which might have led to a clearer picture in this respect.

The poll among the Northern Ugandan population by the ICTJ showed an overwhelming support of international involvement in the process of dealing with the violent past (84%). However, this support does not necessarily indicate a judicial involvement of the international community. Instead, this was favoured only by 32% while other participants were pointing to other involvements such as technical advisory (33%), monitors (18%), and donors (18%) in the process of holding accountable those responsible for human rights violations (ICTJ: 2005: 32).

'Setting the Account Straight' – The Role of the Victim in Prosecution

From what has been said so far, it became apparent that victims – as well as the polled populations in the available studies – are in favour of rights-based and institutionalised prosecutions of war crimes. This is an indicator for a related expectation regarding certain modes of justice. At the same time we find the

23 Ten per cent of the respondents indicated that both, 'own and foreign' courts, should be in charge of a prosecution. Only 7% of all participants were in favour of their own courts followed by 6% opting for their own government. Another 6% indicated that international courts and their own courts should prosecute offenders. The latter combination can be regarded as being in compliance with procedures applied for instance in Bosnia where the 'big fish' are prosecuted in The Hague while the 'less serious' cases are being dealt with on a domestic level. Note that Stover (2003: 111) observes a related dissatisfaction by the interviewed victims and witnesses criticising that the ICTY focuses only on some key individuals instead of (also) holding responsible those who actually committed the crimes.

victims' role in ICrimJ procedures gradually changing.[24] The international tribunals for Rwanda and the former Yugoslavia were still drawing on victims mainly as the 'suppliers' of evidence in their function as witnesses to the court, the prosecutor, or the defence (Stover: 2005; Rohne: 2005), leaving victims to play only a minor role (Rombouts: 2002: 218). Or to put it with Findlay: 'little is said at the international level about the access by victims to justice within the trial context, beyond peripheral concerns such as protection for victim witnesses and victim compensation' (Findlay: 2002: 253).

The establishment of the ICC seems to mark a turning point. A more inclusive approach was developed, increasing the victims' participatory role in the procedure. Article 68(3) of the Rome Statute states: 'where the personal interests of the victims are affected, the Court shall permit their views and concerns to be presented and considered at stages of the proceedings [...]'[25] which also includes the presentation at an early stage to the Pre-Trial Chamber (see Art. 15(3)). Although these mechanisms are subjected to the wide discretionary power of the judiciary (Henham: 2004: 49; Garkawe: 2003: 362; Drumbl: 2007: 41 ff.), to a certain extent, they might be interpreted as a testimony for the increasing awareness of the importance of the victims' participation in international criminal justice (Henham: 2007: 459).

It is of little surprise that outside the narrower field of ICrimJ, particularly in the discussions on restorative approaches (Bloomfield et al.: 2003), the role of the victim is considered to be of paramount importance. For instance, in the South African Truth and Reconciliation Commission (TRC) great emphasis was placed upon the role of victim testimonies in the truth-finding process. The memories of individuals were gathered and fashioned into a sort of collective memory providing for a common narrative of the counties' past (Giroux: 2003).[26] Interestingly, the debate about victim participation goes on without asking the affected persons about their views. As a result, the question to what extent (war-) victims desire to be part of the responsive process is almost completely unexplored (Rohne: 2007: 14).

Addressing this lacuna, in our project the participants were asked if victims should participate in the prosecution of perpetrators or not. The findings support the thesis that victims actually *do* want to participate in prosecution. 72% of all

24 Criminology has to critically keep track of these developments in order to avoid a misuse of positive and important intentions to integrate the victim's perspective: Within the scope of 'normal' crime we have faced dynamics that were termed as 'the politics of victimisation' (Elias: 1986), diminishing the due process principle for the accused, fostering a general trend of criminalisation accompanied with a lower tolerance towards (petty) crime. On an international level an unbalanced focus on victims could support the tendency of 'governing through international crime', i.e. the rise of a 'dominant global political hegemony as 'policing' international security against crime' (Findlay: 2006: 2).

25 For a full account see Damocles Network and Reporters without Frontiers 2003.

26 From a constructivist point of view, a widely accepted narrative is a precondition for the formation of a common identity (e.g. Anderson: 1983) and therefore holds great potential for (re)conciliation.

participants indicated that victims should have a role in this process. Only 14% stated this should not be the case. Another 14% gave no comment, did not know or did not provide any information.

In order to inquire about their perceptions on the desired level of involvement, in a second step the participants were asked to indicate what kind of role victims should have in prosecution. A majority of participants (56%) thought victims should participate in prosecution as witnesses – a quite traditional role of participation. However, from what has been observed in the context of witnessing before the ICTY, it can be doubted that the victims would also agree to the court's discretion about the necessity to hear a victim or to dismiss it before being heard (for example, due to other evidence) (see Stover: 2005; Rohne: 2005). Another 46% of the respondents saw a major role for victims in granting them the opportunity to 'tell their story'.[27] Finally, 29% of all respondents opted for a more active role for victims indicating that they should be part of the prosecution itself. The latter pointed to a related desire among a considerable number of respondents of ensuring an effective control over the process and the outcome as highlighted by the early procedural justice research (Thibaut and Walker: 1975).

A total of 16% of all respondents did not comment, did not know or did not provide any answer to the question, while 3% provided other or additional answers. Besides the small proportion of the latter, the additional comments were revealing further specifics. The few punitive and vengeful comments on the desired role of the victim in the prosecution of the offender(s) underlined the desperate situation of the respondents (for example, 'shoot the bullet' (participant from Israel), or 'an eye for an eye' (participant from the Palestinian Territories)). Other comments illustrated a desire to be heard and become part in the process of dealing with the past (for example 'to tell the story and what has changed [after the victimisation]' (participant from Israel); 'to tell and inform everybody what I go through every single day' (participant from Israel), or 'to be a part in reconstructing what happened' (participant from Bosnia).

In order to identify frequent combinations of answers, once again a profile analysis (threshold 5%) allows further insight. The results clearly support the finding that victims should have the opportunity to tell their story and act as a witness against the perpetrator during prosecution. While 77% of all answer profiles indicated that victims were willing to play an important role in the prosecution process, 17% of combinations were too heterogeneous to form a meaningful profile.

In summary, the participants of our study stressed the importance of integrating victims in the process of dealing with the offender. A majority stated that victims should contribute as witnesses but should also be given the opportunity to tell their personal story. The results clearly point to a prevalent desire of being heard and given a personal voice during the process, allowing for identification with the proceeding and for a certain amount of control. A considerable proportion even

27 Note that this question was set up as a multiple response question.

opted for a more active role for the victim by becoming part of the prosecution. This attitude, however, was confined mainly to a limited number of regions (see Kiza et al.: 2006: 102 ff.). While these findings are basically in line with the provisions of the Rome Statute the practical test for this type of commitment is still pending and we will see how the judicial bodies are managing in walking the tightrope between procedural justice and the politics of victimisation (Elias: 1986).

While most of our participants were dealing on a rather theoretical basis with the participation-question – since they were not heard as witnesses in courts – the study done by Eric Stover was concerned with victim-witnesses only, providing for some insight into the actual experiences of witnesses at the ICTY. Stover found that for most of witnesses testifying in The Hague was not a quest of vengeance – since too much time had passed – but rather to appear in an international court in order to 'set-the-record-straight' about what happened during the war (Stover: 2005: 2). However, the witnesses wanted to see the offender exposed and aimed for 'recognition for their own endurance and dignity' which Stover summarises in the observation that 'what the witnesses sought was public acknowledgement in the presence of the accused that what happened to themselves and their families and communities was wrong' (Stover: 2005: 1). Once again, the findings of this study are basically corroborating our own and hence allowing us to formulate the hypothesis of a prevalent desire of victims to partake in the prosecution process.

Meting out Punishment – Forms of Sanctions

The prevalent form of punishment for serious crimes in today's liberal democratic societies is incarceration. Incarceration is connected to several principles of deprivation that serve as the substance of punishment. First of all the offender is deprived of his or her right to move freely, being confined to a limited space and controlled all the time. Secondly, he or she is extracted from and deprived of participation in society. But also other forms of punishment are based on deprivation. For instance the payment of a fine deprives the perpetrator financially. Finally, the mere process of being arrested by the states executive organs and being tried in a court can be understood as type of punishment as it stigmatises the offender even before any judgment is made.

The victims' attitudes towards the adequacy of particular sanctioning measures certainly adds an important empirical perspective to the broader discussion about sanctions in the criminal process. Thus, our participants were asked what should happen to the people who have victimised them.

To begin with, our question design included the option to put the offender on trial as well as the explicit option not to do so. The inclusion of this rather procedural measure first served to clarify and verify the respondents' attitudes towards criminal prosecution that they previously commented on. Second, it allowed them to stress the importance of imposing the punishment like effects, which an accusation and conviction can have such as publicly stigmatising the offender. Further, this item allowed those respondents who were indecisive about a particular sanction to limit their answer to the support of a trial without leaving the question unanswered. We found that the proportion of those people supporting the trial option was somewhat lower than in the previous 'prosecution' question (see above). However, the percentages of the option 'not to put the offender on trial' was even lower than the previous rejection of a criminal prosecution. Thus, the reduced support for 'trial' is likely to stem from the fact that the respondents wanted to stress other options instead of the trial, rather than from a change of mind.

From a wide range of sanctions the most commonly chosen option was the imprisonment of the offender (36%), followed by the payment of money to the victims (34%). Also the payment of a fine to the state was considered (11%). The fact that only 4% of all respondents were in favour of amnesty was not surprising in regard of the atrocities the respondents experienced and are quite in line with the hypothesis of a basic need for punishment ingrained into modern societies (Durkheim: 1895: 69 ff.). However, in a local context we can find some variation regarding the refusal of punishment. For instance, Sudanese respondents (17%) and the DRC (16%) were expressing the highest support for an amnesty while all respondents from the Israeli and the Palestinian sample were rejecting this option altogether. Furthermore, the overall low support for amnesty deviates also from the results of other population based studies (see below). This deviation may be interpreted as an indicator for the need to distinguish between the results stemming from victim surveys on one hand and those from population studies on the other hand.

Judging from this, in the view of the victims surveyed, an adequate response to the crimes committed definitely involves punishment to a significant degree. Even the call for the death penalty was higher than that for amnesty, discrediting the concept of the latter in the eyes of our participants.

The overall demand for the offender's execution was found among a noticeable number of respondents (4%). However, as it is known from criminological research, respondents tend to choose their answers from the options provided rather than using the option of an open answer (Kury et al.: 2004). Thus, the demand for the offender's execution would possibly have been higher if it were included in the original answer catalogue.[28] Finally, 11% of all participants did not comment, did not know or gave no answer.

Once again an analysis of typical answer profiles was done in order to find out about the most commonly used item combinations. The threshold applied to limit the combinations of answers was 5%. Unsurprisingly, the most frequent choice was to 'be put on trial' without combining it with other options (26%). This number indicates that for each fourth of our respondents a criminal trial in itself had a crucial importance. To what extent this also indicates indecisiveness among this group towards further forms of sanctions cannot be determined here.

---

28 Which we did not do due to the (quite biased) fact that we are proponents of the abolition of death penalty.

As to the application of particular sanctions, we found three answer profiles to be mentioned equally frequent (9%). These were the combination of trial, imprisonment and monetary payment to the victims, of trial and prison and lastly the combination of trial and payment of money to the victims. Only 6% opted for the offender's imprisonment without naming another option. Deducing from these results, monetary payment was perceived as an important and necessary supplement to the trial option, indicating the punitive dimension of a payment to the victims, as well as pointing towards the perceived need of financial reparation. Finally, 41% of all answers were too heterogeneous to form a meaningful profile.

Following from the frequent combination of sanctions it could be deduced that in cases where war-criminals or human rights offenders are standing trial the applied sanctions should not only include imprisonment but also a rather 'interpersonal' dimension of sanctioning, such as the punitive monetary transfer from the offender to the victim.

The basic trends found in our research were mainly confirmed by other available studies. When people in the Uganda were asked what they would like to see happen with the LRA (Lords Resistance Army) leaders, they mainly divided into two groups. A majority of all respondents constituted a rather punitive group (66%) demanding punishment for the responsible parties by imposing trials, imprisonment or even execution. Although considerably smaller, another faction (22%) favoured a rather forgiving stance, opting for the perpetrators' reintegration and reconciliation. A quite similar picture was found in regard to the responses to those members of the Ugandan Army (UPDF) who committed abuses. The majority of respondents favoured their trial (51%) while a third of the sample (also) favoured a form of punishment (33%) such as imprisonment or dismissal from their posts. A smaller number of respondents stated that they wanted them to receive amnesty (18%).

Although the respondents generally supported the amnesty process for LRA members (65%), the ICTJ found that the amnesty procedure needs to be reformed. Only 4% opted for an unconditioned amnesty, while the vast majority favoured a complementary form of acknowledgement by apology (56%) or confession (34%); others demanded trial (13%) or victim compensation (7%) as a precondition for granting amnesty. This finding points to the fact that even under a politically bargained amnesty affected populations do not want perpetrators of serious crimes to get 'of the leash' too easily.

Within a wider international scope the ICRC study ended up with similar results regarding the denial of amnesty to war-criminals. While 76% of all respondents wanted offenders to be punished, 16% were looking for 'closure' – as the ICRC puts it (ICRC: 1999: 46). Unfortunately the study did not ask about the types of sanctions to be applied. Therefore, we are not able to gain meaningful information from this study about this particular issue.

Attributing Guilt – Accountability for Acts Committed during War

In theory, as well as in empirical terms, the need for an 'anti-impunity approach' and accountability for international crimes was clearly established. While this is useful information, it is essential to ask who should be held accountable for the acts committed during war. Hence, our study addressed this important question.

On the overall level only 24% of all participants indicated individuals should be held accountable for the acts committed during war. This was a surprisingly low proportion of all participants. However, a clear majority of the respondents also indicated that political leaders should be held accountable (71%), an option that might have absorbed the support for the more general option 'individuals'.[29]

The same was true for military leaders (42%) but to a lesser extent. Supposedly the perception of the participants was taking into account the 'chain of command' with political leaders deciding the fate of communities and military leaders being their willing accomplices. Nevertheless, it was recognised that military leaders have a high responsibility during times of war, as they are foremost responsible to control the actions of their subordinates concerning their conduct.

But not only were the elites deemed accountable, 14% of all respondents indicated that 'a certain part of the society' was perceived as being responsible for the things that happened during war. Due to the collective dimension of macro conflicts this result was expected, though on a much higher level since all of the regions were shattered by internal conflict involving opposing parts of the society. As a result of political 'otherisation' and stigmatisation, which regularly were the precursors of conflict, it was expected that the blaming of the opposing group would be prevalent. From this point of view the support for collective responsibility was rather low sending out the message that primarily leaders were identified as the ones responsible for the acts committed and not necessarily the 'opposing' collective, namely those people who were following the respective leaders.

Finally, 12% of all participants expressed the opinion that the whole society was to be blamed and held accountable for the things that happened during war. It might be argued that this comparatively low number might stem from the internal nature of many conflicts which makes it unlikely that the victims would blame the whole (their own) society. However, even in the cases of inter-societal conflict such as the Israeli–Palestinian case the blaming of the collective 'other' as such was low as well.

Overall the participants were decisive in terms of accountability for the things that happened during war. Only 7% did not comment, did not know, or did not provide any answer.

29 This guess is reasonable due to the fact that the option 'political leaders' does include both individual accountability as well as the notion of collective responsibility since the leaders typically represent the group under their lead.

Once again the high aggregate number of total answers gave a reason to inquire into typical profiles or answer combinations. The applied threshold was a limit of 5% including 58% of all participants.

Our findings suggest that 22% of all participants attached accountability solely to political leaders, which was a rather high proportion indicating that more than one-fifth of all participants blamed political leaders for the things that happened during war. Another 18% expressed the attitude that military and political leaders should be held accountable. The combination of individuals, military and political leaders was represented by 7% of all participants; 5% of all participants ascribed accountability to individuals and political leaders, and another 5% indicated that the whole society should bear the responsibility for what happened during war.

The message behind the attitudes expressed is quite clear. First of all it is the elites and key persons of warfare – the 'architects' of the violent fate of societies – who are identified as those who should be held accountable for what happened during war. This attitude generally supports the course taken by the international community to primarily hold those persons accountable who were in charge of organising collective violence and mass atrocities. In accordance with the prevalent attitudes of the participants of this study that impunity was no option, this provides for a fertile ground to push forward in the established direction but to refine the applied mechanisms.

Other available studies basically confirm the finding that guilt for atrocities committed during war is mainly attributed to (political) leaders. The comment made by a participant of the AIHRC study in Afghanistan sums up the basic notion quite nicely: 'Today, the same war criminals are ruling the people and have the affairs of the state in their hands' (a man from Zarbul) (AIHRC: 2005: 12). However, the study does not look explicitly into the attribution of guilt according to leadership. Nevertheless, it becomes quite clear that attribution of guilt is basically externalised in the sense, that leaders or foreign powers are blamed but not the society.

A similar outcome was found in Petrovićs's study. In terms of accountability almost all respondents answered that politicians were responsible for the outbreak of war and the atrocities that happened thereafter. The explanation for this decision was based on the insight the leading politicians had, and the power they held that was not used to positively intervene in the course of the armed conflicts. Instead of taking responsibility for their populations they were all trying to fulfil their egoistic goals (Petrović: 2005: 172). But not only the political leaders – namely Tudjman, Milošević and Izetbegović – were named; instead the international community was also held accountable for the bloody course of the war – once again pushing the question of guilt away from the wider population.

In sociological or criminological terms these findings implicate that populations have developed a quite common mechanism of 'externalisation' and neutralisation of guilt. As we know from research on the Third Reich as well as on more recent conflicts, such as Rwanda (Drumbl: 2007), there definitely *is* a collective dimension to atrocities – in the vein of Hannah Arendts' hypothesis of the 'banality of evil'

– which is obviously largely denied by victims and other populations in affected countries.[30] In a critical way of thinking, the prosecution of key figures, solicitors, and 'architects' of armed conflicts means perverting the collectivity of violence and choosing the easy way out of the post-conflict dilemma. This is not to say that prosecution of those in power to put an end to such violence is per se wrong, but it constitutes only one part in the process of (re-)conciliation, and – while it is certainly better than doing nothing at all about atrocities – it even may contribute to the protraction of conflict in certain cases.[31]

'A wound does not heal without ointment'[32] *– Reparative Measures*

Once again, a simple but wise quote from an Afghan citizen who participated in the AIHRC study sums up our findings on the issue of reparations as perceived by victims and populations affected by armed conflict. While we have already learned that reparations are desired by victims (see above), we do not know what types of reparations are considered important by victims. And while there is some literature on this topic it is, as usually, mainly of a theoretical nature. Therefore, our study takes a closer look into this unexplored field.

Since there is a wide variety of possible reparative measures that can be thought of – such as medical or psychological support – the study had to limit itself to certain forms of reparation known from transitional justice processes in order to achieve its goal of collating basic information on different topics of transitional justice. According to the International Court of Justice (ICJ) reparation should: '[…] as far as possible, wipe out all the consequences of the illegal act and re-establish the situation which would, in all probability, have existed if that act had not been committed' (Van Boven: 1995: 506).[33] However, it is reasonable to have doubts about this goal '[…] since reparations can never make full amends. In fact, all reparations are symbolic since human life and suffering cannot be measured monetarily' (Evaldsson: 2003: 2). Nevertheless, reparation is perceived as an

30 Note that this seems to be a general finding; independent from conflict setting, duration or status.

31 Petrovic found out that there was a high willingness to forgive the opposing party in Former Yugoslavia. However, a major obstacle to reconciliation was found to be the problem that no party had the willingness to admit its own guilt, always waiting for the 'other' to admit guilt before forgiveness was considered (Petrovic: 2005).

32 Male respondent from Baghlan, Afghanistan (AIHRC: 2005: 32).

33 Quoted in Evaldsson: 2003: 2.

important part of the reconciliation process.[34] This is also reflected in the inclusion of reparations in the conception of the ICC.[35]

In a multiple response set our answer catalogue offered both material and immaterial forms of reparations. The latter were divided in a commemorative element, namely the construction of a memorial for the victims and a verbal act of acknowledgement by apologies. Corresponding to the previously elaborated perception of accountability, the apology can stem from different sources. Thus, the respondents were provided with the options of an apology by the offender, as well as by officials.[36] Regardless, whether reparation was collective or individual, material or symbolic, the acknowledgement of the victimisation as injustice is a central and common feature of all stated reparation types (Vandeginst: 2003: 145; Minow: 1998: 91–117).

The response set also included the option to 'forget what happened'. Although not a measure in itself its inclusion allowed the respondents to emphasise their desire to find closure to the past by forgetting what happened. This might be facilitated by other reparative measures or expressed as an option by itself. Additionally, the respondents were given the option to mention further measures that in their view were deemed to be helpful to cope with their victimisation.

First of all, our findings revealed a high level of support for reparative measures throughout the whole sample. But there was a wide heterogeneity concerning the desired forms of reparations, especially on the regional level. According to the attitudes expressed by the participants the most important measure was – unsurprisingly, since many of the persons interviewed had lost most of their possessions – monetary compensation (42%).

The second most popular choice was the construction of a memorial for victims (29%), although it was substantially behind material reparation. Surprisingly, 24% of all respondents expressed the opinion that simply forgetting what happened during war would hold the greatest utility for them. Another 22% of all respondents opted for an apology by the offender to be helpful in their situation and another

34 This was also recognised in the provisions of the Statute of the ICC. In respect to this the Rome Statute contains the following provisions: '[a] Trust Fund shall be established by decision of the Assembly of States Parties for the benefit of victims of crimes within the jurisdiction of the Court' (Article 79 of the Rome Statute 1998). Furthermore the Court may 'make an order directly against a convicted person specifying appropriate reparations to, or in respect of victims, including restitution, compensation and rehabilitation. Where appropriate, the Court may order that the award for reparations be made through the Trust Fund' (Article 75 of the Rome Statute 1998).

35 For further reading and the implications of the reparation system and Victim Trust Fund of the ICC see Keller: 2007; Ferstmann: 2002.

36 An example for the latter was the 1970 visit and emotional act of falling to his knees by the German then-chancellor Willy Brandt at the monument for the victims of Holocaust in Warsaw (Evaldsson: 2003: 2). For a fuller account of the impact of symbolic acts of signalling reconciliation in the context of armed conflict see Long and Brecke: 2003.

19% said so in regard of an apology by an official. The latter findings indicate that for those participants, the personal acknowledgement of the guilt and possibly the interpersonal factor in an apologetic situation would be helpful possibly providing for a somewhat cathartic effect.

The option of an open answer resulted in the categorisation of those cases in which the respondents were prone to retributive attitudes (3%) in order to help them to cope with their respective position. Retributive positions included the punishment of the offenders, inflicting the same harm on them and taking their lives. Finally, another 9% of the participants provided for additional comments such as: 'that our children will live in a peaceful state' (participant from the Palestinian Territories); 'to get the truth' (participant from FYROM); 'nothing can change the situation and bring me back what has been before' (participant from Israel); 'a general change of people's attitudes and a change of society' (participant from Croatia).

The analysis of typical answer profiles using a threshold of 5% and covering 45% of the sample population revealed that the most typical answer profile was the sole mention of monetary compensation. A total of 13% of all participants chose monetary compensation as a single type of reparation. Another 10% indicated that they simply wanted to forget. A memorial for victims as the only measure was named by 8% of all participants, followed by the combination of a memorial and monetary compensation (7%). Yet another 5% combined monetary compensation and forgetting what happened. Judging from these results, the most important type of reparation, that is, monetary compensation, should be supplemented by other reparative means. Those cases (55%) that were not encompassed in the display of answer profiles using a low threshold of 5% indicate that the question about helpful measures is a very complex one and varies a lot; probably due to the multifaceted experiences and needs of the respondents.

A regional analysis confirms this statement (Kiza et al.: 2006: 119ff.), indicating that the implementation of reparative measures has to be adapted to the particular setting of the conflict. Failing to do so may cause the situation that the needs of the population – which the reparative measures are typically designed to serve – will be missed. Even regarding the fact that monetary compensation was the most important form of reparation on the overall level, there were huge regional differences. Remarkably, in some regions immaterial measures, such as the construction of a memorial or an apology – both of which are of symbolic *and* collective nature – were seen to be of higher importance in the views of the victims surveyed. In many cases the combination of different means was indicated. These findings support the theoretical assumption of the important role reparations play in states of transition and in the social process of dealing with the past. Especially in regard to immaterial reparation the results also hint to the importance of public recognition of victimisation and suffering.

Similar to our findings the AIHRC found a large portion of the Afghani population to be in favour of reparative measures. A total of 88% of respondents in the survey indicated that reparations should be awarded to victims of past crimes.

Only 9% did not agree with the granting of support to victims. And while the AIHRC was defining reparation in a broader sense as victim assistance, making a detailed comparison to our own results impossible, there are still some preferences to be found among the Afghani population. Amongst these were compensation with 13%, the provision of basic needs with 23%, education with 16%, and work opportunities with 16%.

These findings were also confirmed by the ICTJ study in Uganda. When asked what should be done for the victims of the conflict in Northern Uganda, the majority of respondents said they should get some form of reparations. Only 2% stated that nothing should be done for the victims. More particularly 52% said victims should be provided with financial compensation, 40% mentioned foods, 26% wanted education, 26% chose counselling, 17% mentioned cattle and goats, 8% of the respondents said justice, 9% chose apologies, and 6% mentioned reconciliation. Addressing the collective versus the individual level the majority (58%) of the respondents said that reparations should benefit the community rather than individual victims.

Conclusions

Our quest for information on victims' attitudes towards dealing with a violent past has revealed a couple of very interesting findings. First of all we can state that post-war populations and particularly victims of war-crimes and mass atrocities are demanding accountability. From the empirical information at our disposal we can say that an overwhelming majority of affected populations favour the prosecution of offenders and that they are opposed to the idea of amnesties, even if these are politically bargained or at the heart of a strategy of peace-building – for example, in South Africa or in Uganda (Kiza: 2008). Also most of the respondents of all studies covered in our chapter are proponents of formalised proceedings incorporating international, that is, universalised, norms in order to punish offenders. Even in our study, which was solely taking into account the opinions of people who have suffered from gruesome war-crimes (see Kiza et al.: 2006: 80–90), the wish to exact revenge through vigilantism was very low. Obviously, people were aware that this type of retribution would not contribute to the reconstruction of shattered societies but rather generate new cycles of violence instead of (re)conciliation and societal peace. This finding by itself is a very positive and encouraging sign that, although in a very painful manner, lessons were learned by those who most often provide for the necessary fuel for the conflict and at the same time suffer the most in armed conflicts.

As to the question of who should prosecute offenders of international crimes, we dare say that there exists a broad majority amongst those people who have suffered from wars legitimising international or internationalised organs of prosecution. On the macro-level all available data suggests that populations affected by armed conflict tend to put great hope in international courts or mixed courts in order to achieve justice in the aftermath of war. Nevertheless, we can also identify a certain demand for the development of national structures, especially with regard to specific circumstances and regional peculiarities. This finding is not to be understood as an antagonism but rather as a demand for complementary measures in the aftermath of armed conflict. In the end, the message that can be read between the lines is that international involvement is fine for the beginning but that a stable society can only be achieved through a just judiciary and functioning state institutions. For instance, this finding is exemplified by the case of Bosnia and Herzegovina (BiH). Jan Meernik (2005) found that the actions of the ICTY basically did not have any consequential – or if at all negative – influence on the re-establishment of societal peace in BiH. Furthermore, it can be demonstrated that the special war crimes proceedings in BiH also do nothing to alleviate the still hostile interethnic relations (Freeman: 2004). Obviously, both strategies were communicated in a very counterproductive way. The opportunity to introduce a positive narrative was carelessly thrown away – although the support for such institutions is theoretically very high!

This antagonism leads us to one possible explanation which is found in the fact that the participants in our study stated that victims should play an important role in criminal proceedings, furthermost as witnesses, but not only as 'providers of evidence'. Instead about a half of all participants stated victims should be granted the opportunity to tell their story and give an accurate account of the things that happened. While the demand for such a role is high, the factual role they played in ICTY procedures as well as in national procedures[37] was exactly that of 'providers of evidence'. This was often disconnecting them from the trial resulting in a very unsatisfying experience (Stover: 2005). And while we recognise that process-economics demand concise and short testimony, we also advocate the implementation of supplementary institutionalised opportunities for truth-telling, that is, truth commissions.[38] Basically, our findings support the hypothesis that criminal trials should first and furthermost serve to eradicate impunity and punish high-level offenders, while truth commissions should be applied mandatorily in order to deal with the mass of wrongdoing. Also a positive and transparent communication of how and why perpetrators are going to be prosecuted is of uttermost importance, if the existing support for such proceedings is to be utilised in a positive way. Finally, and this seems to be a positive step regarding ICrimJ, many victims think they should play a more active role in prosecution. The ICC will probably provide for such a chance, but the reality-test is still pending.

The above-formulated hypothesis is emphasised by the fact that a majority of the respondents in our study as well as those in other international surveys are underlining the importance of political and military elites in 'misleading' their

---

37 There is yet no publicly available evidence for this but one of the authors received information confirming this assertion.

38 In fact, in your final report we are able to show that the concept of truth commissions finds wide support throughout the whole victim sample (Kiza et al.: 2006: 106 ff.).

respective societies to waging war against each other and committing gruesome atrocities that are unthinkable under peaceful conditions. While this diagnosis is supporting the strategy to implement personal accountability, even for the heads of states – breaking the longstanding tradition of impunity and inviolable immunity based on state sovereignty – at the same time it is worrying. It suggests that there is a tendency by 'normal' people to externalise guilt, to turn it away from themselves and attribute it to someone else, who was officially in power at that time. And while we do not want to deny that there are certainly many victims who did not actively partake in the conflicts, it is nevertheless problematic to learn that the understanding about the dynamics of conflict and its prerequisites – namely that there is no conflict without enough support in the population – seems to be quite underdeveloped.

Returning to the expectations toward post-conflict justice we were also able to identify that people in post-conflict situations are retributive or punitive in the sense that they demand punishment. The by far preferred form of sanction is the imprisonment of the offenders. Once again, we found that amnesty is the least desired outcome of transitional justice procedures. Instead, many persons affected by war – and of course many victims – are combining the sentence of imprisonment with a demand for monetary compensation; as a means of reparation as well as a means of punishing the offender. Another important aspect of punishment was altogether skipped in our own study – the matter of vetting. However, the other studies introduced in this chapter were convincingly conveying the message that removing officials from their privileged posts was deemed a necessary precondition for post-war stability and was interpreted as a form of punishment. This position correlates with the finding that guilt for armed conflict in general and for atrocities committed in particular is mainly attributed to political leaders. Hence, it would be quite logical to remove them from office and incarcerate those who were furthermost responsible for the violence. However, the past and the present show that vetting is a very problematic issue since peace agreements are often bargained on the basis of keeping in power exactly those persons who have orchestrated violence. In addition, as for instance the de-Nazification in post WWII-Germany demonstrates, it is hard to find educated functionaries and bureaucrats in a sufficient quantity in order to rebuild a functioning state structure. Therefore, vetting is a very limited transitional justice aspect, basically reserved for those persons that were at the top of the system when atrocities were committed – and in this context holding a strong symbolic capacity.

As concerns reparations, the victims' trust fund of the ICC seems to grasp the right idea. However, it will not be able to meet the demands as found in empirical studies encompassing the issue of reparations. It is hard to imagine that the ICC will be able to distribute monetary compensation on an individual basis, as demanded by about a half of all respondents in our study. Supposedly compensation will take the form of collective support, community projects, schooling opportunities and reconstructive measures in general. And while this does not meet the actual demands of war victims, it holds a great transformative potential, as the findings from other studies are clearly indicating. For instance, the AIHRC study or the ICTJ study find that the general population in war torn countries (in these cases Afghanistan and Uganda) is very positive about reparations to victims, thinking beyond the scope of individual monetary compensation. Reparations for victims should encompass education, jobs, and economic help to restart a self-sustained life in the aftermath of conflict, turning the terrible events into something at least marginally positive for the victim, at the same time acknowledging his or her victimisation. Nevertheless, a systematic scheme of monetary compensation on a national basis should be considered and executed where possible. A possible starting point for the funding of such an expensive scheme could be the confiscation of illegitimately gained profits and their redistribution.

Also the installation of a memorial for the victims of atrocities is a very important means of reparation. Almost one third of the participants in our study were suggesting that victims should be remembered and acknowledged through a visible marker.

Probably the most surprising result to us was that many victims were stating that they actually would like to simply forget what happened and carry on with their lives. As a singular statement this finding would only make sense if we redefined every participant into a 'survivor' who was resilient enough to cope with the past and then just leave it behind. However, this result hast to be seen in context with previous statements by the participants. Taking into account that most of the participants were favouring prosecutions of leading figures, we can then interpret this statement as the will to abandon the demand for reparations, since the prosecution of the victimiser is enough to bring closure to the victim.

Finally, the apology by officials and/or offenders was deemed quiet important, pointing to the fact that no matter which type of reparation is considered it certainly hast to carry the public acknowledgement of the suffered victimisation in order to take effect. This is probably the most important rationale of awarding reparations to victims of armed conflict.

At the end of our contribution a closing word of caution needs to be said: While we have some data on the demands and needs of victims and post-conflict populations we are far from understanding the actual underlying process of gaining societal peace. There certainly exists a spectrum of universalised or standardised approaches to deal with a violent past. However, there is *always* a situational perspective to be considered in every single attempt to provide for transitional justice. In terms of a practical approach to transitional justice a careful consideration of the specific needs of victims and affected populations is a *necessary* precondition for the development of potentially successful programs. Basically, every attempt to rebuild a community after violent conflict should be based on a serious empirical assessment of the populations needs. At first this might be considered costly but in the long run it holds the biggest potential to reach the ultimate goal of societal peace.

References

AIHRC – Afghanistan Independent Human Rights Commission (2005), *A Call for Justice* <http://www.aihrc.org.af/Rep_29_Eng/rep29_1_05call4justice.pdf>, (accessed 21 April 2008).

Akhavan, P. (2001), 'Beyond Impunity: Can International Justice Prevent Future Atrocities?', *The American Journal of International Law* 1, 7–31.

Albrecht, H. et al. (eds) (2006), *Conflicts and Conflict Resolution in Middle Eastern Societies: Between Tradition and Modernity* (Berlin: Duncker & Humblot).

Albrecht, H. (2002), 'Preliminary Remarks', *European Journal of Crime, Criminal Law and Criminal Justice* 10, 2–3, 87–9.

Anderson, B. (1986), *Die Erfindung der Nation. Zur Karriere eines folgenreichen Konzepts* (Frankfurt: Campus Verlag).

Banks, C. (2004), *Criminal Justice Ethics: Theory and Practice* (Thousand Oaks: Sage Publications).

Bloomfield, D. et al. (eds) (2003), *Reconciliation after Violent Conflict. A Handbook* (Stockholm: International Idea).

Calließ, J. (ed.) (2001), *Europa nach dem Kosovo-Krieg. Loccumer Protokolle, 17/00* (Rehburg-Loccum: Evangelische Akademie Loccum).

Chomsky, N. (2000), *Der neue militärische Humanismus. Lektionen aus dem Kosovo* (Zürich: edition 8).

Coupland, Robin (2007), 'Security, Insecurity and Health', in *Bulletin of the World Health Organization 2007* 85, 181–4: internet (accessed January 2011) http://www.who.int/bulletin/volumes/85/3/06-037135.pdf

Drumbl, M.A. (2003), 'Toward a Criminology of International Crime', *Washington and Lee Public Law and Legal Theory*. Research Paper Series No. 03–07.

Drumbl, M.A. (2007), *Atrocity, Punishment, and International Law* (New York: Cambridge University Press).

Durkheim, E. (1895/1938), *The Rules of Sociological Method*, translated by S.A. Solovay and J.H. Mueller (New York: The Free Press).

Elias, R. (1986), *The Politics of Victimisation. Victims, Victimology, and Human Rights* (New York: Oxford University Press).

Evaldsson, A.-K. (2003), Reparations after Violent Conflicts: Problems and Possibilities, Paper presented at the training workshop 'Senses of right and wrong', Copenhagen, 15–16 December 2003.

Ewald, U. (2008), 'Large-Scale Victimisation and the Jurisprudence of the ICTY – Victimological Research Issues', in Ewald, Uwe and Turkovic, Ksenija, *Large-Scale Victimisation as a Potential Source of Terrorist Activities: Importance of Regaining Security in Post-Conflict Societies* (Amsterdam: IOS Press).

Ewald, U. and Turkovic, K. (2006), *Large-Scale Victimisation as a Potential Source of Terrorist Activities: Importance of Regaining Security in Post-Conflict Societies* (Amsterdam: IOS Press).

Ferstman, C. (2002), 'The Reparation Regime of the International Criminal Court: Practical Considerations', *Leiden Journal of International Law 15*, 667–86.

FIDH (2006), Victims' Rights before the International Criminal Court: A Guide for Victims, their Legal Representatives and NGOs, <http://www.fidh.org/article.php3?id_article=4208> (accessed 16 March 2008).

Findlay, M. (2006), 'Governing through Globalised Crime', contribution for 'Government of the Shadows: Global governance, para-politics and organised crime', draft version.

Findlay, M. (2002), 'Internationalised Criminal Trial and Access to Justice' *International Criminal Law Review* 2, 237–59.

Fletcher, G.P. (2000), 'The Place of Victims in the Theory of Retribution', in *Buffalo Criminal Law Journal* 3, 52–63.

Freeman, M. (2004), *Bosnia and Herzegovina: Selected Developments in Transitional Justice*. ICTJ Case Studies Series, <http://www.ictj.org/images/content/1/1/113.pdf> (accessed 14 March 2008).

Fukuyama, F. (1992), *The End of History and the Last Man* (New York: The Free Press).

Garkawe, S. (2003), 'Victims and the International Criminal Court: Three Major Issues', *International Criminal Law Review* 3, 345–67.

Giroux, S. (2003), *The South African Truth and Reconciliation Commission: A Perspective on Memory, Violence, Discourse and Testimony*, <http://laurentian.ca/mahumanities/english/events/miniconference/03essays/stephanie_giroux.htm> (accessed 12 December 2006).

Hagan, J. and Kutnjak Ivković, S. (2006), 'War Crimes, Democracy, and the Rule of Law in Belgrade, the Former Yugoslavia, and Beyond', *The ANNALS of the American Academy of Political and Social Science* 605, 129–51.

Hagan, J. et al. (2005), 'The Criminology of Genocide: The Death and Rape of Darfur', *Criminology* 3, 525–61.

Hagan, J. (2004), 'Social Skill, the Milosevic Indictment, and the Rebirth of International Criminal Justice', *European Journal of Criminology* 4, 445–75.

Henham, R. (2007), 'International Sentencing in the Context of Collective Violence', *International Criminal Law Review* 7, 449–68.

Henham, R. (2004), 'Procedural Justice and Human Rights in International Sentencing', *International Criminal Law Review* 4, 185–210.

Huntington, S.P. (1997), *The Clash of Civilisations and the Remaking of World Order* (New York: Simon & Schuster).

ICRC (1999): The People on War Report, <http://www.icrc.org/Web/Eng/siteeng0.nsf/html/p0758> (accessed 15 March 2008).

ICTJ (2005): Forgotten Voices – A Population-Based Survey on Attitudes about Peace and Justice in Northern Uganda. International Center for Transitional Justice and Human Rights Center, University of California [website], <www.ictj.org/downloads/ForgottenVoices.pdf>, (accessed 12 May 2006).

Kegley, Ch. and Wittkopf, E. (2006), *World Politics: Trend and Transformation*, 10th edition, (New York: Wadsworth Publishing).

Keller, L.M. (2007), 'Seeking Justice at the International Criminal Court', <http://www.tjsl.edu/files/faculty/Keller_reparations_ICC_final.pdf>, (accessed 15 March 2008).

Kiza, Ernesto (2008), 'Post-War Societies and Punitivity: The Inquiry into an Underexplored Field of Research', in Kuty, Helmut and Ferdinand, Theodore N., *International Perspectives on Punitivity*, pp. 139–60 (Bochum: Universitaäsverlag Brockmeyer).

Kiza, E. (2001), 'Humanitäre Intervention – Gewalt des Friedens Willen?' in Jörg Calließ (ed.), *Europa nach dem Kosovo-Krieg. Loccumer Protokolle, 17/00* (Rehburg-Loccum: Evangelische Akademie Loccum).

Kiza, E. et al. (2006), *Victims of War – An Empirical Study on War-Victimisation and Victims' Attitudes towards Addressing Atrocities* (Hamburg: Hamburger Edition).

Krauth, J. and Lienert, G. (1973), *Die Konfigurationsfrequenzanalyse (KFA) und ihre Anwendung in Psychologie und Medizin* (Freiburg, München: Alber).

Kury, H. et al. (2004), 'Worüber sprechen wir, wenn wir über Punitivität sprechen? Versuch einer konzeptionellen und empirischen Begriffsbestimmung', in *KrimJ* 8, 51–88.

Licklider, R. (1995), 'The Consequences of Negotiated Settlements in Civil Wars, 1945–1993', *The American Political Science Review* 3, 681–90.

Long, W. and Brecke, P. (2003), *War and Reconciliation. Reason and Emotion in Conflict Resolution* (Cambridge: MIT Press).

Luedtke, R.-M. and Strutynski, P. (2007), *Von der Verteidigung zur Intervention. Beiträge zur Remilitarisierung der internationalen Beziehungen* (Kassel: Jenior).

McMichael, P. (2004), *Development and Social Change: A Global Perspective*, (Thousand Oaks: Pine Ford Press).

Mearsheimer, J.J. (2003), *The Tragedy of Great Power Politics*, (New York, London: W.W. Norton & Company).

Meernik, J. (2005), 'Justice and Peace? How the International Criminal Tribunal Affects Societal Peace in Bosnia', *Journal of Peace Research* 42, 271–89.

Minow, M. (1998), 'Between Vengeance and Forgiveness: South Africa's Truth and Reconciliation Commission', *Negotiation Journal* 14: 4, 319–55 (337).

Neubacher, Frank (2005), *Kriminologische Grundlagen einer internationalen Strafgerichtsbarkeit* (Tübingen: J.C.B Mohr (Paul Siebeck)).

Nozick, R. (1981), *Philosophical Explanations*, (Cambridge: Harvard University Press).

Olson, M. (1982), *The Rise and Decline of Nations: Economic Growth, Stagflation and Social Rigidities*, (New Haven: Yale University Press).

Petrović, N. (2005), *Psiholoske osnove pomirenja ismedju Srba, Hrvata I Bosnjaka*, (Belgrade: Stubovi Kulture).

Roberts, Brad (ed.) (1995), *Order and Disorder After the Cold War* (Cambridge: MIT Press).

Roberts, P. and McMillan, N. (2003), 'For Criminology in International Criminal Justice', *Journal of International Criminal Justice* 1: 2, 315–38.

Rohne, Holger-C. (2007), *Opferperspektiven im interkulturellen Vergleich. Eine viktimologische Studie im Kontext der Al-Aqsa-Intifada* (Hamburg: Verlag Dr. Kovac).

Rohne, Holger (2005), *The Victims and Witnesses Section at the ICTY*. An Interview with Wendy Lobwein (Freiburg: working paper Max Planck Institute), internet (accessed January 2011) http://www.iuscrim.mpg.de/shared/data/pdf/the_victims_and_witness_section_at_the_icty_%28rohne%29.pdf

Rombouts, Heidy (2002), 'Importance and Difficulties of Victim based Research in Post Conflict Societies', *European Journal of Crime, Criminal Law and Criminal Justice* 2–3, 216–32.

Rome Statute (2002), International Criminal Court [website] <http://www.icc-cpi.int/php/show.php?id=basicdocuments>, (accessed 15 March 2008).

Ruf, W. (1994): *Die neue Welt-UN-Ordnung: vom Umgang des Sicherheitsrates mit der Souveränität der 'Dritten Welt'* (Münster: Agenda-Verl., 1994).

Sebba, L. (2006), 'Formal and Informal Conflict Resolution in International Criminal Justice', in Hans-Jörg Albrecht et al. (eds), *Conflicts and Conflict Resolution in Middle Eastern Societies: Between Tradition and Modernity* (Berlin: Duncker & Humblot).

Sebba, L. (1996), *Third Parties. Victims and the Criminal Justice System* (Columbus: Ohio State University Press).

Spiro, P.J. (1995), 'New Global Communities: Nongovernmental Organizations in International Decision-Making Institutions', in Brad Roberts (ed.), *Order and Disorder After the Cold War* (Cambridge: MIT Press).

Stover, E. (2005), *The Witnesses. War-Crimes and the Promise of Justice in The Hague* (Philadelphia: University of Pennsylvania Press).

Teitelbaum, M.S. (2002), 'The Role of the State in International Migration', *The Brown Journal of World Affairs* 2, 157–67.

Thibaut, J. and Walker, L. (1975), *Procedural justice: A Psychological Analysis* (New Jersey: Lawrence Erlbaum).

Vandeginste, S. (2003), 'Reparation', in Bloomfield, D. et al. (eds), *Reconciliation after Violent Conflict. A Handbook* (Stockholm: International Idea).

Van Dijk, J.J.M. et al. (1990), *Experiences of Crime Across the World: Key findings from the 1989 International Crime Survey* (Deventer: Kluwer Law and Taxation).

Weiss, T.G. et al. (eds) (2004), *Wars on Terrorism and Iraq: Human rights, unilateralism, and U.S. foreign policy* (New York: Routledge).

Young, A. (2006), 'The Self-Traumatized Perpetrator: From Vietnam to Abu Ghreib', in Uwe, Ewald and Ksenija Turkovic, *Large-Scale Victimisation as a Potential Source of Terrorist Activities: Importance of Regaining Security in Post-Conflict Societies* (Amsterdam: IOS Press).

Chapter 5
Making International Criminal Procedure Work: From Theory to Practice

Richard Vogler

After two decades of debate and experimentation it is still not clear whether a definitive model of 'international' criminal procedure has emerged from the ad hoc Tribunals for Yugoslavia and Rwanda (ICTY and ICTR), the Internationalised Tribunals (ITs) or the International Criminal Court (ICC). Initial hopes that the scientific deliberations of the world's leading jurists, followed by a period of rigorous testing in practice, would lead us rapidly to the holy grail of a procedure which was both efficient and rights-respecting, have been dashed. So too have the hopes that the procedures emerging from these new tribunals would enable them 'to set paradigmatic fair trial standards' (Temminck Tuinstra: 2006: 63) and provide a practical model for criminal justice reform everywhere. Instead the tribunals have been widely attacked as 'too costly, too inefficient and too ineffective' (Zacklin: 2004: 545; Higgins: 2007) and have demonstrated a procedural instability characterised by sudden and sometimes damaging changes in direction over a very limited period of time.

This is not to suggest that no progress has been made or to diminish the real achievements of the existing tribunals, especially since, as many early commentators noted, the obstacles to success were daunting (Jorda: 2004). On the contrary, the learning process has been rapid and huge efforts have been invested to correct the mistakes of the early models. But the disappointment of original hopes and the confusion which has arisen as procedure was extemporised, point to the failure of the academic community to provide coherent and principled guidance. What is extraordinary about the development of procedure in the international criminal tribunals is not only the rapidity of change and the constant innovation but the fact that while the rest of the world is moving inexorably towards more adversarial forms of process, the tribunals apparently are moving in exactly the opposite direction.

The task of assessing these new prototypes of international criminal justice is urgent if the whole project of defeating impunity for grave international offending is to survive beyond its infancy. The aim of this chapter is to review some of the available scholarship in order to identify the principles which can help us evaluate what has already been achieved and to plan for the future. It will begin with a brief overview of the history of procedural developments at the tribunals and the so-called 'fall of adversarial criminal process'. It will then review some of the attempts to theorise these developments from the standpoints both of the sociology of law and, more significantly in this context, comparative law, before concluding that a fresh approach is clearly needed. Based on this analysis, an attempt will be made to suggest some of the principles on which future evaluations and reform of procedure could be based.

The International Criminal Tribunals and 'Inquisitorial Drift'

Existing accounts of the procedural evolution of the international tribunals have relied heavily on the supposed opposition between the 'adversarial' and the 'inquisitorial' methodologies,[1] attempting to show how the original adversarial model has buckled and collapsed under the special demands of international procedure.

The narrative[2] usually takes 1945 as the starting point, noting that the USA and the UK were able to lay down their own principles of adversarial procedure for the conduct of the Nuremburg Military Tribunals simply because they had physical custody of the leading Nazi defendants. In the same way, 50 years later, the dominant position of the USA as guarantor of the Dayton Accords which ended the Yugoslav conflict, allowed it to do exactly the same for the trials before the ICTY. Judge McDonald, the first President of the ICTY, it was asserted, came to the original drafting sessions for the Rules of Procedure and Evidence (RPEs) with a complete set of rules proposed by a committee of the American Bar Association tucked under her arm and many of these provisions were incorporated directly (Tochilovsky: 2002: 269). According to McDonald 'we merged elements of common and civil law into 129 rules' (2001: 158) but the North American model, as Morris et al. put it, proved 'particularly influential' (1995: 177). The outcome was a strongly adversarial format in which evidence collection and presentation was party-driven (May and Wierda: 1999: 737; Combs: 2002: 70; McClelland: 2002: 1; Tochilovsky: 2002: 269; Fairlie: 2004: 243; Langer: 2005: 857–58). The only significant concession to civil law practice, was the principle of 'flexibility' (Boas: 2001; Murphy: 2010) which permitted the court under Rule 89(c) to 'admit any relevant evidence which it deems to have probative value', This enabled a court to find any kind of evidence (including double or triple hearsay) admissible.

The first full trial began in May 1996. By this time a second tribunal, the ICTR had been created in November 1994 to deal with the atrocities committed in the Rwandan genocide of that year, adopting almost identical RPEs to those of

1 Analyses and critiques of this familiar dichotomy are too numerous for convenient citation here but for a recent exposition, see Jackson, J.D. (2005) 'The Effect of Human Rights on Criminal Evidentiary Processes: Towards Convergence, Divergence or Realignment?', *Modern Law Review* 68(5): 737–64.

2 This section is largely an updated version of the account given in Vogler, R.K. (2005). *A World View of Criminal Justice*. Aldershot, Ashgate.

the ICTY. A 'second generation' of tribunals, notably including the ICC, which was established after 2002, adopted RPEs based upon the experience of the first generation. It is widely supposed that the original 'adversarial' model quickly proved inadequate for the task, falling victim to the combined impact of three major forces; political, financial and practical.

Among the many political difficulties which beset the new tribunals was one which has been described by Gordon as the 'fragmentation of enforcement' (Gordon: 2007: 672–80). As non-state jurisdictions created by the authority of the international community acting through the Chapter VII powers of the United Nations Charter, and depending on the states parties for funding and logistical support, the ad hoc tribunals were from the outset, chronically vulnerable to pressure. For example, in the *Blaškić* trial before the ICTY, evidence tending to suggest innocence was withheld by the Croatian government until after conviction (Cogan: 2002: 122–3). In the *Todorović* case, a ruling by the Appeal Chamber calling for evidence on the alleged illegal detention of the accused was successfully rejected by the NATO countries, who reminded the tribunal that it relied upon them for the apprehension of alleged offenders (ibid.: 124–7). In the *Barayagwiza* case, the ICTR ruled that the defendant should be returned to the Cameroon since the excessive detention which he had suffered, infringed his rights, pointing out that 'nothing less than the integrity of the Tribunal is at stake' (cited in ibid.: 135). Faced with the consequent non-cooperation from Rwanda, which would have made its work impossible, the tribunal backed down and reversed its ruling (ibid.: 134–6; Fairlie: 2003: 57–8). As Cogan has pointed out, 'silent coercion' may also be exerted by the financially supporting states (2002: 133). This vulnerability, so it is alleged, encouraged the progressive imposition of bureaucratic and authoritarian control mechanisms over the procedure.

Financial problems affected the procedure primarily because the United Nations and the contributing powers, conscious of the vast cost of the tribunals, placed considerable emphasis on the expeditious conduct of cases; an objective which clearly threatened the adversarial character of the trial. A typical ICTY trial lasts for a year. However, the *Kordić* trial occupied 20 months and involved 241 witnesses, 4,665 exhibits, and a transcript of more than 28,000 pages (Combs: 2002: 90). Worse still, the case of *Milošević* was in trial for no less than four years (Hotis: 2006). Of course, international trials are endemically lengthy. As Combs points out, they are often located away from the scene of the original events, making witness appearance difficult, they rely upon a new and complex law featuring ill-defined offence categories which require proof of special elements of intent and they may cover numerous events over a lengthy period of time (2002: 94–102). The tribunals have been subjected to intense pressure from the international community to shorten the process and the blame for much of the delay has inevitably been attributed to the 'adversarial' features of the original model (Bonomy: 2007: 349–50).

Finally, since the judges from civil law countries at any given time outnumber those from common law countries by at least three to one, it is inevitable that they should find the adversarial rules difficult to operate during their relatively brief secondments and seek to modify them (Tochilovsky: 2002: 270). Judges interviewed by the Expert Group in the ICTY and ICTR have attributed the delay in proceedings primarily to their inability to exercise sufficient directive control (ibid.: 271). Moreover, Pakes (2003) has shown how civil law judges have adopted a much more directing and active role in trials than their common law colleagues and has noted that 'it is not unreasonable that judges might bring their domestic legal culture with them' (cited in ibid.: 313). In the *Akayesu* case before the ICTR, pre-trial disclosure was covertly delivered to a civil law judge to enable him to take a more familiar directing (rather than reactive) role in the proceedings.[3] In the ICTY case of *Dokmanović*, the judges called for this material openly in court (Tochilovsky: 2002: 271; Fairlie: 2004: 300–5). Equally, the guilty plea provisions have been successfully subverted by a combination of cultural factors, the misunderstandings of civil lawyers and the failure to achieve consistency in giving sentencing discounts (Combs: 2006).

All these pressures have, so it is argued, contributed to produce a significant 'drift' of the tribunal procedures away from the adversarial. This has occurred not merely as the result of judicial subversion, as noted above but by major reformulations of the rules of the ad hoc tribunals in 1998, 2000 and 2006. Moreover, many of the procedural innovations championed by the ICTY and ICTR have found their way into the rules of the 'second generation' tribunals. Broadly speaking, the changes fall into three categories relating to the position of the judge, the nature of evidence and the position of victims.

The position of the judge, both in the pre-trial and the trial, has changed dramatically since the inception of the international criminal tribunals, from neutral arbiter to directive manager (Meron: 2004: 522–3; Langer: 2005). The ICTY now appoints a pre-trial judge to expedite the procedure, establish a work plan and timetable for case preparation and the filing of documents, in order to identify the points at issue. Both ad hoc tribunals now require pre-trial conferences and strict case-management procedures which, although not unheard of in the common law, nevertheless 'resemble (those) of many Continental countries' (Combs: 2002: 74–9; Ambos: 2003: 10–11). From 2000, a defendant was required to set out his written response to the prosecution case before trial (Boas: 2001: 88). In 2005, the Pre-Trial Chamber of the ICC, over the objections of the Prosecutor, established a status conference to enable it exercise a measure of directive control over investigations. According to Schabas:

> The whole controversy was part of an ongoing struggle between the Office of the Prosecutor and the judges, one that is underpinned by the great cultural debates in comparative criminal procedure. (2007: 257)

3 Schabas, W. (2004) *A Convergence of Two Systems*, Harris Institute, http://law.wustl.edu/igls/Conferences/CentennialUniversal/videoindex.html.

There have been repeated calls for further widening of judicial intervention (Harmon: 2007; Jackson: 2009) and even the involvement of the iconic figure of 'inquisitorial' practice; the 'investigating magistrate' (Robinson: 2005: 1046; de Hemptinne: 2007).

As noted above, the directing role of the judge at trial has also been enhanced by the availability of witness statements and the investigative dossier (Tochilovsky: 2002: 271–2) which has enabled the judges to embark on a 'civil law type of examination' (ibid.: 272). There also seems to be increasing evidence that the ICC trial judges will use their powers to call evidence of their own initiative, in the interests of finding the 'truth'; a principle which is expressed as taking precedence over 'fairness'. (Schabas: 2007: 295)

Next, the trial phase has undergone a significant shift away from orality, which Fairlie has described as 'the demise of live testimony' (2003: 48). At the 23rd session of the judges' plenary of the ICTY in December 2000, the judges adopted a new rule entitled 'Proof of Facts Other than by Oral Evidence' (Boas: 2001: 73). A previous rule had already been introduced in 1998 to allow affidavits to be used to corroborate facts in dispute (Fairlie: 2003: 64) and after 2000, deposition evidence could be introduced without 'exceptional circumstances' (ibid.). Equally, under a new rule 92 *bis*, affidavits could be used in lieu of oral testimony to establish background and peripheral matters (Robinson: 2005: 1041–6; Bassin: 2006: 1777). Even these mild restrictions were abandoned in the *Milošević* case when extensive affidavit evidence was admitted to prove material facts (Fairlie: 2003: 67–9). This development was sanctioned in September 2006, when new rules 92 *ter* and *quater* allowed affidavit evidence from persons present in court or from those who were unavailable due to death, disappearance or medical condition to be admitted as evidence of material facts (Gordon: 2007: 683–7).[4] Predictions made by Fairlie and Boas that much of the live testimony in the prosecution case may disappear, to be replaced as DeFrancia has put it, by 'trial by affidavit' (2001: 1424) are probably overstated but clearly there has been a significant change of approach. As US Judge Wald has suggested, there has been a '180 degree turn from earlier emphasis on the 'principle' of live testimony' (cited in Ambos: 2003: 27). The problem with the creation by stealth of a 'document-dominated' trial in this manner is that many of the safeguards appropriate for such a procedure have not been put in place (Kay: 2004). The 'free-proof' system adopted at the outset has also contributed to the courts being overwhelmed with what Murphy describes as 'evidential debris' (2010: 552). Taken together, these changes represent a significant change in emphasis:

4 Following concerns that witnesses were being murdered to prevent them testifying.

> the proceedings now bear a much closer resemblance to the official inquiries of Continental jurisdictions, which are predominantly directed from above, by the court, rather than propelled from below, by the parties. (Combs: 2002: 103)

Finally, although the role of the victim in the ad hoc tribunals was extremely limited, as in an adversarial procedure, '(o)ne of the great innovations of the Rome Statute', according to Schabas (2007: 328) was to allow direct participation on the model of the continental civil party. Moreover, a decision by the Pre-Trial Chamber of the ICC in January 2006, permitted the direct participation of the victim in the investigation stage (de Hemptinne and Rindi: 2006; Stahn, Olasolo et al.: 2006; Zappalà: 2010).

Some commentators, such as Pakes, have welcomed the shift away from adversariality (Pakes: 2003: 319), others, noting the 'obfuscation and delay' of trials such as that of *Milošević*, have gone further, calling for an even more radical strengthening of the inquisitorial features (McClelland: 2002; Tochilovsky: 2002; Nice and Vallieres-Roland: 2005; Jackson: 2009). The outcome has been described as both 'tempered adversariality' (Keen: 2004) and 'cafeteria inquisitorialism' (Fairlie: 2003: 82). Whatever view is taken, it is clear that managerial and bureaucratic considerations have gained very significant ground over due process ones. To make sense of this dramatic procedural revolution, which has been accomplished within a remarkably short time, it will be helpful to consider recent attempts at analysis.

The International Criminal Tribunals and the Sociology of Law Tradition

Authors working within the sociology of law tradition have made an important contribution to the evaluation of the international criminal tribunals, although it must be conceded that this is largely because their work has been adopted by comparative lawyers. There is space here to consider only two of the most important perspectives which have been used in these evaluations; those of Herbert Packer (1968) and Mirjan Damaška (1973; 1975; 1986).

Packer's lasting contribution, which has itself become something of an orthodoxy in criminal justice studies, was to offer two ideal types of criminal justice process; two normative models (1968: 153) which he hoped would help explain the choices which underlie the details of criminal justice practice. The two alternative models were the '*crime control model*' (CCM) and the '*due process model*' (DPM). According to Packer, the CCM 'requires that primary attention be paid to the managerial efficiency with which the criminal process operates to screen suspects, determine guilt and secure appropriate dispositions of persons convicted of crimes' (ibid.: 158). 'If the crime control model resembles an assembly line', continues Packer, 'the due process model looks very much like an obstacle course' (ibid.: 163). This model erects procedural barriers and is based upon a presumption of fallibility and error and a distrust of informal fact-finding methods. Although the two concepts have been widely criticised (see, e.g. Vogler: 2005: 5–8) they have also been used as a tool of analysis for the international tribunals and international procedural norms (Safferling: 2001: 20; Mansoor: 2005). Warbrick, for example concludes that '(t)he fact that one of the prominent aims of the … international criminal courts is the vindication of the victims, does make the 'crime control' objective an important aspect of any proposed procedure' (1998: 52–3).

Damaška's pairing of organisational models, which he terms 'hierarchical' and 'coordinate' (1973) has also been used for similar exercises in analysis. Where Packer looked at the normative principles underlying the procedure, Damaška has argued that it is the nature of the institution which operates the procedure which is most important. If a 'hierarchical' authority resembles a pyramid composed of carefully ranked officials, the 'coordinate' authority is a horizontal ordering of non-official participants who derive their social authority from outside the judicial system. From this central distinction between different relations of authority, all procedural forms follow. This taxonomy has been enormously influential, despite its theoretical shortcomings, and recent scholarship has specifically addressed the implications of this approach for the international tribunals (Combs: 2002; Langer: 2005; Jackson: 2008). Swart argues, for example, that the international tribunals represent a hybrid of the hierarchical and the coordinate models but that there is insufficient clarity about the corresponding goals of international criminal justice as well as about the use of procedural means to pursue them. The main task of the tribunals, the establishment of historical facts, he claims, is best served by a hierarchical, problem-solving approach (Swart: 2008).

The International Criminal Tribunals and the Comparative Law Tradition

Whilst these analyses emerging from the sociology of law had been influential, they cannot remotely compare with the impact of comparative law scholarship. In many senses the international criminal tribunals are the specific creation of lawyers and administrators trained in comparative law methodology. For authors such as Roberts, the contribution of the discipline to international criminal justice is both 'invaluable' and all pervading:

> By extending comparative method, perspectives and insight into every phase and corner of international criminal justice policy-making and practice, including institutional design, legislation, adjudication, operational policy-making and transborder cooperation in policing, mutual judicial assistance, legal harmonisation, and scholarly theorising, commentary and research. (Roberts: 2007: 365)

The international tribunals represents to many a highly significant consummation for comparative law: not only a grand dynastic marriage between the common law and civil law 'families' but a major rapprochement between comparative law and international criminal law which, up until 1948 at least, had been highly compartmentalised (Delmas-Marty: 2003: 15).

Nevertheless, it will be argued here that the debates over the creation of the international tribunals and their subsequent procedural instability have revealed starkly the poverty of comparative law discourse regarding criminal justice. In order to understand why the discipline has so signally failed the international community in this way, it is necessary to look briefly at some of its most obvious and fundamental shortcomings. To begin with, comparative law has been dominated until very recently by the analysis of civil law and substantive law models only (Twining: 2007: 80–81), delegating criminal justice and procedural justice to its periphery (Vogler: 2005: 3–5). Worse still, it has been fixated for over a century by neo-Darwinist 'family' typologies which have had very unfortunate consequences for the design and assessment of contemporary justice forms. This genealogical approach to categorisation, abandoned long ago in most other disciplines, still dominates the literature and leading comparativists such as Zweigert and Kötz (1998) and De Cruz (2007) continue to typologise legal systems on this basis. Even theorists such as Örücü, who are anxious to adapt the discipline to contemporary needs, cannot free themselves from this tendency to botanise amongst legal systems, looking earnestly for 'parentage':

> Today, what is needed is an entirely fresh approach within which legal systems can be classified according to parentage, constituent elements and the resulting blend, and then may be re-grouped on the principle of predominance. (2007: 169–70)

The problems with this approach have been widely discussed (e.g. Twining: 2007: 80–3) and attempts to reconceptualise the legal family as 'legal culture' (Nelken: 1997) or 'legal tradition' (Glenn: 2004) do not necessarily address the fundamental issues. First it is absurd to regard a 'legal system' as a unitary whole and not an amalgam of diverse units and sub-systems, many of which will have been affected by widely differing influences and ideologies at different periods. Second, a taxonomy based upon supposed genetic 'family origins' is necessarily ahistorical, ignoring the profound changes which have occurred at different stages of development. By emphasising 'parentage' (whatever that may mean in a historical context) the approach diminishes the significance of contemporary change, resulting in sterile and circular debates about 'legal transplants'. It is not surprising, given the origins of the discipline in the work of nineteenth century comparativists such as Esmein and Saleilles, that the evolutionist conception of legal systems remains unremittingly Euro-centric. Although some work emerging from the comparative law paradigm has succeeded in transcending these limitations (Twining: 2007: 79–80), nevertheless the dominant '*Grands Systèmes*' approach, locked as it is into a Victorian concept of human development, cannot possibly meet the urgent needs of communities all over the world for fair and rapid justice in the face of gross violations of human rights.

Recent Evaluations of the International Criminal Tribunals

As indicated above, much of the debate over the success or failure of the international criminal tribunals has revolved around the issue of whether the adversarial (common law) approach or the inquisitorial (civil law) approach has achieved dominance in the tribunals. Given the Darwinian conceptual heritage of the comparative law movement, this is not surprising. However, a further controversy has emerged in recent years. Here the question is whether the outcome of the development of the tribunals is not so much the domination of one model over another but rather a sophisticated amalgam or 'hybridisation' of the two. Some authors, such as Delmas-Marty, Ambos and Jackson, amongst others, have hailed the outcome of this process as a distinct and *sui generis* creation, representing a unique synthesis of the best features of the common and civil law models; in short an entirely new type of international 'super-procedure'.

According to Delmas-Marty, harmonisation is a 'progressive, evolutionary process' which should also involve a 'descending integration (from international law to domestic law)' and lead to a 'more pluralist conception of international criminal law' (2003: 21; 2008). Drawing on Cassese's opinion in the *Erdemović* case, she explicitly rejects the 'domination' thesis in favour of her 'hybridisation' approach. Her belief is that the new hybridised international laws, detached from their national origins by the alchemy of 'combination/fusion' will have 'acquired a new dimension, independent of their original meaning' (2003: 20). These proposed transformations seem, at least on the face of it, to offer a comforting exit strategy from the eternal competition of the adversarial and inquisitorial, supposedly avoiding the dangers of 'hegemonic universalism based on an imperialist model' (ibid.: 25).

A similar alchemy has been observed by Jackson in the caselaw of the European Court of Human Rights (ECtHR) which has, he claims:

> … developed its own distinctive brand of jurisprudence … which is transforming rather than merely mixing together the two traditions. … a vision of participation in the decision-making of the justice system which is rooted both in common law principles of natural justice and due process and in what is known on the continent as *la théorie de la procédure contradictoire*. (2005: 758)

Jackson has extended this analogy to the problem of finding the 'best epistemic fit' (2008; 2009) for ICC procedures. His specific proposal is a renewed commitment to the principles of equality of arms and adversarial procedure, coupled with an enhancement of the investigatory powers of the Pre-Trial Chamber to enable it to prepare a single dossier 'containing all relevant evidence, inculpatory and exculpatory, against the accused'[5] (ibid.: 38). In this way he hopes to create a model

5 The syntax used here neatly reveals the essence of the problem. Exculpatory evidence can scarcely be used 'against' the accused!

which will 'straddle the common law, civil law divide' (ibid.). Unfortunately the implications of such a hybridisation, both practical and theoretical, have not been confronted adequately. Long experience has shown that a dossier-based pre-trial subverts an adversarial trial, whereas equality of arms and adversariality (with their diversity of vision) cannot flourish in a unitary, judge-led enquiry. So far from providing an epistemic 'fit', Jackson's hybridisation suggestions represent a mere bolting together of two trial processes with inconsistent methodologies, objectives and epistemologies.

Similar critiques have been trenchantly expressed by a succession of other authors. Orie suggests that as a result of a 'many-headed compromise' between adversarial and inquisitorial in the ICTY, 'basic elements of the procedure have lost their anchorage in a coherent system' (2002: 1494) while for Warbrick, compromise leads to a fatally unbalanced and 'bastardised process' (1998: 53). DeFrancia talks of the 'pitfalls inherent in blending adversarial and inquisitorial systems' (2001) while Casey (2001: 868) and Zappalà (2003: 15) both point out that, however well they may work in their own national contexts 'they do not mix well together'. Adopting gothic imagery to express their distaste, Gordon, amongst many others,[6] is alarmed that due process rights have been 'sacrificed on the altar of this artificial union' (2007: 639) while Skilbeck (2010) and Murphy (2010: 573) both see the outcome as a 'Frankenstein's monster'.

Apart from these practical objections, the 'hybridisation' thesis raises a fundamental conceptual problem which has serious implications for any realistic appraisal of the procedure of the international tribunals. Put simply, procedures which are supposedly polar opposites, or 'antimonies' existing in a dialectical relationship with each other (Zappalà: 2003: 15), cannot be amalgamated. As Zappalà puts it, they represent:

> … two opposing epistemological beliefs: while for the inquisitorial paradigm there is an objective truth that the 'inquisitor' must ascertain, for the accusatorial approach the truth is the natural and logical result of a pre-determined process. (ibid.: 16)

If the adversarial and the inquisitorial represent conflicting epistemologies, 'hybridisation', makes no sense. Nevertheless, what appears to have been happening in practice in the international tribunals and elsewhere is exactly the kind of illicit amalgamation which should be impossible between two opposites. A slightly puzzled Delmas-Marty, for example, concedes that '(s)uch major divergences would exclude any attempt at hybridisation, if comparative study did not show convergent evolution in practice' (2003: 19). Unfortunately, she doesn't

6 See e.g. Fairlie, M.A. (2003). 'Due Process Erosion: The Diminution of Live Testimony at the ICTY', *California Western International Law Journal* 34(1): 47–84; Fairlie, M. (2004). 'The Marriage of Common and Continental Law at the ICTY and its Progeny, Due Process Deficit', *International Criminal Law Review* 4(3): 243–319.

conclude from this that it is the 'oppositional' mode of analysis itself, which is flawed.

There is a further and equally fundamental problem for the 'hybridisation' thesis for which neither Delmas-Marty, nor its other proponents, have given any adequate answer. Like them, she acknowledges but does not address the difficulty that the supposed 'polarity' of laws between the adversarial and the inquisitorial, is necessarily confined to western law and hence, encourages the re-emergence of the obnoxious concept of 'the civilised nations' (ibid.). Safferling, to take one example, begins his influential study on the construction of a new 'international' procedure with the completely unjustified assertion:

> The search for an international criminal procedure has to be based on the two main systems of national criminal procedure, namely the Anglo-American and the Continental European traditions. (2001: 5)

He proceeds to carry out this project by an exhaustive examination of individual steps of prosecution and trial as they derive from the two traditions, in order to find the structure which would suit the International Criminal Court (ibid.: 53). His view is echoed by Gordon whose new and 'truly international procedure' is no more than a judicious attempt 'to mix and match the best features that each system (the adversarial and inquisitorial) has to offer' (2007: 707). This is hardly internationalism. Unlike the ECtHR, the international tribunals are intended to be truly global and it is extraordinary that the debates over procedure have remained so Atlanticist and introspective. As a result, the practice of the international tribunals increasingly gives the impression that defendants from the developing world, and in particular from Africa, are being dragged unwillingly before alien, western courts. Delmas-Marty's hope that the laws of the developing world may eventually enter the procedural equation, looks improbably optimistic.

Not all enthusiasts for hybridisation have assumed that the mechanisms for achieving it are unproblematic, Findlay, for example, calls for the clear identification of procedural 'sites for decision-making' (2001: 33) to enable the development of appropriate levels of 'synthesis' and insists that it should take account of the ideologies of the procedural styles (ibid.: 34–37) their personnel (ibid.: 37–40) and methodologies (ibid.: 40–43). While sharing the hybridisation thesis, Ambos adopts a more sensitive approach than Delmas-Marty or some of the others mentioned, to the adversarial/ inquisitorial typology. After concluding that the existing terminology is misleading, he opts for a functionalist approach derived from the work of Damaška:

> In this sense, the civil law model can more accurately be described as 'judge-led' (*instruktorisch*) or – following Damaška's more structural approach – 'hierarchical', while the common law model is adversarial – prosecution and defence being 'adversaries' – or 'coordinated'. (2003: 4)

These concepts are then used to examine the investigation, the pre-trial and the trial phases of ICTY procedure in turn, dwelling particular on the rules of evidence. His conclusion is that at the level of international criminal procedure, the traditional common-civil law divide has been overcome and replaced with a model which is *sui generis*, exactly as Delmas-Marty had asserted. Moreover, an 'issue-oriented' approach would consider which model of procedure was most appropriate in each of the three different phases of the process (ibid.: 35). Like Delmas-Marty, he predicts a more 'harmonic convergence of both systems', an optimism which is undermined, as was hers, by nagging concerns about the exclusion of other justice systems, notably the Islamic (ibid.: 37).

There are increasing signs, moreover, that some authors are beginning to look beyond the confines of the comparative law typologies. Like Delmas-Marty, Jackson and Ambos, Langer rejects the 'sterile debates about the triumph or defeat of adversarial or inquisitorial models' (2005: 836). However, unlike them, he refuses to identify ICTY procedure as a hybrid between the adversarial and the inquisitorial. Such an approach, he argues, offers little in the way of analytical insight, and instead he proposes the concept of 'managerial judging' which is based upon a claimed structural similarity between the procedure of the ICTY and US civil procedure. Before doing so, however, he offers some interesting reflections on the possibility of consolidating comparative law and sociological concepts, suggesting that '(t)he most promising way to capture these basic distinctions is to describe the adversarial and inquisitorial systems as organised according to two opposing pairs of sub-systems or models'(ibid.: 838). The first opposition is between the 'dispute' and the 'official investigation', while the second is between Damaška's 'coordinate' and 'hierarchical' models (ibid.: 838–47). To Langer the creation of the ICTY was characterised by the competition between the adversarial and the inquisitorial, operating at the levels of culture, legal identity and the distribution of powers and responsibilities. At the outset, the judges chose a dispute model for procedure but a more even balance between the 'hierarchical' and 'coordinate' models for the organisation of authority (ibid.: 868). However, caseload pressures soon brought about 'the fall of adversarial criminal process in the ICTY' (ibid.: 868–74). This evolution, suggests Langer, is very reminiscent of the changes which occurred in US civil procedure in the second half of the twentieth century and which was characterised by the American scholar Resnik as the advent of 'managerial judging' (1982). Langer glosses this theoretical concept to indicate a form of procedure which cuts across the adversarial and inquisitorial, giving a powerful role to the judges to expedite and manage cases without extinguishing the active participation of the parties. He goes on to explain how the introduction of such reforms as pre-trial judges, status conferences, the obligation to file submissions and the move towards written evidence, all indicate the creation of a 'managerial judging' model of process at the ICTY.

Megret, adopting a more sociologically informed approach, proposes a model which he describes as 'becoming international', suggesting that it is the process of adaptation of domestic forms of justice to the 'diversity, distinctness, and dynamism of its international context' which has become the defining characteristic of international criminal justice (Megret: 2009: 75).

A Three Dimensional Approach to International Criminal Procedure

These authors point the way towards a more strategic analysis of international criminal justice procedure. I have argued elsewhere (Vogler: 2005) that rather than relying on the comparative law typologies, domestic criminal justice is better understood as the arena in which disputes between the three fundamental interests in the social order; the individual, the community and the state are negotiated and resolved. For criminal justice to function successfully it must ensure that none of these legitimate elements is excluded from the procedure or significantly impaired in their ability to represent their particular interests. Procedure, therefore, must facilitate this encounter by ensuring that whereas the interests of the state may well be dominant in the early stage of investigation and pre-trial, the interests of the individual at trial and the community at the level of judgement, none is ever excluded from any stage. In particular I have associated the interest of the individual with adversarial methodology and its ideology of legal rationality, the interests of the community with the methodologies of popular justice and common sense understanding and the interests of the state with inquisitorial methodology and its ideology of forensic investigation and bureaucratic efficiency. By examining their historical and intellectual origins, I have tried to show how each of these different approaches is an essential and legitimate element in any successful system of criminal justice (ibid.).

No analysis based upon domestic criminal justice can easily be transferred to the international level without a good deal of reconstruction. As has been repeatedly asserted, international justice involves much more serious crimes than are usually encountered in the domestic courts and it bears a much heavier political responsibility for conflict resolution and for establishing the collective history of conflict. Nevertheless, the essential role of criminal justice remains the same and post-conflict judicial strategies which have ignored this, have encountered serious difficulties. Excessive adversarialism, privileging the role of the individual, disfigured the trial of Milošević. An excessive reliance on popular justice methodologies in the Rwandan *Gacaca* courts seriously compromised individual rights whereas a failure to regard the state's legitimate interest in retribution undermined the legitimacy of the 'Truth and Reconciliation' approach in South Africa. In order to determine the strategic objectives of the reform process, it may be helpful, therefore, to consider briefly the role of the three elements which I have identified, in developing a legitimate international criminal procedure.

Individual Rights in International Criminal Procedure

The position of individual defendants within the tribunals has been the subject of considerable debate, particularly as a result of the degradation of adversarial party control in the pre-trial and trial, described above. It might be assumed, given that the conduct of trials without fair trial guarantees for the accused can of itself constitute a crime against humanity,[7] that individual due process rights would be more robustly defended in the international criminal courts than in any other forum (Megret: 2009: 49–58). As the Secretary-General of the UN announced in 1993 in his commentary on procedural issues, it 'is axiomatic that the International Tribunal must fully respect internationally recognised standards regarding the rights of the accused at all stages of its proceedings.'[8] Nevertheless, despite the verbatim adoption by both the Statutes of the ICTY/ICTR and the ICC of much of the relevant wording of Articles 9 and 14 of the 1966 International Covenant on Civil and Political Rights (ICCPR), this does not seem to be entirely the case. Two areas, in particular, have given cause for concern.

The application of the right to liberty has dramatised the inadequacies of Article 9 rights of the ICCPR in the context of international proceedings conducted at a distance from the events complained of. Deceit used to lure a defendant across a border in order to effect an arrest[9] and even kidnap[10] apparently present no problem of abuse of process (DeFrancia: 2001: 1402–4) any more than the ill-treatment of detainees by custody states.[11] Provisional release under Article 9(3) of the ICCPR is another acutely problematic area and the Netherlands, host for the ICTY and ICC, has vigorously opposed the idea of defendants being bailed onto its territory (Warbrick: 1998: 57–8; Zappalà: 2003: 115). The burden of proof remains with the defendant and, unlike any domestic jurisdiction (even where grave offences are concerned) there are no specific guidelines on the use and scope of pre-trial detention (Zappalà: 2003: 66–75; Gordon: 2007: 690–91) and possibly a presumption in favour of custody (Murphy: 2010: 456–7).

Equally, it might be assumed that an individual's right to counsel would be exceptionally well protected in the context of international criminal proceedings but again this has proved not to be the case (Temminck Tuinstra: 2010). The right

7 Both Nazi prosecutors and judges (see *United States of America v Alstötter* et al. (1948) 3TWC 1; 6 LRTWC 1; 14ILR 274) and, more recently, Saddam Hussein, have faced such allegations.

8 Report of the United Nations' Secretary-General, submitted to the Security Council 3 May 1993, pursuant to operative paragraph 2 of Security Council Resolution 808, (s/25704, 3 May 1993).

9 *Dokmanović* (IT-95-13a-PT) 22 October 1997.

10 In the cases of *Todorović* (see ICTY Eight Annual Report, UN doc. A/56/352, 17 September 2001, paras 141–4) where the application to challenge was withdrawn and *Nikolić* ((IT-95-2-PT) 2 October 2002).

11 *Barayagwiza v Prosecutor*, Cases No. ICTR 97-19 and ICTR 98-44 but see Article 51(1)(d).

is formally provided for in the statutes of both the ICTY[12] and ICC[13] in terms which reflect explicitly the wording of Article 14(3)(d) of the ICCPR: '(t)o be tried in his presence, and to defend himself in person or through legal assistance of his own choosing'.

However, specific provisions for a functioning bar formed no part of the administrative concept of the ICTY and it took some time before arrangements were made to fund legal teams.[14] The result was a heterogeneous collection of legal practitioners from around the world, many of whom had no experience of the kind of proceedings which were taking place at The Hague, with dire consequences for their clients (Ellis: 2002: 955–9).[15] Some counsel, such as a Serbian member of the Tadić defence team, were allegedly secretly working against the interests of their clients (Zappalà: 2003: 26) while allegations of corruption and 'fee-splitting' raised the horrifying prospect of alleged perpetrators of war crimes profiting financially from the trial process (Ellis: 2002: 964–8). Serious attempts have been made to address these problems and a Code of Ethics was in place by 1997 (Ellis: 2002: 968–72) while a Code of Conduct was developed,[16] together with a Disciplinary Panel. The ICC required the establishment of an Office of Public Counsel for the Defence (OPCD) which is able to provide counsel during the investigation stage to represent the interests of an accused who is not yet aware of the proceedings (Scharf: 2005).

While access to counsel has proved problematic in this context, so too has the right to self representation, which has been progressively eroded since 2001, when it was initially upheld in the *Milošević* case (Jorgensen: 2005; Sluiter: 2005; Hotis: 2006). As a result, although it is clear that the defendant enjoys many of the rights necessary for a fair trial, there are still significant areas, of which the above are merely a sample, in which they fall short of what can be expected in a domestic court.

Community Rights in International Criminal Procedure

The concept of 'community' seems the most difficult to transfer into international criminal justice. At the same time, however, it is the complete absence of any

12 Article 21(4)(d).

13 Articles 55(2)(e) and 67(1)(d).

14 By 2007 the ICTY defence bar comprised 257 members, half of whom were drawn from the former Yugoslavia. McMorrow, J.A. (2007). 'Creating Norms of Attorney Conduct in International Tribunals: A Case Study of the ICTY', *Boston College International and Comparative Law Review* 30(1): 139–173.

15 Counsel in the Erdemović case advised their client to plead guilty without understanding either the concept of the guilty plea or the substantive law involved. See *Prosecutor v Erdemovic* IT-96–22-A, 7 October 1997.

16 See http://www.adcicty.org/documents/icc-codeconduct.pdf for a defence commentary.

serious engagement with communities which has formed one of the gravest indictments of the current tribunals (Peskin and Boduszyn'ski: 2003; Arst: 2006; Klarin: 2009). Unless the tribunals can find a practical means of involvement with the communities which they serve, their legitimacy will always be compromised and they will never begin to fulfil their reconstructive mandate.

The main problem of course is that it is hard to identify the 'community' which is specifically offended by international crimes. To involve citizens of the country where the offences have occurred might invite the continuation of hostilities in the courtroom, whereas to include representatives of different countries strains the concept of 'community'. The 'international community', on the other hand, involves states parties rather than real communities. But these difficulties are not insuperable and the Rwandan *Gacaca* jurisdictions have shown clearly that popular participation in the trial of grave crimes is at least possible, even in a deeply traumatised and conflicted community.

The most obvious means of involving and empowering communities directly in the judgement phase of criminal procedure is through the jury, an institution which has been vigorously resisted by academic and judicial elites, particularly since the democratisation of jury practice in the 1970s (Vogler: 2005: 214). This resistance has been even more implacable at the international level. For Safferling, the jury is 'a more than dubious institution' and 'entirely out of the question' for any international court (2001: 216) and Taman (2003) has rejected the role of the jury in any post-conflict society. Powell, on the other hand, argues that the creation of a jury could significantly improve the ICC's flagging legitimacy and prevent abuses of power (2004). She reviews different means to empanel jurors, drawn from either the country where the offences were committed or other countries or mixtures of both. Moreover the jury is not the only means of engaging popular participation in international trials. In terms of formal procedure, lay scrutiny of pre-trial or trial procedure is possible, for example through citizens' panels.

More broadly Drumbl (2007) has attacked the legitimacy of 'individualised liberal-legalist criminal trials' and called for a more pluralised and multivalent approach to transitional justice which would involve popular participation. There are models both in the Township and Village courts (Vogler: 2005: 255–76) as well as in 'Truth and Reconciliation' (Gibson: 2004) and *Gacaca* jurisdictions (Corey and Joireman: 2004; Schabas: 2005) for popular justice which is mobile, much closer geographically to the affected communities and to community values. Combinations of various forms are also possible (Schabas: 2004) as are procedures which encourage restorative justice (Lin: 2005). Legitimate criticism of these existing forms of justice should not undermine the importance of the search for effective forms of community participation in international criminal justice which do not compromise individual and state interests.

States' Rights in International Criminal Procedure

The 'fragmentation' of statal authority, which Gordon refers to as the 'disjunction between authority and control' (2007: 672) presents an almost equally challenging obstacle to the creation of a functioning international criminal law tribunal. The accountability of prosecution authorities and their *propria motu* powers in the ICC (Gallavin: 2006: 45–6; Schabas: 2007: 159–66) has been the subject of intense debate, as have the growing managerial powers of the judiciary, especially since the ICTY judges have been required to act as an international legislature to amend the rules which they are themselves to apply. There is a serious failure of separation of powers in the international tribunals (Meron: 2004: 521) and routes of accountability are unclear, particularly in this era of dispersed international sovereignty or 'plurachy' (Kuper: 2004). This is not the place to discuss the form that such structures should assume but merely to note that the creation of an ever-enlarging civil law bureaucracy within the tribunals (McMorrow: 2007: 152) is no substitute for genuine accountability and the separation of powers.

Equally, it is no substitute for a functioning international police with a degree of operational separation from the prosecution. The tribunals currently exist at a perilous level of international voluntarism, utterly dependent on the goodwill of supporting states. Although the history of attempts to create a global police agency has not been auspicious (Deflem: 2002) and more recent strategies under UN Mandate in Kosovo and elsewhere (Hansen: 2002) to create paramilitary UN forces (Caygill: 2001; Lutterbeck: 2004) raise serious concerns about the accountability and operational styles of international police, nevertheless the transnationalisation of policing is probably an unstoppable process (Sheptycki: 1995) and there is no reason why the tribunals should not take advantage of the new structures being created at the international and regional level.

Conclusion

Attempts to remedy the serious deficiencies affecting the position of each of the three essential participants in the international criminal trial process are not mutually exclusive and advances in one area do not automatically imply retreats in the others. Successful reform, it has been argued here, requires a close look at the purposes of procedure at each stage and a determination to ensure that none of the legitimate actors are excluded from genuine participation, even though involvement cannot always be equal at each point. It also requires sensitivity to the jurisprudential traditions of the region involved and the establishment of regional chambers to reflect those traditions.

The purpose of this chapter has been to suggest that existing comparative law scholarship has failed to offer guidance to the international tribunals in their struggle to develop a truly global concept of justice capable of mobilising universal aspirations for the defeat of impunity for grave crimes. On the contrary, it has tended to encourage the binary conception of international justice as a conflict between state and individual authority in which enthusiasts for inquisitoriality complain of excessively lengthy trials reduced to near farce by obstructive defendants and lawyers, while enthusiasts for adversariality deplore the growing bureaucracy and inertia. Both collude in a procedure which is becoming more and more complex and separated from the interests of the communities which have suffered the ravages of gross criminality. Indeed, the radical exclusion of popular participation is the most damaging legacy of existing comparative law scholarship and, as I have argued elsewhere, justice without real community involvement is a sham.

In short, the existing comparative law typologies fail to establish either a practical or a normative basis for reform. They cannot do this because they are unable to link the nature and design of the procedure which is operated with the purposes of the tribunals at each stage. It is only by identifying the essential constituencies whose conflicted interests provide the necessity for the existence of international tribunals, and analysing their participation at each stage, that a clearer picture of the type of procedure which we need to develop can begin to emerge.

Bibliography

Ambos, K. (2003). 'International Criminal Procedure: "Adversarial", "Inquisitorial" or "Mixed?"' *International Criminal Law Review* 3(1): 1–37.

Arst, D.E. (2006). 'Views on the Ground: The Local Perception of International Criminal Tribunals in the Former Yugoslavia and Sierra Leone', *The Annals of the American Academy of Political and Social Science* 603(1): 226–39.

Bassin, A.S. (2006). '"Dead Men Tell No Tales": Rule 92 Bis – How the Ad Hoc International Criminal Tribunals Unnecessarily Silence the Dead', *New York University Law Review* 81(5): 1766–99.

Boas, G. (2001). 'Creating Laws of Evidence for International Criminal Law: The ICTY and the Principle of Flexibility', *Criminal Law Forum* 12(1): 41–90.

Bonomy, I. (2007). 'The Reality of Conducting a War Crimes Trial', *Journal of International Criminal Justice* 5(2): 348.

Casey, L.A. (2001). 'The Case against the International Criminal Court', *Fordham International Law Journal* 25(1): 840–72.

Caygill, H. (2001). 'Perpetual Police?: Kosovo and the Elision of Police and Military Violence', *European Journal of Social Theory* 4(1): 73–80.

Cogan, J.K. (2002). 'International Criminal Courts and Fair Trials: Difficulties and Prospects', *Yale Journal of International Law* 27(1): 111–40.

Combs, N.A. (2002). 'Copping a Plea to Genocide: The Plea Bargaining of International Crimes', *University of Pennsylvania Law Review* 151(1): 1–157.

Combs, N.A. (2006). 'Procuring Guilty Pleas for International Crimes: the Limited Influence of Sentence Discounts', *Vanderbilt Law Review* 59: 69–151.

Corey, A. and S.F. Joireman (2004). 'Retributive Justice: The Gacaca Courts in Rwanda', *African Affairs* 103(410): 73–89.

Damaška, M. (1973). 'Evidentiary Barriers to Conviction and Two Models of Criminal Procedure: A Comparative Study', *University of Pennsylvania Law Review* 121(3): 506–89.

Damaška, M. (1975). 'Structures of Authority and Comparative Criminal Procedure', *Yale Law Journal* 84(3): 480–544.

Damaška, M. (1986). *The Faces of Justice and State Authority: A Comparative Approach to Legal Process.* New Haven, Yale University Press.

De Cruz, P. (2007). *Comparative Law in a Changing World.* London, Cavendish.

de Hemptinne, J. (2007). 'The Creation of Investigating Chambers at the International Criminal Court: An Option Worth Pursuing?' *Journal of International Criminal Justice* 5(2): 402.

de Hemptinne, J. and F. Rindi (2006). 'ICC Pre-Trial Chamber Allows Victims to Participate in the Investigation Phase of Proceedings', *Journal of International Criminal Justice* 4(2): 342–50.

Deflem, M. (2002). *Policing World Society: Historical Foundations of International Police Cooperation.* Oxford, Oxford University Press.

DeFrancia, C. (2001). 'Due Process in International Criminal Courts: Why Procedure Matters', *Virginia Law Review* 87(7): 1381–1439.

Delmas-Marty, M. (2003). 'The Contribution of Comparative Law to a Pluralist Conception of International Criminal Law', *Journal of International Criminal Justice* 1(1): 13–25.

Delmas-Marty, M. (2008). Reflections on the 'Hybridisation of Criminal Procedure. *Crime, Procedure and Evidence in a Comparative and International Context. Essays in Honour of Professor Mirjan Damaška.* J. Jackson, M. Langer and P. Tillers. Oxford, Hart: 251–60.

Drumbl, M.A. (2007). *Atrocity, Punishment and International Law.* Cambridge, Cambridge University Press.

Ellis, M.S. (2002). 'The Evolution of Defense Counsel Appearing before the International Criminal Tribunal for the Former Yugoslavia', *New England Law Rev*. 37: 949–73.

Fairlie, M. (2004). 'The Marriage of Common and Continental Law at the ICTY and its Progeny, Due Process Deficit', *International Criminal Law Review* 4(3): 243–319.

Fairlie, M.A. (2003). 'Due Process Erosion: The Diminution of Live Testimony at the ICTY', *California Western International Law Journal* 34(1): 47–84.

Findlay, M. (2001). 'Synthesis in Trial Procedures? The Experience of International Criminal Tribunals', *International and Comparative Law Quarterly* 50(1): 26–53.

Gallavin, C. (2006). 'Prosecutorial Discretion Within the ICC: Under the Pressure of Justice', *Criminal Law Forum* 17(1): 43–58.

Gibson, J.L. (2004). 'Truth, Reconciliation, and the Creation of a Human Rights Culture in South Africa', *Law and Society* 38(1): 5–40.

Glenn, H.P. (2004). *Legal Traditions of the World*. Oxford, Oxford University Press.

Gordon, G.S. (2007). 'Toward an International Criminal Procedure: Due Process Aspirations and Limitations', *Columbia Journal of Transnational Law* 45(3): 635–710.

Hansen, A.S. (2002). *From Congo to Kosovo: Civilian Police in Peace Operations*. Oxford, Oxford University Press.

Harmon, M.B. (2007). 'The Pre-trial Process at the ICTY as a Means of Ensuring Expeditious Trials: A Potential Unrealised', *Journal of International Criminal Justice* 5(2): 377–93.

Higgins, G. (2007). 'Fair and Expeditious Pre-trial Proceedings: The Future of International Criminal Trials', *Journal of International Criminal Justice* 5(2): 394–401.

Hotis, C. (2006). 'A "Fair and Expeditious" Trial: A Reappraisal of Slobodan Milosevic's Right to Self-Representation before the International Criminal Tribunal for the Former Yugoslavia', *Chicago Journal of International Law* 6(2): 775–89.

Jackson, J.D. (2005). 'The Effect of Human Rights on Criminal Evidentiary Processes: Towards Convergence, Divergence or Realignment?' *Modern Law Review* 68(5): 737–64.

Jackson, J.D. (2008). Faces of Transitional Justice: Two Attempts to Build Common Standards Beyond National Boundaries. *Crime, Procedure and Evidence in a Comparative and International Context. Essays in Honour of Professor Mirjan Damaška*. J. Jackson, M. Langer and P. Tillers. Oxford, Hart: 221–50.

Jackson, J.D. (2009). 'Finding the Best Epistemic Fit for International Criminal Tribunals: Beyond the Adversarial-Inquisitorial Dichotomy', *Journal of International Criminal Justice* 7(1): 17–39.

Jorda, C. (2004). 'The Major Hurdles and Accomplishments of the ICTY What the ICC Can Learn From Them', *Journal of International Criminal Justice* 2(2): 572–84.

Jorgensen, N.H.B. (2005). 'The Right of the Accused to Self-Representation before International Criminal Tribunals: Further Developments', *The American Journal of International Law* 99(3): 663–68.

Kay, S. (2004). 'The Move from Oral Evidence to Written Evidence. "The Law Is Always Too Short and Too Tight for Growing Humankind"', *Journal of International Criminal Justice* 2(2): 495–502.

Keen, P.C. (2004). 'Tempered Adversariality: The Judicial Role and Trial Theory in the International Criminal Tribunals', *Leiden Journal of International Law* 17(4): 767–814.

Klarin, M. (2009). 'The Impact of the ICTY Trials on Public Opinion in the Former Yugoslavia', *Journal of International Criminal Justice* 7(1): 89–96.

Kuper, A. (2004). *Democracy Beyond Borders: Justice and Representation in Global Institutions*. Oxford, Oxford University Press.

Langer, M. (2005). 'The Rise of Managerial Judging in International Criminal Law', *American Journal of Comparative Law* 53(4): 835–910.

Lin, O. (2005). 'Demythologizing Restorative Justice: South Africa's Truth and Reconciliation Commission and Rwanda's Gacaca Courts in Context', *ILSA Journal of International and Comparative Law* 12(1): 41–86.

Linton, S. (2001). 'Cambodia, East Timor and Sierra Leone: Experiments in International Justice', *Criminal Law Forum* 12(2): 185–246.

Lutterbeck, D. (2004). 'Between Police and Military: The New Security Agenda and the Rise of Gendarmeries', *Cooperation and Conflict* 39(1): 45–68.

Mansoor, F.Z. (2005). 'Reassessing Packer in the Light of International Human Rights Norms', *Connecticut Public Interest Law Journal* 4(2): 262–80.

May, R. and M. Wierda (1999). 'Trends in International Criminal Evidence: Nuremberg, Tokyo, The Hague, and Arusha (1999)', *Columbia Journal of Transnational Law* 37: 725–65.

McClelland, G.A. (2002). 'A Non-Adversary Approach to International Criminal Tribunals', *Suffolk Transnational Law Review* 26(1): 1–38.

McDonald, G.K. (2001). 'Reflections on the Contributions of the International Criminal Tribunal for the Former Yugoslavia', *Hastings International and Comparative Law Review* 24(2): 155–72.

McMorrow, J.A. (2007). 'Creating Norms of Attorney Conduct in International Tribunals: A Case Study of the ICTY', *Boston College International and Comparative Law Review* 30(1): 139–73.

Megret, F. (2009). 'Beyond "Fairness": Understanding the Determinants of International Criminal Procedure', *UCLA Journal of International Law and Foreign Affairs* 14: 37–235.

Meron, T. (2004). 'Procedural Evolution in the ICTY', *Journal of International Criminal Justice* 2(2): 520–5.

Morris, V. and M.P. Scharf (1995). *An Insider's Guide to the International Criminal Tribunal for the Former Yugoslavia: A Documentary History and Analysis* New York, Transnational Publishers.

Murphy, P. (2010). 'No Free Lunch, No Free Proof: The Indiscriminate Admission of Evidence is a Serious Flaw in International Criminal Trials', *Journal of International Criminal Justice* 8(2): 539–73.

Nelken, D. (1997). *Comparing Legal Cultures*. Aldershot, Dartmouth.

Nice, G. and P. Vallieres-Roland (2005). 'Procedural Innovations in War Crimes Trials', *Journal of International Criminal Justice* 3(2): 354–80.

Orie, A. (2002). Accusatorial v Inquisitorial Approaches to International Criminal Proceedings. *The Rome Statute*. A. Cassese, P. Gaeta and J. Jones. Oxford, Oxford University Press: 1439–95.

Örücü, E. (2007). A General View of 'Legal Families' and 'Mixing Systems'. *Comparative Law. A Handbook*. D. Nelken and E. Örücü. Oxford, Hart: 169–88.

Packer, H.L. (1968). *The Limits of the Criminal Sanction*. Stanford, Stanford University Press.

Pakes, F.J. (2003). 'Styles of Trial Procedure at the International Criminal Tribunal for the Former Yugoslavia', *Perspectives in Law and Psychology* 17: 309–20.

Peskin, V. and M.P. Boduszyn'ski (2003). 'International Justice and Domestic Politics: Post-Tudjman Croatia and the International Criminal Tribunal for the Former Yugoslavia', *Europe-Asia Studies* 55(7): 1117–42.

Powell, A. (2004). 'Three Angry Men: Juries in International Criminal Adjudication', *New York University Law Review* 79: 2341–80.

Resnik, J. (1982). 'Managerial Judges', *Harvard Law Review* 96(2): 374–448.

Roberts, P. (2007). Comparative Law for International Justice. *Comparative Law. A Handbook.* D. Nelken and E. Örücü. Oxford, Hart: 339–70.

Robinson, P.L. (2005). 'Rough Edges in the Alignment of Legal Systems in the Proceedings at the ICTY', *Journal of International Criminal Justice* 3(5): 1037–58.

Safferling, C.J.M. (2001). *Towards an International Criminal Procedure*. Oxford, Oxford University Press.

Schabas, W.A. (2004). 'Conjoined Twins of Transitional Justice?: The Sierra Leone Truth and Reconciliation Commission and the Special Court', *Journal of International Criminal Justice* 2(4): 1082–99.

Schabas, W.A. (2005). 'Genocide Trials and Gacaca Courts', *Journal of International Criminal Justice* 3(4): 879–95.

Schabas, W.A. (2007). *An Introduction to the International Criminal Court.* Cambridge, Cambridge University Press.

Scharf, M.P. (2005). 'The Perils of Permitting Self-Representation in International War Crimes Trials', *Journal of Human Rights* 4(4): 513–20.

Sheptycki, J.W.E. (1995). 'Transnational Policing and the Makings of a Postmodern State', *British Journal of Criminology* 35(4): 613–35.

Skilbeck, R. (2010). 'Frankenstein's Monster: Creating a New International Procedure', *Journal of International Criminal Justice* 8(2): 451–62.

Sluiter, G. (2005). '"Fairness and the Interests of Justice": Illusive Concepts in the Milosevic Case', *Journal of International Criminal Justice* 3(1): 9–19.

Stahn, C., H. Olasolo et al. (2006). 'Participation of Victims in Pre-Trial Proceedings of the ICC', *Journal of International Criminal Justice* 4(2): 219–38.

Swart, B. (2008). 'Damaška and the Faces of International Criminal Justice', *Journal of International Criminal Justice* 6(1): 87–114.

Taman, E. (2003). 'Lay Participation in Criminal Justice: Enhancing Justice System Legitimacy in Post-Conflict States', *Dalhousie Journal of Legal Studies* 12: 33–62.

Temminck Tuinstra, J. (2006). 'Assisting an Accused to Represent Himself Appointment of Amici Curiae as the Most Appropriate Option', *Journal of International Criminal Justice* 4(1): 47–63.

Temminck Tuinstra, J. (2010). 'Defending the Defenders: The Role of Defence Counsel in International Criminal Trials', *Journal of International Criminal Justice* 8(2): 463–86.

Tochilovsky, V. (2002). 'Proceedings in the International Criminal Court: Some Lessons to Learn from ICTY Experience', *European Journal of Crime, Criminal Law and Criminal Justice* 10(4): 268–75.

Twining, W. (2007). Globalisation and Comparative Law. *Comparative Law. A Handbook*. D. Nelken and E. Örücü. Oxford, Hart: 69–89.

Vogler, R.K. (2005). *A World View of Criminal Justice*. Aldershot, Ashgate.

Warbrick, C. (1998). 'International Criminal Courts and Fair Trial', *Journal of Conflict and Security Law* 3(1): 45–64.

Zacklin, R. (2004). 'The Failings of Ad Hoc International Tribunals', *Journal of International Criminal Justice* 2(2): 541–45.

Zappalà, S. (2010). 'The Rights of Victims v. the Rights of the Accused', *Journal of International Criminal Justice* 8(1): 137–64.

Zappalà, S. (2003). *Human Rights in International Criminal Proceedings*. Oxford, Oxford University Press.

Zweigert, K. and H. Kötz (1998). *Introduction to Comparative Law*. Oxford, Clarendon Press.

Chapter 6
Should States Bear the Responsibility of Imposing Sanctions on its Citizens who as Witnesses Commit Crimes before the ICC?[1]

Sylvia Ngane

Introduction

This chapter focuses on the responsibility of States to impose sanctions on witnesses[2] for offences, against the International Criminal Court's (ICC) administration of justice. It considers the reasons why States are justified in imposing sanctions on witnesses rather than the ICC. The Rome Statute[3] and jurisprudence of the ICC gives the Court inherent authority over witnesses once they accept to provide testimony. As a moral Court the Statute provides for sanctions against witnesses who breach the Court's administration of justice. If a witness is in contempt of the Court, the ICC has authority and jurisdiction to prosecute and impose sanctions on the said witness. However, in prosecuting crimes of witnesses the ICC relies on State parties to accept jurisdiction if their nationals as witnesses are in contempt of court. State Parties are required to extend their criminal laws penalising offences against the Court's administration of justice committed on its territory or by one of its nationals. It is a universal practice that witnesses are sanctioned for crimes of contempt or perjury; in most domestic legal systems there are laws which prescribe for the sanctioning of crimes contempt and of perjury.

In this article, the author argues that the ICC was created by States and every witness before this Court is a national of a particular State. As a national of the State, the State can accurately determine what sanction that witness deserves for violations before the ICC. The State has been elected by the people, nationals of that State have given their consent to any laws or legislation passed and ratified

---

1 This article was given as part of a presentation during the UCC Law CCJHR Postgraduate Conference April 2009.

2 Note, the mention of witnesses throughout this chapter has nothing to do with the accused as a witness, but rather with all other types of witnesses e.g. crime-based and expert witnesses.

3 Rome Statute of the International Criminal Court, adopted by the United Nations Diplomatic Conference of Plenipotentiaries on the Establishment of an International Criminal Court of 17 July 1998, UN Doc. A/CONF. 183/9 (Rome Statute).

by the State. Therefore, witnesses who come before the Court are bound by the Statute and should be punished by their States for crimes against the Court. As nationals of State witnesses are systemic to the global legal system, they provide the facts in cases before the ICC which assist the Judges in dispensing justice and contribute in developing the law. States have the prescriptive act of penalising the conduct of their nationals who are witnesses, thus having the legal duty to impose criminal sanctions.

Part I examines the responsibilities and duties witnesses have before the ICC, citing instances of failure to carry out this duty and where relevant the jurisprudence of other tribunals to illuminate this obligation. Part II attempts to justify the importance of witness sanctions for offences against the Court's administration of justice, arguing that moral claims such as upholding the integrity of the Court justify the reason for punishing these crimes. Part III examines the authority of the ICC to actually prosecute these crimes and obstacles they may face in exercising this authority. Finally Part IV is an analysis of why the State should accept jurisdiction in prosecuting their nationals who as witnesses are in contempt and why the State should bear responsibility of imposing sanctions on them.

I. Responsibilities and Duties of Witnesses before the ICC

Witnesses have an obligation to testify and tell the truth, Article 69(1) of the Rome Statute provides that 'Before testifying, each witness shall, in accordance of the Rules of Procedure and Evidence, give an undertaking as to the truthfulness to be given by that witness.'

Everyone who appears before the ICC will be presumed to be competent to give evidence at the time they make the solemn declaration, which will usually be done immediately before they testify.[4]

The ICC Rules of Procedure and Evidence[5] provides for the responsibilities of witnesses, Rule 65(1) provides that 'a witness who appears before the Court is compellable by the Court to provide testimony, unless otherwise provided for in

4 Stuart Beresford, 'Child Witnesses and the International Criminal Justice System: Does the International Criminal Court Protect the Most Vulnerable?' (2005) *Journal of International Criminal Justice*, 721, 738; see also William A. Schabas, The International Criminal Court: A Commentary on the Rome Statute (Oxford University Press 2010) pp.838–9.

5 ICC Rules of Procedure and Evidence, UN doc. PCNICC/2000/1/Add.1 (2000) (ICC Rules), available online at http://www.icc-cpi.int/docs/basicdocs/rules, Rule 87(3)(c) (visited 30 December 2004); Claus Kress, 'Witnesses in Proceedings Before the International Criminal Court', in Horst Fischer, Claus Kress and Sascha Rolf Luder (eds) *International and National Prosecution of Crimes under International Law: Current Developments* (Berlin Verlag Arno Spitz GMBH 2001) pp. 309–83 at p. 313.

the Statute and the Rules, in particular Rules 73, 74 and 75'.[6] Rule 66(1) provides that 'except as described in sub-rule 2, every witness shall, in accordance with article 69, paragraph 1, make the following solemn undertaking before testifying: 'I solemnly declare that I will speak the truth, the whole truth and nothing but the truth.' Frank Terrier[7] observes that the oath before the Judges, to tell the truth the whole truth and nothing but the truth is a worldwide immemorial practice. It is held to rid the witness of all feelings of resentment, revenge or antipathy or on the contrary of friendship or sympathy.[8]

An exception to this law is found in Rule 66(2) which is applicable to vulnerable witnesses such as children if unable to understand the scope of the obligations resulting from the oath should be exempted from it. According to Stuart Beresford a child who does not understand the nature of the solemn declaration may be permitted to testify without that formality if the Chamber is satisfied that the child is able to describe the matters of which they had knowledge and understands the meaning of the duty to tell the truth.[9]

ICC trials have recently been plagued with questions about the integrity and truthfulness of witnesses during proceedings at The Hague. In the *Lubanga case*[10] for instance some witness testimony has been inaccurate; some of the witnesses have been accused of coming to The Hague with intention of providing false testimony. Some have claimed to have lied as to their names, age or as to being child soldiers, some have said their false testimonies were in part due to being afraid of seeing the accused in Court and the fear of being prosecuted.[11] In addition, there

---

6 Rules 73, 74 and 75 dealing with Privileged communications and information, Self-incrimination by a witness and Incrimination by family members respectively.

7 Frank Terrier, 'The Procedure before the Trial Chamber' in A. Cassese, P. Gaeta and J.R.W.D Jones, *The Rome Statute of the International Criminal Court: A Commentary*, (vol. II. Oxford University Press, 2002) pp. 1277–318 at p. 1301.

8 Ibid.

9 Stuart Beresford, 'Child Witnesses and The International Criminal Justice System: Does the International Criminal Court Protect the Most Vulnerable?' (2005) *Journal of International Criminal Justice*, 721, 738.

10 Case *The Prosecutor v. Thomas Lubanga Dyilo* ICC-01/04-01/06.

11 See Lubanga Transcripts 8 February 2010 http://www.icc-cpi.int/NR/exeres/05B30F9E-82FC-4B77-8BF8-D623B1C7FFF6.htm, (last visited March 2010); AEGIS, Lubanga Chronicle No. 71 'Truth or Lies? The Questions continue', 22 March 2010 available at http://www.aegistrust.org/Lubanga-Chronicles/lubanga-chronicle-71-truth-or-lies-the-questions-continue.html, (last visited April 2010); see also Lubanga Chronicle No. 58: Defence Witness 04: 'Child soldiers were enlisted in the UPC but it wasn't Thomas Lubanga who recruited them.' 10 February 2010- available at http://www.aegistrust.org/Lubanga-Chronicles/lubanga-chronicle-58-defence-witness-04-child-soldiers-were-enlisted-in-the-upc-but-it-wasnat-thomas-lubanga-who-recruited-them.html (last visited March 2010); Lubanga Chronicle 69-Prosecution intermediaries in the eye of the storm 17 March 2010 available at http://www.aegistrust.org/Lubanga-Chronicles/lubanga-chronicle-69-prosecution-intermediaries-in-the-eye-of-the-storm.html or generally http://

are accusations of 'intermediaries' inducing witnesses to supply false statements to ICC investigators which do not reflect the truth of what happened.[12]

Most of the witnesses at the *Lubanga* trial are children who were former child soldiers – understandably this is because Lubanga is charged under Articles 8(2)(b)(xxvi) and 8 (2)(e)(vii) with the war crimes of conscripting and enlisting children under the age of 15 years into his *Forces patriotiques pour la libération du Congo* [Patriotic Forces for the Liberation of Congo] (FPLC) and using them to participate actively in hostilities.[13] Following the *Lubanga case* it is demonstrated that children do lie and make allegations they know to be untrue.[14] Beresford suggests that in addition to testing a child's competence by inquiring into whether they understand what truth is and that they may be punished if they tell a lie, the Chamber will be able to require the child to explain the difference between truth and lies.[15] He questions whether the competence test set out in the ICC Statute can accurately predict whether a child will give complete and honest evidence. Since it is clear that not everyone who makes a solemn declaration will tell the truth even when they are aware that providing false testimony is an offence. Understanding the importance of telling the truth cannot guarantee that testimony will be truthful; conversely, it does not follow that failing to adequately explain

www.aegistrust.org/Lubanga-Trial/ (last visited March 2010); Times online, Chaos reigns at International Criminal Court trial of Thomas Lubanga January 29, 2009 http://www.timesonline.co.uk/tol/news/world/africa/article5606892.ece (last visited March 2010); reparation Centre for Victims of War Crimes, Lubanga Defense Described as 'Witnesses Lied, Lubanga Not Guilty', available at http://warcrimesreparations.info/blog/2010/02/13/lubanga-defense-described-as-witnesses-lied-lubanga-not-guilty/ (last visited March 2010); Racheal Irwin, Witness admits to false Statements, June 19 2009 available at http://www.lubangatrial.org/2009/06/19/witness-admits-to-false-statements/ (last visited March 2010).

12 *The Prosecutor v. Thomas Lubanga Dyilo*, Decision on the prosecution's 'Request on the Manner of Questioning of Witness DRC-OPT-WWWW-0015' and contact by the Prosecution with Court witnesses, ICC-01/04-01/06, 1 February 2010, see for paras 3, 11, 17; see also Racheal Irwin, Witness admits to false Statements, June 19 2009 available at http://www.lubangatrial.org/2009/06/19/witness-admits-to-false-statements/ (last visited March 2010); Defense Witnesses Claim ICC Agents Concocted Evidence available at http://allafrica.com/stories/201002150005.html (last visited March 2010).

13 See ICC Situation and Cases, democratic Republic of Congo Thomas Lubanga Dyilo ICC-01/04-01/06 available at http://www.icc-cpi.int/Menus/ICC/Situations+and+Cases/Situations/Situation+ICC+0104/Related+Cases/ICC+0104+0106/Democratic+Republic+of+the+Congo.htm, (last visited April 2010).

14 Note that not only child witnesses may tell lies under oath, adult witnesses may as well provide false testimony.

15 See discussion in Stuart Beresford, 'Child Witnesses and The International Criminal Justice System: Does the International Criminal Court Protect the Most Vulnerable?' *Journal of International Criminal Justice* (2005): 721, 738.

the difference between truth and lies will result in the child lying or making inaccurate statements.[16]

Before starting to testify at the ICC, the witness is informed of the sanctions applicable under Article 70(1) (a)[17] which provides for the Court to have jurisdiction over offences against its administration of justice when committed intentionally:

> Giving false testimony when under an obligation pursuant to article 69, Paragraph 1, to tell the truth.

However, in *Lubanga* the Judges felt it would be wholly inappropriate at the beginning of a witness's testimony (many of whom are nervous) for the Judges to issue a warning of the possibility that they could be charged with an offence of giving false testimony if they do not tell the truth[18] and decided instead that such advice should be given by a lawyer in a private setting, coolly and quietly and in an unhurried manner.[19] It is evident that these witnesses before the ICC do not have mistaken beliefs about the facts; following the allegations of providing false testimony they are aware or know their statements are untrue. A child witness, who lies about his age in cases such as *Lubanga*, commits perjury or commits an offence against the ICC's administration of justice because the age of such a witness is a factor necessary to determine the legal fact that the accused is guilty of conscripting and enlisting children under the age of 15 into his FPLC.

The practice and reasoning of other international tribunals may prove illuminating to ICC cases, the Judges of the International Criminal Tribunal for Rwanda (ICTR) in *Rutaganda*, have defined false testimony as a false statement made in Court under oath or solemn declaration.[20] They enumerate four constituent elements of false testimony: the witness must make a solemn declaration; the false statement must be contrary to the solemn declaration; the witness must believe at the time the statement was made that it was false; and there must be a relevant relationship between the statement and a material matter within the case.[21]

The assessment of testimonial evidence lies ultimately on the credibility of witnesses, the Judges of the Special Court for Sierra Leone (SCSL) held in *Fofana et al.* that in assessing the credibility and reliability of oral witness testimony, the Chamber considers factors such as the internal consistency of the witness testimony, its consistency with other evidence in the case, any personal interest

16 Ibid., 739–40.

17 Rule 66(3).

18 Lubanga (ICC-01/04-01/06) Transcript 28 January 2009 pp. 1–6.

19 Ibid., p.5.

20 *Prosecutor v. Rutaganda*, Decision on the Defence Motion To Direct The The Prosecutor To Investigate The False Testimony By Witness 'E' *Case No.: ICTR-96-3-T, T CH I*, 10 March 1998 (Hereinafter Rutaganda decision on defence motion on matter on matter of false testimony).

21 Ibid.

a witness may have that may influence his motivation to tell the truth, as well as observational criteria such as the witness' demeanour conduct and character.[22] The fact that a witness gives evidence honestly is not in itself sufficient to establish the reliability of that evidence. The issue is not merely whether the evidence of a witness is honest; it is also whether the evidence is objectively reliable.[23] In addition, the Judges have held that they may accept or reject the evidence of a witness in part or in whole and may find a witness to be credible and reliable about certain aspects of their testimony and not credible or reliable with respect to others.[24]

The onus may be on the party pleading a case of false testimony to prove the falsehood of the witness statements; that these statements were made with harmful intent, or at least that they were made by a witness who was fully aware that they were false; and the possible bearing of the said statements upon the Judge's decision.[25] The ICTR Appeals Chamber in *Simba*[26] stated a credibility determination may be based, but does not necessarily depend, on a judicial finding that a witness has given false testimony. The Chamber stressed that the mere existence of discrepancies between a witness' testimony and his earlier statements does not constitute strong grounds for believing that a witness may have knowingly and wilfully given false testimony.[27]

Given the controversy surrounding the credibility of some of these witnesses in *Lubanga* and other cases before the ICC, it is necessary that such persons if guilty be prosecuted for perjury and for the Judges to disqualify any testimony given by such witnesses for the determination of the case. However, it is still left to be seen what the Judges' position will be on this isssue; given the experiences of other international tribunals, less importance is being placed on witnesses who actually commit crimes of perjury; critics have condemned the handling of contempt cases with regards to witnesses before the Ad Hoc Tribunals.[28]

---

22 *Prosecutor v. Fofana et al.*; Judgement, Case No.SCSL-04-14-T; 2 August 2007, para 256.

23 Ibid., para 257.

24 Ibid., para 258.

25 See Rutaganda decision on defence motion on matter of false testimony.

26 *Prosecutor v. Simba*, Judgment, Case No. ICTR-01-76-A, Appeals Chamber, 27 November 2007.

27 Ibid., paras 31–2.

28 See Alexander Zahar, 'The Problem of false Testimony at the International Criminal Tribunal for Rwanda', in Andre Klip and Goran Sluiter (eds), *Annotated Leading Cases of International criminal Tribunals, vol. 25: the International Criminal tribunal for the Former Yugoslavia 2006–2007*, (Intersentia, 2010) available at http://papers.ssrn.com/sol3/papers.cfm?abstract_id=1443124; see also Goran Sluiter, 'The ICTY and Offences against the Administration of Justice', (2004), *Journal of International Criminal Justice*, 631–41 at 637–41; William A. Schabas, T*he International Criminal Court: A Commentary on the Rome Statute* (Oxford University Press 2010) pp. 855–6.

Furthermore, pursuant to Rule 65(2) a witness who appears before the Court is compellable by the Court to provide testimony; this obligation can be enforced with a fine.[29] Article 71 provides that the Court may sanction persons present before it who commit misconduct, including disruption of its proceedings or deliberate refusal to comply with its directions. The offence of contempt of court which is not a statutory crime before the International Criminal Tribunal for Former Yugoslavia (ICTY), for instance, was inserted by the Judges; the practice has been for the Judges to make or expand the substantive or procedural law.[30] Rule 77(A) (i) of the Ad Hoc Tribunals provides that the Tribunals in their exercise of inherent power may hold in contempt those who knowingly and wilfully interfere with its administration of justice, including any person who being a witness before a Chamber, contumaciously refuses or fails to answer a question.[31]

In the ICTY *Haradinaj et al.* case a witness who appeared to testify did not answer any questions put to him by the prosecution or the Judges on the substance of the case. Following a warning, he persisted in his refusal to answer questions. The Judges ordered the prosecution of the witness for 'knowingly and wilfully interfering with the administration of justice by contumaciously refusing or failing to answer questions while being a witness before the Trial Chamber' under Rule 77(A) ICTY RPE.[32]

Otto Trifferer[33] suggests that the Court ought to take into consideration the traumatisation or the sufferings a witness has been exposed to and which may have to be at least partly recalled for reasons of evidence. A mere warning therefore may be more adequate especially when victim-witnesses commit misconduct during cross-examination.[34] Nontheless, it is the responsibility of witnesses to follow Court orders and to tell the truth because the Judges also rely for the determination of guilt of the accused on evidence presented by their testimony. It might be argued that the ICC does not have core jurisdiction over persons other than the accused and therefore the ICC has no authority over persons other than the accused or that witnesses are usually nationals from different jurisdictions and are not to be subjected to the jurisdiction of the ICC. According to Alexander Zahar, the practice of the Ad Hoc Tribunals has taught that an international Court will rapidly assume powers over individuals, other than the accused, that are not always mediated or

29 See Rule 171.

30 Alexander Zahar, 'International Court and Private Citizen', (2009) *New Criminal law Review*, 569 at 578.

31 For details, see Goran Sluiter *International Criminal Adjudication and the Collection of Evidence: Obligations of States* (Antwerp, Oxford, New York: Intersentia, 2002), pp. 264–68.

32 *In The Contempt Case Of Shefqet Kabashi*, Order in Lieu of Indictment on Contempt Concerning Shefqet Kabashi, (IT-04-84-R77.1), 5 June 2007.

33 Otto Trifferer, 'Sanctions for Misconduct Before the Court,' in Otto Trifferer (ed.) *Commentary on the Rome Statute of the International Criminal Court: Observers Notes, Article by Article* (Baden-Baden: Nomos, 1999) pp. 925–35.

34 Ibid.

moderated by the laws of the subject's State but leave the individual exposed to the whims of the supranational body.[35]

With the imposition of criminal sanctions by the Court for offences against its legal rule, it may also be argued that the imposition of criminal sanctions may give rise to negative reactions on the part of the witnesses and many may be unwilling to testify. The argument may be that witnesses assist the Court in providing evidence for some of the most heinous crimes of international law and why should they be punished for a petty crime? Should they go unpunished if they bring the Court into disrepute? What is the justification for imposing sanctions on witnesses who commit crimes before the ICC?

II. Reasons for Imposing Sanctions on Witnesses Who Commit Crimes before the ICC

Does the punishment of a witness for crimes against the ICC administration of justice stand in need of justification? According to John Rawl, Judges justify the punishment of individual offenders on the non-consequential ground that he or she violated a legal command.[36] Hart defines criminal sanctions as sanctions that involve 'pain or other consequences normally considered unpleasant' which are inflicted upon 'an actual or supposed offender for his offence' and which must also be imposed for 'an offence against legal rules'.[37]

Witnesses have an influence in judicial decision-making of the ICC; they are usually important parties in the giving of evidence before the Court to assist the Judges to make important decisions and judgements against perpetrators' grave crimes under the Court's jurisdiction. False testimony, for instance, against an accused may infringe the rights of the accused or lead to wrongful conviction; a breach of truth telling constitutes a breach to a legal rule and sanctions confirm the moral legitimacy of the ICC. Crimes of perjury defined in moral terms are offences against the Court's legal rules and should not be left unpunished when the system has the capacity to punish them at reasonable cost.

According to Frank Terrier[38] reasons for lying are many and the causes of error in good faith are numberless. For most witnesses the requirement of justice exceeds

35 Alexander Zahar, 'International Court and Private Citizen', (2009) New Criminal law Review, 569, 589. NB, The ICC's authority is discussed below in subsequent section.

36 John Rawls, 'Two Concepts of Rules', (1955) *Philosophical Review 64*, 3–32.

37 H.L.A. Hart, 'Prolegomenon To The Principles of Punishment in Punishment and Responsibility: essays in the philosophy of Law' 1, 4–5 (1968) see also Alon Harel, 'Why only the State may inflict criminal sanctions: the case against privately inflicted sanctions', (2008) *14 Legal Theory* 113, 116.

38 Frank Terrier, 'The Procedure before the Trial Chamber' in A. Cassese, P. Gaeta and J.R.W.D Jones, *The Rome Statute of the International Criminal Court: A Commentary*, (vol. II. Oxford University Press, 2002) pp. 1277–318 at p. 1301.

the requirement for truth and the oath to tell the truth has obligations attached to it that are perhaps harder to escape than one might think. Being involved in conflict some of the witnesses heard may have belonged either on the victim's side or the side of the accused. Resentment may cloud testimony or reduce its scope but also the commitment the person has had during the conflict.[39]

André Klip observes that perjury hinders the course of justice and might even lead to miscarriages of justice. Especially in the serious cases pending before the International Criminal Tribunal it is important that the Judges can rely on those giving evidence. He suggests that, whenever this trust is abused it deserves a reaction.[40] Again, the ICTR Judges in *Rutaganda* have held that false testimony is a deliberate offence, which supposes wilful intent on the part of the perpetrator to mislead the Judge and thus to cause harm. According to the Judges a false testimony may consist of either an affirmation of a false fact or a negation of a true fact implicated in crimes and may lead a witness to distort the pure truth.[41] In addition, they have reiterated to the parties, to witnesses and to others connected to proceedings before the Tribunal, that the Tribunal will not tolerate occurrences of false testimony.[42]

As already observed the assessment of testimonial evidence lies ultimately on the credibility of witnesses. In accepting to give testimony, a witness accepts the jurisdiction of the Court and accepts to adhere to the laws and regulations of the Court. Imposing criminal sanctions on witnesses reinforces the norm of the ICC being a moral court; the ICC Statute seeks the truth, the Judges have a mission of assessing witness testimony. Article 69(3) provides that the Court shall have the authority to request the submission of all evidence that it considers necessary for the determination of the truth. Regulation 43 of the Regulations of the Court also provides that the Court shall determine the mode of questioning witnesses, to ensure fairness and to determine the truth effectively.

Again, the influence of witness-based truth in judicial decision-making is of great importance; there is a moral obligation for a witness to tell the truth. Perjury may lead to an unjust conviction, or unjust acquittal of an accused. In *Prosecutor v. GAA*,[43] the ICTR Judges held that although all perjury is serious, the Chamber is

---

39 Ibid.

40 A. Klip, 'Commentary on Decisions Relating to the false Testimony of Dragan Opacic', in André Klip and Goran Sluiter, *Annotated Leading Cases of International Criminal Tribunals, vol. 1: the International Criminal tribunal for the Former Yugoslavia 1993–1998* (Intersentia, 1999) p. 214.

41 Rutaganda decision on defence motion on matter of false testimony.

42 *Prosecutor v. Kamuhanda* Oral Decision Rule 115 and Contempt of False Testimony, Case No.ICTR-99-54A-A, Appeals Chamber Rutaganda decision on defence motion on matter of false testimony.

Prosecutor v. Kamuhanda Oral Decision Rule 115 and Contempt of False Testimony, Case No.ICTR-99-54A-A, Appeals Chamber, 19 May 2005.

43 The Accused was a protected witness who testified in *Kamuhanda* trial under the pseudonym GAA. GAA admitted that he willingly gave the false testimony when

of the view that the most serious category is where the perjured evidence is being given to lead to the conviction of an innocent person and the second most serious category is where, as in this case, the perjured evidence is given in the hope of procuring the acquittal of a guilty person. The Judges considered that the gravity of the offence requires that a custodial sentence should be imposed taking into account the mitigating factors that have been established.[44]

As it is important to protect the witness it is equally important to protect the accused's rights to a fair trial. Any international Tribunal or Court which endeavours to prosecute violations of and enforce international law must concurrently provide for and protect the proper administration of justice. Again, in *GAA*, the Chamber held false testimony under solemn declaration and contempt of the Tribunal as a very grave offence, as it constitutes a direct challenge to the integrity of the trial process. Maintaining the integrity of the administration of justice is particularly important in trials involving serious criminal offences. It is therefore necessary for general deterrence and denunciation to be given high importance in sentencing policies.[45] Similarly the ICTY convicted a potential witness Zuhdija Tabaković[46] for Contempt of the Tribunal Rule 77(A) and sentenced him to three months' imprisonment.

ICC Articles 70 and 71 provide for a means for the Court to protect itself, preserve its authority, credibility and protect the Court's evidence. Article 71 gives the Court a degree of control over a recalcitrant witness who is in contempt of the Court and allows the imposition of a fine.[47] Otto Trifferer[48] suggests that Article 71 serves the

---

he appeared before the Appeals Chamber on 18 May 2005 in the case of Jean de Dieu Kamuhanda who appealed against his conviction and sentence. See *The Prosecutor v. GAA*, Case No. ICTR-07-90-R77; *Prosecutor v. Jean de Dieu Kamuhanda*, Case No. ICTR-99-54A-A; *The Prosecutor v. GAA* Judgement and Sentence Case No. ICTR-07-90-R77 4, T.CH III December 2007, para 5 *(Hereinafter GAA* Judgement and Sentence).

44 *GAA* Judgement and Sentence para 10.

45 GAA was then sentenced to nine months imprisonment for contempt of the Tribunal and false testimony under solemn declaration See *GAA* Judgement and Sentence paras 10, 12–13; ICTR Press Release, Former Witness Sentenced to 9 Months for Contempt ICTR/INFO-9-2-541.EN3 December 2007 available at http://www.ictr.org/ENGLISH/PRESSREL/2007/541.htm (last visited November 2009).

46 Zuhdija Tabaković was a potential witness in the case of *The Prosecutor v. Milan Lukić and Sredoje Lukić*. See ICTY press release Tabaković Pleads Guilty, Sentenced to Three Months' Imprisonment, 15 March 2010 available at http://www.icty.org/sid/10359 (last visited March 2010); *Prosecutor v. Zuhdija Tabaković*, Indictment, IT-98-32/1-R77.1; *Prosecutor v. Zuhdua Tabakovic*, Sentencing Judgement Case No. IT-98-32/1-R77.1, 18 March 2010.

47 Rule 75, 65 and 171(1); see William A. Schabas, *An Introduction to the International Criminal Court* (Second Edition, Cambridge University Press, 2004) p. 152.

48 Otto Trifferer, 'Sanctions for misconduct before the Court,' in Otto Trifferer (ed.) *Commentary on the Rome Statute of the International Criminal Court: Observers Notes, Article by Article* (Baden-Baden: Nomos, 1999) pp. 925–35 at p. 928.

purpose of preventing obstructions to the administration of international criminal justice and of enabling the Court to exercise its jurisdiction properly undisturbed by illegal influences from witnesses. It is also to avoid or exclude any behaviour which may have a negative impact on the smooth running of the case especially by exercising an impartial jurisdiction according to the applicable law.[49]

The ICC has to uphold its standing as a moral Court. Punishing witness contempt enhances the denunciation of the act as does a call for witnesses to refrain from crimes against the Court's administration of justice. Hence, moral claims justify the reason or practice of punishing witnesses. False testimony for instance leads to miscarriages of justice; witness sanctions maintain the dignity and credibility of ICC proceedings, and thus its standing as a moral court, and as a court which protects the rights of all who come before it.

III. Authority of the Court and the Obstacles to That Authority to Actually Punish Witnesses Before It

The ICC has inherent judicial authority to prosecute crimes of contempt of court and for giving false testimony by witnesses. The ICC has jurisdiction over persons other than the accused; the Judges have held in *Lubanga*[50] that witnesses should not be considered as witnesses of the Prosecution nor of the Defence but as witnesses of the Court.[51] Rule 165 sets out the Procedure for 'investigation, prosecution and trial' of offences against the administration of justice under Article 70. Rule 165(1) provides that the Prosecutor may initiate and conduct investigations with respect to the offences defined in Article 70 on his or her own initiative, on the basis of information communicated by a Chamber or any reliable source.[52] If conduct covered by Article 71 also constitutes one of the offences defined in Article 70, the Court shall proceed in accordance with Article 70 and Rules 162 to 169.[53]

The Judges of the ICTY have maintained that contempt power is inherent to the Courts.[54] in *Delalic*, Judge Antonio Cassesse noted that 'the judges acting in plenary had the authority to adopt a rule on contempt only by virtue of this

49 Ibid.

50 Situation in The Democratic Republic of Congo in the Case of the *Prosecutor v. Lubanga Dyilo*, The Public Document Decision on the Practices of Witness Familiarisation and Witness Proofing No.: ICC-01/04-01/06, Date: 8 November 2006.

51 Ibid., para 26.

52 Rule 165(1), Note Articles 53 and 59, and any rules there under, shall not apply.

53 Rule 172.

54 Alexander Zahar, 'International Court and Private Citizen', (2009) *New Criminal Law Review*, 569, 578.

inherent power …'.[55] In *Tadić*,[56] it was held that the Tribunal possesses an inherent jurisdiction, deriving from its judicial function, to ensure that its exercise of the jurisdiction expressly given to it by the Statute is not frustrated and that its basic judicial functions are safeguarded. As an international criminal Court, the Tribunal possess the inherent power to deal with conduct interfering with its administration of justice. The content of that inherent power may be discerned by reference to the usual sources of international law.[57] Finally, in *Simic et al.*, the Judges held that the inherent power is to hold in contempt those who knowingly and wilfully interfere with the Tribunal's administration of justice and that inherent power exists independently of the terms of Rule 77 and the amendments made to that Rule from time to time do not limit that inherent power.[58]

According to ICTY/R Rule 91(B) if a Chamber has strong ground for believing that a witness has knowingly and wilfully given false testimony, or at the request of a party, it may direct the Prosecutor to investigate the matter with a view to the preparation and submission of an indictment for false testimony. ICTY Rule 77 (G) of the Rules provides that the maximum penalty that may be imposed on a person found to be in contempt of the Tribunal shall be a term of imprisonment not exceeding seven years, or a fine not exceeding 100,000 euros, or both. The ICTY Rule 91(G) provides more draconian punishment than the ICTR Rule 91 (G); ICTY Rule 91 provides that a witness who gives false testimony may be punished for perjury with a fine of up to 100, 000 euros and or up to seven years imprisonment, while the ICTR Rule 91 provides for a fine of up to US$ 10,000 and or 12 months' imprisonment.[59]

Enforcement of sanctions imposed with respect to offences defined in Article 70 shall be subject to a period of limitation of 10 years from the date on which the sanction has become final. The period of limitation shall be interrupted with the detention of the convicted person or while the person concerned is outside the territory of the States Parties.[60]

55 *Prosecutor v. Delalic et al.*, Decision of the President on the Prosecutor's Motion for the Production of Notes Exchanged between Zejnil Delalic and Zdravko Mucic, Case no. IT-96-21-T, 11 November 1996; see also discussion on inherent power by Micheal Bohlander, 'International Criminal Tribunals and Their Power to punish Contempt and False Testimony', (2001) Criminal Law Forum 91; Goran Sluiter, 'The ICTY and Offences against the Administration of Justice', (2004), Journal of International Criminal Justice, 631, 633–5.

56 *Prosecutor v. Tadic*, Judgement on Allegations of Contempt against Prior Counsel, Milan Vujin, Case No. IT-94-1-A-R77, 31 January 2000.

57 Ibid., para 13.

58 *Prosecutor v. Simic et al.*, Judgement in the matter of Contempt Allegations Against an Accused and his Counsel, Case No. IT-95-9-R77, 30 June 2000 at IV.

59 See Micheal Bohlander, 'International Criminal Tribunals and Their Power to punish Contempt and False Testimony', (2001) 12 *Criminal Law Forum*, 91, 95.

60 Rule 164(3).

In imposing a fine the Court shall allow the convicted person a reasonable period in which to pay the fine. If the convicted person does not pay a fine imposed in accordance with the conditions set forth in Rule 166(4), appropriate measures may be taken by the Court pursuant to Rules 217 to 222 and in accordance with Article 109. Where, in cases of continued wilful non-payment, the Court, on its own motion or at the request of the Prosecutor, is satisfied that all available enforcement measures have been exhausted, it may as a last resort impose a term of imprisonment in accordance with Article 70(3). In the determination of such term of imprisonment, the Court shall take into account the amount of fine paid.[61] If conduct covered by Article 71 also constitutes one of the offences defined in Article 70, the Court shall proceed in accordance with Article 70 and Rules 162 to 169.[62]

At the Rome conference, States expressed concern about the ICC itself having jurisdiction over these crimes. It was noted that the ICC should refer this cases to the State concerned and such a State should take action, treating the cases with all diligence. Delegates recognised that it will be impracticable to leave prosecution of these offences exclusively to the jurisdiction of States Parties; they were also mindful of the fact that the Court might have insufficient time and resources to pursue all such offences or might have difficulty exercising jurisdiction or that it might otherwise be more appropriate in a particular case for prosecution to be carried out by the State.[63] The ICC may be faced with certain obstacles which

61 Rule 166(4)(5).

62 Rule 172.

63 See the following reports during the drafting years; Article 48. Evidence, Commentary, International Law Commission draft: Document A/48/10: Report of the International Law Commission on the work of its forty-fifth session (3 May–23 July 1993), ICC Legal Tools Doc. No. 19930901_A4810(E); See also Perjury; punishable by national Courts versus ICC, Report of the Preparatory Committee on the Establishment of an International Criminal Court Volume II (Compilation of proposals) General Assembly Official Records Fifty-first Session General Assembly Official Records Fifty-first Session Supplement No. 22A (A/5 1 /22) United Nations p.102, ICC Legal Tools Doc. No. 19960913_A5122 [VOL.II] (SUPP) (E); USA Proposal: U.S. Non-Paper On Rules Of Investigation, Procedure And Evidence For The International Criminal Court footnote.77, ICC Legal Tools Doc. No. 19950821_ST_UNITEDSTATES_UD(E); United Kingdom Mission to the United Nations New York : Ad Hoc Committee On The Establishment Of An International Criminal Court Summary of observations made by the Representative of the United Kingdom of Great Britain and Northern Ireland on 3, 4, 5, 6 and 7 April 1995, p. 9 19950407_ST_UNITEDKINGDOM(E) (853 kb); Report of the Preparatory Committee on the Establishment of an International Criminal Court, UNGAOR, 51st Session, Supplement No. 22A, U.N. DOC A/51/22 (1996) vol. II, pp. 210–13; SECTION 3. Contempt Of Court, Misconduct And Perjury Report of the Preparatory Committee on the Establishment of an International Criminal Court Volume II (Compilation of proposals) General Assembly Official Records Fifty-first Session General Assembly Official Records Fifty-first Session Supplement No. 22A (A/5 1 /22) United Nations p. 102–3, ICC Legal Tools Doc. No. 19960913_A5122[VOL.II](SUPP)(E); Rule 77 Contempt of the Tribunal Report of the

may prevent it from exercising its inherent authority over witness crimes against its administration of justice. The following section will analyse briefly some of these factors.

Firstly, some provisions in the Statute may make it difficult for the ICC to prosecute; for instance, Article 93(1) provides that *States Parties shall, in accordance with the provisions of this Part and under procedures of national law, comply with requests by the Court to provide the following assistance in relation to investigations or prosecutions: (e) facilitating the voluntary appearance of persons as witnesses or experts before the Court.* The term 'facilitate' referred in this provision connotes voluntariness and does not imply an obligation on the part of the State Party to provide sanctions according to its national law, if a witness or an expert refuses to appear before the Court.[64] The voluntary nature of the cooperation under Article 93(1) (e) is underscored by the fact that a witness failure to respond to a summons is not an offence against the administration of justice in Article 70.[65] Following the interpretation of the article, the adoption of this

---

Preparatory Committee on the Establishment of an International Criminal Court Volume II (Compilation of proposals) General Assembly Official Records Fifty-first Session General Assembly Official Records Fifty-first Session Supplement No. 22A (A/5 1 /22) United Nations p.102, ICC Legal Tools Doc. No. 19960913_A5122 [VOL.II](SUPP)(E); Report of the Inter-Sessional Meeting from 19 to 30 January 1998 in Zutphen, the Netherlands, U.N. Doc. A/AC.249/1998/L.13, Article 63, p.119. Final Act of the United Nations Diplomatic Conference of Plenipotentiaries on the Establishment of an International Criminal Court, U.N. Doc. A/CONF.183/10, Annex 1, para. 6. Apprehension and surrender, Cooperation between States and the ICC Remarks of the U.S. Delegation April 8, 1996 – afternoon session Para 4. p. 3, ICC Legal Tools Doc. No. 19960408_ST_UNITEDSTATES_UD(E). Press Release L/2780 Preparatory Committee On International Criminal Court Discusses Draft Articles On Arrest, Pre-Trial Detention, 9 April 1996, ICC Legal Tools Doc. No. 19960409_L2780(E). See also Kenneth Harris, 'Offences against the administration of justice,' in Otto Triffterer (ed.) *Commentary on the Rome Statute of the International Criminal Court: Observers Notes, Article by Article* (Baden-Baden: Nomos, 1999) pp. 917–23 at p. 919. Kenneth Harris, 'Offences against the administration of justice,' in Otto Triffterer (ed.) *Commentary on the Rome Statute of the International Criminal Court: Observers Notes, Article by Article* (Baden-Baden: Nomos, 1999) pp. 917–23 at p. 919; See also, Otto Triffterer, 'Sanctions for misconduct before the Court,' in Otto Triffterer (ed.) *Commentary on the Rome Statute of the International Criminal Court: Observers Notes, Article by Article* (Baden-Baden: Nomos, 1999) pp. 917–23 at pp. 921–35. See, Otto Triffterer, 'Sanctions for misconduct before the Court,' in Otto Triffterer (ed.) *Commentary on the Rome Statute of the International Criminal Court: Observers Notes, Article by Article* (Baden-Baden: Nomos, 1999) pp. 925–35 at p. 927–8.

64 See Kimberly Prost and Angelika Schlunck, 'Other Forms of Cooperation', *Observers Notes Article by Article, Commentary on the Rome Statute of the International Criminal Court*, (Otto Triffterer ed.: 1999) p. 1108.

65 See, Karim Khan and Rodney Dixon, Archbold *International Criminal Courts: Practice, Procedure and Evidence*, (Thomson, Sweet and Maxwell: 2005: 2nd Edition) p. 138; see also for details, Goran Sluiter *International Criminal Adjudication and the*

principle of voluntary appearance of a witness, indicates that the non-appearance of a witness is not an offence against the ICC administration of justice. Furthermore, there is the practical problem of arrest and detention of witnesses; the ICC provides for safe conduct measures which guarantee that a witness will not be prosecuted shortly before, during and after his testimony. Article 93(2) provides an assurance that witnesses would not be 'prosecuted, detained or subjected to any restriction of personal freedom by the Court in respect of any act or omission that preceded the departure of that person from the requested State'. This provision makes it difficult for the Court to punish any witness who has committed an offence against the Court's administration of justice; the article is contrary to Article 70(1) (a). Some witnesses are privileged under Rule 73 which stipulates rules governing privileged communications and information. Any information given to the ICC by some organisations is meant to be confidential when this information has not been made public or collected by another source. Therefore, witnesses from these organisations may not be sanctioned pursuant to Article 71 if they fail to follow the Court's direction, for instance failing to provide before the Court testimony which is said to be confidential or testimony they provided to the Prosecutor in a confidential agreement.

Secondly, the fact that the Court does not have the same jurisdiction as the regime contemplated for core crimes may make it difficult for the Court to impose sanctions. The ICC Prosecutor's office already has a considerable amount of work in investigating and prosecuting core crimes which requires a vast amount of resources; this may hinder the office from effectively prosecuting these crimes. Furthermore, there is the important factor of prosecutorial discretion; the ICC prosecutor has considerable discretion whether to prosecute or initiate investigations against witness contempt before the ICC. He may have a conflict of interest with regards to his relationship with victim witnesses; however it is still left to be seen if the ICC prosecutor will use his discretion to prosecute.

Finally, Rule 162(1) provides that before deciding whether to exercise jurisdiction, the Court may consult with States Parties that may have jurisdiction over the offence. However, in making a decision whether or not to exercise jurisdiction, the Court may consider, in particular (a) the availability and effectiveness of prosecution by a State Party, and (b) the seriousness of an offence.[66] According to Rule 162(3), the Court shall give favourable consideration to a request from the host State for a waiver of the power of the Court to exercise jurisdiction in cases where the host State considers such a waiver to be of particular importance. The

---

Collection of Evidence: Obligations of States (Antwerp, Oxford, New York: Intersentia, 2002), p. 254. William A. Schabas, *An Introduction to the International Criminal Court* (Cambridge University Press 2001) p. 127, Alexander Zahar argues that the concept voluntary means no more than the formal instrument of compulsion, such as a Subpoena, it does not mean the absence of compulsion. See Alexander Zahar, 'International Court and Private Citizen', (2009) *New Criminal Law Review* 569, 587.

66 Rule 162(2).

Court has the option of not assuming jurisdiction itself but instead requiring States Parties to prosecute such offences if committed on their territory or by one of their nationals. To implement this duty Article 70(4) (a) provides that each State Party shall extend its criminal laws penalising offences against the integrity of its own investigative or judicial processes to offences against the administration of justice committed on its territory or by one of its nationals.

IV. Why Should a State Bear Responsibility to Impose Criminal Sanctions for Offences against the ICC Committed by their Nationals before a Court out of its Jurisdiction?

Should State Parties bear responsibility of imposing criminal sanctions on their nationals who as witnesses commit crimes before the ICC? What is the likelihood that the national Courts take up these cases? Will witnesses accept the jurisdiction of their national Courts for crimes they have committed in the ICC?

Generally States have an obligation to cooperate with the ICC and this obligation must not only be limited to arrest, detention and surrender of accused persons; it should also extend to prosecuting witnesses who have committed crimes at the Court. Pursuant to Rule 167(1). The Court may request a State to provide any form of international cooperation or judicial assistance with regard to offences under Article 70, corresponding to those forms set forth in Part 9 of the Statute.[67] In any such request, the Court shall indicate that the basis for the request is an investigation or prosecution of offences under Article 70. The conditions for providing international cooperation to the Court with respect to its proceedings under this article shall be governed by the domestic laws of the requested State.[68]

The ICC was created by States and its legal jurisdiction is dependent on powers granted to it by the States which established it. State Parties are bound by the Rome Statute; it is therefore appropriate for the States to impose sanctions for violations committed by witnesses. Witnesses may argue that they have not entered into a mutually advantageous agreement with other States or with the ICC or that they owe no responsibility or obligation to the Court and should not be punished. However, as a national of a State Party, a witness is bound by any treaties ratified by that State Party.

67 Part 9 refers to part 9 of the Statute dealing with international cooperation and judicial assistance.

68 Article 70(2) and Rule 167(2).

What is the General View for State Inflicted Sanctions?

According to Alon Harel,[69] the justification for States to inflict sanctions could be that the power to inflict criminal sanctions is an agent-dependent power, a power that can be successfully exercised only by the State. State-inflicted sanctions are designed to realise goals or perform tasks that cannot in principle be performed successfully by the ICC. International cooperation with prosecutions for offences against the Court's administration is governed by the domestic laws of the State requested to furnish cooperation.[70]

Kenneth Harris suggests that the requirement that States make punishable such offences committed by their nationals will enable prosecution to take place where the witness is found in many cases and is particularly important if the State in question has a legal prohibition against the extradition of its nationals.[71] Roger O'Keefe[72] observes that a State's jurisdiction refers to its authority under international law to regulate the conduct of persons, natural and legal in accordance with its municipal law. Thus, as nationals of the State, the State can accurately determine what its nationals deserve for violations before the ICC and inflict a just sanction successfully. They do have the prescriptive act which consists of penalising the conduct of a witness within its legal order by way of adoption of the applicable international legal rule into the domestic legal order; this has been done by many State Parties by way of ICC Implementing Legislation.

Why is the State Justified in Coercing Its Citizens?

Why should the State regulate the conduct of its nationals who testify before the ICC? Citizens of a State have consented in any laws or legislation passed and ratified by the State because it is the citizens who have elected the officials who enact these laws. Thus, they have agreed to any decisions taken by legislators or the government. Noah Feldham observes that the traditional liberal answers to why the State is justified in coercing its citizens through the law and why there is a corresponding duty to obey the law relies on consent.[73] He argues that scepticism about the mechanism of consent has given rise to a set of liberal arguments designed to ground the justifiability of State coercion in some other moral framework. He

69 See Alon Harel, 'Why Only The State May Inflict Criminal Sanctions: The Case Against Privately Inflicted Sanctions', (2008) *14 Legal Theory*, 113–33.

70 Article 70(2).

71 Kenneth Harris, 'Offences against the administration of justice,' in Otto Trifferer (ed.) *Commentary on the Rome Statute of the International Criminal Court: Observers Notes, Article by Article* (Baden-Baden: Nomos, 1999) pp. 917–23 at p. 923.

72 Roger O'Keefe, 'Universal Jurisdiction: clarifying the basic concept', (2004) *Journal of International Criminal Justice*, 735–60 at 736.

73 Noah Feldham, 'Cosmopolitan Law?' (2007) *The Yale Law Journal*, 1024–68 at 1049.

observes that such theories do not rely on traditional notions of consent but rather on some other feature of membership in a political community that is thought to provide a ground for justifying coercion.[74]

Feldham mentions Ronald Dworkin's influential theory of law, which argues that 'associative or communal obligations' provide the basis for justified state coercion. When certain conditions of mutual concern and respect apply, people in communities have these associative obligations 'whether or not they want them.[75] The State has been elected by the people and they have the powers to carry out sanctions for crimes committed by a Court created by them. Feldham reiterates the fact that associative membership is necessary to justify coercion and observes that according to the political conception of law a State could not justifiably enact or enforce laws governing the conduct of persons who have never been in political association with it.[76] Therefore, State Parties may justifiably instruct their nationals or impose legal duties on their nationals who are witnesses, prohibiting them from engaging in acts of perjury or contempt before the Court.

State Obligation to Prosecute and ICC Implementing Legislation

Could the national Courts take up these cases of offences against the ICC administration of justice by a witness? State parties are obliged to take necessary measures to ensure that their legal system sanctions offences against the Court's administration of justice where the offences are committed on its territory or by one of its nationals.[77] Article 70(4) (b) provides that upon request by the Court, whenever it deems it proper, the State Party shall submit the case to its competent authorities for the purpose of prosecution. Those authorities shall treat such cases with diligence and devote sufficient resources to enable them to be conducted effectively. State Parties should have adequate procedures to assist the Court in criminalising offences against its administration of justice. State Parties are under a legal obligation to enact laws to criminalise such offences in their national laws.

Three States currently under ICC investigation have actually extended their domestic laws to cover crimes of false testimony and contempt of the Court. The Kenyan Legislation[78] provides in section 12(1) that a person who, with intent to mislead, makes a false statement under oath or solemn affirmation before a Judge of the ICC or an official of that Court who is authorised by the Court to permit statements to be made before him, knowing that the statement is false, is guilty of the offence of perjury and liable on conviction t o imprisonment for a term of not

74 Ibid., 1050.

75 Ibid., see also Ronald Dworkin, *Laws Empire* (Harvard University Press, 1986) p. 196.

76 Ibid., pp. 1050, 1052.

77 Article 70(4).

78 The International Crimes Act 2008.

more than seven years.[79] According to Section 18 a person who is alleged to have committed an offence under Section 12 may be tried and punished in Kenya for that offence if *(a) the act or omission constituting the offence is alleged to have been committed in Kenya or on board an aircraft or vessel which is registered in Kenya; or (b) at the time the offence is alleged to have been committed, the person was a Kenyan citizen or was employed by Kenya in a civilian or military capacity; or (c) the person is, after commission of the offence, present in Kenya.* Finally, pursuant to section 19(1) (a) If the ICC makes a request for assistance in any investigation or proceedings involving an offence against the administration of justice, that request shall be dealt with in the case of a request for surrender in the manner provided in Parts III and IV, which Parts shall apply with any necessary modifications and subject to any contrary provision in the Rome Statute or the ICC Rules.

Clause 13 of the Ugandan Bill[80] provides that a person who gives evidence for the purposes of a proceeding before the ICC or in connection with a request made by the ICC that contains an assertion that, if made in a judicial proceeding in Uganda as evidence on oath, would be perjury, gives false evidence. That person is liable, on conviction on indictment, to imprisonment for a term not exceeding seven years who, in Uganda or elsewhere, gives false evidence. Furthermore, if the false evidence is given in order to obtain the conviction of a person for an offence for which the maximum punishment is not less than 3 years' imprisonment, the punishment may be imprisonment for a term not exceeding 14 years.[81]

The Democratic Republic of Congo[82] provides '*Paragraphe 5 Atteintes à l'administration de la justice devant la Cour pénale international: Article 9 Il est inséré à la section V du Titre III du Livre II du Code pénal un article 132 ter et un article 132 quarter ainsi libellés: Article 132 ter Les articles 128 à 132 bis s'appliquent, mutatis mutandis, aux procédures intentées devant la Cour pénale internationale et conformément au Statut de cette Cour.*'[83]

---

79 See also Section 12(2) Subsection (1) shall apply – (a) whether or not the statement is made in judicial proceedings of the ICC; and (b) whether the statement is made by affidavit, solemn declaration or deposition or orally. (3) Subsection (1) shall not apply to a statement that is made by a person who is not specially permitted, authorized or required by law to make that statement; see also Section 13.

80 The International Criminal Court Bill, Bill No 18 2006.

81 Ibid., clause 13(1)–(3) see also clause 14.

82 Loi modifiant et completant certaines dispositions du code penal, du code de l'organisation et de la competence judiciaires, du code penal militaire et du code judiciaire militaire, en application du statut de la cour penale internationale *Kinshasa, September 2005.*

83 Article 128(4) Le faux témoignage fait sous serment devant les tribunaux, un officier du ministère public ou un officier de police judiciaire agissant en execution d'une commission rogatoire est puni de 2 à 5 ans de servitude pénale principale et de cent mille Francs congolais constants d'amende. Si l'accusé a été condamné soit à la servitude pénale à perpétuité, soit à la peine de mort, le faux témoin qui a déposé contre lui peut être condamné

Other State Parties such as[84] the United Kingdom treat these offences in the same way as those offences against the administration of British justice.[85] Section 54(1) of the UK implementing legislation provides that a person who commits Article 70 offences may be dealt with as for the corresponding domestic offence committed in relation to a superior Court in England and Wales. It further extends the giving of false testimony when under an obligation to tell the truth an offence against Section 1(1) of the Perjury Act 1911.[86] Section 12 of Norwegian Implementing law[87] extends its national laws to cover offences against the ICC. Section 163 to 167 of the Norwegian Penal Code applies correspondingly to criminal liability for giving false testimony before the ICC. Section 12 also applies to offences committed abroad by Norwegian nationals. Subdivision J of the Australian Implementing law[88] provides proposed sections 268.102 to 268.114 and creates a series of offences in Australian law that constitute crimes against the administration of the justice of the ICC; for example, Proposed Section 268.102: Perjury, namely where a person makes a false sworn statement in a proceeding before the ICC ('an ICC proceeding') and is reckless as to whether or not the statement is true.[89] Australian law provides that if guilty of the above offence the penalty will be 10 years' imprisonment.[90] Article 3(2) (f) of Swiss Implementing legislation provides that The Central Authority shall have the following responsibilities in particular. It shall forward to the competent authorities requests of the Court to undertake prosecutions in accordance with Article 70 paragraph 4 subparagraph b of the Statute.[91]

In order to extend its domestic laws to crimes against the Court, Finland added some clarifying provisions to the Penal Code concerning the jurisdiction in Finland

---

à la peine de servitude pénale à perpétuité. Toutefois, le faux témoin est exempt de peine s'il a rétracté spontanément son témoignage avant la décision mettant fin à la procedure d'instruction ou par la juridiction de jugement.

84 Note that the author has no particular reasons for choosing the implementing legislation of these countries; these are countries that have included provisions for these offences in their legislation. See also Roy S. Lee, 'States' Responses: Issues and Solutions', in Roy S. Lee (ed.) *States' Responses to Issues arising from the ICC Statute: Constitutional, Sovereignty, Judicial Cooperation and Criminal Law* (Transnational Publishers, 2005) p. 35.

85 United Kingdom, International Criminal Court Act 2001.

86 Ibid., Section 54(3)(a).

87 Act No. 65 of 15 June 2001 relating to the Implementation of the Statute of the International Criminal Court of 17 July 1998 (the Rome Statute) in Norwegian law.

88 Subdivision J – Crimes against the administration of the justice of the International Criminal Court, International Criminal Court (Consequential Amendment) Act 2002.

89 Ibid.

90 Subdivision J 268.102(1).

91 Swiss Federal Law of 22 June 2001 on Co-Operation with the International Criminal Court.

for the offences against the administration of justice.[92] It provides in Section 12(a) that 'for the purposes of application of the provisions on false statement, false denunciation, falsification of evidence, and threatening a person to be heard in the administration of justice, 'a court of law' shall also mean the International Criminal Court and 'criminal investigations' shall also mean an investigation referred to in the Statute of the International Criminal Court'.[93]

The above State Parties have extended their domestic laws to violations against the Court; they create in their citizens a national duty not to engage in acts of perjury and contempt of the Court and a legal duty to the ICC in so far as they act as witnesses before it. These States are therefore better capable of determining the appropriate severity of sanctions against their nationals who come testify before the Court. All State Parties should develop a common practice of prosecuting and imposing criminal sanctions on witnesses who have committed crimes before the Court. It is important that those State Parties who have not included provisions for offences against the ICC administration of justice should amend their legislations. It is very essential that all States determine the extent of their obligations to cooperate and implement legislation which is consistent so as to produce consistent practice.

It is established through the ICC Implementing Legislations that national Courts can impose sanctions on nationals who as witnesses commit crimes before the ICC. If the national Courts can, then why will it be unlikely for them to do so? It will be difficult to determine to what degree national legal systems will comply and punish crimes committed by their nationals who testify before the ICC. Given the experiences of other tribunals it has been difficult for these Courts to obtain the cooperation of States when it comes to extraditing witnesses who have been in contempt of the Court or to enforce orders compelling such witnesses to come testify.[94]

Importantly, State Parties should have the political will to enforce these sanctions. A State has resources to enforce sanctions; the variant of this argument is that State-inflicted sanctions are justified because the States cost in establishing the relevant institutions or sustaining them are lower than those of international organisations.[95] According to Malcolm Shaw, international organisations are

92 Acts on the Implementation of the provisions of a Legislative Nature of the Rome Statute of the International Criminal Court and on the Application of the Statute, see at http://www.nottingham.ac.uk/shared/shared_hrlcicju/Finland/Act_on_the_Implementation_of_the_Provisions_of_a_Legislative_Nature_of_the_Rome_Statute_.pdf. (last visited April 2010).

93 Chap. 15: Sect. 12a Offences against the administration of justice by the International Criminal Court (1285/2000), Extracts from the Finish Penal Code Act No. 1285/2000).

94 See Alexander Zahar, 'International Court and Private Citizen', (2009) *New Criminal Law Review* 569, 572–8.

95 See Alon Harel, 'Why Only The State May Inflict Criminal Sanctions: The Case Against Privately Inflicted Sanctions', (2008) *14 Cambridge Legal Theory*, 113–33 at 118.

unlike States that possess a general competence as subjects of international law. They are governed by the principle of speciality, so that, as the International Court has noted, 'they are invested by the States which create them with powers, the limits of which are a function of the common interests whose promotion those States entrust to them'.[96] Hence, States created the ICC and they have a vital interest in ensuring, maintaining and enforcing the adherence to international fair trial standards and integrity of the Court. As already mentioned, as nationals of a State these sanctions can be best administered in their home countries, arguably justice will be better served if States themselves take responsibility to address these violations and local Courts can easily apply rules relating to perjury and enforce readily defined penalties.

According to James Cockayne, the norms that States usually seek to enforce do reflect a larger, supranational consensus prohibiting conduct of which individuals may reasonably said to have been given notice.[97] At the start of trials, witnesses are given such notice as not to commit perjury, for instance, pursuant to Rule 66(3); the need for predictability is satisfied. The witness is aware if he/she provides false testimony, he/she will be prosecuted; it is therefore open to the competent national authorities to enforce the norm. The cosmopolitan conception of legal duty to punish witness contempt could be used to expand universal jurisdiction to cover crimes of perjury and contempt of the ICC. In addition, political authority and moral power to submit to legal processes should be extended to the ICC, thus witnesses are bound by the laws of the ICC and the States should take full responsibility to impose criminal sanctions.

What about Non-State Parties such as the United States (USA) who have peacekeepers and military officers working in conflict areas around the World? Would they prosecute their nationals who act as witnesses and are in contempt of the Court? Given the aggressiveness towards the Court already by such countries, who do not accept the jurisdiction of the ICC to prosecute their nationals for ICC core crimes, it will be very unlikely for them to assist the Court when it comes to prosecuting nationals who have committed crimes as witnesses before the ICC.

States not Party to the Rome Statute are not bound in principle to punish crimes committed against the Court; they are under no obligation to cooperate with the Court.[98] However, Article 12(3) provides for a non-State party to accept the jurisdiction of the Court and cooperate with the Court in accordance with Part 9 of the Statute. Arguably, the referral of cases to the ICC can be done by the United Nations Security Council (UNSC) acting under Chapter VII of the UN Charter, an example being the referral of atrocities in Dafur Sudan.[99] The UNSC is

96 Malcolm N. Shaw, *International Law* (Cambridge University Press 1998) pp. 915–16.

97 See James Cockayne, 'On the Cosmopolitanization of Criminal Jurisdiction', (2005) *Journal of International Criminal Justice*, 514–24 at 523.

98 Article 79.

99 See Article 13(a); see also ICC Press Release SG/SM/9797 AFR/1132; Secretary-General Welcomes Adoption of Security Council Resolution Referring Situation in Darfur,

made up of countries who are not parties to the ICC Statute; again countries like the USA did not expressly show their support for referral of the Darfur situation to the ICC. Nonetheless, it can be argued that they impliedly did so by not using veto powers against the UNSC Resolution 1593.[100] It may be argued, these Non-State Parties did recognise the jurisdiction of the Court to prosecute international crimes by referring a serious situation of violations of international law to the Court. Importantly, because of global trend or interaction, many witnesses who come to testify will be nationals of States not Party to the ICC. In recognising the Court's jurisdiction for core crimes, these States should recognise and punish offences committed by witnesses before the ICC for contempt; they must embrace certain universal moral commitments. According to Feldham[101] to be a legitimate legal system requires satisfying some basic moral requirements; the act of establishing a legal system that exercises coercive power subjects the system itself to certain moral duties, among them the duty not to make morally arbitrary distinctions among persons. These States should have the legal and moral duty to prosecute an individual who is also in breach against the Court's administration of justice.

Finally, there is the possibility of State Parties to be reluctant in accepting jurisdiction and prosecuting a national who is a perjured witness before the ICC. It is still left to be seen if national Courts will automatically accept jurisdiction and prosecute a national who in their view assists a foreign Court in providing testimony but is in contempt of the latter Court. Again, State Parties should have the political will to prosecute and accept jurisdiction in order to protect the integrity and moral standing of the ICC. In the presence of clear State practice and opinion juris evidencing such duty of prosecuting contempt and of perjury under customary international law,[102] all States arguably have a permissive right, jurisdiction and obligation to impose criminal sanctions on witnesses who commit crimes against the ICC administration of justice. Again, it may be argued that the gravity of the crimes committed by witnesses is not as grave as international

---

Sudan, To International Criminal Court Prosecutor 31/03/2005 available at http://www.un.org/News/Press/docs/2005/sgsm9797.doc.htm, (last visited April 2010).

100 See Amy E. Eckert, 'The Cosmopolitan Test: Universal Morality and the Challenge of the Darfur Genocide', in Steven C. Roach, *Governance, Order, and the International Criminal Court* (Oxford University Press 2010) pp. 205–24, see especially p. 214.

101 Noah Feldham, 'Cosmopolitan Law?', (2007) *The Yale Law Journal*, 1024–68 at 1062–3.

102 Looking at general principles of law common to the major legal systems of the world, the law of contempt originated and has remained a creature of the common law. The general concept of contempt is said to be unknown to the civil law, but many civil law systems have legislated to provide offences which produce a similar result. See *Prosecutor v. Tadic*, Judgement on Allegations of Contempt against Prior Counsel, Milan Vujin, Case No. IT-94-1-A-R77, 31 January 2000, para 15; Goran Sluiter, The ICTY and Offences against the Administration of Justice, (2004), 2 *Journal of International Criminal Justice*, 631–41 at 631–2.

crimes; however, in maintaining universal fair trial standards and the integrity of the ICC it is important that these crimes should not be left unpunished. All States should take the necessary steps to prosecute, suggesting a universal condemnation of breaches which affect the Court's credibility, fair trial standards and justice to victims. Furthermore, the creation of a universal rule that specifically punishes witnesses for crimes such as perjury and consistent and uniform State practice in the prosecution of these crimes.

PART II
International Criminal Justice as Governance

Chapter 7
Exclusion and Inclusion: Bio-Politics and Global Governance through Criminalisation

Edwin Bikindo

Introduction

This chapter is an exercise in theorising and is neither policy formulation nor a descriptive overview. It aims to create a theoretical framework to illuminate some obscure connections between international crime and global governance. A major theme of the chapter is to introduce the shorthand term 'bio-legality' active as a form of global governance. Two minor themes addressed are aggression and abuse of process. The links between these themes are that bio-legality connotes law with life as its referent and justification, while criminal aggression is the taking and degrading of life contrary to law in a scenario involving sustained armed force, and the abuse of process is the taking or degrading of life under the colour of law nevertheless contrary to legality.

This chapter investigates where the themes of bio-legality, aggression and abuse of legal process overlap and intersect as the ensuing global process of monopolising force by criminalising rival violence through the law becomes clearer because it gradually becomes entangled less in local particularities and parochial concerns. That is, when globalisation utilises criminalisation as a technique of governance it lays bare the links constructed between law, life and death because it ignores cultural differences and erases political boundaries.[1] As outlined in the chapter's structure below, through criminalisation, governing stretches from localised individuals below the state and its territory all the way to the entire globe and all of humanity. Torture provides a sounding board to interrogate the issues arising when law is linked directly to life and death by excluding and including individual lives within its ambit and protection. This globally governing process is then examined as it operates upon people and places incidental with instituting a distinction between force and violence and thereby a monopoly on legitimacy that is mediated through and by the law.

---

1 See Mark Findlay, *Governing through Globalised Crime: Futures for International Criminal Justice*, Devon, 2008, especially at pp. 152–54.

Torture in the Global War on Terror

The narration below is taken verbatim from a report of the International Committee of the Red Cross (ICRC) chronicling treatment meted out to one Abu Zubaydah, a suspected high-level member of al Qaeda.[2]

> After the beating I was then placed in the small box. They placed a cloth or cover over the box to cut out all light and restrict my air supply. As it was not high enough even to sit upright, I had to crouch down. It was very difficult because of my wounds. The stress on my legs held in this position meant my wounds both in the leg and stomach became very painful. I think this occurred about 3 months after my last operation. It was always cold in the room, but when the cover was placed over the box it made it hot and sweaty inside. The wound on my leg began to open and started to bleed. I don't know how long I remained in the small box, I think I may have slept or maybe fainted.
>
> I was then dragged from the small box, unable to walk properly and put on what looked like a hospital bed, and strapped down very tightly with belts. A black cloth was then placed over my face and the interrogators used a mineral water bottle to pour water on the cloth so that I could not breathe. After a few minutes the cloth was removed and the bed was rotated into an upright position. The pressure of the straps on my wounds was very painful. I vomited. The bed was then again lowered to horizontal position and the same torture carried out again with the black cloth over my face and water poured on from a bottle. On this occasion my head was in a more backward, downwards position and the water was poured on for a longer time. I struggled against the straps, trying to breathe, but it was hopeless. I thought I was going to die. I lost control of my urine. Since then I still lose control of my urine when under stress.
>
> I was then placed again in the tall box. While I was inside the box loud music was played again and somebody kept banging repeatedly on the box from the outside. I tried to sit down on the floor, but because of the small space the bucket with urine tipped over and spilt over me. I remained in the box for several hours, maybe overnight. I was then taken out and again a towel was wrapped around my neck and I was smashed into the wall with the plywood covering and repeatedly slapped in the face by the same two interrogators as before.
>
> I was then made to sit on the floor with a black hood over my head until the next session of torture began. The room was always kept very cold. This went on for approximately one week. During this time the whole procedure was repeated five times. On each occasion, apart from one, I was suffocated once or twice and was put in the vertical position on the bed in between. On one occasion the suffocation was repeated three times. I vomited each time I was put in the vertical position between the suffocation.

---

2 ICRC Report on the Treatment of Fourteen 'High Value Detainees' in CIA Custody by the International Committee of the Red Cross, February 2007, at pp. 30–31.

> During that week I was not given any solid food. I was only given Ensure to drink. My head and beard were shaved everyday. I collapsed and lost consciousness on several occasions. Eventually the torture was stopped by the intervention of the doctor.
>
> I was told during this period that I was one of the first to receive these interrogation techniques, so no rules applied. It felt like they were experimenting and trying out techniques to be used later on other people.

'Torture'. The very word invokes images of medieval bestiality and primitive cruelty. Yet this is precisely how the ICRC characterised the allegations of ill-treatment towards detainees held by the United States pursuant to the global war on terror.[3] The US position was that although the Torture Convention applied it was only according to US understanding of torture which would not include the kind of coercive interrogation described above.[4]

These allegations are currently before a Spanish court against six members of the Bush administration, all lawyers who, as lawyers, are suspected of having given legal advice that justified, caused or led directly to torture.[5] Along with this, US lawyers also provided legal advice recommending the inapplicability of the Geneva Conventions and claiming a Presidential authority to suspend them.[6] In other words, their alleged 'offence' entails their manipulation or abuse of the law and legal process in order to 'legalise torture'. When put in that way the questions is: but is it 'torture'? In the 'ICRC's view the victims were placed outside the protections of law'.[7] This begs the question as to whether the perpetrators of these acts were also simultaneously placed outside the prohibitions of the law (which is their argument). But this exclusion and inclusion has another strand because the victims are included in regard to prohibition of their actions by law yet simultaneously excluded from the usual protections of the law. Essentially the USA has arrogated to itself the power to make law and immunity from breaking it while denying its adversaries from the protections of law at the same time as holding them to legal accountability.

---

3 ICRC Report on the Treatment of Fourteen 'High Value Detainees' in CIA Custody by the International Committee of the Red Cross, February 2007, at p. 26.

4 See Memorandum of 'Working Group Report on Detainee Interrogations in the Global War on Terrorism: Assessment of Legal, Historical, Policy, and Operational Considerations', 4 April 2003, in Karen J. Greenberg and Joshua L. Dratel (eds), *The Torture Papers: The Road to Abu Ghraib*, at pp. 288–90.

5 Scott Horton, 'The Bush Six to Be Indicted'. http://www.thedailybeast.com/blogs-and-stories/2009-04-13/the-bush-six-to-be-indicted/ (last visited 14 April 2009).

6 See Memorandum from G.W. Bush to Vice President and others dated 7th February 2002 in Karen J. Greenberg and Joshua L. Dratel (eds), *The Torture Papers: The Road to Abu Ghraib*, at p. 134.

7 ICRC Report on the Treatment of Fourteen 'High Value Detainees' in CIA Custody by the International Committee of the Red Cross, February 2007, at p. 24.

By omitting to address this and merely citing provisions of the law, the ICRC tends to assume as proven precisely what is in dispute. That is the applicability of the law itself as the standard of judging, distinguishing or discernment.

According to Article 1 of the United Nations Convention Against Torture, torture is:

> any act by which severe pain or suffering, whether physical or mental, is intentionally inflicted on a male or female person for such purposes as obtaining from him, or a third person, information or a confession, punishing him for an act he or a third person has committed or is suspected of having committed, or intimidating or coercing him or a third person, or for any reason based on discrimination of any kind, when such pain or suffering is inflicted by or at the instigation of or with the consent or acquiescence of a public official or other person acting in an official capacity. It does not include pain or suffering arising only from, inherent in, or incidental to, lawful sanctions.

For emphasis, according to the legal definition at a minimum torture does not include pain or suffering arising *only* from, inherent in, or incidental to, *lawful* sanctions. The battleground then is the boundaries of lawfulness. That is not the actual occurrence of these acts but their characterisation as lawful/unlawful.

The 'global war on terror' is difficult to adequately characterise. It is at once an event, justification and specific set of techniques and tactics in accordance with a strategic plan and long-term objective. According to Julian Reid, the war on terror is in reality not defending the integrity and security of human life against an enemy with a nihilistic will to destroy of human life but it is fought over the political constitution of life pitting liberalism principally against Islam as an alternative belief system.[8] Race, as the Australian David Hicks' beatings and other physical maltreatment showed, is not really the issue[9] and the idea that this could be an egregious example of 'a few bad eggs' is not borne out by the documentary record.[10]

The US National Security Strategy of 2002 is a case in point. It regarded the war on terror as an 'opportunity to extend the benefits of freedom across the globe' and 'democracy, development, free markets, and free trade to every corner

8 See generally Julian Reid, *The Biopolitics of the War on Terror: Life Struggles, Liberal Modernity and the Defence of Logistical Societies*, Manchester University Press, 2006.

9 See Affidavit of David Hicks dated 5 August 2004 in S. Rasul et al. v. G.W. Bush et al. Civil Action No. 02-299 (CKK) United Sates District Court of Columbia in Karen J. Greenberg and Joshua L. Dratel (eds), *The Torture Papers: The Road to Abu Ghraib*, at p. 1234.

10 Philippe Sands QC Torture Team: The Responsibility of Lawyers for Abusive Interrogation (2008), *Melbourne Journal of International Law* 13.

of the world'.[11] This meant that weak states were as much a danger to US national interests as strong states and poverty, weak institutions, and corruption can were linked directly to terrorist networks and even drug cartels.[12] This is an explicit link if one were needed of criminalisation as a tool of global governance.

The US Administration reorganised its government by creating a new Department of Homeland Security and a new unified military command ensuring 'the homeland encompasses every level of government and the cooperation of the public and the private sector'.[13] This strategy meant that emergency management were to 'cope not just with terrorism but with all hazards', both 'bioterror' and 'all infectious diseases and mass-casualty dangers'.[14] Here crime, war and disease are simultaneously the defined enemy in a war waged on the terrain of life itself.

Modernising public health infrastructure means an enhanced ability to respond to pandemic public health threats and countering the threat of biological warfare.[15] For instance, the Department of Health and Human Services got a thirty-fold increase in funding for bioterrorism research.[16] The blueprint for the future biodefense program, 'Biodefense for the twenty-first century', fully integrates national and homeland security and the 'medical, public health, intelligence, diplomatic, and law enforcement communities'.[17]

The 'war against global terrorism' is ultimately for the USA about fighting for 'democratic values and way of life'.[18] Furthermore, the campaign against terrorism forges new international relationships and redefines existing ones in a future oriented manner.[19] Violence is therefore being deployed to found new revolutionary legal orders. Giorgio Agamben's notion of the state of exception describes how sovereignty now paradoxically defends the law from outside the law in the name of security thereby blurring, distorting or erasing the lines between law and lawlessness.[20] Due to its efficacy in addressing extraordinary circumstances, this state of exception gradually becomes the rule. Governments increasingly rely on this seemingly bottomless source of power and legitimacy which, when coupling security and risk, means that even modern democratic societies are not exempt from a state domination that approaches the totalitarian.

---

11 The National Security Strategy of the United States of America, September 2002, at p. 4.

12 Ibid.

13 Ibid, at pp. 6–7.

14 Ibid., pp. 6–7.

15 The National Security Strategy of the United States of America, March 2006, at pp. 21–2.

16 'Biodefense for the 21st Century', at p. 3.

17 Ibid.

18 The National Security Strategy of the United States of America, September 2002, at p. 7, emphasis added.

19 Ibid.

20 See generally Giorgio Agamben, *State of Exception* (Translated by Kevin Attell), Chicago and London, University of Chicago Press, 2005.

What do we make of all this? Torture as a political issue encompasses both what Michel Foucault would call 'disciplinary' and 'regulatory' aspects of power. Foucault demonstrated how sex could come to be at the forefront of wielding power because it 'was at the pivot of two axes along which developed the entire political technology of life' and 'was a means of access both to the life of the body and the life of the species'.[21] Torture occupies an analogous position in the war on terror. It too is 'tied to the disciplines of the body but applied to the regulation of populations'.[22] It therefore fits both categories because it applied to 'man-as-body' and 'man-as-species'.[23] Whereas discipline orders a multiplicity of individualised persons by surveillance, training and punishment, regulation is addressed to a multiplicity of men as 'a global mass' affected by the processes of birth, life, illness, death and the like.[24] So torture links 'the anatomo-politics of the human body' to 'a 'biopolitics' of the human race.'[25]

With regard to war that could be characterised as aggression, Melinda Gates has identified the issue as not only the securitisation of human life (incorporating 'humanitarian warfare'), but that U.S. defence discourse is integrating '*the whole of life*, from the micro- to the eco-systemic level, within its strategic vision.'[26] This 'war is no longer waged in the defense of the state … but rather in *the name of life in its biospheric dimension, incorporating meteorology, epidemiology, and the evolution of all forms of life, from the microbe up*.'[27] 'The extension of preemptive warfare to include the sphere of environmental (sic) and biopolitics conflates the externalisation of war with the evolution of life on earth – as if permanent war were simply *a fact of life*, with no other end than its own crisis-driven perpetuation.'[28]

When the ICRC report is juxtaposed with the National Security Strategy these points become clearer:

a. 'Torture' or 'coercive interrogation' is done at both bodily-disciplinary and group-regulatory levels.
b. Biopolitics is operating at the level of the human species and confined to that species given the supersession of race by ideology.
c. Law is given as the justification for violence and violence is given as justification for the suspension of legal provisions.
d. We see the creeping development of 'bio-legality' as law relating to protecting lives from death by exposing other lives to death.

---

21 Michel Foucault, *History of Sexuality*, vol. 1, pp. 145–6.

22 Ibid.

23 Ibid.

24 Michel Foucault, *Society Must be Defended*, pp. 242–3.

25 Ibid.

26 Melinda Cooper, *Life as Surplus: Biotechnology and Capitalism in the Neoliberal Era*, at p. 80, emphasis in original citation omitted.

27 Ibid., at p. 98, emphasis in original.

28 Ibid., emphasis in original citation omitted.

Law, Life and Death

Friedrich Hegel, when speaking of 'Law, Life, and Death' said that the administration of penal justice was the force of law exerted over individual life.[29] Foucault in turn said: 'For millennia, man remained what he was for Aristotle: a living animal with the additional capacity for a political existence; modern man is an animal whose politics places his existence as a living being in question.'[30] This chapter builds on these and argues that the law not only regulates both the states of life and death but also defines the boundary between them. The law does this by assigning rights and duties among the living to create different forms of life. Law additionally abandons life to the exposure of conditions that lead to death by deciding what life is worth living, which is not, and even when a person is as good as dead or deserves death. I refer to this process as bio-legality.

The aim of the project is to explain partially law's relationship to violence in the context of criminalising aggression in international law. This aspect of the argument works through examining the calibration of legal responses that alternately protect and expose persons and populations to degrees of violence. The argument is that law is the only practicable division and divisor between life and death.[31] Law is indeed the differentiator between life and death even as it regulates forms of life, distinguishes levels of death,[32] and ultimately condemns to death. Extending this applicability directly from legal entitlement to life onto entitlement

29 G.W.F. Hegel, *Hegel and the Human Spirit*. A translation of the Jena Lectures on the Philosophy of Spirit (1805–6) with commentary, by Leo Rauch; published by Wayne State University Press, Detroit 1983; translated from G.W.F. Hegel *Gesammelte Werke*, vol. 8: Jenaer Systementwürfe III; also known as *Realphilosophie II*, first published 1931, at p. 145.

30 Michel Foucault, *The History of Sexuality: An Introduction*, vol. 1, (translated by Robert Hurley) at p. 143. Also cited in Anne Orford, 'Trade, Human Rights and the Economy of Sacrifice' in Anne Orford (ed.), *International Law and Its 'Others'*, at p. 183.

31 See '... in any ethical debate of topics involving life and death, one is forced to introduce cultural constructs such as, on the one hand, the concept of clinical death and, on the other, the concept of existence.' Giovanni Boniolo and Pier Paolo Di Fiore, 'A Defining Analysis of the Life and Death Dyad: Paving the Way for an Ethical Debate', *Journal of Medicine and Philosophy* 33: 609–34, 2009, at p. 611 and '... or perhaps it is better to say that, in contemporary medicine, life and law have always been indistinguishable' Jeffrey P. Bishop 'Biopolitics, Terri Schiavo, and the Sovereign Subject of Death', *Journal of Medicine and Philosophy* 33: 538–57, 2009, at p. 539.

32 See press reports e.g. Julia Medew, 'Donors Not Truly "Dead" When Organs Removed, http://www.brisbanetimes.com.au/news/national/donors-not-truly-dead-when-organs-removed/2008/10/19/1224351091401.html (last visited 20 October 2008); *Defining death: O death, when is thy sting?* http://www.economist.com/science/displayStory.cfm?source=hptextfeatureandstory_id=12332939 (last visited 5 October 2008), and *Debate: When to Declare Donors Dead* http://www.time.com/time/health/article/0,8599,1832688,00.html?iid=336x280_health2 (last visited 18 August 2008).

to take life legally seems logically implicit. The criminal law is just a narrow aspect of various possible approaches but it is the focus of this project.

In pursuing its object this discussion concludes in the final section that law and violence are bound together so intimately that they cannot be viably distinguished without reference to each other. This leads to the enigmatic explanation that violence always defers to law except when it does not (because the state generally has both a factual preponderance of and normative monopoly of force over violence) and law never defers to violence except when it does (because there are exceptional circumstances such as successful revolutions and coup d'états where erstwhile governments are overthrown). The task set out is to broadly map out these shifts as they occur in legal contexts and examine their effect on human life and death as both protections and penalties are excluded and included principally through the wielding of the criminal law.

Niklas Luhmann conceptualised the legal system as the social system's immune system that sought to avoid 'violent resolution of conflicts' by providing alternative means of communication for every conflict.[33] Linking this characterisation to force as the social system's ultimate sanction and violence as the greatest threat to the social system renders the malady (violence) and the remedy (force) identical. Thus, it makes force a healing poison or a health giving disease against violence, which are in any event each other's closest kin and worst adversary. To stretch the analogy to cover auto-immunity as well, terrorism (viewed as violence) and the military counter-reaction (constructed as force) just like Jacque Derrida noted, appear to be the effects of social auto-immunity on a global scale.[34] Within the context of a life and death struggle some lives are necessarily valorised and protected while others are devalued and run the gamut of progressive privations running all the way to exposure to death through being excluded from legal protections while included in legal sanction.

Exclusion and Inclusion

The mechanism of inclusion and exclusion is generally how the law meaningfully applies force or allows violence. The law may either exclude persons and populations from or include them within the penalties or protection of the law and thereby violently expose or forcefully protect them. Frédéric Mégret has identified the hyper-inclusivity of international humanitarian Law that nevertheless contains

33 Niklas Luhmann, *Social Systems*, Stanford University Press, Stanford, 1995 (translation by John Bednarz Jr and Dirk Baecker of *Soziale Systeme: Grundriß einer allgemeinen Theorie* Suhrkamp Verlag Frankfurt am Main 1984), at pp. 374–5.

34 See Giovanni Borradori, *Philosophy In A Time Of Terror: Dialogues With Jurgen Habermas And Jacques Derrida*, University of Chicago Press, 2004, at p. 94 and cited in Roberto Esposito, *Bios: Biopolitics and Philosophy*, translation by Timothy Campbell of *Bios: Biopolitica e filosofia* Minnesota, Minnesota University Press 2008, at pp. xvi–xvii.

the logic of exclusivity as well.[35] Carl Schmitt too traced an exceptional zone that was excluded from law, which took the shape of a 'free and juridically empty space' in which sovereign power was no longer bound by the limits fixed by the rules governing the normal territorial order. In classical international law, this zone corresponded to the New World and European colonies, which were assimilated with the state of nature in which nothing was prohibited and therefore everything was permitted including unbridled violence. In domestic law through declarations of emergencies or states of exception, the state frees up the restrictions on the use of force to meet immediate threats that are repressed as treason or mutiny, and so on.

Both Luhmann and Agamben in constructing society's relationship to the human agree that any inclusion of aspects of humanity necessarily implies exclusion of others.[36] This is so despite that humanity is on both sides of the distinction even and especially when using descriptors like inhuman or subhuman. The distinction used can make a re-entry and it then becomes impossible to distinguish between who are inside and who are outside when outside appears as inside and inside as outside.[37] William Rasch sees Agamben as indicating that Hobbes' sovereign saves us from the state of nature only for the selfsame sovereign to plunge us into the analogous situation of the state of exception.[38] To paraphrase this in systems theoretic terms the initial distinction between society and a state of nature re-enters in society to produce the state of exception (as distinct from the state of normality) that for all intents and purposes mirrors the state of nature. Therefore the justification of the law in keeping the state of nature at bay as society's environment is fundamentally undermined by the society producing the state of exception at its core even as it keeps the state of nature at its periphery.

What Agamben calls the political Hobbes called the state of nature.[39] This is because Agamben concludes from the above that the state of nature and state of exception are 'two sides of a single process in which what was presupposed as external (the state of nature) now reappears, in the inside (as the state of

35 See e.g. Frédéric Mégret, 'From "Savages" to "Unlawful Combatants": A Postcolonial Look at International Humanitarian Laws'; 'Other' in *International Law and its 'Others'*, Anne Orford (ed.), Cambridge, Cambridge University Press, 2006, at p. 265.

36 See Urs Stäheli and Rudolf Stichweh, 'Inclusion/Exclusion –Systems theoretical and Poststructuralist Perspectives', in *Soziale Systeme* vol. 8 (2002), Issue 1, Special issue on Exclusion and Socio-cultural Identities: Systems Theoretical and Poststructuralist Perspectives, at p. 5.

37 Ibid., at pp. 4–5.

38 See William Rasch, 'A Completely New Politics or Excluding the Political? Agamben's Critique of Sovereignty', in *Soziale Systeme* vol. 8 (2002), Issue 1, Special issue on Exclusion and Socio-cultural Identities: Systems Theoretical and Poststructuralist Perspectives, at pp. 44–8.

39 Ibid., at p. 46.

exception)'.[40] For Agamben, life is what appears both inside and outside the law as 'bare life' and 'the good life'.[41] The outside is viewed as the environment and conveyed as excluded yet this environment is produced by the society itself through its functional subsystems of law, politics, economics, and so on. The concrete manifestation of this for Agamben is Guantanamo Bay while for Luhmann it was Brazil's Favelas or shantytowns.[42] Therefore, for both Luhmann and Agamben all of humanity as such is initially and as a matter of default excluded until it is included in certain limited capacities such as customer or consumer, citizen or refugee, combatant or civilian, and so on, so forms of living are like statues carved out of the marble block of life.

In essence this 'bio-legality' has always been inscribed in law's reference to and protection of life because law has been organised around and upon life at least since the signing of the Magna Carta.[43] The protection of humanity is the protection of life itself and not individual lives.[44] International criminal law is the epicentre of this development in at least two of the following ways. First, genocide is the paradigm example of this in protecting whole groups against total or partial death against other groups. Conceptually speaking, condemnation of genocide cannot be grounded in each group individually but only on all groups collectively as an all inclusive 'group of groups' that has purchase over everyone not just within singular groupings. Second, crimes against humanity are by definition inhuman acts. The enemy of humanity is necessarily inhumane and their acts and standards inhuman. It follows that the total enemy of humanity is again necessarily a criminal and the worst of the category at that. These crimes are viewed as deserving the most extreme repression society can muster up as it acts in the name of supreme good against supreme evil. International criminal law is therefore at the forefront of this and the crime of aggression is the leading edge of the criminalising sword because it monopolises the means through which life is either protected or exposed to death. Genocide and crimes against humanity (among others) are what are sought to be repressed through suppressing aggression.

40 Giorgio Agamben, *Homo Sacer: Sovereign Power and Bare Life*, Stanford, 1998, at pp. 36–7.

41 Ibid., at pp. 1–12.

42 See Friedrich Blake, 'Tristes Tropiques and Systems Theory and the Literary Scene', in *Soziale Systeme* vol. 8 (2002), Issue 1, Special issue on Exclusion and Socio-cultural Identities: Systems Theoretical and Poststructuralist Perspectives, at p. 27.

43 See Giorgio Agamben, *Homo Sacer: Sovereign Power and Bare Life*, translated by Daniel Heller-Roazen, 1998, Stanford, at p. 123.

44 See 'At this point, humanity emerges as the organising concept of our symbolic space', Costas Douzinas, 'Speaking Law' in Anne Orford (ed.), *International Law and its 'Others'*, Cambridge, 2006, at p. 54.

Grounding Legality in Life to Simultaneously Protect and Expose Lives

As outlined above, bio-legality refers to the law active upon human life itself as a supreme principle. In seeking to ground fundamental human values and rights as all transcending, distinctions have long been sought to be drawn between the secular and the religious with the secular being derived from the religious.[45] For instance, in words attributed in the Bible to Jesus, he exhorted his followers to 'render unto Caesar what belonged to Caesar and to God what belonged to God'. Carl Schmitt famously wrote that for sociological considerations '[a]ll significant concepts of the modern theory of the state are secularised theological concepts' because of their historical development and systematic structure.[46] It follows then that life and death issues are simultaneously classifiable into biology, theology, and law to name but a few possible subject areas.[47] While biology may define and describe these issues scientifically, theology provides a transcendental explanatory or ethical view, and law provides both a mechanism for decision and a regulatory framework. Following on from Schmitt's observation that the modern state has politicised *everything* and therefore vastly expanded the range of the political[48] it is only through the political process that law may gain its deserved prominence.

We can therefore perceive that the opposition between secular and religious originally derives from differentiating heavenly from secular on the one hand, and religious from earthly on the other. Thus the distinctions between the sacred and profane or religious and secular can be identifiable as 'nested oppositions' which are oppositions that 'involve a relation of dependence, similarity, or containment between the opposed concepts'.[49] This is not idle theorising because it has definite implications when applied to social categories especially when comparing and contrasting theology and politics.[50] It opens up the space for a 'Biopolitics' that

45 See e.g. Judith Grbich, who traces the structural identity and intimate relationship between Christian messianic thought and international law in 'Secrets of the Fetish in International Law's Messianism', in *International Law and its 'Others'*, Anne Orford (ed.), Cambridge, Cambridge University Press, 2006, at p. 202.

46 Carl Schmitt, *Political Theology: Four Chapters on the Concept of Sovereignty*, at p. 36.

47 See e.g. Alex J. Bellamy saying recourse and conduct of war 'originated in Western traditions of theological, legal and philosophical reasoning' in *Just Wars*, at p. 4.

48 Carl Schmitt, *Concept of the Political*, Chicago University Press, 1996, p. 22. See also 'Nothing is Political, Everything Can Be Politicized: On the Concept of the Political' in Michel Foucault and Carl Schmitt Astrid Deuber-Mankowsky, *Telos* 142 (Spring 2008): 135–61.

49 Jack M. Balkin. 99 Yale L.J. 1669 (1990). Nested Oppositions Book Review of *Against Deconstruction*, by John M. Ellis, at p. 3.

50 See e.g. Carl Schmitt *Political Theology: Four Chapters on the Concept of Sovereignty*, trans. George Schwab, Chicago University Press, 2005; Michel Foucault, *Hermeneutics of the Self: discussing the confessional;*, Giorgio Agamben, *The Time that Remains on the Pauline legacy*; Slavoj Žižek, *Why is the Christian Legacy Worth Fighting*

refers to techniques of power linked to life that are prevalent in society and utilised for subjugating bodies and controlling populations.[51] This is accompanied by a concomitant 'Thanatopolitics' referring to the power to expose to death or kill that necessarily accompanies the power to foster life.[52]

Both systems theory and discourse analysis are post-foundational in that foundations are not abolished as such but are rendered radically contingent and contextual.[53] Anne Orford points out the placeholder Father/God/Market to who decision-makers are beholden.[54] Foucault too traced the shift in the genealogy of government of the organising principle from God to the King to the People and then to the market.[55] This process whilst changing the overarching justification over time leaves the underlying activities intact. The modern equivalent of this ultimate rationality and supreme benchmark is probably the democratic free market State that respects human rights. Globalisation then can readily export or replicate this model all over the world even through force.

This supreme 'authority' over life and death retains a distinctly religious or quasi-theological air. Even the contemporary prevalence of atheism does not necessarily abolish the notion of God in disavowing belief in the existence of a supernatural being. Instead, it opens up possibilities for humans to play the role previously reserved for a god.[56] In addition, in so doing it secularises the ultimate decision-maker. God is not dead *pace* Nietzsche. He has just changed sides from

---

For?. On modern politics' debt to religion, see *Black Mass: Apocalyptic Religion and the Death of Utopia* by John Gray, London, Allen Lane, 2007.

51 'Biopolitics' as coined by G.W. Harris in 'Bio-Politics' *The New Age: A Weekly Review of Politics, Literature, and Art*, 1911, 10(9), p. 197, developed by Rudolf Kjellén, extended by Michel Foucault and further developed by Giorgio Agamben in *Homo Sacer: Sovereign Power and Bare Life*, Stanford, Stanford University Press, 1998, and Roberto Esposito, *Bios: Biopolitics and Philosophy*, translation by Timothy Campbell of *Bios: Biopolitica e filosofia* Minnesota, Minnesota University Press, 2008. See e.g. Michel Foucault, *The History of Sexuality vol.1: The Will to Knowledge*, London, Penguin, 1998, at p. 140.

52 Giorgio Agamben, *Homo Sacer: Sovereign Power and Bare Life*, Stanford (1998), at p. 122. See also Paul Rabinow and Nikolas Rose, 'Biopower Today', *BioSocieties* (2006), 1, 195–217.

53 See Oliver Marchart, 'On Drawing a Line. Politics and the Significatory Logics of Inclusion/Exclusion' in *Soziale Systeme* vol. 8 (2002), Issue 1, Special issue on Exclusion and Socio-cultural Identities: Systems Theoretical and Poststructuralist Perspectives, at p. 74.

54 Anne Orford, from 'A Jurisprudence of the limit' in *International Law and its 'Others'*, Anne Orford (ed.), Cambridge, Cambridge University Press, 2006, 1 at p. 18.

55 Michel Foucault, *The Birth of Biopolitics*, especially at pp. 87–8.

56 As James Watson, co-discoverer of DNA structure, said: 'People say we are playing God. My answer is: 'If we don't play God, who will?'' Kam Patel, *God's little helper* 14 March 1997

http://www.timeshighereducation.co.uk/story.asp?storyCode=101663andsectioncode=26 (last visited 5 October 2008).

religious to secular and from divine spirit to human endeavour.[57] However, what is the point of this metaphorical apostasy? One effect is that of sophisticated ambivalence where human rights are still defensible by stating they remain the best available alternative simply as a matter of pragmatism.[58]

Yet another more ominous effect is it strips human life of any pretence of an intrinsic value separate and apart from that granted or recognised by social consensus. Merit or utility is the new touchstone and individual life's mere existence can be construed as either a nuisance (inviting targeted assassinations or euthanasia) or an opportunity (to conduct experiments, for stem cell research, or harvest organs, and so on). This is because life as a supreme value can always be pitted against itself with individualised *lives* bearing the brunt of this high-stakes contest. The law provides both the meaning and the means to drive this social process. The criminal law in particular enforces the process both at first instance and as a last resort. With criminal law extending to the international use of force in the name of humanity and for the purpose of protecting life, the process receives a global aspect and bursts its banks beyond the nation state onto the global stage. The powers of life and death are then wielded globally in the name of, on behalf of, and representative of 'humanity' in whose name life as a general principle is both protected and exposed to death.

For instance, in both Walter Benjamin's and Giorgio Agamben's work the view expressed is that the violence of law is ultimately a power over life.[59] Actually, Benjamin believed that law originated in its ability law to decide over life and death.[60] His argument was that, in condemning someone to death, law is not merely punishing an offence, but affirming its rule: 'in the exercise of violence over life and death more than in any other legal act, law reaffirms itself'.[61] This is because, in Agamben's view, supreme power is, in the final analysis, 'nothing other than the capacity to constitute oneself and others as life that may be killed but not sacrificed'.[62]

Carl Schmitt cited Alberico Gentili as offering the first clear case of a clearly juridical as opposed to theological treatment of the nature of war when he asked

57 Anne Orford, from 'A Jurisprudence of the limit' in *International Law and its 'Others'*, Anne Orford (ed.), Cambridge, Cambridge University Press, 2006, 1 at p. 18.

58 See e.g. Florian F. Hoffman who utilises Richard Rorty's pragmatic human rights defence in 'Human Rights the Self and the Other' in *International Law and its 'Others'*, Anne Orford (ed.), Cambridge, Cambridge University Press, 2006 at p. 240.

59 Rachel Magnuson, 'Just Barely: Agamben's Reading of Bare Life from Benjamin's 'Critique of Violence', *Strategies of Critique*, vol. 1 No. 1, Spring 2008.

60 Walter Benjamin, 'Critique of Violence', *Reflections: Essays, Aphorisms, Autobiographical Writings*, at p. 286.

61 Ibid.

62 Giorgio Agamben, *Homo Sacer: Sovereign Power and Bare Life*, Stanford (1998), at p. 101.

theologians to be silent in what did not concern them.[63] In so doing, justification for the use of force was shifted from the justice or otherwise of the cause to the identity of the perpetrators of force. This substituted an objective standard for a subjective stance where actors in their capacity as states could utilise force with impunity as just another political tool at their disposal.

However, through legality, objective humane ends as exceptions to the prohibition on the use of force could be the ultimate legitimation for the use of force. These would oppose the subjective standard of reason of State. In a sense, it is the geographical and political culmination of the logic of the state in monopolising the legitimate use of physical force in a given territory extended to the globe. Given the global ramifications of modes of social control that are unbound by national boundaries, the underlying rationality can only be underpinned by replacing the reason of *State* for a reason of *humanity*. Where the territory in question is the entire globe and the community under reference is humanity. In criminalising some violence as illegal, the criminal process becomes purified of and less entangled in local peculiarities and parochial concerns.

The next line of inquiry below opens into how the principles of distinction between spaces (war zones, the New World and colonies) and individuals (pirates, terrorists, barbarians and savages) open to violence[64] and those places and persons not so readily amenable.[65] A space is an empty place just as a person stripped of rights remains an individual. Space therefore matches to the individual and place to the person. Whereas the former pair is open to domination, the latter is inviolate. This describes the inclusion/exclusion mechanism of the law in concrete, historical, conceptual and empirical application as the right to life is denied a whole swathe of humanity.

Persons and Spaces Abandoned to Violence

Particularly in this context, to act is to dominate and conversely to be acted upon is to be dominated.[66] Leading on this, the section argues that the representative notion in law of person as a bearer of rights and duties within a legal system is a social construct and therefore without any inherent content. The notion is only

---

63 Carl Schmitt, *The Nomos of the Earth in the International Law of the Jus Publicum Europaeam* at p. 12.

64 See e.g. Frédéric Mégret, 'From "Savages" to "Unlawful Combatants": A Postcolonial Look at International Humanitarian Law's "Other"' in *International Law and its 'Others'*, Anne Orford (ed.), Cambridge, Cambridge University Press, 2006, especially at pp. 394–5.

65 See e.g. Antony Anghie, 'On Critique and the Other', in *International Law and its 'Others'*, Anne Orford (ed.), Cambridge, Cambridge University Press, 2006, at p. 265.

66 See Anne Orford, from 'A Jurisprudence of the Limit', in *International Law and its 'Others'*, Anne Orford (ed.), Cambridge, Cambridge University Press, 2006, 1 at p. 27.

a form upon which society can act, in order to endow or deny status to human lives. Giorgio Agamben defines his notion of *Homo sacer* or 'sacred man' as human life included in the juridical order solely in the form of its exclusion.[67] *Homo sacer* is excluded from the protections of law while being included in its condemnation at the same time. This figure mirrors the sovereign who stands, both within law (exercising constitutional and statutory powers) and outside the law (exercising prerogative power including suspending law itself).[68] To relate the two more succinctly: *homo sacer* ultimately is the figure to whom everyone is sovereign while the sovereign is the person to whom everyone is ultimately *homo sacer*.[69] When humanity is the conceptual category, foetuses in the abortion debate, human-animal hybrids[70] in the scientific debate, refugees in the immigration debate, detainees in the terrorism debate and human-machine sentient beings in science fiction are mere staging posts in the journey to post-humanism. Luhmann foresaw this in describing social processes that were both reflexive and recursive analogous to cell processes and therefore 'life' which utilised communication as the unit of analysis instead of human actors as the drivers of this process.

Giorgio Agamben extends his study of the inner workings on power from people to places when he states that 'the state of exception is the opening of a space in which application and the norm reveal their separation' where law applies in 'ceasing to apply' leaving only the force formerly associated with the law.[71] To sum up, the state of exception is a frame while *homo sacer* is a canvas, with the law as the paintbrush and the artist the politician. Force and violence are indispensable to this.

Foucault wrote that 'the ancient right to *take* life or *let* live was replaced by a power to *foster* life or *disallow* it to the point of death'.[72] He cited Hobbes stating 'Take a newborn child. Its parents (its father in a civil society, or its mother in the state of nature) could simply allow it to die, or quite simply have it put to death.'[73]

67 Giorgio Agamben, *Homo Sacer: Sovereign Power and Bare Life*, Stanford (1998), at pp. 83–5.

68 Ibid.

69 See William Rasch, 'A Completely New Politics or Excluding the Political? Agamben's Critique of Sovereignty' in *Soziale Systeme* vol. 8 (2002) Issue 1, Special issue on 'Exclusion and Socio-cultural Identities: Systems Theoretical and Poststructuralist Perspectives', at p. 44.

70 UK, US scientists look to genetically modified pigs for organs. http://www.smh.com.au/news/science/uk-us-scientists-look-to-genetically-modified-pigs-for-organs/2008/09/08/1220725898653.html (last visited 5 October 2008).

71 Giorgio Agamben, *State of Exception* (2005), at p. 40.

72 Michel Foucault, *The History of Sexuality: An Introduction*, vol. 1, at p. 138.

73 Michel Foucault, *Society Must be Defended*, trans. David Macy, Penguin, London, 2003, at p. 96.

This indicated to him that the law that affords protection is the same as that which allows violation. Agamben noted this as well:[74]

> The first time we encounter the expression 'right over life and death' in the history of law is in the formula *vitae necisque potestas*, which designates not sovereign power but rather the unconditional authority [*potestà*] of the *pater* over his sons. Not simple natural life, but life exposed to death (bare life or sacred life) is the originary political element.

Agamben carried this forward saying 'the first foundation of political life is a life that may be killed, which is politicised through its very capacity to be killed'.[75] Agamben relies on Foucault to hold that because of modernity, man moved from an animal with the additional capacity for political existence to 'an animal whose politics calls his existence as a living being into question' and both the human species and individual become 'what is at stake in a society's political strategies'.[76] This development is moreover not limited to the domestic space and its citizens.

Classical international law mirrors this process when it divides into the 'Law of War' and the 'Law of Peace'. This distinction between war and peace provides differentiated regimes of applicable laws. The use of force is allowed in extreme cases to affect entire populations and groups not only military but to a certain extent, allows accidental or proportionate civilian casualties as well. Because the United Nations Charter was born in the wake of the necessity to prevent war, it represents the collective pooling of force among its members. The international system as well indicates when the prohibition is inapplicable such as in self-defence for the lawful use of force following a breach or a threat to the peace especially in Chapter VII and article 52 of the UN Charter. Such legalisation through United Nations resolutions that authorise force in the language of 'by all necessary means' exposes whole populations to death while prescribing no penalty for their dying.

The Law of War splits in turn between the *Jus ad Bellum* (justification for the use of force) and the *Jus in Bello* (regulation of armed conflict).[77] The *Jus in Bello* also referred to as 'Hague Law' (generally derived from the 1907 Hague Conventions) governs the conduct of hostilities and 'Geneva Law' (principally derived from the 1949 Geneva Conventions) provides for the protection of the victims of war. Hague Law renders military personnel and military targets open to the application of deadly force while Geneva Law stipulates when military personnel may no longer to be targeted even as it protects civilians from the brunt of the *deliberate* use of force. Although both the Hague and Geneva regimes are

74 Giorgio Agamben, *Homo Sacer: Sovereign Power and Bare Life*, Stanford (1998), at p. 87.

75 Ibid., at p. 89.

76 Ibid., at p. 3.

77 See Adam Roberts and Richard Guelff, *Documents on the Laws of War*, Oxford (2000), at pp. 1–3.

of course not applicable prior to force being used, the two are considered discrete areas of the law with no bearing on the legality of the *resort* to force as opposed to its *use*.

The Law of Peace allows, for instance, for the general applicability of human rights law. However, even dedicated human rights instruments only protect recognised rights when it is appropriate and those not legally recognised therefore do not exist for them. Further, these instruments in any case allow derogation from the recognised rights and remain open to different regimes of the law in situations of conflict or emergency. However, there is a tendency to straddle (without erasing) the divide between war and peace for certain laws. These include non-derogative human rights and the prohibition on torture. The Hague and Geneva law regimes, while limiting the means and methods of war and assigning protections to non-combatants respectively for example, simultaneously open the use of force upon combatants and civilians. Moreover, this indicates that the law does not ignore the state of exception but attempts to capture it as well. An example is the Convention against Torture and Other Cruel, Inhuman or Degrading Treatment or Punishment (CAT) that explicitly states, 'No exceptional circumstances whatsoever, whether a state of war or a threat of war, internal political instability or any other public emergency, may be invoked as a justification of torture'.[78]

It follows then that international law has an inside and an outside that mirror each other. That is, the international legal structure resembles a doughnut with an outer boundary and an inner core. The outer boundary allows all which international law does not forbid (represented by the *Lotus* case deciding 'restrictions upon the independence of States cannot be presumed').[79] The inner core holds any and all legal obligations are subject to the actions of the Security Council in addressing breaches of and threats to the peace (represented by the *Lockerbie* case where the International court of Justice ruled that Security Council Resolutions under Chapter VII of the United Nations Charter prevailed over treaties and domestic laws).[80] These actions taken by the Security Council in addressing aggression and breaches of the peace are paradoxically unbound by law but sanctioned by the law.[81]

---

78 Article 2.2 of the Convention against Torture and Other Cruel, Inhuman or Degrading Treatment or Punishment (Convention against Torture or CAT), adopted 10 December 1984, G.A. res. 39/46, annex, 39 U.N. GAOR Supp. (No. 51) at 197, U.N. Doc. A/39/51 (1984), entered into force 26 June 1987.

79 S.S. Lotus (Fr. V. Turk.) (1927), Permanent Court of International Justice Publications, Series A, No. 9, at 18 (Sept. 7).

80 Questions of Interpretation and Application of the 1971 Montreal Convention arising from the Aerial Incident at Lockerbie (Libyan Arab Jamahiriya v. United Kingdom) – Provisional Measures Order of 14 April 1992, particularly at p. 15, paragraph 39.

81 See Gregor Noll, 'The Miracle of Generative Violence. René Girard and the Use of Force in International Law' (2008), 21 *Leiden Journal of International Law* 563–80, especially at pp. 578–9.

International law's inside is the Security Council acting in exceptional circumstances to suspend the ordinary law while the outside is the not yet prohibited sphere of state action that approximates and indeed renders actual the 'state of nature'. This inside and outside mirror each other in their openness to violence although in a state of nature there is no distinction between force and violence. This legal constantly expanding self-referential boundary and ever contracting core of international law are crucial in resolving the ongoing tension between anomie (being completely without norm) and anarchy (being completely without rule).[82] It necessarily follows that complete freedom is only temporary and is subject to constraint in the lack of freedom from freedom itself, as it were, given unavoidable restraints in terms of the limited choices available externally. Law is then the origin and fountain of freedom and thus not subject to it. As the law expands, it reduces the chaos external to itself and the anomie internally shrinks all in accordance with its idiosyncratic logic of assigning the code legal/illegal as sovereignty dialectically applies the inclusive exclusion and the exclusive inclusion.[83]

The process of opening or closing to violence may be mapped in terms of time. This casts the past as a violent time to be moved way from to a utopian peaceful future through a present forceful struggle against violence. Individuals may be characterised as civilians, terrorist and so on, while space may be categorised into war zones, contact zones, hospital zones, safety zones, demilitarised zones,[84] or both into 'rogue' or 'failed' states[85] either excluded or included by law from the effects of conflict. While normative judgments leading to applying force include declarations of, failed states, oppressive regimes, piracy and so on. The implicit assertion uniting the punitive and/or revolutionary applier of force is 'I enforce rights while you violate them'. Law enforcement is then a matter of course and the violation is a circumstance taken exception to.

Melinda Cooper is a perspicuous observer of this contemporary phenomenon linking the law, life and violence/force:[86]

> The preemptive strike has been decried as a departure from all existing principles of legitimate warfare. But it would be better understood (and countered) on its

---

82 See Sara E. Davies, 'International Law and the State of Exception' in Alex J. Bellamy et al., *Security and the War on Terror*, especially at p. 78.

83 Giorgio Agamben, *Homo Sacer: Sovereign Power and Bare Life*, Stanford (1998), at pp. 21–2.

84 See Regulation 5 annexed to Hague Convention IV, Hague Convention IX articles 1 and 2, Annex I to Geneva Conventions I and IV as well as Additional Protocol I to the Geneva Conventions in Articles, 8, 18, 26, 59, 60 and 85.

85 Richard Devetak calls this 'strategic cartography in 'Failures, Rogues and Terrorists: States of exception and the North/South divide', in Alex J. Bellamy et al., *Security and the War on Terror*, especially at p. 126.

86 See Melinda Cooper, *Life as Surplus: Biotechnology and Capitalism in the Neoliberal Era*, at p. 89.

> own terms, as a radically new formulation of law, one that founds the legitimate use of violence on 'our' collective apprehension of the future, however uncertain rather than the predictive calculus of risk. ... Both Preemption and precaution endow our suspicions, fears and panics with an active force of law.

Governmental practice thus appears to be a creative wielding of productive and destructive powers underpinned by a legal regime with criminalisation at the forefront. This practice of governing by production and destruction of life through wielding or withholding force and allowing or preventing violence finds itself unleashed by the forces of globalisation directly onto the globe and humanity through and above state, territory and population.

Governing as Reflecting, Producing and Destroying

Thomas Hobbes used the image of the Leviathan as a striking metaphor for the state apparatus. Foucault too addressed an essentially Hobbesian description of the state as that 'artificial man who is at once an automaton, a fabricated man, but also a unitary man who contains all real individuals, whose body is made up of citizens but whose souls is sovereignty.[87] This fusion of man and machine in the Leviathan according to Schmitt enabled the mechanisation of man to follow the mechanisation of the state.[88] In addition, dividing human from animal shows that the state is an 'anthropological machine' that produces a gradation of humans, for example slave, barbarian or foreigner, and so on, by the means of an exclusion (which is always already a capturing) and inclusion (which is always already an exclusion).[89] This is 'a ceaselessly updated decision' that moreover operates on 'bare life'.[90] Human beings in civil society are cultivated and not naturally sociable as per Hobbes, Pufendorf and Foucault.[91]

These insights articulate the claim that the political community (exemplified in but not monopolised by the state) is a machine that fosters and manipulates life and dispenses death through the mechanism of law. Giorgio Agamben has developed further Foucault's biopolitics to cover this ground. Examples include cloning, human experimentation, euthanasia, and the death penalty. Additionally, with colonialism and state building, the state has come to replicate itself as it

---

87 Michel Foucault, *Society Must be Defended*, trans. David Macy, Penguin, London 2003, at p. 34.

88 Carl Schmitt, *The Leviathan in the State Theory of Thomas Hobbes*, trans. George Schwab and Erna Hilfstein, 1996, Westport and London, pp. 91–100.

89 Giorgio Agamben, *The Open: Man and Animal,* 2004, translation of *L'aperto: L'uomo e l'animale*, 2002, by Kevin Attell, Stanford, at p. 37.

90 Ibid., at p. 38.

91 Richard Devetak Foucault, 'Discipline and Raison d'Etat' in *Early Modern Europe International Political Sociology*, vol. 2, Issue 3, at p. 271.

produces humans (through the construct of legal personality) as well. According to Agamben, law captures life not by sanction but by guilt through being indebted to the law. That is 'the condition of being included through exclusion'.[92] This 'guilt refers not 'to the determination of the licit and the illicit, but to the pure force of the law, to the law's simple reference to something'.[93]

Foucault noticed that although Hobbes seemed to proclaim that war was everywhere and ever present, Hobbes in fact meant quite the opposite as he believed that it was the subjects who (with or without war and defeat) constituted the sovereign that represented them.[94] In sum, through constant divisions the state produces life and death by creating human personality while feeding off human life with the consent of humans. Democracy is government in our name, for our benefit and by us. Sovereignty is only the organising principle along which the process of inclusion and exclusion rules by opening and closing persons and populations to potentially deadly violence. This cascades into regulation of all forms of life. It ordinarily does not impose or recommend violence as such. It at most merely removes the consequences attached to the deliberate deprivation of life or denial of living conditions along the continuum from discomfort gradually onwards to death. The logic of this process links to a political community that may resemble but need not coincide with the State.

Governmentality beyond the State

Foucault defined 'Governmentality' as 'a strategic field of power relations in their mobility, transformability, and reversibility'.[95] He also urged the abandonment of the leviathan model, juridical sovereignty and the State in favour of analysing the 'techniques and tactics of domination in studying.[96] Agamben's own work too relies on this setting aside of traditional approaches in order to examine how power acts on actual bodies.[97]

The conceptual apparatus of government with humanity as the sovereign and security replacing religion de-links itself from nation-states,[98] which are in fact

92 Giorgio Agamben, *Homo Sacer: Sovereign Power and Bare Life*, Stanford, 1998, at pp. 26–7.

93 Ibid.

94 Michel Foucault, *Society Must be Defended*, trans. David Macy, Penguin, London, 2003, at p. 98.

95 Michel Foucault, *Hermeneutics of The Subject: Lectures at the College de France 1981–1982*, at p. 252.

96 Michel Foucault, *Society Must be Defended*, trans. David Macy, Penguin, London, 2003, at p. 34.

97 Giorgio Agamben, *Homo Sacer: Sovereign Power and Bare Life*, Stanford, 1998, at p. 6.

98 See Barry Hindess, 'Government and Discipline', *International Political Sociology*, vol. 2, Issue 3 (p. 268–70), and Nikolas Rose and Peter Miller, 'Political Power

judged by and do not judge governmentality.[99] For example, human rights are in a sense post-political being neither culturally nor geographically relative. Slavoj Žižek's differentiating of subjective, objective, and systemic violence[100] can underpin the present need for moving international violence from the subjective (the terrorist/freedom fighter false dichotomy) to the objective (a distinction between legal force and illegal violence) and onward to the systemic (an international monopoly on the legitimate use of force).

Efforts to achieve this are ongoing with attempts to include the crime of aggression within international criminal's law ambit. After the Second World War, the victorious Allied Powers criminalised the illegal use of force as a 'crime against peace'. The Nazis and imperial Japanese were the first, and so far the only, convicted and punished 'peace' criminals. The political process leading to the Rome Statute for the International Criminal Court[101] attempted to find or create a definition without complete success. A definition is pending with a special working group considering proposals for the same before the next meeting of the state parties to the statute.[102]

Legalising further the use of force by criminalising objectively illegitimate violence as aggression will be a foundational step towards keeping legal tools for legal ends. This is because it will prevent a rule by law that mimics the rule of law by utilising the legal system for political ends through a preponderance of military force. This ensures a clearer distinction to be drawn between the spheres of law and politics and enables the rule of law to transcend the nation state and apply directly onto the global level with an accompanying identity between the illegal and the inimical.

That is, the friend/enemy political distinction is being mapped onto the legal/illegal criminal conduct distinction. With globalisation, the state is increasingly marginalised and the monopoly on the use *of* force is becoming a monopoly on the use *for* force. That is, humanitarian and security concerns increasingly underpin resort to force and claims to sovereignty in justifying resort to force are no longer legitimate. Because the state predicates itself upon distinguishing force from violence, it essentially justifies the former and penalises the latter even though they are essentially identical. In other words, the law makes a re-entry in

---

beyond the State: Problematics of Government', *The British Journal of Sociology*, vol. 43, No. 2 June 1992, at pp. 176–8.

99 See James D. Faubion (ed.), *Michel Foucault Power: Essential Works of Foucault 1954–1984*, vol. 3, Penguin, London, 2002, at p. 221.

100 Slavoj Žižek, *Violence*, Picador, New York, 2008, at pp. 10–13.

101 Opened for signature 17 July 1998, 2187 UNTS 3, art 83(2) (entered into force 1 July 2002).

102 Special Working Group on the Crime of Aggression, ICC Assembly of States Parties, Informal Inter-Sessional Meeting of the Special Working Group on the Crime of Aggression, 6th sess, ICC Doc ICC-ASP/6/SWGCA/INF.1 (25 July 2007).

order to distinguish between force and violence after emerging from a mythical undifferentiated regime of general and all pervasive war.

Force: The Relationship between Law and Violence

Following on from previous sections that described criminalisation governing the globe and humanity with torture illustrating law linked to life and death through exclusion and inclusion (thereby producing a distinction between force and violence that enables the monopolisation of entitlement to life and ability to give death), this section argues that although force and violence are physically indistinguishable they are legally distinguishable, for example when *violent* riots by striking workers, students or whoever are *forcibly* put down by the authorities. That is to say, only the law provides a viable distinction between them. This is because both force and violence are found at the absolute limit of the law however with a telling difference. Force is inside the law and violence is outside the law. Whether violence not permitted under the law is against the law would depend on the content of the *particular* law in question not the *general* amenability of violence to legalisation. The mechanism of the law itself can be used conceptually, has been used historically, is being used in the domestic law setting, and can be further extended in international law by attaching penal sanctions to the unlawful use of force.

The legal narrative of the emergence from a state of nature may be summarised as violence once the rule, becomes the exception and peace as the exception becomes the rule. This inversion, though lauded in law, has had its critics. Walter Benjamin, for instance, considered that the power of the law was its threat to mere life and therefore, making law was in reality manifesting power and in so doing manifesting violence.[103]

This violence of law does not simply sanction a transgressive act but instead repeats the same act without sanctioning it by treating it as an exceptional case.[104] The law therefore makes possible the distinction between privileged lawful force and illegitimate unlawful violence. The pre-legal state of nature is assimilated to the state of extreme violence of a Hobbesian war of all against all. The state of exception also requires and therefore excuses the use of violence to restore order as an emergency exigency. The emergency is what makes it exceptional. It therefore cannot be permanent because permanent conflict means (for example) no gains or spoils of war could ever be consolidated or enjoyed.

The state of exception simultaneously provides a state of no applicable law with the ordinary distinctions rendered inoperative and an opportunity for a new

103 Walter Benjamin, 'Critique of Violence', *Reflections: Essays, Aphorisms, Autobiographical Writings* at p. 295.

104 Giorgio Agamben, *Homo Sacer: Sovereign Power and Bare Life*, Stanford , 1998, at pp. 26–7.

legal regime to instil these same distinctions anew under a different dispensation. This is then how violence always defers to law except when it does not and law never defers to violence except when it does. The key to this is the *normative* monopoly on the use of force coinciding with a *descriptive* monopoly on the use of force. The ICC as part of the constellation of international criminal justice is therefore shaping up as an apparatus for governing through trying crimes with little explicit debate as to whether this is a proper purpose for it.

Chapter 8
Contrasting Dynamics of Global Administrative Measures and International Criminal Courts: Cosmopolitanism, Multilateralism, State Interests

Nicholas Dorn

Introduction

This chapter is concerned with two intertwined international aspects of governance, engaging with administrative and criminal law in terms of the dynamics between states, international bodies and cosmopolitan actors. The global policy space is not just multi-*level* (government at international, regional, national and local levels, vertically differentiated) but also multi-*source* (juridical interventions, private sector cooperation and hence influences, and civil society). We apply this perspective to aspects of international regulatory/administrative measures and to criminal courts and tribunals, illustrating some of the elements of contingency and surprise that characterise international aspects of governance.

It may be helpful to start by distancing ourselves from any preconception that globalism can be understood as an even process, the consequences of which are uniform. That is far from the case, as will be shown below. Similar in some respects to the approach taken here, Burris et al. (2005) draw on their work on international relations and local security to elaborate a notion of 'nodal governance' as highly contingent, saying that 'Whether it produces 'goods' or 'bads' is an empirical and contingent question' (Burris et al. 2005: 58). We concur with this evaluation, even though we would quibble over 'nodal' language, since it may underestimate the solidity, bureaucratisation and persistence of much that we see in states and international bodies. Nor would we adopt the more commonly used term 'multi-level governance' (Rosenau: 1992; Paterson: 1992; Stubbs: 2005; Jessop: 2004). In our view, 'multi-level' governance has equal but opposite problems to that of 'nodes': it is too vertical and state-centric a concept. The term fails to articulate the 'horizontal' influences in governance – private sector, civil society and NGOs, communications including the internet, cultural formations and so on.

Our preferred term, multi-source governance, acknowledges influences from sovereign states and their federal variants, multilateral systems of implementing administrative measures and criminal law, and the cosmopolitan influences of the private sector and civil society. Sovereignty is acknowledged to be alive and kicking – as some of the examples below will illustrate – and has if anything been selectively strengthened by global bodies and networks (cf. Picciotto: 2006: 1).

The structure of the chapter is as follows. First, looking for conceptual tools, we review some sociological and legal approaches to globalisation, settling upon an approach that looks at synergies and contradictions between actions by states, actions by international bodies (such as the World Bank) and cosmopolitan networks. For hints about the application of these concepts to current developments, we are indebted equally to advances in global administrative law and in the sociological study of regional and international criminal courts (see below). Although these traditions have trodden somewhat different tracks, we aim to show that they are parallel and broadly compatible approaches. Each in its way is a conflict and power analysis, with normative concerns around conflict-resolution, legitimacy, negotiation and fairness. Borrowing freely from these traditions, we examine international governance in some of its administrative and regulatory forms – sanction-making by states meeting in the UN Security Council and other international fora, the attempted direction of countries' social and economic policies by the World Bank and IMF, and current problems of (lack of) legitimisation of the actions of those bodies. In a broadly parallel analysis of regional and international criminal courts and tribunals, we explore cosmopolitan, multilateral and inter-state influences around the International Criminal Tribunal for the Former Yugoslavia (ICTY) and the International Criminal Court (ICC). Finally we conclude on the challenges that multi-source governance poses both analytically and politically.

Approaches: Criminology with an International Perspective?

In a paper entitled 'Pre-crime and post-criminology', historian Lucia Zedner asks if criminology is capable of grasping contemporary developments in its field (Zedner: 2007). She suggests that criminology faces difficulty because its historical project and knowledge concern criminal justice responses after crimes take place (policing, courts, punishment, rehabilitation, and so on) – yet contemporary policy pays attention to 'pre-crime' questions, that is to say, to the prevention of crime and terrorism. Does a 'pre-crime' policy focus mean that criminology is left behind?

In a parallel fashion, the present author asks whether criminology's main focus on states and national policies may reduce criminology's ability to analyse events with a stronger international dimension. Although trained as a criminologist, the author finds it necessary to partially disengage from that discipline in order to address international issues. Work on globalisation and crime policies, international regulatory regimes and international criminal courts came earlier and more easily to international relations and public law specialists (for example Andreas and Nadelmann: 2006; Slaughter and Zaring: 2006) than to criminologists.

Criminology remains more comfortable with domestic issues – with the result that the increasing salience of international issues and perspectives threatens its command of a fast-expanding subject matter.

Three specific impediments to criminological appropriation of the international dimension can be identified: political aversion, the nation-focussed format of criminology and the specific idea of sovereignty loss by neo-liberal states.

Political Aversion

An initial impediment to criminological analysis of international developments may be termed political aversion. Many criminologists would be keen to distance themselves from discussions couched in terms of globalisation as an inevitable process or in terms of acceptance of a neo-liberal perspective. However, on inspection, the literature on globalisation and crime policies is remarkably varied, both in its scientific assumptions and the normative positions taken; it certainly cannot be written off as being all of one piece. For example, whilst Levy and Sznaider (2006) find in human rights a basis for the normative optimism exhibited by some authors (including Kingsbury et al. to be discussed below), others such as Fischer-Lescano and Teubner (2004) perceive fragmentation and little likelihood of emergence of a global space that could be both unified and just. Indeed, some recent international events suggest that 'Enlightenment values may yet pave the road to hell' (Davies et al. 2006: 73). Authors coming from a Foucauldian position, for example Paul Passavant (2005) and Gabe Mythen and Sandra Walklate (2006), perceive a double oppression of neo-liberal state and market diffusing into the international sphere. Others, having internationalist sympathies and taking a constructivist stance, take offence at 'universal' principles, these being, in the words of Carol Harlow, a 'double colonisation', first in the invention by western interests of purportedly universal principles and second in their insertions into non-western systems (Harlow 2006: 209). All these political minefields instil caution in any approach to international issues.

National Origins

A second impediment to criminology's thinking about international developments is the national (and sometimes local) focus traditionally taken by criminology as its primary analytic point of departure – and perhaps as its normative ideal (policy *should* be made at national or maybe local level). In continental Europe, the discipline has been quite closely related to national law (van Swaaningen: 1997), whilst British and other English-speaking criminology has been intertwined with national social policy and youth studies, from conservative, managerial or critical perspectives (Muncie: 2005). A strand of pan-European critical criminology underlines the 'downward' focus of much comparative work, focusing on local variations (Edwards and Hughes: 2005). The term 'glocal' (global-local), popularised within criminology by Dick Hobbs (1998), draws our attention to the idea that all international processes are simultaneously local and global; however that strand has had more to say about crime than about policies.

When it has ventured upon international terrain, criminology has commonly done so by construing that terrain as inter-national, with the hyphen implying comparative analysis in which the unit of analysis is the nation. Some contemporary work tries to extend the analysis to include international bodies (Sheptycki and Wardak: 2006). Concerning historical legacies, there is a growing criminology on colonial (Godfrey and Dunstall: 2005) and post-colonial crime policies (Burris et al. op. cit.), construing crime policies in terms of relations between imperial centres and their peripheries. The innovative nature of these approaches to the international sphere suggests that criminology is beginning to part company with one of its founding assumptions analysis: that crime policies can be understood purely in *domestic* terms ('the state's job on the domestic front', Fitzpatrick: 2001: 220). International developments and institutions have undoubted significance – triggering concerns, inter alia, about a dispersal of political accountability (Loader and Walker: 2004).

'Sovereignty Loss'?

A third impediment to criminological analysis of international developments is the popularity within the discipline of the notions of state retreat and sovereignty loss. When policy is articulated by criminology primarily in terms of the nation state, the question arises of the possibility of changes in the willingness and/or capability of states to maintain responsibility for crime control. The work of David Garland stands as an important statement in this tradition, suggesting that an erosion of sovereignty leaves neo-liberal states such as the UK or the USA less able to reduce crime. So, in order to maintain (or recreate) legitimacy, the state shifts attention to criminal opportunities and makes their reduction the responsibility of everyone (Garland: 1985; Fitzpatrick: 215–6). Within that perspective, declining state capability supplies an explanation for a perceived retreat of the state (see also Fulcher, next section).

By contrast, according to others working in the tradition of regulatory studies, such accounts are precarious because they getting ahead of the facts. John Braithwaite (2005), building on the work of Jacint Jordana and David Levi-Faur (2004), suggests that the notion of retreat of the state is a 'neo-liberal fairytale', which has been picked up by criminology from the right and then supported and embellished with Foucauldian theoretical scaffolding. In the view of Braithwaite, Jordan and Levi-Four and others such as Adam Crawford (2006), the role of the state has indeed shifted – 'from rowing to steering' – however, the resulting 'regulatory state' is no weaker for making that strategic transition. In summary, an assumption that globalisation inevitably involves loss of sovereignty by all states cannot be safe – unless one defines globalisation that way, pre-empting theoretical development and empirical enquiry. The possibility must exist that, as in earlier historical periods, some states may get stronger as others weaken. This will be reflected on our analysis of administrative and criminal developments, below.

Sovereignty Reconfigured

Clearly, a closer look at globalisation is needed, stripped of any preconception that is inimical to all sovereignties. In a wide-ranging paper on globalisation and the nation state written before the events of 2001, sociologist James Fulcher characterises globalisation as 'the development of relatively distanceless relationships that extend beyond national units and involve a growing consciousness of the world as a whole' (Fulcher: 2000: 525). Noting familiar arguments purporting to show that globalising processes weaken the nation-state, Fulcher draws on a variety of sources (see, for example, Hirst and Thompson: 1996: 189–90) to argue that the 'lean state is a more not less effective apparatus because it has unloaded some of the problems that the state had accumulated' (Fulcher: 2000: 531). Indeed, neo-liberalism, far from being a stake driven through the heart of the state, may strengthen some states (ibid.). Furthermore, following the events in the United States of September 2001, some writers suggest that globalisation has offered challenges which, being taken as opportunities by some, have allowed extensions of their sovereignty (Moran: 2005: 335–59).

Moran goes on to make the theoretical claim that social theory on governmentality cannot fully capture the post 9/11 landscape because Foucault's ideas about disciplinary society 'under-determine' state power and politics, including the juridical core of the nation state and the influence of national security (ibid.). We might comment that it is easier to make the sort of remark made by Moran when writing in the shadow of 2001. One analytic and methodological danger here is that, as international political conditions change, so theoretical positions are first knocked over and then rebuilt, in an 'I told you so' fashion. However, analytically, one seeks an understanding that would be helpful in articulating and explaining diverse historical developments. To make an analogy with the scientific modelling of climate change, one seeks a model that is good for dry and wet seasons.

Usefully summarising the wider canvass of social scientific theorising about the international sphere, Tony Fitzpatrick identifies three broad mindsets (Fitzpatrick: 2001: 217). The first approach, 'resistance', may be identified with post modernist approaches and other relativistic approaches that construct globalisation as an effect of pro-market ideology that would crumble if people did not believe in it. A second approach, 'absorption', is quite the opposite – it sees globalisation as the only viable game on the planet – 'a self-propelling force into which we can make little intervention' (ibid.). A third alternative, drawing upon sociologists such as Giddens (1990) and Castells (1996), constructs globalisation as made up of real social processes, however their 'effects' are contingent. For example, 'cybertechnology may have been spawned both by the American military (leading to the Internet) and by post-industrial entrepreneurs (leading to Microsoft, and so on), but 'the parent does not thereby necessarily dictate the future of the offspring'

(Fitzpatrick: 2001: 217, see also Rainbow and Rose 2003: 7 and 10). It is this third position of contingency that we find helpful. The question is how to articulate it in relation to international administrative and criminal policy processes.

Borrowing from Global Administrative Law and Sociology of Law

In defining methodological tools capable of grasping multi-source governance, we are indebted equally to recent advances in global administrative law and in the sociological study of regional and international criminal courts. In both cases, the researchers' analytic assumptions are of conflict and their normative commitments include conflict-resolution. From the administrative law perspective, there are demonstrations of the ways in which 'global governance can be understood and analysed as administrative action: rulemaking, administrative adjudication between competing interests, and other forms of regulatory and administrative decision and management' (Krisch and Kingsbury: 2004: 10). This analytic strand is taken from the global administrative law research programme of Benedict Kingsbury and colleagues at New York University School of Law and his co-workers Nico Krisch at the London School of Economics and Sabino Cassese at the University of Rome. In this chapter we draw particularly on work by Kingsbury, Krisch and Stewart, taking up their claim that global administrative law amounts to a distinct sphere, which is separate from national law (although the latter typically is involved in implementation) and also separate from inter-national, treaty-based law that is agreed directly between states (Kingsbury et al. 2004: 13).

Hailing from a more sociological direction, work by John Hagan at Northwestern University, together with his international co-workers Sanja Kutnjak Ivković, Ron Levi and Gabrielle Ferrales, examines the strategies of international criminal courts in response to crimes such as genocide (for sources, see below). Again here the analysis is one based on conflict assumptions, not just in the obvious sense of relationships between courts and those they may or may not prosecute but also (and more at issue here) in terms of the interplay of international and local forces, both outside and inside the legal institutions concerned, which produces judicial priorities, ways of working and sometimes disengagements (Hagan: 2005; Hagan et al.: 2006; Burke-White: 2006).

Starting with the administrative aspects of international law, according to Kingsbury et al. (2004) there are five types of bodies populating this space ('ideal types', sociologists might say): international administrations, transnational network administrations, distributed administrations, hybrid intergovernmental-private administrations and purely private bodies (Kingsbury et al.: 2004: 8–10). The authors analyse the resulting governance space under three conceptual headings, drawn in part from the English School of international relations (Linklater and Suganami: 2006) as well as from legal and regulatory studies. We shall use their three concepts of governance throughout this chapter, referring to them as inter-state relations, multilateral mechanisms and cosmopolitan networks. We shall show that it is the dynamics between these strands that make up international governance.

- *Inter-state* aspects of governance constitute the minimal expression of a common administrative/regulatory space. This aspect of international governance is state-centric: it is based on agreements, treaties and ways of working that are formulated directly between states, with implementation undertaken by the states concerned and through obligations placed by them upon private sector actors. The UN Security Council's declarations on sanctions and states' implementation of them provide an example discussed below.
- *Multilateralism*. A deepening of the space occurs with what Kingsbury et al. term solidarism, where policy making and/or implementation is undertaken by or at least led by an international or regional body with multilateral and 'solidaristic' (a key term for Kingsbury et al.) characteristics. Whilst the present author finds that consideration of multilateral bodies and mechanism essential (see following pages), he finds that their actions cannot be reasonably predefined in the glowingly positive manner implied by use of the term 'solidaristic'. Some things done by multilateral bodies may be done in a spirit of solidarity and received in the same spirit – yet this can hardly be the case in every case, as illustrated by the discussion of sanctions below. In this chapter it is therefore proposed to replace Kingsbury et al.'s 'solidaristic' by the simple and normatively-open multilateral mechanisms and bodies. In this spirit, some administrative or regulatory actions of the UN, World Bank and the IMF will be discussed. In the sphere of criminal law, we will discuss trajectory of the International Criminal Tribunal for the Former Yugoslavia and the International Criminal Court.
- *Cosmopolitanism* 'envisages global governance that is not essentially the result of inter-state bargaining, but draws also from cross-border networks of civil society actors, private regulatory and media institutions, and markets' (Kingsbury et al.: 2004: 29; see also Kingsbury: 2003). A diversity of views on the political colours and practical potential of cosmopolitanism can be found in the classic and politically liberal work of James Rosenau (1992; for a review see Paterson: 1992), in pro-market approaches such as Fratianni and Pattison (2002), in approaches from the left both optimistic (Hardt and Negri: 2000) and more critical (Jessop: 2001 and 2004), in philosophical and historical work (Thibault: 2001) and in jurisprudence (Eleftheriadis: 2003).

The value of an inter-state/multilateral/cosmopolitan approach to multi-source governance can now be illustrated. In what follows on some recent developments in international regulatory/administrative measures, the presentational order is first inter-state relations, then multilateral mechanisms and finally cosmopolitan influences. The reverse order is taken in relation to international and regional criminal courts. The reason for this reversal of ordering is that, whilst administrative actions of states and global bodies' increasingly are being challenged by cosmopolitan demands, the converse dynamic can be seen in international criminal courts in recent years, which have gone from cosmopolitan beginnings to greater management by states.

Administrative/Regulatory Aspects of International Governance

UN Sanctions: Inter-State Relations in Coercive Form

The possibility that, within the sphere of international administrative/regulatory measures, late modern states draw strength from the networked international environment will now be explored, with special reference to the power of initiative of states in relation to administrative/regulatory action. (This possibility will be contrasted later with the dynamics of international criminal law and tribunals, to be described in terms not of initiatives of states but rather of states' appropriation and management of the initiatives of cosmopolitan actors.) Our interests in the present section of the chapter include state positions that are adopted within multilateral organisations – focusing first on the Security Council – the ways in which those policies are implemented, their perceived consequences and legitimacy, and to what extent they can escape challenge by other parties (those adversely affected and also review bodies and the courts). The aim is not to give a technical or historical outline of the origins, competencies and functions of this international body but rather to explore some consequence of its rulemaking in one particular area – sanctions. Many authors point to the importance of the Security Council within the UN structure and, within that, the influence of the United States (Puchala: 2005). One aspect of this is the ability of the US to block action. As a French diplomat acknowledged in 2002, 'Nothing can be done without the concurrence of the United States,' this reflecting 'the reality of the world' (cited in Puchala: 2005: 574). Even so, there is a negotiating process and some suggest that it is not solely the USA but more widely 'the West' that is the hegemon within the UN, as within other bodies such as the World Bank and OECD (ibid.).

On the topic of UN sanctions against countries or persons (Biersteker and Echert: 2006), the declared objectives may include bringing pressure to bear to induce them to change their policies, their rulers and/or their political and economic systems. The political attractions of sanctions may include a sense of 'doing something' and expressing disproval, even when history gives many examples of such measures being low or even counterproductive. Daniel Drezner suggests that sanctions are most likely to be used under conditions where they will produce the feeblest results, because under such conditions relations are most strained and the target county's resistance is highest (Drezner: 1999). What, then, are the wider consequences? Characterising the 1990s as 'a decade of sanctions', David Cortright and George Lopez point to quite varied outcomes, depending on approaches and contexts (Cortright and Lopez: 2000). Looking specifically at Yugoslavia and Iraq – two instances in which in Drezner's terms the wish to resist was very strong – the balance of evidence suggests that unexpected and frankly negative consequences may have outweighed the expected and positive ones.

> Regimes like Milošević's and Hussein's are propped up not only by official state institutions but also by sprawling and overlapping matrixes of underworld criminal groups, shadowy commercial clans and quasi-legal paramilitary units. International sanctions and embargoes like those imposed on the FRY and Iraq tend to strengthen these elements, which are adept at the smuggling and subterfuge necessary to keep the economy puttering along. (Whitmore: 2003, cited in Andreas: 2005: 354)

Peter Andreas finds that sanctions can 'unintentionally contribute to the criminalisation of the state, economy, and civil society of both the targeted country and its immediate neighbours, fostering a symbiosis between political leaders, organised crime and transnational smuggling networks. This symbiosis, in turn, can persist beyond the lifting of sanctions' (Andreas: 2005: 335). One possible response might be to enhance the UN's ability to enforce sanctions. However, based on the Yugoslavian experience, tougher enforcement 'may simply push out small-time freelance operators while further inflating profits and enhancing market position for the most sophisticated and well-organised smugglers' (Andreas, op. cit.: 357–8).

Good Governance as Bypassing and Undermining State Capacity

Faced with the negative fallout from sanctions in relation to the Balkans and the Middle East, western governments have tried to refine and focus measures in order to attain a political end whilst not having unfortunate side effects in humanitarian and criminalisation terms (Swiss Federal Office: 1998). These developments drive specific developments in multi-source governance. For example, in 2006 and early 2007, concerted attempts were being made to isolate an elected Palestinian government. Given the need perceived by the so-called Quartet (UN, US, EU and Russia) not to be seen as responsible for the deepening of suffering that would follow a long-term cutting off of all aid, a 'Temporary International Mechanism' (TIM) was designed (Delegation of the European Commission: 2006a). This aims to channel money directly to recipients in the public and private sectors (Delegation of the European Commission: 2006b), bypassing the Palestinian government and, in doing so, making a political point to the general population (that as voters they made the wrong choice). In the event, some reports suggest that the TIM has had the unintended but unsurprising effect of strengthening the position in the region of other givers of aid (Financial Times: 2007). Central to our concerns here, NGOs have been critical of the TIM because of alleged inefficiencies in delivery, the costs of the scheme (including allegedly high fees paid to a London bank) and the failure to build local capacity (ibid., and see also Oxfam: 2006). It has yet to emerge whether there is any relation between these mechanisms and levels of criminality in the region and/or corruption in the administering 'pipeline'. Nor is it clear what if any relationship obtained between the political and financial bypassing of the elected government and the political fracturing that followed in 2007.

Sitting alongside the state capacity-destruction approach of the international community towards the Palestinian authorities, we can identify an approach in which support for individual politicians in weak states is made highly *conditional* on their behaviour. David Chandler has outlined and criticised this approach in relation to Bosnia.

> In March 2005 the Croatian member of the Bosnian Presidency, Dragan Covic, due to chair the Presidency in June 2005, was dismissed from his post, without appeal, by the [then] international High Representative Lord Paddy Ashdown. [...] Covic was just the most recent of a long line of highly ranked elected politicians to be forced out of office, or barred from running for high office, as a result of anti-corruption and good governance practices. [...] Lord Ashdown has administered the Bosnian protectorate according to rules of 'good governance' which are much tougher than those of many Western democracies [...]. (Chandler: 2006: 86)

Chandler observes that Bosnian politicians are 'caught in a no-win situation'. If they do not do much on the corruption front, then of course they are criticised. However, if they take a more active stance position, for example by ensuring that anti-corruption teams are led by people who are knowledgeable and powerful enough to overcome obstruction, then they are accused of covering things up. Thus whatever they do is construed as evidence of a need for more external regulation. Chandler goes on to suggest that state capacity building that is so highly controlled from the outside is 'even more corrosive of the authority of non-western state than earlier policies which sought to bypass or marginalise the state' (ibid.: 93–4). If correct, then ironically that would imply that the bypass attempts in relation to Palestine may be less damaging in the long run than the 'partnership' activities of the international community in the Balkans. An undermining of nascent government may not the best way to reduce criminality.

Governance, International Bodies, Corruption: World Bank and IMF

The World Bank (henceforth the Bank) and its Bretton Woods 'twin', the International Monetary Fund (henceforth IMF) command less respect than might have been the case when they were set up. These two institutions were set up with the respective aims of safeguarding economic stability at a global level by, for example, ensuring orderly conversion of currencies (IMF) and stimulating economic development of underdeveloped countries by means of loans (Bank). The two institutions now face the prospect of a decline in their business and political influence, due to greater caution amongst prospective borrowers, competition by new lenders such as China and Latin American countries, and the prospect of new regional financial institutions not wedded to a neo-liberal agenda. We explore some governance and corruption aspects of this fast-changing situation.

Over time, both bodies moved from Keynesian to neo-liberal policies, favouring deflation, high interest rates, social spending cuts and privatisation policies. Both bodies have been roundly criticised on the grounds that such policies are counterproductive in under-developed countries and in crisis situations (see for example Stiglitz: 2002). Witness for example the East Asian financial crisis of 1997, which extended to Russia and Latin America by 1998. Here, the IMF support was conditional on economic reforms in line with neo-liberal economic principles – the so-called structural adjustment packages (Barnet and Finnemore: 2004). Cosmopolitan critics however have pointed out that, when the United States entered a recession in 2001, its government pursued quite the opposite policies, namely lowering interest rates, increasing government spending, and cutting taxes, in order to re-expand the economy (Wikipedia entry for IMF). Such apparent 'double standards' have not been overlooked by the countries involved in that crisis and indeed by other countries.

Once burned, twice shy.

> Asian countries have mounted massive foreign reserves to avoid risking a return to the Fund for a bailout. [...] This trend is now moving to Latin America as well. Eventually this may be a mechanism to cope with potential financial crises without involving the IMF. (Bretton Woods Project: 2006)

The situation has been given added piquancy by the fact that China, in particular, has had a rapid economic rise and increasingly is in a position to offer alternative finance, without the conditions favoured by the Bretton Woods 'twins'. This creates the possibility, worrying for the World Bank and IMF, that their 'market' (customer countries) might simply walk away. Indeed that is what many critical NGOs recommend (Institute for Policy Studies et al.: 2006). It is this context that resistance offered to policy developments led by the recently deposed President of the Bank, Paul Wolfowitz, may be seen. First, 'Mr Wolfowitz raised the possibility that the bank and other international institutions could establish incentives "and some disincentives", to ensure countries stayed within sustainable borrowing levels (reported in Financial Times: 2006). In other words, countries taking loans from elsewhere on loan conditions that do not please the Bank might find that they would face less positive appraisals by the Bank – potentially serious, since the Bank's perceptions may be taken into account by rating agencies and market participants when assessing countries' economic status, safety of government bonds, and so on. Second, after years of seeming insouciance to corruption in its lending programmes, under Mr Wolfowitz the Word Bank adopted a more visible stance of fighting corruption (Department of Institutional Integrity: 2006).

> The Bank's plans for a corruption amnesty are contentious. Under the scheme, companies must reveal any misconduct in their involvement in Bank projects over the past five years. The companies would then be subject to three years' monitoring […]. The anti-corruption lobby Transparency International has welcomed the plan but another group, Probe International, says the Bank's plan 'immunises bribers from debarment [exclusion from Bank projects], allows the Bank to cover up its own negligence or complicity, and undermines the administration of justice in countries where it is a criminal offence to bribe a foreign official'. (Africa Confidential: 2006)

Why historically has corruption been such a feature of World Bank programmes and why has the institution 'done little to address the fundamental source of that corruption' (Rich: 2002: 47)? One answer that seems both simple and credible is that inherent in the institution there is 'internal pressure to keep lending in spite of poor compliance' (ibid.: 47). The cause of this pressure is 'chronic 'clientitis' of the bank' (ibid.: 50), that is to say a desire to keep good relationship between the Bank and client countries – in other words, to keep market share and to maintain influence. The institution now faces a balancing act, between the need to at least rhetorically and demonstratively increase its profile on anticorruption activities, whilst not at this delicate time taking action of a sort that would push borrowing countries into the arms of their eastern and southern brethren.

Administrative Legitimacy and Fairness – Problems and Prospects

International bodies such as the IMF, World Bank, and UN Security Council provoke additional controversy because they 'administer' individuals and countries without clear judicial oversight or adequate means of challenge. One response favourably considered by Kingsbury et al. is the emergence of *external* forms of challenge.

> In the case of treaty law, it might be possible to adapt the approach developed by the European Court of Human Rights in dealing with the problem that the European Convention on Human Rights does not formally bind intergovernmental organizations or the European Union. The court requires states parties which are member states of such institutions, when conferring powers on them, to ensure a level of protection within these institutions equivalent to that provided by the ECHR. Applying such an approach more broadly would supply at least a basic set of standards for global administrative bodies […]. (Kingsbury et al.: 2004: 17)

There are some practical examples of similar mechanisms/constraints, for example in relation to the UN's listing of persons whose financial assets are to be frozen for alleged terrorist links. Implementation of Security Council decisions depends on UN member states and on private sector networks. *Thus the measures become open to challenge within these circuits of implementation.* Actions have been brought in EU member states' courts challenging the EU regulations that implement UN Security Council sanctions. (A note on a recent case and an opportunity for updating is given by the American Society of International Law: 2006). Such legal actions might seem frustrating from the perspective of the sanction-makers, however another perspective sees them as essential – not only to safeguard the rights of the individuals concerned but also in order to bring much-needed legitimacy to the Security Council (Cannizzaro: 2005: 5).

Similarly, in 2000 the Bosnian Constitutional Court took the view that it could review decisions of the High Representative governing Bosnia. The Court held that, when acting as domestic rather than international official, the High Representative was not above the constitution (Constitutional Court of Bosnia and Herzegovina: 2000). These examples show that in practice, some degree of oversight is developing through case law by regional and national legal systems. They might be more effective arbiters of the activities of international organisations than the latter's rudimentary and possibly self-serving internal procedures. Over time, this might lead to the consolidation of a consensus on the key procedural aspects of and guarantees in international administrative law (Kingsbury et al.: 2004: 15–16,and 38).

Of considerable interest for the theorising of multi-source governance is looking beyond the formal powers of courts at European or national level (powers that may not extend to the legitimacy gaps within the wider global regulatory space), to grasp the wider influence that courts may have. Reputational pressures and processes are also in play – shaming of international bodies, not totally dissimilar from the pressures brought to bear by NGOs or the media. This reputational aspect of judicial challenge may be articulated as an aspect of cosmopolitanism, concerning lateral rather than hierarchical pressures. As William Burke-White puts it in a parallel context: 'Political effects of numerous courts operating together as a system can cajole, pressure, prod, and even compel states and their institutions to comply with substantive international legal obligations' (Burke-White: 2006: 38). This notion of cajoling and prodding gives us an entrée to international and regional criminal courts.

Evolution of International and Regional Criminal Courts and tribunals

In this section, we explore the extent to which criminal courts, acting at a global or a regional level, can be understood in terms of cosmopolitan networking, multilateral mechanisms and inter-state action. We examine the vicissitudes of the International Criminal Tribunal for the Former Yugoslavia (ICTY) and the International Criminal Court (ICC). Across this field, we will find quite similar dynamics to those described above in relation to international regulatory/ administrative action: blurring and interpenetration of states, international bodies and wider networks and influences; enhancement of the capacities of some states at the expense of others; and the potential for unexpected reverses. However, the historic and developmental dynamics seem to be reversed. In a nutshell, the argument will be that, in relation to the examples discussed, cosmopolitan actors were the primary initiators and also were highly influential in forming the positions of states in formulating the legal mechanisms concerned. Yet as time went on, and as it came to implementation, the roles of the cosmopolitan actors diminished, being overshadowed by the bureaucratic and functional needs of the tribunals set up, and also by the efforts made by (some) states to manage their evolution.

This analysis of the dynamics in play in relation to international criminal law tribunals (cosmopolitan initiatives becoming colonised by states) is not new (see below). However we claim that there is analytic novelty and importance our contrast between it and the converse dynamic described earlier in relation to administrative/regulatory measures (where state initiatives become challenged by cosmopolitan challenged).

ITFY: Cosmopolitan Beginnings, Statist Ends

Cosmopolitan and cross-border networks of civil society actors might sound unlikely in the context of criminal law. However, as is widely recognised in the literature, NGOs and non-legal activists have played crucial roles in the formation of international and regional criminal courts. For example, talking about International Criminal Tribunal on the Former Yugoslavia (ICTY), set up by the UN Security Council in 1993, Gary Bass says that 'NGOs can claim credit, or bear responsibility for the establishment of the tribunal mostly insofar as they were able to persuade the liberal members of the Security Council' (Bass: 2000: 33). Similarly, John Hagan, Ron Levi and Gabrielle Ferrules (2006) point to the importance of NGOs in the early stages of the ICTY.

> One finds at the ICTY two groups of actors active in *creating* the field and in its *continued* sociopolitical development. Social movement activists, and in particular women's groups, were essential in developing public awareness of the civilian casualties of the Balkan wars. [...] The Chair of the Commission that paved the way for the ICTY, Cherif Bassiouni, was able to boast that 'we had almost 30 feminist organizations, mostly from outside the U.S., many German, French and other organizations that had been active in fighting violence against women and rape'. However, once the Tribunal gained funding and contingent support from powerful states, ICTY leadership and staff began to create distance between social movements and the Tribunal. Movement activists were not hired for positions, and once the ICTY attained a more secure footing, the Office of the Prosecutor ceased meeting regularly with activists (Hagan et al.: 2006: 593, *emphasis in original*).

This court's bureaucratic shift of alliances away from NGOs reflected in part the fact that the NGOs were simply no longer needed: the political case had been made, the court was up and running. What the court needed to operate was professional investigators and prosecutors and, crucially, it needed to persuade states to make some arrests of those indicted – otherwise the court would be unable to do anything and might fall into disrepute (ibid.: 593–7).

In time, however, the loss of a close relationship with non-state actors left the court vulnerable to pressure from powerful states, whose nationals became increasingly well represented in its staffing (ibid.: 594–603). An important contextual point is that, during the formative period of the ICTY, the US suffered a change of mood over a permanent international court with wider jurisdiction – the ICC, to be discussed below (Rothe and Mullins: 2006; Schabas: 20). One worrying possibility for the United States was that, under certain conditions, there could be references of its citizens (military personnel, private sector contractors, even responsible political leaders). Due to the limitations placed on the ICTY, actions against NATO states concerning the aerial bombardment of Yugoslavia were dismissed by the tribunal when referred to it (ICTY Committee: 1999; ICTY Prosecutor 2000; see also International Court of Justice: 1999 and 2004). However, the attempts to bring such cases, and the fact that the ICTY prosecutor took them under consideration, 'infuriated opponents of the ICC within the US government' (Cerone: 2007: 290). There was deepening concern in the US administration about the future potential for international courts to be two-edged swords, in evolving circumstances such as Afghanistan, Iraq, Sudan, Sierre Leone or other sites of *jus ad bellum*, humanitarian intervention or other zones of international cooperation (ibid.: 298–308).

In this sense, the Balkans provided a 'preview' of what might happen in other 'theatres' and it, contributing to the *volte face* of the USA in the context of negotiations for, and distancing from, the ICC (see following section). Equally, from other perspectives, there was apprehension that international justice was being 'dismantled' (Aleksandar 2006). The relevance regarding the future of ICTY is that there was western pressure for it to wind down its activities (Hagan et al.: 2006: 608–9). As for the consequences of the earlier defenestration of cosmopolitan supporters of the court, Hagan et al. say this.

> The eagerness of the ICTY to gain legitimacy, by distancing itself from the foundational social movements involved in its creation, has contributed to its ongoing vulnerability to the intrusion of domestic political struggles emanating from influential, sponsoring states – including Great Britain as well as the United States'. (Hagan et al.: 2006: 610)

In related work, Hagan and Ivković (2006) comment that for courts in a post-conflict situation to contribute to the construction of democracy, the courts need not only to meet procedural and due process standards but also to be seen as doing so by members of the public Hagan and Ivković (2006: 132–3) These authors draw upon local surveys to suggest that the modus operandi of the ICTY has led to dissatisfaction with it throughout the former Yugoslavia (ibid.). For example, in Sarajevo a common perception in the general population is that the court's use of punishment has not been consistent (sometimes sentences are perceived as too harsh, others too lenient – perceptions which seem independent of ethnicity (Ivković and Hagan: 2006: 391 and 402–3). It is believed locally that this inconsistency has been at least partly due to the court's keenness on wherever possible striking plea bargains with defendants (ibid.: 391). Because of this, many of those Bosnians surveyed reported that they look forward to a domestication of further trials, seeing that as the way to root justice less in formal procedures and plea bargaining (characteristic of US justice, particularly when it is in a hurry) and more in a substantial sense of justice that has 'an understanding and familiarity with the local setting' (ibid.: 402). It seems, therefore, that in making the transition from support by international NGOs, to time-conscious management of the legal process, the ITCY failed to generate, build or maintain local support, thus making its closure politically non-problematic.

ICC: Political Surprises for All

In response to Serbian objections (Parenti: 2000) and other queries, Richard Goldstone, the first chief prosecutor of the ICTY, had been at a loss to answer the question why, considering all that had occurred in the world, (ex-)Yugoslavia should find itself the focus for the first regional criminal tribunal since Nuremberg. Goldstone conceded that, 'if there was no follow-through and if other equivalent situations in the future were not treated comparably, the people of the former Yugoslavia could justifiably claim discrimination' (cited by Hagan and Ivković: 2006: 132).

This complaint was somewhat addressed by the setting up of the International Criminal Court in 2002 (for background and commentaries see International Criminal Court: 1999; Burke-White: 2002; Weller: 2002). Born out the same broad political moment, the mainspring of the ICC, like that of the ICTY, was much animated by cosmopolitan ideas and actors. Marlies Glasius describes the influence of civil society in the following terms.

> As the negotiations, which had been little more than exchanges of views at the preparatory committee meetings, reached their climax in Rome [conference], the most important thing global civil society contributed to the process was transparency. Traditionally, international law-making has occurred in complete secrecy; all that became available to the public was the final product – and sometimes, there were also secret treaties. It is unlikely that international negotiations will ever be entirely open, but the Coalition for an International Criminal Court took the potential for making international negotiations transparent to its limits. It had a highly developed system of twelve shadow teams to follow negotiations on different parts of the Statute, they debriefed friendly state delegates after closed meetings, and they kept 'virtual vote' tallies on crucial issues. They then sent this information to thousands of national activists by email, and posted it on their website. Thus, an interested citizen

> with an Internet connection could almost exactly follow which country took which views on which issues on a daily basis. Incidentally, this also levelled the playing field for poor countries, whose mostly small delegations could only follow every aspect of the negotiations thanks to the NGOs. (Glasius: 2003; see also Glasius: 2004 and Simpson: 2004)

Thus cosmopolitan actors were as important in the conception and early development of the ICC as they were for the ICTY. However, the interests of states are clearly reflected in the way in which the powers of the court are circumscribed. The general condition under which the ICC operates is 'complementarity', which means that the court can find admissible only cases where the state concerned is 'unwilling or unable' to take action; it is a 'consent regime' (Burke-White: 2002: 8–9). In these terms the birth of the ICC disappointed some who had looked forward to a possibility of global justice for all those accused of the gravest crimes.

As is well known, the United States worked hard to circumscribe the legal basis of the ICC during negotiations, indicated when signing the resulting treaty that it would not ratify, and has subsequently most energetically made bilateral agreements with roughly one hundred states to deny the ICC jurisdiction (Cerone: 2007; Burk-White: 2002). There is some historical consistency in this, as John Cerone points out: for 80 years 'The US has tended to support international criminal courts where the US government has (or is perceived by US officials to have) a significant degree of control over the court, or where the possibility of prosecution of US nationals is either expressly precluded or otherwise remote' (Cerone: 2007: 27). The USA has not been alone in having concerns about the ICC, with Islamic states seeing it as having a potential for interference in domestic and cultural affairs (Roach: 2005) and with China also ambivalent (Yang: 2005).

Yet subsequent developments go beyond what was expected of the ICC and articulate key themes of multi-source governance. It was not expected that many states would refer themselves. That expectation was confounded by an invitation extended to the ICC by the President of the Democratic Republic of Congo in 2004 (Burke-White: 2005). Following this, by 2007 one case was under way (International Criminal Court: 2007: 1–3). Much of the literature on international law and tribunals revolves around notions of abstract and pure legality ('clean') *versus* political interests ('dirty'). The decision of the President of the Congo that the country should refer itself to the ICC – on the grounds of insufficient capacity of its domestic legal system to prosecute perpetrators of crimes committed on its territory – requires us to move beyond that opposition of terms. Burke-White (2005: 564) argues that it requires us to peer into the 'black box' of government, which in the Congo is constituted by four power-sharing groups, in an uneasy balance. He further suggests that 'the existence of the Court sufficiently shifted the incentive structure for the national government such that President Kabila perceived it to be in his own interests to refer the case' (ibid.: 564). The surmise is that Kabila himself is less likely to be prosecuted than many of his political competitors, partly because his record is cleaner than theirs (ibid.: 564–6) and partly because his initiative makes his own prosecution unlikely. In these circumstances the acceptance by the ICC of a role in the Congo inevitably takes particular political partners as it constructs justice.

> Kabila's referral may well be indicative of a broader phenomenon of weak states self-referring situations to the ICC, when sitting governments can benefit from prosecutions [...] While there are benefits, cooperative complementarity also carries with it significant difficulties, namely that the ICC may alter a delicate domestic political balance. The ICC must recognize that it is part of a system of global governance in international law enforcement, that its policies will alter incentives at the national level, and that in responding to actions by national governments it may be engaging in a potentially dangerous political game. (Burke-White: 2005: 567)

In such developments can be seen a breaking down of the received categories of sovereign state and higher court. The ICC Congo case so clearly involves cooperation between 'levels' (in contra-distinction to the ICTY, whose process is somewhat top-down) that is would be inappropriate to try to analyse it using the hierarchical concepts of multi-level governance. As Burke-White suggests, the ICC–Congo relationship looks like 'complex sharing of authority and multi-dimensional influences between national and international structures [as] suggested by the global governance literature' (ibid.). We can add that it is not so far from the 'pluralist, heterarchical [*sic*] model' of relations as described in global administrative law (Krisch et al.: 2006: 10). Thus, in the emergent practices of international and regional criminal courts – as in the workings of administrative/ regulatory measures – multi-source governance helps us to capture the spirit of developments.

Conclusions

Dynamics

One received conception of globalisation is that it is the flip-side of a generalised process of erosion of capability of states. We show that a more open and contingent analysis of international governance is emerging from studies of administrative and criminal aspects of governance and law. Interplays occur between late modern and other states, multilateral bodies including international courts, and cosmopolitan networks. These interactions are contingent (depending not only on power but also on how all concerned strategise and 'play' situations) – yet some regularities can be observed. Cosmopolitan networks provide both challenges and opportunities, for example in relation to late modern states, networks provide resources and opportunities for strategies, rather than displacing such states (cf. Jessop: 2001: 166). At the same time and, somewhat contrary to expectations, 'pariah' states that are targeted by sanctions and other coercive measures may be maintained and even strengthened, state criminality being part of their resistance. Dispersal of sovereignty is the fate of those weaker states that, variously penetrated by sanctions and regulation, are opened up to strong states, multilateral bodies and networks working in tandem. Faced with such varied circumstances and contingent outcomes, a sovereignty decline thesis is too general and insufficiently nuanced.

Sitting between states and networks – and in interaction with both – multilateral bodies such as the World Bank have to contend not only with states but also with the private sector and with independent think tanks, NGOs, research, media and other knowledge producers and reputation spoilers. Judgments of national or regional courts, whilst not necessarily having direct legal effects on international bodies, nevertheless have to be attended to, because of the reputational and shaming potential for all concerned. Thus courts may take a cosmopolitan role, alongside NGOs and media, in shaping non-binding but politically persuasive boundaries of governance.

Analysis

This chapter has brought together within two bodies of scholarship – on international administrative measures (the IR-inspired legal analysis of Kingsbury et al.) and on international criminal courts and tribunals (the sociology and law of Hagan et al.). Some distinct regularities and some contrasts emerge.

- Acknowledging that international administrative or regulatory measures may take either 'disciplinary' forms such as sanctions or 'supportive' forms such as capacity-building, the claim is made that, in all such measures, *inter-state relations* constitute the initial drivers. As the political and practical difficulties inherent in 'selling', legitimising and implementing such measures mount, they typically 'morph' into more multilateral arrangements. Moving on in time, it is quite typical for a wide range of international administrative/regulatory measures to be strongly challenged by cosmopolitan and independent actors (NGOs, pressure groups, non-aligned media), on the grounds of fairness, ineffectiveness and negative side effects. One can clearly see such a trajectory in relation to sanctions, targeted aid, the Bretton Woods institutions, as discussed above.
- What is analytically interesting (and may have practical importance) is that, in relation to international and regional criminal courts and tribunals, the historical dynamic seems to be reversed. The ICTY and the International Criminal Court owed their genesis to campaigning by cosmopolitan networks and media (campaigns against impunity); developed organisational solidity and capabilities required to function (professional, dedicated and well-connected prosecutors, the capability to investigate effectively and make arrests); then attracting much closer management and demands for closure or at least curtailment by concerned states (notably the USA).

One question, which we cannot answer here, is why international multi-source governance measures of an administrative or regulatory nature should see a dynamic running from state bargaining, through multilateral management, towards cosmopolitan challenge (s-m-c) – whilst the evolution of the administration of international criminal courts and tribunals experience the converse dynamic (c-m-s).[1]

That question cannot be settled in this chapter, which remains at the point of making some preliminary and hopefully provocative observations.

Further Research

That one framework – on shifting relations between states, multilateral bodies and cosmopolitan networks – can be applied both to administrative/regulatory and to criminal law aspects of international governance, observing differing dynamics in these fields, demonstrates the analytic power of this approach. Further applications could extend multi-source governance analyses from international and regional administrative/regulatory mechanisms and criminal courts to other areas. For example, there are links to be forged between contemporary developments and historical scholarship on colonial crime policies (Dupont et al.: 2005). In making these links, socio-legal research can build upon its best traditions in terms of empirical work, paying careful attention to conflict and negotiation, continuing to bring together material from different disciplines, and moving between detailed studies and attempts at synthesis.

Acknowledgements

Various iterations of this work have benefited from the author's involvement on behalf of Cardiff University in the HUMSEC project (2006–2009), an EU Sixth Framework Programme Coordination Action, coordinated by the European Centre for Training and Research Centre for Human Rights and Democracy. Within that context, academics and practitioners from the Balkan region and more widely in Europe offered helpful comments, as did student participants at the 2007 Summer Academy in Graz. In particular Jelena Jolic critically commented on a draft and pointed out some non-sequiturs and possible improvements. The work also benefited from the wider perspectives offered at a conference on organised crime in Asia, organised by Narayanan Ganapathy and Marc Craig on behalf of the National

1 Is it somehow in the socio-legal or political 'nature' of these two legal cousins that their developments are mirror images? *Must* administrative measures be something that states initiate and cosmopolitan actors attack? *Must* innovations in criminal law be the business of private actors – who then get shouldered aside by states? Such questions could be approached both empirically (a search for disconfirmation of the relations described) and theoretically.

University of Singapore and the Queensland University of Technology. The author is also grateful to Henk van de Bunt, Damián Zaitch and René van Swaaningen for an opportunity to open up this as a new area of teaching in comparative criminology at Erasmus Rotterdam University, and to masters students who discussed the issues in class. Thanks also to Tom Vander Beken at Ghent University, who has been a helpful interlocutor, and to Michael Levi at Cardiff for comments on a final draft. Needless to say, not all the suggestions made by those mentioned above have been followed in full, all responsibility remaining the author's.

References

Africa Confidential, 2006, 'Crying Wolfowitz', *Africa Confidential Newsletter*, 47, 19, 22 September, 1–8. London: www.africa-confidential.com.

Aleksandar, J., 2006, 'Introduction: Yugoslavia Dismantled and International Law', *International Journal for the Semiotics of Law*, 19, 339–46. http://www.springerlink.com/content/xt401m6271481077.

American Society of International Law, 2006, [Case Note on] Court of First Instance of the European Communities: Chafiq Ayadi v. Council of the European Union, Faraj Hassan v. Council of the European Union and Commission of the European Communities (July 12 2006), in Editorial Staff of International Legal Materials (eds), *International Law In Brief*, July 25, Washington: American Society of International Law. http://www.asil.org/ilib/2006/07/ilib060725.htm#j3.

Andreas, P. and Nadelmann, E., 2006, *Policing the Globe: criminalisation and crime control in international relations*. Oxford: University Press.

Andreas, P., 2005, 'Criminalising Consequences of Sanctions: Embargo Busting and Its Legacy', *International Studies Quarterly*, 49, 335–60.

Bass, G., 2000, *Stay the Hand of Vengeance: The Politics of War Crimes Tribunals*. Princeton: Princeton University Press, 2000, pp. 368.

Barnett, M. and Finnemore, M., 2004, *Rules for the World: International Organisations in Global Politics*. Ithaca: Cornell University Press.

Biersteker, T. and Eckert, S., 2006, *Strengthening Targeted Sanctions Through Fair and Clear Procedures*, White Paper prepared by the Watson Institute Targeted Sanctions Project at Brown University, 30 March. Providence: Watson Institute for International Studies.

Braithwaite, J., 2005, *Neoliberalism or Regulatory Capitalism*, RegNet Occasional Paper 5, October, 1–48. Canberra: Regulatory Institutions Network. http://ctsi.anu.edu.au/publications/nontaxpubs/ROP5.pdf.

Braithwaite, J., 2000, 'The New Regulatory State and the Transformation of Criminology', *British Journal of Criminology*, 40, 2, Spring, 222–38.

Bretton Woods Project, 2006, *Tinkering at the Edges of Governance Reform: IMF quota proposals*, 11 September. London: Bretton Woods Project. http://www.brettonwoodsproject.org/art.shtml?x=542308.

Burke-White, W., 2002, 'A Community of Courts: Toward a System of International Criminal Law Enforcement', *Michigan Journal of International Law*, 24, 1, Fall, 1–101. http://jsmp.minihub.org/Reports/otherresources/Burke-White per cent20ITP2.pdf

Burke-White, W., 2005, 'Complementarity in Practice: The International Criminal Court as Part of a System of Multi-level Global Governance in the Democratic Republic of Congo', *Leiden Journal of International Law*, 18, 557–90. http://journals.cambridge.org/action/displayAbstract;jsessionid=02E12E88B977C6886B56099B8E41C8C1.tomcat1?fromPage=online&aid=348843#

Burke-White, W., 2006, 'Double Edged Tribunals: The Political Effects of International Criminal Tribunals', *Guest Lecture Series of the Office of the Prosecutor*, 28 July, 1–39. The Hague: International Criminal Tribunal for the Former Yugoslavia.

Burris, S., Drahos, P. and Shearing, C., 2005, 'Nodal Governance', *Australian Journal of Legal Philosophy*, 30, 30–58.

Cannizzaro, E., 2005, *Machiavelli, the UN Security Council and the Rule of Law*, Global Law Working Paper 11/05, 1–32. New York: NYU School of Law. http://www.nyulawglobal.org/workingpapers/documents/glwp0106cannizzaro.pdf

Castells, M., 1996, *The Rise of Network Society*. Oxford: Blackwell.

Chandler, D., 2005, International State-Building: Beyond Conditionality, Beyond Sovereignty, Guest Seminar of the Royal Institute for International Relations (IRRI-KIIB), Brussels, 17 November 2005. http://www.wmin.ac.uk/sshl/pdf/CSDCHandlerInternationalState-Building180206.pdf

Chandler, D., 2006, 'Building Trust in Public Institutions? Good governance and anti-corruption in Bosnia-Herzegovina', *Ethnopolitics*, 5, 1, 85–99. http://taylorandfrancis.metapress.com/media/2gpmvwqrrnwmaxjlkq5r/contributions/l/6/h/0/l6h0466105m2q748.pdf

Cerone, J, 2007, 'Dynamic Equilibrium: The Evolution of US Attitudes toward International Criminal Courts and Tribunals', *European Journal of International Law*, vol. 18, No. 2, 277–315.

Constitutional Court of Bosnia and Herzegovina, 2000, *Decision U-9/00, Having Regard to Article VI(a) on the Constitution [...]*, 3 November, 1–9. Sarajevo: Constitutional Court of Bosnia and Herzegovina. http://www.ccbh.ba/eng/odluke/povuci_pdf.php?pid=22419

Cortright, D. and Lopez, G., 2000, *The Sanctions Decade: Assessing UN Strategies in the 1990s*. Boulder: Lynne Rienner.

Cortright, D., 2001, 'A Hard Look at Iraq Sanctions', *The Nation*, reproduced December 3. Bonn: Global Policy Forum Europe. http://www.globalpolicy.org/security/sanction/iraq1/sanclook.htm

Crawford, A., 2006, 'Networked Governance and the Post-Regulatory State?: Steering, rowing and anchoring the provision of policing and security', *Theoretical Criminology*, 10, 4, November 1, 449–79. http://tcr.sagepub.com/cgi/content/abstract/10/4/449

Davies, P., Dumbrell, J., Meehan, E., Hames, T. and Williams, S., 2006, 'The Grinding Reality of Realpolitik: Current and future directions in the UK, USA and Europe', *21st Century Society*, 1, 1, June, 73–98. http://taylorandfrancis.metapress.com/content/m113wj670u603qp7.

Delegation of the European Commission, 2006a, Temporary International Mechanism for Assistance to the Palestinian people: Implementation modalities applying to the European Community contribution, memo pp. 3. Cairo: European Commission and others. http://www.delegy.ec.europa.eu/en/TIM per cent20US-EC per cent20June per cent2015 per cent202006 per cent20rev.pdf

Delegation of the European Commission to the USA, 2006b, *Middle East: EU-Crafted Temporary International Mechanism Fully Operational*, Press Release, No. 75/06, September 1. Washington: EU. http://www.eurunion.org/News/press/2006/20060075.htm

Department of Institutional Integrity, 2006, *Annual Integrity Report – Fiscal Year 2005/06*, 1–64. Washington: World Bank. http://siteresources.worldbank.org/INTDOII/Resources/complete.pdf

Drezner, D.,1999, *The Sanctions Paradox: Economic Statecraft and International Relations*. Cambridge: Cambridge University Press, 1–362

Dupont, B., Grabosky, P. and Shearing, C., 2005, 'The Governance of Security in Weak and Failing States', *Criminology and Criminal Justice*, 3, 4, 331–49. http://crj.sagepub.com/cgi/content/abstract/3/4/331

Edwards, A. and Hughes, G., 2005, Editorial, *Theoretical Criminology* (special issue on The Governance of Safety in Europe), 9, 3, 259–263.

Eleftheriadis, P., 2003, 'Cosmopolitan Law', *European Law Journal*, vol. 9, No. 2, 241–63.

Financial Times, 2006, 'World Bank Move to Reclaim Stolen Funds', Krishna Guha in Washington, *Financial Times*, September 7. http://www.ft.com/cms/s/9166fd4a-3e9a-11db-b4de-0000779e2340,dwp_uuid=2114d450-df62–11da-afe4–0000779e2340.html

Financial Times, 2007, 'Palestinian Aid Policies "Backfiring"' (newspaper report), by Harvey Morris in Jerusalem, *Financial Times*, February 7. http://www.ft.com/cms/s/ae85d588-b62a-11db-9eea-0000779e2340.html

Fischer-Lescano, A. and Teubner, G., 2004, 'Regime-Collisions: The Vain Search for Legal Unity in the Fragmentation of Global Law', *Michigan Journal of International Law*, 25, Summer, 999–1046.

Fitzpatrick, T., 2001, 'New Agendas for Social Policy and Criminology: Globalisation, Urbanism and the Emerging Post-Social Security State', *Social Policy and Administration*, 35, 2, 212–29.

Fratianni, M. and Pattison, J., 2002, 'International Financial Architecture and International Financial Standards', *The Annals of the American Academy of Political and Social Science*, 579, 183–99.

Fulcher, J., 2000, 'Globalisation, the Nation-State and Global Society', *Sociological Review*, 48, 4, 522–43.

Garland, D, 1985, *Punishment and Welfare*, Aldershot: Gower.

Ghani, A., Lockhart, C. and Carnahan, M., 2005, *Closing the Sovereignty Gap: An Approach to State-Building*, September, 1–20. London: Overseas Development Institute. http://www.odi.org.uk/Publications/working_papers/wp253.pdf

Giddens, T., 1990, *The Consequences of Modernity*. Cambridge: Polity Press.

Glasius, M., 2003, 'How Activists Shaped the Court', *The Magazine*, December, Washington: Crimes of War Project. http://www.crimesofwar.org/icc_magazine/icc-glasius.html.

Glasius, M., 2004, *The International Criminal Court: A Global Civil Society Achievement*. London: Routledge (Advances in International Relations and Global Politics).

Godfrey, B. and Dunstall, G., 2005, *Crime and Empire 1840–1940: criminal justice in local and global context*. Cullompton: Willan.

Goldstone, R., 2000. *For Humanity: Reflections of a war crimes investigator*. New Haven, CT: Yale University Press.

Hagan, J. and Ivković, S.K., 2006, 'War Crimes, Democracy, and the Rule of Law in Belgrade, the Former Yugoslavia, and Beyond', *Annals of the American Academy of Political and Social Science*, 605, 1, 129–51. http://ann.sagepub.com/cgi/content/abstract/605/1/129.

Hagan, J., 2005, 'Crimes of War and the Force of Law', *Social Forces*, vol. 83, No. 4, June, 1499–1534.

Hagan, J., Schoenfeld, H. and Palloni, A., 2006, 'The Science of Human Rights, War Crimes, and Humanitarian Emergencies', *Annual Review of Sociology*, August, 32, 329–49.

Hagan, J., Levi, R. and Ferrales, G., 2006, 'Swaying the Hand of Justice: The Internal and External Dynamics of Regime Change at the International Criminal Tribunal for the Former Yugoslavia', *Law and Social Inquiry*, vol. 31, Issue 3, summer, 585–616.

Hardt, M. and Negri, A., 2000, *Empire*. Cambridge, MA; London: Harvard University Press. http://www.angelfire.com/cantina/negri

Harlow, C., 2006, 'Global Administrative Law: The Quest for Principles and Values', *European Journal of International Law*, 17, 1, 187–214. http://ejil.oxfordjournals.org/cgi/content/abstract/17/1/187.

Hirst, P. and Thompson, G., 1996, *Globalisation in Question*. Cambridge: Polity Press, 186–9.

Hobbs, D., 1998, 'Going Down the Glocal: the Local Context of Organised Crime', *Howard Journal of Criminal Justice*, 37, 4, November, 407–22.

ICTY Committee Established to Review the NATO Bombing Campaign Against the Federal Republic of Yugoslavia, 1999, Final Report to the Prosecutor by the Committee Established to Review the NATO Bombing Campaign Against the Federal Republic of Yugoslavia, unpagenated. The Hague: International Criminal Tribunal for the Former Yugoslavia. http://www.un.org/icty/pressreal/nato061300.htm.

ICTY Prosecutor, 2000, *Prosecutor's Report on the Nato Bombing Campaign*, 13 June, PR/ P.I.S./ 510-e, 1 page. The Hague: International Criminal Tribunal for the Former Yugoslavia, Office of the Prosecutor. http://www.un.org/icty/pressreal/p510-e.htm.

Institute for Policy Studies et al. 2006, *The IMF: Shrink it or Sink it: A Consensus Declaration and Strategy Paper*, Monday, 24 July. Bangkok: Focus on the Global South/CUSRI. http://www.focusweb.org/content/view/985/27/.

International Court of Justice, 1999, Legality of Use of Force (Yugoslavia v. United States of America): the Court rejects the request for the indication of provisional measures submitted by Yugoslavia and dismisses the case, Press Release 99/33. The Hague: International Court of Justice. http://www.icj-cij.org/icjwww/ipresscom/iPress1999/ipresscom9933_iyus_19990602.htm.

International Court Of Justice, 2004, *Case Concerning Legality of Use Of Force (Serbia and Montenegro v. United Kingdom) Preliminary Objections*, General List No. 113, 15 December. The Hague: International Court of Justice. http://www.icj-cij.org/icjwww/idocket/iyuk/iyukframe.htm.

International Criminal Court, 1998 (2002 entry into force), *Rome Statute of the International Criminal Court*, 1–77. The Hague: International Court of Justice, Public Information and Documentation Section. http://www.icc-cpi.int/library/about/officialjournal/Rome_Statute_120704-EN.pdf.

International Criminal Court, 2007, Pre-Trial Chamber I commits Thomas Lubanga Dyilo for trial, *ICC Newsletter*, 12, January, 1–8. The Hague: International Court of Justice http://www.icc-cpi.int/library/about/newsletter/files/ICC-NL12–200701_En.pdf.

Ivković, S.K. and Hagan, J., 2006, 'The Politics of Punishment and the Siege of Sarajevo: Toward a Conflict Theory of Perceived International (In)Justice', *Law & Society Review*, 40, 2, June, 369–410. http://www.ingentaconnect.com/content/bpl/lasr/2006/00000040/00000002/art00004.

Thibault, J.-F., 2001, 'As if the World Were a Virtual Global Polity: The political philosophy of global governance', *First Press*, 4, Sussex University. http://www.theglobalsite.ac.uk/press/108thibault.htm.

Jessop, B., 2001, 'Bringing the State Back In (Yet Again): Reviews, Revisions, Rejections, and Redirections', *International Review of Sociology/Revue Internationale de Sociologie*, 11, 2, 149–73. http://eprints.lancs.ac.uk/171.

Jessop, B., 2004, 'Hollowing out the 'Nation-State' and Multilevel Governance' in Kennett, P., (ed.), *A Handbook of Comparative Social Policy*. Edward Elgar Publishing, Cheltenham, UK. Lancaster: Lancaster E-Prints.

Jordana, J. and Levi-Faur, D. (eds), 2004, *The Politics of Regulation: Examining Regulatory Institutions and Instruments in the Governance Age*. Cheltenham: Edward Elgar.

Kingsbury, B., 2003, The International Legal Order, IILJ Working Paper (History and Theory of International Law Series). New York: N.Y. University School of Law, http://www.iilj.org/papers/2003/2003.1 per cent20Kingsbury.pdf.

(Original source: same author, title and date, chapter 13 in Cane, P. and Tushnet, M. (eds), *Oxford Handbook of Legal Studies*, Oxford University Press.)

Kingsbury, B., Krisch, N. and Stewart, R., 2004, The Emergence of Global Administrative Law, IILJ Working Paper, 2004/1, 1–13. New York: New York University. http://www.iilj.org/papers/2004/documents/2004.1Kingsbury KrischStewart.pdf.

Krisch, N. and Kingsbury, B., 2004, 'Introduction: Global Governance and Global Administrative Law in the International Legal Order', *European Journal of International Law*, 17, 1, 1–13. http://www.ejil.org/journal/Vol17/No1/art1.pdf.

Levy, D. and Sznaider, N., 2006, 'Sovereignty Transformed: A sociology of human rights', *British Journal of Sociology*, 57, 4, 657–76.

Linklater, A. and Suganami, H., 2006, *The English School of International Relations: A Contemporary Reassessment*, in the series Cambridge Studies in International Relations, number 102. Cambridge: Cambridge University Press.

Loader, I. and Walker, N., 2004, 'State of Denial? Rethinking the governance of security', (Review of: *Governing Security: Explorations in policing and justice*, Les Johnston and Clifford Shearing. London: Routledge, 2003), *Punishment and Society*, 6, 2, 221–8. http://pun.sagepub.com/cgi/content/refs/6/2/221.

Moran, J., 2005, 'State Power in the War on Terror: A Comparative Analysis of the UK and USA', *Crime, Law and Social Change*, 44, 4–5, December, 335–59.

Mythen, G. and Walklate, S., 2006, 'Criminology and Terrorism: Which thesis? Risk society or governmentality?' *British Journal of Criminology*, 46, 379–98.

Muncie, J., 2005, 'The Globalisation of Crime Control – The case of youth and juvenile justice: neo-liberalism, policy convergence and international conventions', *Theoretical Criminology*, 9, 1, 35–64. http://tcr.sagepub.com/cgi/content/short/9/1/35.

Orakhelashvili, A., 2006, 'The Idea of European International Law', *European Journal of International Law*, 17, 2. http://www.ejil.org/journal/Vol17/No2/art1.pdf.

Oxfam, 2006, *EU Must Resume Aid to Palestinian Authority*, Press Release, 14 September. Oxford: Oxfam International Secretariat. http://www.oxfam.org/en/news/pressreleases2006/pr060914_palestine.

Parenti, M., 2000. *To Kill a Nation: The attack on Yugoslavia*. London: Verso.

Passavant, P., 2005, 'The Strong Neo-liberal State: Crime, Consumption, Governance', *Theory & Event*, 8, 3, 1–48.

Paterson, M., 1992, International Affairs (Royal Institute of International Affairs 1944–), 68, 4, October 1992, 733–4.

Picciotto, S., 2006, Regulatory Networks and Global Governance, extract from proceedings of W.G. Hart Legal Workshop, 27–29 June 2006, London, 1–14. Lancaster: Lancaster E-Prints. http://eprints.lancs.ac.uk/232.

Puchala, D.J., 2005, 'World Hegemony and the United Nations', *International Studies Review*, 7, 571–84.

Rainbow, P. and Rose, N., 2003, *Thoughts on the Concept of Biopower Today*, 1–25. Berkeley: Molecular Sciences Institute. http://www.molsci.org/files/Rose_Rabinow_Biopower_Today.pdf. Also available at: http://www.lse.ac.uk/collections/sociology/pdf/RabinowandRose-BiopowerToday03.pdf.

Rich, B., 2002, 'The World Bank under James Wolfenson', in Pincus, J. and Winters, J. (eds), *Reinventing the World Bank*, 20–53 of 288. New York: Cornell University Press.

Roach, S., 2005, 'Arab States and the Role of Islam in the International Criminal Court', *Political Studies*, 53, 143–61.

Rosenau, J., 1992, 'Governance, Order and Change in World Politics' in Rosenau, J. and Czempiel, E.-O. (eds), *Governance without Government: Order and Change in World Politics*. Cambridge and NY: Cambridge University Press (out of print).

Rothe, D. and Mullins, C., 2006, 'The International Criminal Court and United States Opposition: A structural contradictions model', *Crime, Law & Social Change*, 45, 201–26.

Schabas, W., 2004, 'United States Hostility to the International Criminal Court: It's All About the Security Council', *European Journal of International Law*, 15, 4, September, 701–20.

Sheptycki, J. and Wardak, A., 2006, *Transnational and Comparative Criminology*. Abingdon: GlassHouse Press.

Slaughter, A.-M. and Zaring, D., 2006, 'Networking Goes International: An Update', *Annual Review of Law and Social Science*, vol. 2, December, 211–29. http://arjournals.annualreviews.org/doi/abs/10.1146/annurev.lawsocsci.1.041604.120026?journalCode=lawsocsci

Stiglitz, J, 2002, *Globalisation and Its Discontents*. New York: Norton.

Simpson, G., 2004, 'Politics, Sovereignty, Remembrance' in McGoldrik, D., Rowe, P. and Donnelly, E. (eds), *The Permanent International Criminal Court: Legal and Policy Issues*, pp. 47–60, Oxford: Hart Publishing (Studies in International Law).

Stubbs, P., 2005, 'Stretching Concepts Too Far? Multi-Level Governance, Policy Transfer and the Politics of Scale in South East Europe', *Southeast European Politics*, VI, 2, November, 66–87.

Swiss Federal Office for Foreign Economic Affairs (ed.), 1998, *Report on the Expert Seminar on Targeting UN Financial Sanctions*, 17–19 September, Interlaken, 1–140. Bern: Swiss State Secretariat for Economic Affairs SECO. Available at: http://www.seco.admin.ch/themen/00513/00620/00639/00641/index.html?lang=en.

Van Swaaningen, R., 1997, *Critical Criminology: Visions from Europe*. London: Sage.

Weller, M., 2002, 'Undoing the Global Constitution: UN Security Council action on the International Criminal Court', *International Affairs*, 78, 4, 693–712. http://www.blackwell-synergy.com/doi/abs/10.1111/1468–2346.00275?journalCode=inta.

Whitmore, B., 2003, 'Letter from Belgrade', *The Nation*, 276, 17, May 5. http://www.thenation.com/doc/20030505/whitmore.

Wikipedia, 2007, International Monetary Fund, *Wikipedia*, http://en.wikipedia.org/wiki/Imf.

Winters, J., 'Criminal Debt', in Pincus, J. and Winters, J. (eds), *Reinventing the World Bank*, 1–288. New York: Cornell University Press. http://www.cornellpress.cornell.edu/cup_detail.taf?ti_id=3861.

Yang, L., 2005, 'On the Principle of Complementarity in the Rome Statute of the International Criminal Court', *Chinese Journal of International Law*, 4, 1, 121–32.

Zedner, L, 2007, 'Pre-crime and post-criminology?', *Theoretical Criminology*, 11, 2, 261–81.

Chapter 9
Governing through Globalised Crime: Thoughts on the Transition from Terror

Mark Findlay

Introduction

Crime and criminalisation are constantly employed by the nation state as discriminatory governance tools. Currently, the global political hegemony (Findlay: 2008: chap. 7) advances crimes against humanity, and terrorism in particular, as instrumental in the promotion of the 'new' global risk/security agenda, and consequent *para-justice* control regimes (Duffy: 2005). Along with the argued utility of crime in global governance (Findlay: 2008: chaps 1 and 9), the fear of crime and the valorisation of crime victims are identified as vital forces over the crime/governance nexus (Findlay: 2006). With international terrorism the contemporary justification for a risk/security nexus for global governance criminal justice is both relied upon and contorted for the achievement of violent control agendas (Aksu and Camilleri: 2002).

While it is accepted that crime may frame the broader role of regulatory power (Garland: 2001) it is now apparent in the global context that crime and control have become central planks of international governance, in a divided world. Essential for this is:

- the magnification of crime (through terror) as a threat to legitimate world order;
- the construction of the crime victim as 'humanity';
- the representation of the victim as the idealised citizen subject of the global community;
- the responsibility of the representatives of the 'global community' to fight crime as part of the process to restore post-conflict societies, and
- to take the political subjects of the global community beyond idealised fictions, into a realm of security, away from terrorist threat as defined by the dominant political hegemony.[1]

---

1 Due to the constraints on this chapter there is not space here to fully argue the nature of this hegemony or to appropriately problematise its entity and significance. This is attempted in Findlay, 2008. Against the war on terror metaphor (post 9/11) and accepting the place of western 'neo-liberal' economic and political dogma behind the modernising era

Central to this domain of threat and security is the vast and imagined possibility of victimisation. Having said this it would be incorrect to assume that the crime/global governance nexus is founded on a victim constituency, or even aspirations for humanity (Findlay: 2009; Findlay and Henham: 2010). The place of the victim in global governance remains declaratory. It is a key to the claimed legitimacy of a global hegemony that it retains the authority to distinguish and valorise victims (Findlay: 2006). In global governance, as yet, victimisation is a political rather than practical utility. This admission may become less viable as global risk moves away from the sectarian metaphor of terror, to more encompassing harms consequent on economic collapse and environmental degradation which are inevitable and in train.

If the fear of crime and terror as a prevailing threat predetermines global political control agendas, then any dominant hegemony claiming the right to identify the terrorist, and the capacity to protect the citizen, will retrieve their political currency even if this does not progress beyond narrative representation (Findlay: 2006). Further, as the recent relationship between global governance and international criminal justice suggests (Findlay: 2008), the fragile legitimacy of dominant political alliances has inspired concurrent resort to *para-justice*[2] strategies wherein violence and oppression run contrary to the protective limitations which demark conventional justice responses.

Jonathan Simon has developed the paradigm that crime metaphors are crucial to state-centred governance. This chapter moves outside a state-centred jurisdictional focus to engage with globalisation, international criminal justice, and global crime as contexts for global governance. While metaphor is relevant for conceptualising governance through crime, morphology is a more incisive paradigm from which to address crime and governance in globalisation.

Simon (2001–2002) identified two metaphorical directions crucial to a particular legislative reliance on crime as governance:[3]

- the rise of the 'street' as the nexus for a war on crime style governance and as a consequence,
- the extraordinary emphasis this placed on policing in managing virtually all organisations, public and private (Simon: 2001–2002: 1053).

---

of globalisation, this hegemony is equated with the loose (and often unwilling) coalition supporting the US Iraqi intervention.

2 As with *para-politics*, the concept of *para-justice* has no definitional certainty. Here we are employing the notion to encapsulate those control responses which follow on from proscribed behaviours which in other circumstances might be processed through conventional criminal justice. Violence, intimidation and a denial of due process are characteristic of *para-justice*. Rather than being dismissed as institutional injustice *para-justice* makes claims for institutional and process credibility through the determinations of military tribunals in particular, and justifies excessive responses through the necessities of war.

3 President Johnson's *Safe Street's Act*.

From an international/global as opposed to a local/jurisdictional/state-based perspective this chapter augments these directions towards:

- the rise of the 'global community' as the habitas for crime (and eventually control);
- the indication of 'humanity' as the global crime victim, and
- the particularisation of a dominant global political hegemony as 'policing' international security against crime, especially terrorism.

International crime control has become the discourse of the 'liberal democratic' interlocutor. The idealised political subject (the 'global community' or 'humanity') is realised through the definition of 'actual' threats, and legitimate responses (Findlay: 2006). Presidents and prime ministers speak on behalf of victim communities and determine what qualifies as crimes of aggression and crimes against humanity. These political discriminations accord legitimacy to idealised victims and alienate and delegitimise the motivations and actions of those who challenge the dominant political hegemony (Findlay: 2009).

The dependencies of global governance on international criminal justice, and in turn on a risk/security environment for globalisation have developed reactively. They are repressive, recursive and regressive. International terrorism has necessitated for the dominant political hegemony a shift away from late-modern economic culturation and towards a containment model which relies on criminalisation and justice/control supports (often following military or violent intervention) to counter the challenge of alternative cultural and political alignments. This is about to change. With the challenge to the dominant economic model of free-market capitalism by the financial collapse of 2008/2009, international security concerns (and their internationalising capacity) have shifted from terror to commercial survival. Globalisation as a recursive paradigm both advances and retreats in the face of economic risk. Modernisation is on hold. If the Westernised international financial framework weathers the storm then the risk on the horizon is global warming and its dire consequences for economic stability and modernisation.

This evolution to a contemporary globalisation of terror/risk criminal justice/security has not been without its radical coincidences, or its longstanding antipathies. The destruction on September 11, grounded in part in the struggle between fundamentalism and the 'liberal' ideologies and perceived economic imperialism of the West, has become the backdrop for a *new age of globalisation*. Crime and control within this transition appear as:

- a process to consolidate political victory for an coalition of dependant states, through an emergent and formal international criminal justice (Findlay and Henham: 2005);
- a consequence where an opposed political alignment, wherein religion, economy and morality are determined as the enemy for war discourse at many levels;

- a recognition of the need by the dominant hegemony for legitimacy through 'justice' as well as force, in the face of violent challenge;
- a critical growth in specialised technologies and exclusive knowledge that in turn fuel governing through crime/control, and
- the defining of a new set of privileged subjects for government, and an old set of enemies for exclusion.

Valorisation counterbalances demonisation. The 'streets' to be 'policed' are now populated by the global community and are beyond state jurisdiction, legislation and dominion (Roberts: 2005). The security of the idealised citizen/victim is the justification for meeting the terrorist risk. Thereby, the local/cultural relative motivations for terrorist violence are subsumed in a more simplistic anti-crime discourse. The indicia of good global governance are successes in the 'war on terror' fought in the tribunals and not the trenches.

Yet legitimacy is fragile. This hegemony is a loose and negotiated order. It lacks true legislative, juridical or executive authority beyond metaphor or concession. This has profound significance for the embryonic institutional forms of international criminal justice (such as the International Criminal Court) which are struggling for authority without the benefit of a grounded and confirmed constitutional legality (Clark: 2002). The citizenship which institutions of global governance are said to serve is ceded to them rather than democratically included. Their normative foundations have few deep or common cultural roots (Findlay and Henham: 2010: chap. 1). The institutions and formal processes of global governance are searching for a framework of governability beyond military might (Findlay: 2008: chap. 1). The risk/security nexus particularly mirrored in international terrorism has to some extent recently provided this. It is now a governance founded in fear and the assurance of the protection that selective citizenship accords, dependent as it does on sectarian loyalty (Findlay: 2006).

However, the legitimating potential of international criminal justice has, in certain control contexts, been supplemented by the dominant global political alliance, with a *para-justice* paradigm. The violent and oppressive nature of this second level of 'justice' has challenged the legitimacy of control interventions as a consequence of denying some central justice 'balances' which international criminal justice propounds, particularly where 'rights' are at issue (Duffy: 2005). The assumed necessity and expediency of *para-justice* has made the legitimating capacity of international criminal justice more potent and less negotiable (Wilson and Lindsey: 2009).

In the context of *para-politics* (wherein both organised crime and terrorism are said to have their place) the characteristics of *para-justice* are predominant in control strategies. The adoption of *para-justice* by the dominant political alliance in this contemporary phase of globalisation reveals an intriguing intersection between the aims and activations of both political forms. It also suggests in a political sense, the limitations inherent in conventional criminal justice, with an enunciated rights dimension, as a governance tool. This is particularly so when the authority of the global hegemony remains connected to violence and militarism. As the risk/security dimension of globalisation moves on to concerns for economic stability and environmental sustainability the challenge to ICJ as a governance tool may also move from violent justice to an essential engagement with pluralism.

The conflict language of this dominant political alliance sees international criminal justice as well as military intervention engaging both the moral political hegemony, and the emergence of its strong military imagery in its control discourse (*para* and conventional), are paradoxical at a global level. Wars against crime are designed to replace military intervention with criminal justice. While war imagery invokes a simplistic and dominant process of demonisation as a consequence of 'victors justice', systematic measures against the criminalised enemy and political threats which they represent.

Accepting the potential for crime to facilitate governance at the state level, this chapter explores the current and apparent synergy between globalisation, a risk/security nexus, and the structure and form of international criminal justice and governance, particularly in the context of international terrorism. It also speculates on the tension between the legitimating capacity of international criminal justice as a crucial agency of governance, against the reversion to violent and intimidatory control practices of *para-justice*. From here, the analysis questions whether a shift in the conceptualisation of global risk/security will produce a consequent repositioning of criminal justice in global governance.

The 'New' Globalisation[4]

In the *Globalisation of Crime* (Findlay: 1999) we envisaged globalisation as the 'collapsing of time and space', in a political age where modernisation and materialism promoted common culturation through economic development. The 'new' globalisation considered here takes mass communication as a given and modernisation as the medium for the advancement of international political hegemony. A risk/security nexus which has emerged from the domination by (and violent challenges to) this hegemony, provides a contemporary international context for both crime control and governance issues. With the present (somewhat limited) legitimating potential of international criminal justice above military intervention in post-conflict states (Findlay and Henham: 2005: esp. chap. 7) the connection between criminalisation and governance, in a world where legitimacy is violently contested, is inextricable.

Today is an age of risk and security wherein global terror is the focus. Tomorrow it will be economic stability and environmental sustainability, although some might say tomorrow is upon us.

---

4 For the purposes of this argument I am not critiquing the reality or utility of 'globalisation' as an analytical concept.

From the perspective of 'liberal' Western democracies vying for global hegemony, 9/11 was the crunch point – the apocalypse now. In these scenarios of terrorism lie the seeds of the 'new' globalisation. The radical conflation which was '9/11' complemented long-standing antipathies and ushered in a regime of 'war' against ideology, dominion and a redefinition of global citizenship. The restructuring of jurisdiction, standing, citizenship, humanity, community and exclusion, essential for the new age of globalisation, have their justifications and projections in 9/11. Global governance through reaction became the reluctant priority. Battle lines were redrawn. Global crime agendas were re-ordered. Security priorities are realigned. States of war were more universalised. Crime victimisation and the legitimate claims to global citizenship were conflated. The fissures of exclusion and inclusion were drawn against criminality and victimisation across global communities. Governance became defined by criminalisation and the restoration of global security.

Along with this, the 'risk society' has surpassed modernisation as the organising framework for globalisation. 'Victim communities' identified at risk and valorised as without blame require the intercession and security proffered by the dominant political 'culture', as with modernisation the 'underdeveloped' and transitional cultures required material advancement through the dominant economy (Findlay: 1999: chap. 2).

The common push to a mono-culture in globalisation, similar to earlier mercantile epochs, has had to defer an economic priority in order to address the violent challenges of contesting cultures.[5] Rather than engage with the complexity of this resistance, a methodology of criminalisation is employed by the dominant political hegemony, and the immediate motivations for globalisation become redefined in response to crime risk, as security/control.

Can Globalised Crime Construct Governance?

About governance Foucalt suggests that the task of acting on the actions of others (government) is bound up with ways of *reasoning* about governing (Foucault: 2002). In the sense of globalised governance within the 'new' globalisation, the dominant political hegemony has tended to define what is *knowable* and 'more importantly to produce truth selectively' (Simon: 2001–2002: 1063). This 'truth' has emerged as a bi-product of its own strategies of intervention, and their legitimacy through the earlier-argued crime/security nexus. A particular notion of

5 The similarities might be extended in contrast with the militaristic mercantile companies in Asia and the New World, chartered by their sponsoring states to make war, colonise, and deliver criminal justice along with the predominant commitment of wealth creation. None of this, however, operated in the same atmosphere of internationalisation as we see it today.

governance has been rationalised both through challenges to international security and 'exclusive' approaches to its restoration.

Therefore, the *ways of reasoning about governing* in the recent global context have in significant measure focused around:

- new emergent crime risks
- consequent challenges to international security
- actual harm of the global citizen and global communities
- requiring a force-based response from the 'democratic' international hegemony
- legitimating a particular form of international justice intervention
- repositioning ongoing concepts of sovereignty, citizenship, legal standing and alien attack (Findlay: 2006)

The translation of this reasoning through epithets and campaigns such as the 'war on terror' has moved the nexus between crime and governance from the politics of the ideal, into processes whereby criminal justice and the control potentials it offers significantly reconstruct and determine the legitimate interlocutors of global conflict (Findlay and Henham: 2005). In fact, global conflict, and the re-institution of post-conflict states are in part now depend on the arena of international criminal justice for legitimate resolution (Findlay: 2008). Resistance through violence no matter how destructive is marginalised and relegated by the determination of the criminal liability of its principal perpetrators. The tribunal has become essential to the restoration of governability post-military intervention.

The importance of military intervention in contemporary global governance cannot be underestimated. Even when, through economic sanctions, the collapse of civil regulation is identified as the reluctant trigger to military muscle, the heavy hand of global hegemony in the form of war is now the established precursor to formal international criminal justice resolutions (Brownsword: 2004).

Global governance around a political discourse of the *war on terror* seems now reliant on risk/security balances. An investigation of the structures which are said to achieve and maintain these balances (morphology) align with and support the central structures and institutions of global governance where globalisation addresses risk (crime) concerns for security (control).

The structures of the relationship between risk and security, mirrored in contemporary global governance include:

- jurisdiction – international alliances beyond 'super' states and regions
- location – the global 'community'
- citizenship – idealised members of that community
- standing – power to determine the legitimate victim, to empower the interlocutor, to authorise the judiciary and to disenfranchise the perpetrator
- dominion – the dominant political hegemony

- authority – control over the institutions of international justice first through 'victor's' status and then through control of international organisations
- enforceability – initially through violent military intervention followed by monopoly over investigation, policing, trial and punishment
- amnesty – monopolisation over rewarding complicity and awarding mercy
- reconciliation – meter the availability of retributive and restorative outcomes

Employing the example of terrorism and its containment (from the perspective of the dominant hegemony):

- jurisdiction is the attack against democracy and 'liberal' values
- location is within those communities which enjoy democratic government
- citizenship is accorded the idealised victim and denied the perpetrator
- standing is only as a consequence of victimisation within the context of citizenship
- dominion comes as a consequence of 'liberal' democracy
- authority is initially force-based but eventually legitimated through the monopoly over justice paradigms
- enforceability comes from superior force, widest communication and control over 'knowledge', and through the support of alliances and coalitions with mutual risk/security agendas
- amnesty is denied as a consequence of terror, except where it is perpetrated within the hegemony
- reconciliation is marginalised in favour of retribution and deterrence

This summarises a passage of crime control and governance within the contemporary international risk/security agenda. To move on and detail the institutions and processes responsible for international criminal justice resolutions of risk would identify further the synergy between justice in this context and identifiers of global governance (Findlay and Henham: 2005). These would include (but not exhaustively):

- prevailing constitutional legality
- 'supra-national' legislative power
- a set of rules and regulations for administering criminal liability and punishment
- a fabric of public and private policing
- state monopoly over prosecution
- power to appoint and authorise judges
- executive responsibility for the nature and duration of penalty

It is not difficult to determine the separation of powers implicit in this structure which is said to confirm democratic government.

This too holds for the consideration of *para-justice* responses to crimes such as terrorism:

- prevailing authority to create and maintain alternative 'legalities'
- 'supra-national' exclusion of both the perpetrators and the mechanisms for their containment beyond the conventional jurisdiction of the state
- extraordinary rules and regulations for administering criminal liability and punishment, which in turn rely on complex discretionary delegations and largely anonymous activation
- a process of investigation and policing which is covert, co-optive, compulsory and confrontational[6]
- state monopoly over prosecution, and more importantly when to detain and punish without prosecution
- power to sanction and penalise without the confirmation of judicial authority
- enforceability through superior force and through the construction of control 'technologies', plus the clandestine application of terror against terror, torture against aggression
- collapsing of military and quasi-judicial powers, and the translation of perpetrators into combatants
- executive responsibility for the nature and duration of penalty

The application of conventional and para-justice paradigms is not essentially a question of choice. But insofar as they may be known to operate against the same 'risk' for the restoration of global security, they may tend to challenge legitimacy, each to each.

From the perspectives of crime control and governance justice and para-justice responses are not designated or activated in terms of the nature and extent of harm to humanity (Findlay and Henham: 2010). Were this the case then there might be some confidence in the continued significance of international criminal justice for global governance as concepts of risk shift from terror. Where the cause of risk isn't inextricably connected to criminalisation (such as with environmental degradation) is crime control the determinant of global security responses?

Can Crime Control Determine Considerations of Risk and Security?

Garland (2001), as did Cohen (1985) before him, argues that community protection is now the dominant theme of penal policy. The risk here is unidirectional. Crime poses a threat to the security of the individual and the community, therefore the state is obliged to minimise that risk through control. The public supports this. On the other hand:

6 For a discussion of these styles of policing, see Findlay and Zvekic (1993), chap. 2.

> In these matters (harsh state control interventions) the public appears to be (or is represented as) decidedly risk-averse, and intensely focused on the risk of depredation by unrestrained criminals. The risk of unrestrained state authorities, of arbitrary power and the violation of civil liberties seems no longer to figure prominently in public concern. (Garland: 2001: 12)

Garland says more than that new crime control developments have 'adapted' and 'responded' to the late modern world and to its political and cultural values. He advances these developments as 'creating that world, helping to constitute the meaning of late modernity' (p. 194). Along with managing problems of crime and insecurity, he argues, crime control 'institutionalises a set of responses to these problems that are themselves consequential in their social impact'.

Transposed to a global context, and with the risk being terrorism, and the control response being both violence and 'justice' (Findlay: 2006), strong messages for the managing of risk and the 'taming of chance' travel through the new institutions of international criminal justice. These in turn lead on to an environment of international governance in which the citizen accepts restrictions of liberty which would have been intolerable in an era of globalisation outside this risk/security nexus, particularly when democracy was marketed as the ideology of modernisation. Now:

> Spatial controls, situational controls, managerial controls, system controls, social controls self-controls – in one realm after another, we now find the imposition of intensive regimes of regulation, inspection and control and, in the process, our civic culture becomes increasingly less tolerant and inclusive, increasingly less capable of trust. After a long-term process of expanding individual freedom and relaxing cultural and social restraints, control is now being reemphasised in every area of social life – with the singular and startling exception of the economy, from whose deregulated domain most of today's major risks routinely emerge. (Garland: 2001: 194–5)

Prophetically in the global context Garland identifies, along with the rise of this partial concern for risk/security control agendas, the characteristic of reaction. A new sense of international disorder pervaded the close of the twentieth century and was accompanied by a renewed interest in global order and world governance. Crucial to governance and order internationally, as seen from the perspective of the dominant political hegemony, was addressing:

- dangerously inadequate controls
- rapidly and violently emergent challenges to the control of that hegemony.

Initial responses were militaristic. But as is always the case, these were unsustainable. Criminal justice has been conscripted to take management of the control of global risk (Findlay and Henham: 2005). Of course this is not an exclusive control responsibility, and more violent repression will always be on call in a climate of risk and security where the threat is erratic and incisive. However, international criminal justice is the attractive medium term response because of its perceived potential to enhance the legitimacy of the dominant political hegemony.

Another important feature of the control profile internationally is the redefinition of 'community' and along with it notions of jurisdiction, citizenship and standing. Immersed in community is the potential both for legitimacy and resistance. This will become more the case as risk is increasingly conceptualised in terms of actual, widespread and experienced harm. As the population of victim communities expands and the nature of global risk becomes more visible and intrusive, security/control responses will be forced from symbolic to applied expectations. In this sense, criminal justice may recede to a declaratory role within a pluralist regulatory agenda. The legitimacy of global governance will in turn more probably be measured against whether a wider citizen base is secure than now where a narrow citizen base fears impending insecurity. In the latter state criminal justice and its retributive/deterrent forms have a more convincing if less tested governance place.

Where does Legitimacy Fit Within this Relationship – Contested Reasoning for Governance?

Predominant and prevailing notions of 'truth' are essential in the struggle over the legitimacy of international governance. Prevailing *reasoning* presupposes predominance over 'truth' as a delineator of the government and the governed.

When it comes to considerations of 'truth' in (for instance) the context of terrorist struggle, the contested nature of truth is obvious if also regularly glossed over. Truth is what the suicide bomber is said to die for and what the military and criminal justice responses are set to protect. Can it be the same truth? If not then its relativity becomes a contested objective of the relationship between terror and 'justice' responses. How is the subjectivity of truth here to be managed beyond the force-based authority and supremacy of victor's justice?[7]

In the terrorism/response context it is not so much the nature of truth but its contest which is the connection. The protection of truth is the common justification for the exercise of violence on both sides. Even violent retaliation against say 'genocide' through terrorism claims its legitimacy against 'guilty' or 'blameworthy' violence where truth is at risk. Yet again the relativity of guilt and blame challenge the advance and democratic dominance of a single 'truth' on which the justice response relies.

7 There is a need here for a more detailed consideration of Weber's conditions for the authority of the state.

'Moral standing' is contested where responses to terrorism make exclusive claim to the legitimate use of violence. Those on the other hand who promote reintegrative techniques as against retribution, to more effectively manage original violence, recognise that restorative justice relies on the context of a supportive community if shaming is to be positively applied to offenders (Braithwaite: 1989). Without a supportive context, dependent on a common acceptance of the moral standing of the preferred response, attempts at shaming break down as stigmatic rather than reintegrative. Resort to violence is soon reiterated.

However, in the situation of terrorism/response relationships, moral standing is at the centre of the contest for legitimacy. Reflective communities, in which both the terrorist and the justice responses are marketed, may oppose the moral legitimacy of each other. These are communities in part galvanised through resistance to the external and oppositional claims for moral standing.[8]

Particularly damaging to the justice response is the resistance of terrorist 'communities' over the basis of moral standing. Dworkin's components of the moral standing of law (determinacy, integrity, coherence and wholeness)[9] are difficult for the violent justice response to export when new institutions and processes of incarceration, interrogation, trial and punishment are directed to the terrorist opponent. These novel entities generally contradict or at least strain some of the central protections which make criminal justice in general fair and 'just'.[10]

Criminal justice declares moral standing from within its homogenous realm of 'principle'. Such declaratory governance capability becomes more difficult to maintain as globalised crime/risk priorities move from political discourse to dimensions of daily-experienced harm.

How Do Globalised Crime Priorities Inform the Political Discourse of Globalisation?

As mentioned previously, concepts of crime have traditionally relied on some cultural or jurisdictional situation for their relevance and impact. Implicit in this is the expectation that crime stops at national borders, or at least that it has localised interests. The growing utility of criminal justice as a tool for global governance is stimulated by the recognition of crime/risks which impact the global community (terrorism, economic collapse, environmental degradation).

This is not a new observation. The jurisdictional boundaries of crime, however, can only be explained in terms of legal convenience and legislative limits. As piracy, smuggling, abduction, gun-running and counterfeiting have been crime

8 Moral standing as a legal/constitutional claim to legitimate voice is discussed in Winter (1988).

9 For a discussion off these, see West (1999).

10 For a discussion of the detail of these changes in US criminal justice and their impact on due process, see Gross (2002).

problems for centuries, so too the laws of individual nations have been powerless to control them.

Transnational crime such as terrorism is new only in its technologies and reach, along with the manner in which law enforcement and international agencies have recently identified it as a priority. Again, the selective political representation of crime is the explanation for such a trend. For instance, as governments realise the potential for criminal enterprise to endanger world market structures, capital transfer, national security, and international transport and communication, crime targets are selected out for cooperative action while others, like environmental degradation on a scale well beyond the reach of harm ever caused through terror attacks, are largely ignored. Strategies have been developed, for example, to prevent and prosecute commodity futures fraud and abuses, but an international approach to crimes against the environment is yet to be convincingly settled.

Interestingly, however, it has not been organised crime which has proved to be the economic 'fifth estate'. As much as proponents of free market capitalism might have us believe otherwise it is the system itself and not the illegitimate forces beneath it that risk global economic security. And this is the danger in a simple causal correlation between crime/risk, criminal justice/security in global governance terms. The financial collapse of 2008/2009 occurred as a result of dangerous but condoned banking practice, mostly not criminal, much deemed to be competitive. In this respect the risk, if not criminalised, cannot be addressed by criminal justice or para-justice strategies on their own.

The other difference with transnational crime, represented as a recent problem for globalisation, is the manner in which crime control is reshaped in order to address the difficulties with jurisdiction. Crime control is, in this context, at least a bilateral endeavour. However, in many control strategies for transnational crime the bilateral efforts are stimulated by globalised representations of crime and control priorities.

It is the threat posed both by terrorism and organised crime motivating local jurisdictions to adopt international control agendas. Normally this would be resisted on the basis of the autonomy of criminal justice as a state domain even in the face of international crime threats (Findlay: 1995). By concentrating on representations of organised crime and terrorism, as well as the state response through criminalisation, the local authorities have translated the international significance of crime threat to justify local interventions which may have little real impact within the jurisdiction concerned. It is an example of the impact of internationalism on localised/criminal justice policy.

The threat of global terrorism as a challenge to 'legitimate' political ordering has stimulated the development of extra-ordinary control responses in a similar fashion that organised crime justified extra-legal state reactions under threat (Findlay: 1999: chap. 5). Organised crime and their economies, enterprises and market manipulations were determined, throughout the last century, as challenging legitimate political and economic governance. Further, the application of violence and intimidation by organised crime in its control aspirations were said to require a response in kind by the state. With global terrorism today, the dominant political alliance emphasises the risk of terrorism to legitimate governance and its capacity to compromise the protections of conventional justice to its own ends. *Para-justice* paradigms are promoted in return and legitimated against the nature of the threat and its own methods of 'governance'.

How Does International Criminal Justice Relate to Global Governance

New levels of law-enforcement cooperation across borders have been fostered in a climate of acute threat and exaggerated retaliation (Viano: 1999). By concentrating on the violent and intimidatory behaviours of terrorism, rather than on their organisational structures or expressed motivations, the community is more ready to accept strong medicine to prevent terror in its midst. Interestingly, the state has employed the 'terror' of fear concept to facilitate what might otherwise be law enforcement responses that would meet vocal resistance (McCulloch: 2003). *Para-justice* paradigms gain similar purchase in the strategies for national, regional and global security against the representation of risk which emphasises the challenge to legitimate governance.

Fear or reality, both justice and governance issues depend on constituencies as well as jurisdiction. For international criminal justice and global governance the focus recently is with 'victim communities'. This notion engages:

- individual victims
- the communities of these victims which share their harm
- where wider communities or groups of victims suffer harm
- where the crime is directed at community cohesion or cultural integrity, and
- when violence is motivated by the destruction of what makes communities or cultures (language, art, religion, family structure and so on)

A justification for international criminal justice is crimes against humanity. In this sense 'humanity' has a community or cultural location. Justice should reflect 'humanitarian' concerns in its mandate to protect humanity. Such concerns are only partial, sectarian, or selective in the way contemporary global governance views 'humanity'. Anything outside the legitimate citizenship of the dominant hegemony tends to be removed from the protective ambit of its humanity. The excluded are worthy of destruction rather than protection. The followers receive the patronage so long as they ascribe to the prevailing order.

The dominant hegemony in this climate of international terrorism (be it manifested in the genocide of Rwanda, the ethnic cleansing of the Balkans, or the anticipated and illusive weapons of mass destruction in Iraq) has significantly transferred militaristic intervention at least in part to the jurisdiction of international criminal justice. This is a transition that carries with it expectations for global governance and the legitimation on which it depends. But in keeping with the agenda and exclusive instrumentation of this political alliance, the morphology of international criminal justice for this purpose is made reliant on common notions of the crimes against humanity, the legitimate victim communities and the appropriate retributive responses. This has in fact meant that the formal institutions of international criminal justice have presented limited pathways of access, and professionally removed representation which in turn have not well integrated and connected with these communities. The consequence for global governance has been to constrain the influence of international criminal justice in restoring post-conflict societies.

But ICJ is not about victims and harm as it is not about governance outside context. Much of what we have explored is at least stimulated by the contest of legitimacy. As international criminal justice transforms to better address the needs of victim communities, then its legitimacy, and its power to legitimate as a crucial component of global governance, will be enhanced.

The connection between international criminal justice and global governance is both symbolic and applied (Findlay: 2008). Let's leave symbolism aside for another day. As risk conceptualisations transform from terror to economic stability and environmental sustainability the victim base will expand massively and the influence of symbolic control will exponentially contract. For the present, and in terms of its designated and located context in an age of global terror/risk, the power of international criminal justice in global governance is in recuperating the tattered authority of the dominant hegemony as a consequence of military intervention. And at this level, the justice/governance link is reliant on and determined by the failings of the hegemony as much as the transformational strength and consistency of international criminal justice.

Crime, Control and Governance – More than Metaphor

Roberts' (2005) 'cultural assemblage' well covers the dominant political hegemony which is currently master of international governance, at least at a formal/economic level. It has come together largely within projects of regional government. Its claims to the indicia of *government* are as yet fragile and primitive beyond military victory. The international organisations said to house global governance while representative, are without authority, without the support of this hegemony. The legislature, judicial institutions and executive bureaucracies emergent from these international organisations are dependant (particularly in resource terms) on this hegemony. The endorsement and protection of global citizenship currently resides with the hegemony, not in terms of democratic inclusion and representation, but rather through patronage.

Roberts rightly cautions against rewarding these 'negotiated orders' with the established juridical, legal or jurisdictional order required of the nation state.

> Today, under an onslaught of jural discourse and institutional design, the distinctive rationalities and values of negotiated order, while arguably deserving to be celebrated, are effectively effaced. (Roberts: 2005: 1)

Globalisation invites the discussion of governance in terms such as law, justice, and bureaucracy, without or above the state. For law at least this requires severance from a narrow notion of legislative jurisdiction. In the 'war on terror' discourse there is an invocation to protect 'civilisation' and 'democracy' against violent assault. It is compatible with this celebration of preferred international political paradigms, to view law as 'cosmology'. In this sense, law and its institutions are engaged in the enterprise of 'imagining and articulating what we want the social world to be' (Roberts: 2005: 6). Law in governance in this sense links the discursive formulation of rules and process to an articulation of preferred world order.

At the declaratory level, I would argue, criminal justice can retain a key role in a pluralist regulatory strategy even where global risk moves away from the sectarian and symbolic (terror) and towards the uniformly harmful and culturally indiscriminate (environmental degradation). There is no doubt that politics will continue its fascination with governing through penal provision. The challenge will be for lawyers and justice professionals to argue their relevance in a more pluralist regulatory world beyond the status of normative proscription or 'show-trial' intervention.

Law as cosmology is also supportive of governance through 'leaders and followers' which goes well beyond the inclusive occupation and responsibilities of democracy. While democracy is celebrated as worthy of protection by the dominant international hegemony, its aspirations to global governance are not democratic but oligarchic. Justice within this oligarchy tends to be institutionalised, formal, non-accountable and professionalised. It is thereby consistent with and supportive of oligarchic governance.

If globalisation even in an age of risk and security retains a commitment towards a single culture perpetration (risk) single culture victimisation (sectarian securitisation) (Findlay: 1999), the preferred justice may continue to be exclusive and not pluralist in its authority, coverage or outreach. Such a version of 'justice' also tends to legitimate oligarchic governance rather than to seek legitimacy from it. This is because the paradoxical 'due process' trajectory of conventional international criminal justice (even if not its procedures) is towards a concern for humanity and its communities of victims. This then becomes another ground on which the dominant political hegemony claims the legitimacy of its constituency and their patronage.

As risk and security concerns become more universalised, actual and intrusive across the globe the legitimating potential of ICJ will be tested. In turn, hegemony and governance will be drawn into realities of risk rather than metaphors of risk/security. The law and its institutions will struggle for purchase in global governance if they cannot change the dynamics and not just the discourse of risk (O'Malley: 2008).

Presumptuous as it may seem in fact, the dominant political hegemony has represented its version of global order as legal order, and this is supported by a crude but emergent general jurisprudence.[11] The jurisprudence of international criminal law has a particular place in international governance when compared with other fields of international law. For instance, international commercial law sees courts with national legal orders applying commercial conventions originating at a supra-national level. International criminal law has in contrast had developed for itself a tribunal/court structure which requires the determination of state authority. The negotiated order which will be the province of the International Criminal Court will act as law at least for subscribing states, and will operate across a ceded international jurisdiction. A globalised legal order managing criminal justice is not simply taken for granted. As with states and their jurisdiction, international criminal justice and its institutions become indicia of governance (local, regional or international).

Foucault's observation on law's decreasing capacity to code power, to serve as its system of representation, does not currently hold for international criminal justice and its jurisprudence. The reasons for this are uniquely contextual and inextricable with terror/risk globalisation and a very particular enterprise of global governance (Findlay: 2008). This is much more than what Robert's explains as the extended space claimed by jural discourse and institutional forms (Roberts: 2005: 24). International criminal justice is now incorporated into the 'reasoning' of global governance much more than Simon gives it credit at a state level as metaphor. Where Foucault's critique will ring true is in a fast approaching age of globalisation where risk is real and widespread.

However, in the contemporary context of a security/risk nexus with global terror at its heart, the 'reasoning' of contemporary governance is created recursively. A formative and fragile institutional hegemony legitimises globalised forms of 'truth' through control mechanisms specifically designed to minimise threats to its authority. Hence, although 'libertarian' arguments trumpet justice as an integral element of the democratic credo (and thereby through their application internationally, as indicia of global governance), the reverse seems to represent reality. Bilateral intimidation, regional coercion and military incursion are the preferred international relations.

The reduction of symbolic and anticipated terror/risk (in whose-ever name) is accompanied by a reduction in civil liberties, a denial of plurality, and a marginalisation of civil society. Individual autonomy, so central to the normative politics of the dominant hegemony and their idealised 'community' is subjugated through the sacrifices required to maintain 'civilisation' and 'humanity'. With a repositioning of global risk towards the realities of universal harm civil society may assume an enhanced role in a more communitarian governance style where ICJ will of necessity be more inclusive, accessible and integrated if it is to represent a

11 Claims for the existence and operation of international criminal law are consistent with this.

more uniformly accepted 'good' within global governance (Findlay and Henham: forthcoming).

The current secularisation of international criminal justice within the terro/risk dominion has led to the emphasis on formal retributive paradigms to resolve conflict, and the abandonment of reason to fear on a globalised scale (Findlay, forthcoming). This may be as much due to fragile and transitional frameworks of global governance, as it is a consequence of the vacuum resulting from relativity and moral pluralism, and failure to find expression in a shared belief system to underpin globalised forms of justice. Dominant political hegemony and ideological oppression fill the gap, so that the institutional control of behaviours which threaten it are justified in amoral terms – terms which do not rely on any notion of a shared reason, experience or shared value system. In this sense, international criminal justice as the theatre in which the crime/risk-control/security nexus is tested has been profoundly compromised. It is a justice largely unconfirmed by universal moralities. As such, it retains limited legitimacy, and its potential to legitimate wider global governance and conflict resolution, while present, will continue to have limited sweep.

Risk and security as threats and needs are presently procured to essentially justify harsh control, and the only morally coherent basis for global governance they can provide is through a reactive denunciation of those who challenge the hegemony. For instance, in order to justify an extreme punishment response, the violence and violent potential of terrorism is highlighted. However, a moral assessment of terrorism in terms of 'mindless' violence is compromised by any corresponding excessive violence of punishment, particularly where this has consequences for innocent communities, in a 'law of war' scenario. In addition, its 'mindlessness' challenges the deterrent impact of violent punishment, which is offered as the reason for requiring violent punishment.

As risk/security considerations globalise into a world of more universalised and experienced harm then the indicia of governance (such as ICJ) will claim a more long-lasting legitimation if they can produce peace and order, and not simply promise its likelihood. The 'new drivers' for globalised justice must of necessity be developed from a renewal of humanistic principles as they find expression in what we have referred to elsewhere as 'communities of justice' (Findlay and Henham: 2005: chap. 7). To sustain and complement these communities, the foundations for international criminal justice need to rediscover the deeper and more grounded rationality for penality as it is expressed in the sharing of values and experiences over time and place.

In this way the 'contexts of control' within the globalisation project may be more convincingly identifiable as coherent and resilient value systems essential to (and more tolerant of) relative forms of human existence. As such, partial and hegemonic justice will be diminished in its role and will no longer provide either a metaphor for, or structural implementations of, justice in global governance. A natural consequence of this transition will be the diminution of the risk/security metaphor in the face of real and immediate engagement with a failing planet.

International criminal justice will be left to offer a more accessible, heuristic and normatively convincing role in global governance and conflict resolution, if it offers the didactic and declaratory backbone for governance and regulation towards survival, not sectarian domination. International Criminal Justice may then become the honest broker for global governance rather than, as it seems now, another agent of political patronage in the struggle for world order.

References

Aksu, E. and Camilleri, J. (eds) (2002) *Democratising Global Governance*, Basingstoke: Palgrave McMillan.

Barker, T. and Simon, J. (2002) *Embracing Risk: The changing culture of insurance and responsibility*, Chicago: Chicago University Press.

Bordier, P. and Wacquant, L. (1992) *An Invitation to Reflexive Sociology*, Chicago: University of Chicago Press.

Brownsword, R. (2004) *Global Governance and the Quest for Justice (vol. 4 Human Rights)*, Oxford: Hart.

Braithwaite, J. (1989) *Crime Shame and Re-integration*, Oxford: Oxford University Press.

Chemerinski, E. (2005) 'Detainees (Wartime Security and Constitutional Liberty)', *Albany Law Review* 68/4: 119.

Clark, G. (2002) 'Military Tribunals and the Separation of Powers', *Suffolk University Law School Faculty Publications*, Paper 111.

Cohen, S. (1985) *Visions of Social Control*, Oxford: Polity Press.

Duffy, H. (2005) 'Case Study: Guantanamo Bay Detentions under Human Rights and Humanitarian Law', in Forrest F. (et al.) (eds) *The War on Terror and the Framework of International Law*, Cambridge: Cambridge University Press: 379–442.

Findlay, M. (1995) 'International Rights and Australian Adaptations: Recent developments in criminal investigation', in *Sydney Law Review* 17/2: 278–97.

Findlay, M. (1999) *The Globalisation of Crime: Understanding transitional relationships in context*, Cambridge: Cambridge University Press.

Findlay, M. (2006) 'Terrorism and Relative Justice' in *Crime Law and Social Change*, 47/1: 57–68.

Findlay, M. (2008) *Governing through Globalised Crime: Futures for International Criminal Justice*, Collumpton: Willan Publishing.

Findlay, M. (2009) 'Activating Victim Constituency in International Criminal Justice', *Journal of Transitional Justice* 3/2: 183–206.

Findlay, M. and Henham, R. (2005) *Transforming International Criminal Justice: Restorative and retributive justice in the trial process*, Collumpton: Willan Publishing.

Findlay, M. and Henham, R. (2010) *Beyond Punishment – Achieving international criminal justice*, Basingstoke: Palgrave.

Findlay, M. and Zvekic, U. (1993) *Alternative Policing Styles: Cross-cultural perspectives*, Deventer: Kluwer.

Foucault, M. (2002) 'Governmentality', in J. Faubion (ed.) *Power: the Essential Works*, vol. 3. London: Penguin.

Garland, D. (2001) *The Culture of Control: Crime and social order in contemporary society*, Oxford: Oxford University Press.

Gross, E. (2002) 'Trying Terrorists – Justification for Differing Trial Rules: The balance between security considerations and human rights', in *Indiana International and Comparative Law Review* 13/1: 1–98.

Kemshall, H. (2003) *Understanding Risk through Criminal Justice*, Milton Keynes: Open University Press.

McCulloch, J. (2003) '"Counter-Terrorism", Human Security and Globalisation – From welfare to warfare state', in *Current Issues in Criminal Justice* 14/3: 283–98.

Meister, R. (2004) 'The Supreme Court, Guantanamo Bay and Justice Fix-it', *Cornell Law School Berger International Speaker Series*, Paper 4.

Murphy, D. and Robinson, M. (2008) 'The Maximiser: Clarifying Merton's theories of anomie and strain', *Theoretical Criminology* 12: 501–21.

O'Malley, P. (2008) 'Experiments in Risk and Criminal Justice', *Theoretical Criminology* 12: 451–69.

Roberts, S. (2005) 'After Government? On representing law without the state', in *Modern Law Review* 68/1: 1.

Shearing, C. and Johnston, L. (2005) 'Justice in the Risk Society', in *ANZ Journal of Criminology* 38/1: 25–38.

Simon, J. (1997) 'Governing through Crime', in G. Fisher and L. Friedman (eds), *The Crime Conundrum: Essays on Criminal Justice*.

Simon, J. (2001–2002) 'Governing through Crime Metaphors', in *Brooklyn Law Review* 35: 1035.

Viano, E. (ed.) (1999) *Global Organised Crime and International Security*, Aldershot: Ashgate.

Wilson, E. and Lindsey, T. (ed.) (2009) *Government of the Shadows: Para-politics and criminal sovereignty*, London: Pluto Press.

Winter, S. (1988) 'The Metaphor of standing and the Problem of Self Governance', in *Stanford Law Review* 40: 1371.

Chapter 10
Evaluating Sentencing as a Force for Achieving Justice in International Criminal Trials[1]

Ralph Henham

Introduction

This purpose of this chapter is to consider the extent to which sentencing in international trials could play a more instrumental role in promoting reconciliation and peace in post-conflict states. The political rhetoric of international relations currently makes it very difficult to visualise exactly what this might mean except in purely abstract terms, because our perceptions of international criminal justice are relative and contextual. Consequently, it appears futile to argue that the procedures and outcomes of sentencing have some kind of instrumental force at either the international or domestic level without exploring these additional contextual dimensions.

However, the trial structures purporting to deliver international criminal justice, and the values it represents, are depicted as universally relevant and its outcomes applicable wherever international crimes are alleged to have been committed, irrespective of context. In order to deconstruct this myth, the chapter begins by highlighting some of the problems which afflict sentencing in international criminal trials. It then goes on to suggest that there are several obstacles which appear to hamper the notion that sentencing in international trials might be viewed as an instrumental force for achieving 'justice'. The analysis then examines whether international sentencing is capable of playing a greater, more constructive, role in achieving 'justice' for victims and communities in post-conflict states, and considers how such an objective might be realised. The chapter concludes with some broader speculation about the capacity of international trial justice to contribute to the objectives of transitional justice strategies.

The chapter's focus on international sentencing[2] is deliberate, because it is chiefly through this mechanism that the values and norms of international trial justice are transformed into something which has significance at both the

1 This chapter is a revised and expanded version of the author's Inaugural Professorial Lecture delivered on 26 November 2008 at Nottingham Trent University.

2 References are restricted to the sentencing practices of the UN International Tribunals for the Former Yugoslavia and Rwanda (ICTY and ICTR, respectively), and the International Criminal Court (ICC).

international and domestic level. As such, it represents a critical point in the trial where the idea of justice can be measured against a concrete outcome. The problem is that the legitimacy of any sentence may be perceived in many different ways. Analysing the theory and practice of international sentencing therefore raises fundamental questions about:

- The rationales which purport to underpin and thereby validate international sentencing outcomes. The issue here is whether they need to be clarified and, if so, how this might be accomplished.
- How to interpret what is going on as an issue of theory and method. This raises questions about the way international sentencing outcomes are perceived by 'relevant audiences',[3] and whether we have adequate tools at our disposal for understanding such a phenomenon.
- The 'legitimacy' of international trial justice and the implications of this for the future development of international sentencing. This suggests that it may be necessary to consider ways of transforming the ideological and normative frameworks that underpin international trial justice.
- Where international sentencing sits in terms of the future role of international trial justice, and international criminal justice more generally as a form of governance. This forces us to consider the extent to which international trial justice can be implicated more directly in transitional justice strategies?

The Rationality of International Sentencing

Contrary to expectations, commentators generally agree that there is substantive irrationality and obfuscation in the penal justifications for international sentencing (Henham: 2003). This kind of analysis exposes the underdeveloped nature of international sentencing as a relatively new form of jurisprudence. The problem of giving concrete effect to the aims of punishment through a principled framework for distributive justice may be due to some structural or procedural deficiency. More fundamentally, however, it may conceal a more deep-seated and intractable difficulty which goes to the core of criminal justice governance; namely, a fundamental lack of connection between the ideology which informs punishment and the perceived legitimacy of its normative expression in the form of sentencing outcomes (Henham: 2007).

This problem is exacerbated in more complex, pluralistic societies where the ideological and physical resources of criminal justice are monopolised by power elites as part of the apparatus of control through the exclusion and stigmatisation of individuals or groups which threaten their hegemony. As Garland (1990) implies, such shifts in governance over time make the task of understanding different

3 The key concern is which contexts are crucial, and how should considerations drawn from different contexts (and various levels of context) be weighed against one another.

punishment rationales and studying the relationship between values, norms and the legitimacy of trial justice in different contexts extremely complex.

The practice of sentencing distorts penal ideology and obscures its moral foundations. Not only is there the difficulty of identifying the ideology itself, but the problem of describing the social reality of sentencing is exacerbated because the process both interprets that ideology and contextualises it through the decision-making process (Duff and Garland: 1994: 16–20). When punishment is imposed through sentencing the moral ideology which informs sentencing law is given substance. This does not mean to say that sentencing distorts these moral values; rather they find concrete expression *through* sentencing. Sentencing can to that extent be described as morally transformative.

This complexity is further magnified where hegemonic ideologies deliberately obfuscate conventional understandings of criminality and punishment within state or regional contexts, as occurred in the Balkans and Rwanda (Cockayne: 2005). Such effects often mirror a profound divergence in the morality which informs penal ideology and criminalises particular actions, and may precipitate a realignment of forms of political and criminal justice governance. This shift may then be projected onto existing paradigms of criminal justice, at the global and local level, distorting and magnifying orthodox conceptualisations of governance.

Similarly, Ewald (2006) describes how the 'approval' of risk as posing a 'relevant threat' may depend on it qualifying as a perceived threat to hegemonic interests. Seen in this light, it may be argued that the structures of international criminal justice are manipulated to selectively appropriate particular moralities in order to accommodate perceived threats to political hegemony. Correspondingly, the morality of the 'victim' has been appropriated to broaden the reach of criminal justice as a response to politically defined threats such as terrorism (Simon: 2006: 268).

In specific terms, although retribution, and to a lesser extent deterrence, have repeatedly been affirmed as the primary objectives for punishment in the ad hoc tribunals, there is considerable evidence of confusion on the part of ICTY and ICTR judges regarding the possible scope and meaning to be accorded to these and other penal justifications in the practice of international sentencing. For instance, one of the five enumerated goals of the ICTY was explicitly to deter future violations of international criminal law. Indeed, in *Erdemovic*,[4] the Trial Chamber of the ICTY discussed the objective of deterrence in the context of the United Nations Security Council's overriding concern to maintain peace and security in the former Yugoslavia. In so doing, it drew clear distinctions between 'general prevention (or deterrence), reprobation, retribution (or 'just deserts'), as well as collective reconciliation', suggesting that these purposes would provide guidance in determining the appropriate punishment for a crime against humanity. Yet, no attempt was made to define these purposes, or explore their meaning in the trial

4 *Prosecutor v Erdemovic* (Case No. IT-96-22-T), Sentencing Judgement, 29 November 1996, para 58.

context. Still less was there any suggestion of exactly how purposes might be linked to guidance in determining the appropriate sentence.

Further instances of such inconsistency revealing a lack of clear principles are common. For example, in *Rutaganda*[5] the ICTR stated that there was a clear dichotomy between retribution and deterrence, but it was not explained how deterrence could be achieved, or indeed, what evidence exists to suggest that deterrence has any impact whatsoever as a consideration in the motivation of offences of mass atrocity. If deterrence alone is not enough, then it may well be asked what its relationship should be to the other possible aims of international trial justice.

The ICTY Trial Chamber itself acknowledged the problem in *Kunarac*,[6] noting the various and interchangeable use of such expressions as 'objectives, purposes, and principles, functions or policy' in previous tribunal decisions, suggesting that the theoretical justifications for imprisonment were often treated as sentencing factors, in the sense that they might consistently affect the length of prison sentences. Such reasoning shows a fundamental failure to distinguish the purposes of sentencing from the purposes at sentencing.

Furthermore, there is the added difficulty that, historically, particularly since Nuremberg, retributive justice has more often been equated with the concept of victor's justice. This view finds favour in the present context where international trial justice has been portrayed as the vindication and the symbolic exculpation of western political hegemony (Bassiouni and Manakas: 1996). This is hardly an ideal foundation for forging penal aims that will command universal allegiance through their moral integrity and principled application.

The principle of offence proportionality, an implicit paradigm for the practice of retributivist forms of sentencing, continues to impose an 'overriding obligation'[7] on the approach of the ICTY and ICTR to sentence determination, and threatens to do the same for the fledgling ICC as the throughput of cases increases. The problem of unjust and disproportionate sentences is addressed by its appeals process, but the ICC Statute does not create a hierarchy of offence categories from which principles of proportionality might easily be developed.

In common with most western systems of criminal justice, ICTY and ICTR sentences are largely determined by the 'gravity' of the offence (Frulli: 2001; Carcano: 2002), and the degree of responsibility of the accused, together with the impact of relevant aggravating circumstances. Although sentencers have access to a broad range of information to assist them in achieving their objectives,[8] the weight

5 *Prosecutor v Rutaganda* (Case No.ICTR- 96-3), Judgement and Sentence, 2 February 1999.

6 *Prosecutor v Kunarac* (Case No. IT-96-23-T and IT-96-23/1-T), Judgement, 22 February 2001, para 836.

7 *Prosecutor v Banovic* (Case No. IT-02-65/1-S), Trial Chamber, Sentencing Judgement, 28 October 2003, paras 33–6.

8 For example, Rule 85(A)(vi) of the ICTY Rules provides that the parties may produce 'any relevant information that may assist the Trial Chamber in determining an appropriate

to be accorded to the evidence remains largely dependant on judicial discretion being exercised according to the circumstances of each individual case, within the overarching constraints of offence proportionality imposed by the predominant retributive paradigm.

In his detailed analysis of the sentencing practices of the ICTY and ICTR, Beresford (2002) identified the following main aggravating factors as commonly taken into account: the scope of the crime; the number and suffering of the victims; form of participation; motive; and superior responsibility. Mitigating circumstances include: the plea of guilty; personal circumstances (emotional condition of the accused, background of the accused, effect of the sentence on others where unusual hardship is likely to result, the conduct of the accused since the commission of the offence); good character; superior orders; and the accused's level of participation in the crimes.

However, Zappalà (2003: 201) has suggested that Rule 101 of the ICTY/ICTR Rules of Procedure and Evidence[9] consists of so vague a reference to aggravating circumstances as to be contrary to the principle of legality. This prompts him to advocate the deletion of such requirements[10] and the substitution of a definitive list of aggravating circumstances to be taken into account at the sentencing stage. Zappalà relates the issue of unspecified aggravating circumstances to the unrestricted use of judicial discretionary power, suggesting that this volatile combination may have possible adverse implications by obfuscating the perceived seriousness of international crimes.

Arguably, both the ICTY and ICTR have failed to differentiate clearly or consistently between notions of gravity and seriousness for the purposes of the

---

sentence if the accused is found guilty on one or more of the charges in the indictment.'

9 Rule 101 of the ICTY Rules of Procedure and Evidence provides:

(B) In determining the sentence, the Trial Chamber shall take into account the factors mentioned in Article 24, paragraph 2, of the Statute, as well as such factors as are:

(i) *aggravating circumstances*;

(ii) any *mitigating circumstances* including the substantial cooperation with the Prosecutor by the convicted person before or after conviction;

(iii) the general practice regarding prison sentences in the courts of the Former Yugoslavia;

(iv) the extent to which any penalty imposed by a court of any State on the convicted person for the same act has already been served, as referred to in Article 10, paragraph 3, of the Statute.

(C) Credit shall be given to the convicted person for the period, if any, during which the convicted person was detained in custody pending surrender to the Tribunal or pending trial or appeal. (These provisions are mirrored by those of the ICTR).

10 Rule 145, paragraph 2(b)(vi) of the ICC Rules of Procedure and Evidence replicates this provision.

trial and sentence. The concept of the 'gravity'[11] of an offence for the purposes of determining guilt depends upon satisfying different criteria from those applicable to sentencing. However, both expressions tend to be used interchangeably in the sentencing context. Notwithstanding, the concept of 'seriousness' is probably more appropriate. The reasons for this are somewhat complex, the most important being that assessing 'seriousness' not only involves thinking about what penalty may be suitable to reflect the harm caused, but also determining the appropriate sentence in that particular case.[12]

The concept of seriousness also determines the relative distance between offence types for the purposes of fixing the appropriate penalty. This involves making crucial decisions about the relative severity of penalties for different offences (cardinal proportionality) and deciding how offences should be ranked according to seriousness within each offence category (ordinal proportionality). There has been obfuscation in resolving these issues in the international context because of the inherent difficulty of reaching agreement about the relative severity of such heinous crimes as genocide and crimes against humanity, not to mention the problem of delineating seriousness levels within offence categories. Again, this has a lot to do with failing to differentiate the consequences of assessing offence gravity for the purposes of criminal liability from that of determining seriousness for sentencing purposes.[13]

Furthermore, despite the fact that the notion of the individualisation of sentences is apparently enshrined in Article 24(1) of the ICTY Statute[14] (Article 23(1) ICTR Statute) through the reference to 'individual circumstances', the exact

11 The concepts of 'offence gravity' and 'offence seriousness' and 'crime' and 'offence' appear to be used interchangeably in the jurisprudence of the ICTY and ICTR.

12 See the example of S143(1), Criminal Justice Act (2003) in England and Wales.

13 As von Hirsch (1976) explains, commensurate desert systems (as personified by the *ad hoc* tribunals) need to recognise that sentencing policy must consider the extent to which deserved punishment is applied in individual cases. However, it is an unresolved weakness in deserts theory that the approach is unable to distinguish convincingly between different degrees of responsibility, *or quantify harm*. It is, therefore, as difficult to establish a relationship between cardinal and ordinal proportionality, as it is to define those moral values which should inform the setting of penalty levels.

14 Article 24 provides as follows:

1. The penalty imposed by the Trial Chamber shall be limited to imprisonment. In determining the terms of imprisonment, the Trial Chambers shall have recourse to the general practice regarding prison sentences in the courts of the former Yugoslavia.
2. In imposing the sentences, the Trial Chambers should take into account such factors as the gravity of the offence and the *individual circumstances* of the convicted person.
3. In addition to imprisonment, the Trial Chambers may order the return of any property and proceeds acquired by criminal conduct, including by means of duress, to their rightful owners.

parameters of this concept are not elaborated. As a result confusion also persists in the sentencing decisions of the ICTY and ICTR regarding the interpretation of 'individualisation' as a sentencing concept. Arguably, Zappalà (2003: 204) has added to this uncertainty since he seems to elevate the notion of 'individualisation' in relation to crimes under international law to the level of a due process right on the basis that it is instrumental in defining the limits of individual criminal responsibility for acts committed during the course of armed conflicts, although falling short of recognising an allied right to rehabilitation on the part of the convicted person. In any event, the precise ambit of the 'individualisation' concept and its relationship to rehabilitation as a possible sentencing objective for the ad hoc tribunals remains conjectural, more particularly since there is no clear statement of what is meant by 'rehabilitation'.

Notwithstanding, it is difficult to see why individualisation as a philosophical approach for resolving the conflicting demands made on international sentencers should be conceived as a legally enforceable right. This would only be possible should the rationale(s) for sentencing international crimes accommodate such an approach. As things stand, the predominantly retributive and deterrent ideological framework for international sentencing suggests a partisan interpretation of individualisation, certainly not one that engages constructively with the wider social context of sentencing. In other words, the focus remains very much on the individual offender rather than the context in which the criminality took place.

The use of plea bargains in international trials provides a further example of how the dynamics of retributive justice coupled with those of a predominantly adversarial trial structure can work together to obfuscate international criminal justice. In the ICTY, for example, plea agreements have been justified on the basis that they can make a significant contribution to truth-telling and thereby aid the process of peace and reconciliation in post-conflict societies.[15] However, it is certainly arguable that a major underlying rationale for the encouragement of guilty pleas and the increasing use of plea agreements in the ICTY is the simple administrative expedient of speeding up the trial process with a consequent saving of resources, especially when faced with an increasing workload and deadline for case completion.

---

15 See, for example, *Prosecutor v Plavsic* (Case No. IT-00-30 and 40/1-S), Trial Chamber, Judgement, 27 February 2003. Here the Trial Chamber concluded that the accused's guilty plea and acknowledgement of responsibility should carry significant weight in mitigation as a 'positive impact' on the reconciliatory process. Despite this, the Trial Chamber was eventually swayed by the heinous nature of what had taken place and its effects. The prosecution was criticised for giving insufficient weight to (inter alia) the accused's guilty plea and her post-conflict conduct, yet there was a distinct lack of clarity in the Trial Chamber's determination of exactly what the effect of the mitigation (described as 'very significant') should be on the sentence. Such an outcome tends to support Zappala's (2003) point, that it may not be appropriate to allow plea-bargaining and plea agreements for crimes of extreme gravity.

The dissenting judgement of Presiding Judge Wolfgang Schomburg in the *Deronjic* case[16] is salutary in this respect. It represents a significant attack on the use of plea agreements by the ICTY on the basis that they diminish the quality of justice by undermining the principle of proportionality. This argument hinges on the capacity for negotiated pleas to distort truth, in that the factual situations which form the basis of the indictments admitted in plea agreements are not only tailored to suit the particular negotiated circumstances, but they are also selective in terms of the truths that offenders are willing to reveal. Plea agreements and guilty pleas often produce sanitised and censored versions of the truth which tend to obfuscate the real extent of individual responsibility for international crimes. More significantly, they may also alienate victims and communities and so hamper the contribution that trial outcomes might otherwise make to transitional justice and the re-establishment of governance following conflict and war.

Finally, the need to rationalise and integrate penal objectives in international criminal justice is evident from the way the ICC's reparations regime appears both conceptually and practically detached from the purposes of the trial proper (McCarthy: 2009). Indeed, one might argue that a rationale for the international criminal trial which envisages its function as a mechanism for providing redress mandates a broad range of possible strategies and structures to achieve them, including those concerned with reparation and punishment. It is arguable that, because reparative justice is elemental to restorative justice,[17] any attempt to detach the reparations regime conceptually from the penal ideology of the trial proper is inappropriate and counterproductive. This is because the extent to which reparative justice can be expected to redress the concerns of victims is severely constrained by the legitimacy attached to the purposes and practices of the trial, including the punishment of perpetrators.

More fundamentally, this debate highlights the complex and wider issue of defining the role of victims and communities within the ICC process. In other words, it questions the extent to which reparations for victims can be effectively separated from the broader demands for 'justice' raised in the aftermath of mass atrocity. Arguably, the only way to ensure that the 'interests' of these groups are satisfied is to modify the rationale for the ICC trial to include a broader notion of redress that embraces both reparative and retributive justice. As it stands, the interrelated purposes of reparations and retributive punishment have not been fully addressed within the normative framework of the ICC trial.

16 *Prosecutor v Deronjic* (Case No IT-02-61-S), Dissenting Opinion of Judge Wolfgang Schomburg, 30 March 2004.

17 On the difficulties of distinguishing between symbolic and material reparation; see Retzinger and Scheff (1996).

The Meaning of International Penality

Clearly, the fact there are serious deficiencies in the aims and practices of international sentencing is a matter for concern. However, it is difficult to make a rational assessment of its contribution to international trial justice because perceptions of 'justice' are relative and depend on context. Consequently, it is vitally important to pin down exactly what we mean when using expressions such as 'international trial justice' or 'international criminal justice'. For this reason, it is worth pausing for a moment to consider whether existing concepts such as 'penality' may be more helpful in advancing our understanding of the international context.

Two commonly accepted definitions of 'penality' may be contrasted. Hudson (2003: 194) defines 'penality' as:

> ... the complex of ideas, institutions, rules, practices and relationships pertaining to punishment.

This suggests a kind of inclusive universe of concrete ideas, relationships, rules and structures centred on punishment and through which particular notions of punishment are promulgated.

Garland (1990: 17) appears to endorse a similar kind of conceptualisation. He refers to 'penality' in terms of:

> ... the networks of laws, processes, discourses, representations and institutions which make up the penal realm.

However, Garland then goes on to elaborate as follows:

> ... penality communicates meaning not just about crime and punishment but also about power, authority, legitimacy, normality, morality, personhood, social relations, and a host of other tangential matters. (Garland: 1990: 252)

On the basis of these definitions, one might argue that 'penality' could be conceptualised in terms of either an exclusive or inclusive paradigm. Paradoxically, the idea of a more exclusive paradigm for 'penality' tends to correspond more closely with Hudson's (2003) implicitly inclusive (that is, system bound) universe of ideas, norms, structures and processes through which the dominant ideology of punishment is promulgated. Garland (1990), on the other hand, hints at a more inclusive (that is, socially reflexive) paradigm for penality; one that invites us to go beyond the semantics of crime and punishment to engage more widely with issues of moral philosophy, psychology and sociology.

In this regard, Garland's (1990: 253) point about the signifying nature of penality – the idea that it communicates meaning – has special resonance because it suggests that international forms of punishment should be reflective of generally understood cultural meanings of crime and punishment and, consequently, the boundaries of morally acceptable behaviour. In other words, this perspective invites us to engage with different contexts in order to understand what the 'legitimacy' of justice actually signifies.

Nevertheless, there is a paradox for 'international' trial justice in generalising from the particular to the universal. Because it occurs outside national contexts, it can be argued that international trial justice has the capacity to alter or distort our ideas about the values which conventionally underpin punishment. Yet, the problem remains of establishing some kind of link between punishment administered internationally in the name of humanity and its perception as a legitimate response to alleged criminality by those citizens who inhabit conflict zones and have experienced the horrors of social conflict.

This paradox transcends debates about legal legitimacy and appeals directly to morality. In other words, it forces us to consider the extent to which international trials are capable of reconciling universal and particular truths, and reflect this in outcomes which have some tangible impact reaching beyond the symbolism of retributive justice. Failure to address this question makes it difficult to decide on what basis we can attach any underlying or essential meaning to 'international penality' and so confirm its utility as a conceptual device. For example, it may be asked whether it represents some kind of international consensus about the value of retribution or deterrence, or just another vehicle for giving effect to the hegemonic ambitions of powerful states (Alvarez, 1999).

Beyond Retributive Justice

The above suggests that we need to consider the normative boundaries of 'international penality' before we can begin to establish clear purposes and effective outcomes for international trials. However, before embarking on this task, it is worth spending a moment to consider the limitations of relying on retributive justice as the 'legitimate' foundation for punishing international crimes and the basis for developing international trial justice. These include:

- the universal criminalisation of behaviour irrespective of context;[18]
- the right to assert modalities and techniques for penal repression;
- the determination of the means for allocating responsibility for criminality

18 As Howland and Calathes (1998: 157) suggest in the case of Rwanda: 'The major reason justice systems fail to respond adequately to crime is that we inadequately think about crime by defining crime only as law-breaking. We then concentrate solely on the resulting adversarial relationship between government and the criminal offender. This existing pattern of thinking fails to address, or even recognise, the other dimensions involved. A human rights crime is not merely an offence against the state. Likewise, justice is more than punishment and incapacitation.'

irrespective of the different historical, social and cultural contexts in which punishment norms are applied;
- the relative autonomy of international trial processes which have developed outside institutional mechanisms of accountability.

Arguably, such dangers might lead us to the conclusion that the only way for international trial outcomes to reach beyond symbolism is for them to engage more directly with 'real' contexts, such as the diverse communities within post-conflict societies. It may be argued that, for this to happen, criminal justice theory needs to adopt a more normative perspective for conceptualising international trial justice; namely, one which looks at the actual impact of decisions in particular contexts. As Tyler (2006) implies, such a perspective leads us to examine the values which underpin internalised norms of justice and obligation, especially the fact that personal experience has a direct effect upon perceptions of legitimacy.[19]

If this conclusion is correct, it has significant implications for understanding the wider impact of international trial outcomes, especially in speculating what forms of international criminal justice might be most conducive to promoting peace.[20]

Relating to International Criminal Justice

Regrettably, such an insight does not automatically overcome the problem of understanding the basis upon which particular individuals or communities might relate to international trial outcomes or the idea of 'international penality' more generally. To put it another way; is it possible to identify and comprehend the reasons why individuals or communities empathise with values they see as implicit in achieving international trial justice? This is a difficult task on two levels because:

1. It involves being able to account for particular (that is, contextual) interpretations of the morality attached to international trial justice and to explain how these have come about, especially their reflection in the attitudes and perceptions of individuals and communities within a particular cultural context; and
2. It raises the possibility that international criminal justice has a universal morality to which all humankind is connected.

---

19 It is important to note the influence of theoretical perspective on approaches to studying the issue of 'legitimacy' (Tyler, 2006: 282).

20 This assumes an acceptance that peace is preferable to war, and a capacity to suggest (or model) scenarios favouring peace.

Durkheim's Moral Individualism

An interesting insight on the second issue is provided by Durkheim's notion of moral individualism (Cotterrell: 1999: 202). This is the idea that individual and collective concern for others is a moral imperative. Such a perspective has significant resonance for national and international human rights movements because it reflects our essential humanity. Cotterrell (1999) suggests that the value system of individualism envisaged by Durkheim can be conceptualised as a shared moral culture which transcends national boundaries. The difficulty remains that of envisaging the moral basis upon which law's authority, in this case sentencing law, is claimed to rest in terms of shared beliefs or sentiments. More specifically, how do we identify transnational values of individualism in forms of international regulatory power, such as structures designed for the implementation of international penal norms, and ground them in principles of fairness and justice.

Weber's Forms of Rationality

Similarly, Weber's analysis of substantive and formal rationality is also insightful when thinking about the significance of trial outcomes (Cotterrell: 1992: 153). According to Weber, the legal norms which regulate punishment are founded on principles of substantive rationality in so far as they are informed by a mixture of moral and other beliefs existing beyond the formalism of the legal rules themselves. However, in reality such norms are highly formalised in structure and there exists a complex balance between formal logical processes which facilitate the recursive reproduction of law as an autonomous system of rules and the extent to which ideology about the moral acceptability of social action informs decision-making.[21] Therefore, in Weberian terms, legal rationality is bureaucratised to the extent that the criminal process recursively perpetuates the development of internally consistent principles which tend to re-enforce dominant political ideologies. A system of formal rationality reproduced in contexts where political and moral ideologies are at odds (as may well be the case both within and between modern pluralistic states) means that legal formalism predominates and increasingly causes the alienation of the criminal process from the outcomes it produces.

However limited, such theoretical insights are useful in helping us to address one of the primary tasks which remain for scholars; that of explaining why retributive and other forms of justice delivery predominate in different contexts, and the functions they satisfy. This work is still in its infancy. This clearly restricts our ability to understand how and why particular trial outcomes are perceived as unjust, discriminatory or oppressive, and to gauge the significance of this for international criminal justice.

---

21 A similar effect noted by some social psychologists is that perceived legitimacy provides a kind of 'reservoir of support' for institutional practices which may override the interests of those whom such structures are meant to serve (Tyler, 2006: 281).

Conceptualising International Trial Justice

Another vital issue to consider when assessing the role of sentencing in the delivery of international trial justice is the practical everyday reality of discretionary decision-making. Strange as it may seem, we know relatively little about the way in which perceptions of 'justice' actually manifest themselves in the daily practice of international sentencing. This raises both theoretical and practical questions. Theoretical concerns include the continuing debate in legal theory as to whether legal norms and legal reasoning are closed systems, and therefore only susceptible to particular forms of analysis, or whether the reverse is true, in which case issues of law and morality are irrevocably intertwined in sentencing. Practical issues include the fact that relatively little is known about how penal norms and values are actually implicated in the everyday processual activity that constitutes sentence decision-making.

Elsewhere, I have argued (Henham: 2005: chaps 3 and 5) that judges effectively operate a kind of sociological methodology in their decision-making; they interpret trial ideologies and the moral values that underpin them selectively (Hogarth: 1971), thereby controlling the ways in which flexible legal concepts are adapted to novel circumstances. Taking this further, Mark Findlay and I (2005) have suggested elsewhere that judicial discretionary power could be utilised to achieve more humanitarian[22] solutions for international criminal justice.

The kind of normative transformation that would be necessary to achieve this relies on the notion that penal ideology is somehow implicated in sentencing outcomes through the process of judicial discretionary decision-making. Accordingly, it may be argued that the moral power of international sentencing to act as a transformative mechanism depends upon its capacity to shape social reality. This is achieved through the recursively organised practice of the trial. Such a perspective suggests that the transformation of normative principles into morally significant aspects of social reality, either through their correspondence with values held about the appropriateness of punishment, or their capacity to influence social behaviour, will depend upon enhancing the capacity of judicial discretionary power to achieve this end (Henham: 2001).

Developing Notions of 'Community'

As suggested, the idea of transforming international trial justice has something to do with making it more inclusive and participative, especially for victims and communities affected by social conflict and war. Hence, it is important to consider exactly what we mean when we invoke notions of 'community' for this purpose.

22 In the sense that outcomes could engage more with the 'justice' aspirations of victims and communities in post-conflict societies.

Cotterrell (2006), for example, asks whether post-conflict societies are potentially holistic communities; what might be the responsibilities and expectations of 'communities' with regard to the trial; and, what do we mean by the 'international community'? We need to improve our understanding of how the perceptions of individuals and communities about international trial justice are constructed and their interrelationship. It is particularly important to investigate how subjective factors, such as feelings and emotions, relate to the ways in which the structures and outcomes of international criminal trials are perceived; in other words, their legitimacy. We do not know, for example, how each community feels about the role of formal punishment rituals, or whether retributive or restorative justice forms are used, either separately or in combination - crucially, whether practices that appear to conform to definitions or understandings[23] derived from other cultures and traditions actually exist at all. In other words, are actions taken by the community in order to restore harmony thought of in retributive, deterrent or restorative terms, or indeed, does the notion of punishment have any significant role in maintaining community coherence? More significantly, there may be no indication of where the line is drawn between resolutions governed by so-called 'law', and those which regulate the infringement of social norms; which (if any) have priority, and why.

For example, the social stigma attached to rape and other forms of sexual violence is clearly something culturally specific. Commonplace assumptions about those factors which determine the status of women are also likely to prove incorrect. The conclusions drawn by the ICTY provide an illustration of this. As de Londras (2007) points out, in the case of *Krstic*[24] the Trial Chamber referred to the fact that it was common knowledge that the Muslims of Eastern Bosnia constituted a patriarchal society. Consequently, women were required to have a clear marital status in order to constitute part of that society, and a woman whose husband was missing did not fit within any of these categories, that is, married, widowed or divorced. In other words, such a woman was effectively a social outcast.

Asserting that international sentencing should reflect different contexts also means that we have to be able to recognise why particular purposes for punishment or certain trial outcomes may be judged morally indefensible by different factions. A case in point is the ICTR decision in *Kambanda*,[25] the former prime minister of Rwanda, whose life sentence was upheld on appeal after he had pleaded guilty to offences of genocide. Not only did the sentence fall well short of the retributive expectations of the victim community, but Rwandan law itself advocated the death penalty for the masterminds of such crimes. To make matters worse, the ICTR Trial

23 Including the rationales which inform the practices in question, and the factors which have shaped them.

24 *Prosecutor v Krstic* (Case No. IT-98-33-T), Judgement, 2 August 2001, para 592; *Prosecutor v Krstic* (Case No. IT-98-33-A), Appeals Chamber Judgement, 19 April 2004.

25 *Prosecutor v Kambanda* (Case No. ICTR-97-23-S), Judgement and Sentence, 4 September 1998.

Chamber compounded this failure for the victim community by not capitalising on Kambanda's confessions and admissions of guilt through encouraging the process of reconciliation at the local level. This arguably served to undermine the educative and reconciliatory purposes of the trial process, and also its legitimacy.

Since the primary function of the international trial process remains that of allocating blame, more constructive and transformative sentences will depend on the explicit identification of the nature and needs of particular communities. As Cotterrell (2002) suggests, these communities may be of shared beliefs or interests which extend beyond the boundaries of the nation state, as well as constituting minorities within them. This is by no means a straightforward issue. For example, some indigenous communities have no concept of blame. Furthermore, within particular states and regions, criminal justice may be portrayed as a key component in the ongoing hegemony of imperialism and colonialism; a crucial part of the ideological and structural apparatus of repression and exclusion, whereby indigenous people are increasingly and disproportionately subject to imprisonment (Sarre and Wilson, 1997). Such accounts view customary forms of dispute and conflict resolution as far removed from the confrontation, guilt and accountability associated with adversarial justice. Consequently, we need to have some idea how different notions of 'community' might impact upon perceptions of 'justice' and its delivery in different contexts, particularly through alternative interpretations of concepts like 'responsibility' and 'liability' and the implications these might have for developing more inclusive forms of trial outcome.

Victimisation and Truth Construction

Alternative structures and processes, such as Truth and Reconciliation Commissions (TRCs) in their various guises, provide alternative and more relative interpretations of truth and justice that are drawn from (and rooted in) *context*, and, therefore, claim to be nearer to historical truth (Cohen: 1995). However, whether TRCs provide a more relevant[26] form of truth is conjectural since it is arguable that international trial justice may have a more enduring impact on victims, because trials contribute more directly to the deconstruction of myths that surround notions of collective responsibility. International criminal trials also provide a symbolic and historically definitive version of truth with legal consequences which assists in achieving closure and a refocusing of efforts on the reconstruction of broken communities. In addition, several so-called internationalised courts and tribunals have been created to exist alongside domestic processes of accountability (including TRCs), such as those in Sierra Leone, East Timor and Kosovo (Bohlander: 2001; Linton: 2001; Strohmeyer: 2001). These normally juxtapose international and domestic structures of criminal justice and frequently display tensions resulting from the failure to develop coherent principles to underpin trial practice.

---

26 Relevant in the sense of victims or communities.

Ewald (2006) describes how victim identity is constructed in international criminal justice through 'societal technologies' that determine the relationship between hegemonic groups and those who are excluded from rights of access and justice. He suggests that such identities of victimisation are 'inevitably linked to interest-based political and global control strategies' and that international criminal justice is crucially implicated in constructing false accounts of victimisation as a consequence. The processing of false victim identities is enabled through the normative framework of international trial justice. An example of this is the focus in international trials on the construction of individual perpetrators and the failure of international criminal law to reflect the collective nature of victimisation through the accountability it provides. Ewald (2006) argues further that the distortion of value relationships by the large-scale victimisation of international criminal law is validated through the value-related dimension of sentencing, since this justifies the ideology of international criminal justice. The consistency of this false labelling amounts to social victimisation because it systematically approves the selective appropriation of false victim status and promotes distorted deviant identities.

More recently, Ewald (2008) has suggested how the 'plausible rationality' that underpins international trial justice produces a form of 'judicial truth' that bears little resemblance to the 'material truth' of commonly shared values. The ideology that informs this rationality comes from the hegemony of the socio-political context of international criminal justice which comprises 'an international political process of global structuring and organisation'. Consequently, the possibility of developing rights or standards aimed at achieving greater 'material truth' is compromised by the partisan westernised definitions of risk perception and threat that inform the ideologies and normative frameworks of international trial justice. These 'regimes of truth' are reproduced through the generation of evidence which sustains their hegemonic ideology, despite the fact that they are accepted only by a relative majority of relevant social actors, including the global 'community'.

Cohen (1995) also highlights the role of social control in manufacturing 'truth' – 'the notion that it is necessary to discover the truth about the past in order to achieve justice in the present'. He posits the possibility that structures of international punishment, for example, provide a form of social control which is instrumental in negotiating and defining what becomes known as truth and counts as justice. Cohen suggests that any discussion involving redefinition, whether resulting from trial justice, truth and reconciliation, lustration, or any other means inevitably has significant implications for social control and governance during and beyond the transitional justice phase. This is because, as Cohen (citing Spitzer) cogently argues, any determination about the facts of what has happened in the past inevitably creates an artificial barrier; a breaking of the relationship between past and future, so that policing the past becomes more a question of making sure that the past remains closed. Social control becomes a process involving the selective control and manipulation of memory.

In the post-modern era, the certainty of this discourse has been replaced by what Cohen (1995: 48) calls the 'centrifugal' falling away of information and memory.

The relativity of values and their controlling ideologies become increasingly difficult to identify, let alone predict, making it harder to prevent the absolution of human rights abuses carried out by totalitarian regimes. In other words, to a greater or lesser extent, we gradually come to accept degrees of denial without necessarily being aware of its insidious effects on our perceptions and actions towards present and future human rights abuses, especially those amounting to international crimes such as genocide and crimes against humanity.

Trial justice appears powerless to counter the social injustices of hegemony; it simply reflects the moral boundaries of the social context that informs the ideology, structure and operation of the international criminal trial process. The future legitimacy of governance structures for international criminal justice will depend on developing ties of horizontal and vertical trust among citizens. It may be argued that the emergence of such shared moral networks will be enhanced through strengthening the framework for achieving fundamental human rights. However, building relationships of trust with excluded and alienated victims and communities is a necessary precursor in restoring legitimacy to international criminal justice.

Delivering International Trial Justice

In *Transforming International Criminal Justice* (2005) Mark Findlay and I suggested that judicial discretionary decision-making in international trials could be viewed as an appropriate context for developing more integrated and inclusive forms of international trial justice. We suggest that the perceived legitimacy of international punishment could be enhanced if trial justice were made more inclusive by reflecting the aspirations of victims and communities within post-conflict societies more effectively.

In our recent work *Beyond Punishment: Achieving International Criminal Justice* (2010) we are concerned with giving substance to these aspirations. Accordingly, in the sentencing context, a number of issues are identified as key areas for transforming international trial justice. These include:

- considering the possibility of introducing intermediate stages and outcomes (such as mediation) for the trial;
- looking at how this might affect issues such as the relationship between trial professionals and the probative value of evidence;
- ensuring greater victim involvement through actual participation in decision-making and corresponding rights protection;
- expanding and recasting the parameters for the exercise of judicial and others forms of discretion (such as that of the prosecutor);
- exploring the potential for mixing lay and professional forms of adjudication where appropriate.

In terms of accountability, the focus is very much on establishing connections, dialogues and representations of justice from within victim communities, so that the idea of access to justice is unequivocally associated with the more holistic and representative justice which is the essence of the transformed trial. Similarly, the notion of trial rights is broadened and interpreted within this democratised framework for accountability, so that the rights themselves are conceived of as an essential component in maintaining the dialogue of justice with victim communities. In this way accountability could extend beyond its conventional role of ensuring the principled enforcement of penal norms by ensuring that rights become more socially responsive. Changing the penal ideology which informs the trial, as we suggest, would enhance the pedagogic mission of the trial in terms of 'truth-finding' and its social context, since the interests of all parties who can establish a legitimate claim to participation would be promoted equally.

However, there remains a need for a principled approach to developing the normative framework for rights to fulfil this changed ideology. This should not only draw a distinction between the foundations for rights and practice, but also promote methodologies that produce a deeper understanding of each social context and the relationship between rights and accountability. Instead of partisan penal ideology delineating access and rights, they are conceived as grounded in context, so that the moral values attaching to them are mirrored in state and international structures for justice delivery. In this way, contextualised understandings of the relationship between participation and rights inform the capacity of sentencing to reconcile competing moral claims for justice.

International Sentencing and the Future of International Criminal Justice

This chapter has suggested that we begin to think about explaining the phenomenon of international trial justice more normatively, so that we are able to provide more convincing accounts of the justice demands of different groups of victims and communities in post-conflict situations, and reflect these in more inclusive and relevant sentencing outcomes. By adopting this kind of approach, we can start to think more creatively about the legitimacy of trial justice, and speculate about its capacity to act as a force for reconciliation and peace.

Some commentators have argued strongly that trial and punishment is an inappropriate paradigm for developing more restorative forms of conflict resolution. For example, at the theoretical level, Christodoulidis (2000) questions the capacity of legal rules to bring about reconciliatory functions such as 'mercy' through process, seeing law as over-deterministic and incapable of proceeding beyond the categories imposed by the reductive nature of legal rules; that essentially complex reflexive ethical decisions cannot be reached solely within a legal context.

Roche (2005) argues that sentencing hearings are more concerned with a victim's physical injuries and material loss than serious emotional or psychological loss, such as loss of dignity, happiness, confidence, security, personal power and sense of self-worth, and that even a modified form of trial more mindful of victims' needs, such as the ICC, 'remains an inherently unsuitable forum for pursuing reparation.'

Parmentier (2003: 213) is equally circumspect about the future potential of the ICC. He suggests that the ICC's role as a complimentary institution is best seen in its capacity to link the primary loci for retributive justice (that is, nation states). He further envisages retributive and restorative forms of justice as generally deliverable by separate mechanisms; as complimentary, each with their specific characteristics and contributions to situations of mass violence.

Finally, Fletcher and Weinstein (2002) make the important point that there are 'no mechanisms to respond to the ways in which bystanders are implicated in the establishment and maintenance of societal structures that facilitate the onset and implementation of mass violence'. In their view, trials single out particular authors and perpetrators, omitting broader initiatives on rule of law, humanitarian assistance, democracy building and economic development. Consequently, Fletcher and Weinstein also advocate multiple interventions, and envisage criminal trials as continuing to perform an essentially retributive punishment role. By only responding to one dimension of the abuse of power, they suggest criminal trials fail to address the phenomenon of collective power and its influence on individuals. We are, therefore, unable to address the social and collective forces that lead to violence.[27]

As these comments suggest, a significant influence on international sentencing is that it operates within a largely adversarial framework which focuses on establishing individual responsibility for legally-defined guilt rather than working towards developing understandings of the relationship between individual and collective forms of responsibility, and what this might mean for reconciliation and peaceful co-existence. Tallgren (2002) rightly regards this tendency for international criminal justice to produce 'unambiguous notions of guilt or innocence' as establishing patterns of causality which conveniently ignore the complexity and scale of multiple responsibilities that signify the social reality of collective violence and mass atrocity.

More recently, Drumbl (2007) has suggested the need for more flexible and alternative paradigms such as tort, contract and restitution so that the universal norms of accountability are rendered relational. He suggests that, whilst rejecting notions of collective guilt, notions of collective responsibility and collective sanction do not recognise the collective nature of the violence. Drumbl goes on to argue that structures of accountability need to be more proactive, rather than simply reactive, through providing incentives for controlling the behaviour of those who promote conflict. Sanctioning of the individual in such a way as is proportionate to their involvement in the collective wrongdoing will more easily

27 This, of course, begs the question as to the extent to which any form of resolution or intervention (including trials) is able to avoid contamination and deliver justice irrespective of power.

facilitate the pursuit of restorative approaches. He calls this an 'obligations based preventative *ex ante* model'.

Drumbl's proposals raise several difficult questions. For example, how does one monitor and control the activities of what he calls 'conflict entrepreneurs'? How can a duty effectively be imposed on individual citizens to prevent the state from 'actualising extraordinary international crimes'? How can a framework of collective sanctions be effective? Realising the potential of individuals or groups to identify and monitor potential sources of collective violence is problematic. Blurring or merging sanction outcomes in terms of civil and criminal possibilities would be very difficult to apply collectively.

Notwithstanding, we can conclude that those sympathetic to restorative forms of justice (Braithwaite: 2002) are more likely to regard international trial justice, and international criminal justice more generally, as important elements in a complex and unique jigsaw for moving forward from war to peace. For example, Braithwaite (2002: 207) suggests that institutional renewal is a precondition for engaging restorative justice in the battle to transform peace and build a society which actually enforces international humanitarian and human rights law. Viewed in this light, the role of international criminal justice to expose 'truth' and define the capacity of those structures which regulate the behaviour of individual citizens in civil society is crucial. This potential lies in its ability to substitute the domestic politics of alienation, exclusivity and social control with a response based on humanitarian values grounded within communities of interest.

Towards Transitional Justice

Thinking through the contribution of international trial justice to transitional justice is equally problematic. As has been argued, the retributive dynamic in international criminal process has acted as a conceptual and normative barrier to engaging with the idea that trial outcomes can form part of a more constructive and inclusive type of penality. Therefore, trial justice is deemed to lack the capacity for truth-telling possessed by structures such as Truth and Reconciliation Commissions, and the international trial structure is seen as an inappropriate locus for pursuing reconciliatory and reparative objectives. True, international trials may manufacture a form of 'truth' and provide legal closure, but many regard this kind of 'truth' as distorted by the limited rationale and objectives set for international trial justice. An example of this compartmentalised thinking about the capacity of international trial justice can be seen in the way in which its relationship within transitional justice is normally conceived. This is illustrated by Bickford's (2004) summary of the main features of transitional justice in terms of prosecutions, truth-telling, reparations, memorialising; reconciliation and institutional reform. Borraine (2004) similarly envisages clear divisions of function when describing the problems of defining transitional justice.

Such perspectives clearly foresee a limited contribution on the part of international trials (as currently conceived) to transitional justice. Both Bickford and Borraine reflect this narrow, one-dimensional view of the instrumental capacity of international trial justice; one that is tied firmly to its conventional retributive and deterrent role. Hence, in order to move forward, the various aspects of transitional justice must be balanced and coordinated, held 'in tension to one another' (Borraine: 2004).

However, I do not endorse such an emasculated role for trial justice. Rather, I would argue for a form of trial justice which is capable of producing 'truth' and outcomes that engage more directly with the values and objectives of inclusion, healing and reconciliation. Within this broader context, the contribution of international trial justice to transitional justice may be seen as one which includes many of the functions of other practices and structures, such as truth-telling and reparations, which are currently treated as self-contained areas. In suggesting this fundamental change in the instrumental capacity of trial justice, the aim is not to detract from other structures and practices of transitional justice. On the contrary, trial justice is envisaged as a more effective and constructive partner for other structures and practices, whether these take the form of truth and reconciliation, or indigenous, or hybridised forms of justice.

To achieve this will require trial outcomes to be evaluated against the objectives set for transitional justice and the development of measures of satisfaction which go beyond those which might impact directly on victims and communities. For example, their perceptions might be influenced by such factors as:

- emotional experiences
- feelings about procedural justice
- whether aspirations for trial justice were satisfied

However, the broader implications of these responses will need to be evaluated within the context of transitional objectives. So, for example, retribution and deterrence may be regarded by certain parties as essential precursors to restoring harmony. In other cases, these purposes might be regarded as part of the mechanism for resolution and transition.

It is also difficult to assess the basis upon which individuals or groups attribute greater satisfaction to one kind of process over another; for example, restorative over retributive and deterrent. Satisfaction may ensue because the process was inclusive and participatory, or because of feelings held about its intrinsic value in resolving conflict and aiding transition. Similarly, the locus and length of trial proceedings; separation of outcome from cause; distinction between high and low-ranking perpetrators; differences between hybridised, internationalised, international and indigenous forms of trial, all affect perceptions of legitimacy. In terms of timing, for instance, the window of opportunity and impetus for reconciliatory motives to be exploited may quickly dissipate.

Consequently, effectively coordinating all the elements of transitional justice, including prosecution, truth-telling, reconciliation, reparation and institutional reform becomes critical. Not least, because, as Borraine (2004) suggests, reconciliation may be triggered at different times in transitional states. Such triggers may range from the indictment and prosecution of particular perpetrators, to the release of political prisoners, whereas the reform of institutional structures to achieve economic justice may be seen as more pressing, or equally significant to the goals of criminal justice.

The interrelationship of each element for achieving transitional justice will depend on the relevant context and its transitional needs. It cannot be assumed that these will correspond to any pre-conceived notions of governance;[28] or the role and structures needed to deliver criminal justice (Teitel: 2000: 224). By comprehending the contexts which inform the reasons for conflict and the perception of justice, it should be possible to move more effectively towards reconciliation and peace. Only then will we begin to understand the *real* relationship between international sentencing and achieving justice in international criminal trials.

References

Alvarez, J.E. (1999) 'Crimes of States/Crimes of Hate: Lessons from Rwanda', *Yale Journal of International Law*, 24: 365.

Bassiouni, M.C. and Manakas, P. (1996) *The Law of the International Criminal Tribunal of the Former Yugoslavia*, Irvington-on-Hudson, NY: Transnational Publishers.

Beresford, S. (2002) 'Unshackling the Paper Tiger: The Sentencing Practices of the ad hoc International Criminal Tribunals for the Former Yugoslavia and Rwanda', *International Criminal Law Review*, 1: 33.

Bickford, L. (2004) *The Encyclopedia of Genocide and Crimes Against Humanity*, vol. 3, USA: Macmillan Reference: 1045.

Bohlander, M. (2001) 'The Direct Application of International Criminal Law in Kosovo', *Kosovo Legal Studies*, 1: 7.

Borraine, A. 'Transitional Justice as an Emerging Field' Paper presented at the 'Repairing the Past: Reparations and Transitions to Democracy' symposium, Ottawa, Canada, 11 March, 2004.

Braithwaite, J. (2002) *Restorative Justice and Responsive Regulation*, Oxford: Oxford University Press.

28 For example, Seils and Wierda (2005) suggest that prosecutions can play a positive role in encouraging a commitment to 'democratic' values. However, these effects are attributed as beneficial outcomes of adhering to the rule of law. They are not based on achieving more inclusive justice for victims and communities in transitional states by enhancing the legitimacy of trial outcomes.

Carcano, A. (2002) 'Sentencing and the Gravity of the Offence in International Criminal Law', *International and Comparative Law Quarterly*, 51: 583.

Christodoulidis, E.A. 'Truth and Reconciliation as Risks' (2000) 9 *Social & Legal Studies* 179.

Cockayne, J. (2005) 'Hybrids or Mongrels? Internationalised War Crimes Trials as Unsuccessful Degradation Ceremonies' *Journal of Human Rights*, 4: 455.

Cohen, S, (1995) 'State Crimes of Previous Regimes: Knowledge, Accountability and the Policing of the Past', *Law and Social Inquiry*, 20: 7.

Cotterrell, R.B.M. (1992) *The Sociology of Law: An Introduction*, London: Butterworths, 2nd edn.

Cotterrell, R.B.M. (1999) *Emile Durkheim: Law in a Moral Domain*, Edinburgh: Edinburgh University Press.

Cotterrell, R.B.M. (2002) 'Seeking Similarity, Appreciating Difference: Comparative Law and Communities' in A. Harding and E. Örücü (eds) *Comparative Law in the 21st Century*, The Hague: Kluwer.

Cotterrell, R.B.M. (2006) *Law, Culture and Society*, Aldershot: Ashgate.

De Londras, F. (2007) 'Telling Stories and Hearing Truths: Providing an Effective Remedy to Genocidal Sexual Violence against Women' in Henham, R. and Behrens, P. (eds) *The Criminal Law of Genocide: International, Comparative and Contextual Aspects*, Aldershot: Ashgate.

Drumbl, M. (2007) *Atrocity, Punishment and International Law*, Cambridge: Cambridge University Press.

Duff, A. and Garland, D. (eds) (1994) *A Reader on Punishment*, Oxford: Oxford University Press.

Ewald, U. (2006) 'Large Scale Victimisation and the Jurisprudence of the ICTY – Victimological Research Issues' in Ewald, U. and Turkovic, K. (eds) *Large-Scale Victimisation as a Potential Source of Terrorist Activities – Importance of Regaining Security in Post-Conflict Societies*, NATO Security through Science Series, E; Human and Societal Dynamics, vol. 13: 171.

Ewald, U. (2008) '"Reason" and "Truth" in International Criminal Justice – A Criminological Perspective on the Construction of Evidence in International Trials' in Smeulers, A. and Haveman, R. (eds) *Supranational Criminology: Towards a Criminology of International Crimes*, Antwerp: Intersentia.

Findlay, M. and Henham, R. (2005) *Transforming International Criminal Justice: retributive and restorative justice in the trial process*, Cullompton: Willan.

Findlay, M. and Henham, R. (2010) *Beyond Punishment: achieving international criminal justice*, Basingstoke: Palgrave Macmillan.

Fletcher, L.E. and Weinstein, H.M. (2002) 'Violence and Social Repair: Rethinking the Contribution of Justice to Reconciliation', *Human Rights Quarterly*, 24: 573.

Frulli, M. (2001) 'Are Crimes against Humanity More Serious than War Crimes?' *European Journal of International Law*, 12: 329.

Garland, D. (1990) *Punishment and Modern Society*, Oxford: Clarendon Press.

Henham, R. (2001) 'Theory and Contextual Analysis in Sentencing', *International Journal of the Sociology of Law*, 29: 253.

Henham, R. (2003) 'Some Issues for Sentencing in the International Criminal Court', *International and Comparative Law Quarterly*, 52: 81.

Henham, R. (2005) *Punishment and Process in International Criminal Trials*, Aldershot: Ashgate.

Henham, R. (2007) 'Developing Contextualised Rationales for Sentencing in International Criminal Trials: A Plea for Empirical Research', *Journal of International Criminal Justice*, 5: 757.

Hogarth, J. (1971) *Sentencing as a Human Process*, Toronto: University of Toronto Press.

Howland, T. and Calathes, W. (1998) 'The UN's International Criminal Tribunal: is it Justice or Jingoism for Rwanda? A call for transformation', *Virginia Journal of International Law*, 39: 135.

Hudson, B. (2003) *Understanding Justice: An introduction to ideas, perspectives and controversies in modern penal theory*, Buckingham: Open University Press, 2nd edn.

Linton, S. (2001) 'Cambodia, East Timor and Sierra Leone: Experiments in International Criminal Justice', *Criminal Law Forum*, 12: 185.

McCarthy, C. (2009) 'Reparations under the Rome Statute of the International Criminal Court and Reparative Justice Theory', *International Journal of Transitional Justice*, 3: 250.

Parmentier, S. (2003) 'Global Justice in the Aftermath of Mass Violence: The Role of the International Criminal Court in Dealing with Political Crimes', *International Annals of Criminology*, 41: 203.

Parmentier, S. (2007) 'Ask the Victims: Towards a 'Bottom-up' Approach to Transitional Justice' Paper presented at Oxford Centre for Criminology Seminar, 9 May 2007.

Retzinger, S. and Scheff, T. (1996) 'Strategy for Community Conferences: Emotions and Social Bonds' in B. Galaway and J. Hudson (eds), *Restorative Justice: International Perspectives*, Monsey, NY: Criminal Justice Press.

Roche, D. (2005) 'Truth Commission Amnesties and the International Criminal Court', *British Journal of Criminology*, 45: 565.

Sarre, R. and Wilson, D. (eds) (1998) *Sentencing and Indigenous Peoples* Proceedings of Roundtable convened by the Australian Institute of Criminology and the University of South Australia on 31 October 1997, Research and Public Policy Series No. 16, Canberra: Australian Institute of Criminology.

Seils, P. and Wierda, M. (2005) *The International Criminal Court and Conflict Mediation*, International Center for Transitional Justice, Occasional Paper Series, June 2005.

Simon, J. (2006) *Governing Through Crime: How the War on Crime Transformed American Democracy and Created a Culture of Fear*, New York: Oxford University Press.

Strohmeyer, H. (2001) 'Collapse and Reconstruction of a Judicial System: The United States Mission in Kosovo and East Timor', *American Journal of International Law*, 95: 46.

Tallgren, I. (2002) 'The Sensibility and Sense of International Criminal Law' *European Journal of International Law*, 13: 561.

Teitel, R.G. (2000) *Transitional Justice*, New York: Oxford University Press.

Tyler, T.R. (2006) *Why People Obey the Law*, Princeton: Princeton University Press.

von Hirsch, A. (1976) *Doing Justice*, New York: Hill and Wang.

Zappalà, S. (2003) *Human Rights in International Criminal Proceedings*, Oxford: Oxford University Press.

Chapter 11
The Paradox of Global Terrorism and Community-Based Security Policing

Clive Walker

Introduction

The phenomenon of terrorism presents us with several apparent paradoxes. There is first the paradox of the United States choosing to embark upon a 'Global War on Terrorism'[1] and seeking to adopt the language of armed conflict, just as the international community has at last managed to define much of terrorist activity as an international crime through the United Nations International Convention for the Suppression of Terrorist Bombings 1997[2] and its International Convention for the Suppression of the Financing of Terrorism 1999.[3] Admittedly, the international community has made less progress in applying to terrorism suitable international law criminal processes through the Rome Statute.[4] Then again, the American alternative, Presidential decrees on detention without trial and military tribunals, have convinced few (including in the US Supreme Court) of their legitimacy or value.[5]

Another paradox is the belief that terrorism, especially Jihadist terrorism, is depicted as an unwarranted assault on our basic values – to liberty, equality, and democracy – only for our own societies to warrant that the same values have to be sacrificed in various ways. Thus, we are embroiled in endless debates

1 The term 'war on terror' was first voiced by President George W. Bush on 20 September 2001: 'Our war on terror begins with al Qaida, but will not end until every terrorist group has been found, stopped and defeated … And we will pursue nations that provide aid or safe havens to terrorists. Every nation, in every region, now has a decision to make: either you are with us, or you are with the terrorists.' (President Bush, Address to a Joint Session of Congress and the American People, http://georgewbush-whitehouse.archives.gov/news/releases/2001/09/20010920-8.html, 20 September 2001).

2 37 I.L.M. 249.

3 39 I.L.M. 270.

4 37 I.L.M. 999.

5 For the latest rejection by the US Supreme Court of the Presidential exercise of war powers, see *Boumediene et al. v. Bush*, 553 US 723 (12 June 2008). President-elect Barack Obama has promised to close Guantánamo Bay detention facilities: Eggen D. and White, J., 'Debate Over Guantanamo's Fate Intensifies', *The Washington Post*, 4 July 2008, p. A01.

about the concocted 'balance' between liberty and security,[6] as witnessed by the erstwhile controversy which raged (until their Parliamentary defeat in October 2008)[7] over proposals in the Counter-Terrorism Bill 2007–08 for 42 day police detention of terrorist suspects. To Gordon Brown, in a speech to the Institute for Public Policy Research in June 2008, because of the possibility of 'a grave and exceptional terrorist threat – detention before charge should be extended from 28 to 42 days'.[8] To David Davis, '42 days is the one most salient example of the insidious, surreptitious and relentless erosion of fundamental British freedom'.[9] In other words, the paradox is that our reaction to terrorism can more undermine our values than terrorism itself, a point famously voiced by Lord Hoffman, who in *A and others v Secretary of State for the Home Department*, the House of Lords' decision on the legality of the detention regime in December 2004, stated:[10]

> Terrorist violence, serious as it is, does not threaten our institutions of government or our existence as a civil community. … The real threat to the life of the nation, in the sense of a people living in accordance with its traditional laws and political values, comes not from terrorism but from laws such as these. That is the true measure of what terrorism may achieve. It is for Parliament to decide whether to give the terrorists such a victory.

Compared to these paradoxes, the paradox to be discussed in this chapter may be of a lesser scale. But it is important, and it might take the form of a more positive paradox in its outcome than those previously mentioned. What will be discussed is the paradox between the perceived globalising nature of the threat of terrorism and the growing localism of the police response. The next two sections will describe each of those elements in turn. Explanations for their origins and implications will then be attempted, as well as future prospects.

Globalising Nature of the Threat

The first element of the posited paradox is relatively easy to demonstrate and need not be dwelt upon at length. The claim is that every jurisdiction in the world is now affected by the working assumption that it is seriously threatened by global

6 See Waldron, J., 'Security and Liberty: The image of balance' (2003) *Journal of Political Philosophy*, 11: 191.

7 See HC Debs. vol. 480, col. 620, 13 October 2008, Jacqui Smith.

8 http://www.pm.gov.uk/output/Page15785.asp.

9 'Davis Resignation: The speech', The *Guardian*, 13 June 2008 p. 4. Davis resigned his Parliamentary seat and won the subsequent by-election on a platform of support for human rights: Wainwright, W., and Stratton, A., 'Haltemprice and Howden Byelection', *The Guardian*, 11 July 2008, p. 2.

10 [2004] UKHL 56 at paras 96, 97.

terrorism. This trend towards risk propagation and standardisation has been brought about by the impact of events of 9/11 and is a novel situation in at least two respects.

First, the perception of threat has become more globally dispersed. Before 9/11, many states disputed in international forums the definitional bounds and policy priority which Western states such as the United Kingdom and United States sought to accord to terrorism.[11] Though, as mentioned previously, some progress was made in international criminal law, that progress was faltering and was counterbalanced by failures in other respects – such as the failures to agree a more ambitious international definition of terrorism or to put terrorism in the Rome Statute. After 9/11, the Western viewpoint prevailed, perhaps best signalled by the United Nations Security Resolution 1368, adopted on 12 September 2001, by which the Security Council:

> 3. … Calls on all States to work together urgently to bring to justice the perpetrators, organizers and sponsors of these terrorist attacks and stresses that those responsible for aiding, supporting or harbouring the perpetrators, organizers and sponsors of these acts will be held accountable;
>
> 4. Calls also on the international community to redouble their efforts to prevent and suppress terrorist acts including by increased cooperation and full implementation of the relevant international anti-terrorist conventions and Security Council resolutions …;
>
> 5. Expresses its readiness to take all necessary steps to respond to the terrorist attacks of 11 September 2001, and to combat all forms of terrorism, in accordance with its responsibilities under the Charter of the United Nations ….

After this point, no state can be left in doubt as to the imperative of dealing with terrorism as a requirement of collective security. This degree of prioritisation is indeed so high that some would say has unbalanced the United Nations and caused it to lose sight of values such as human rights and development.[12] The same may be true at national level, where policies can only be taken seriously when they can be shown to impact on security. Thus, in the United States, more notice seems to be taken of environmental issues after the chairman of the National Intelligence Council told Congress that climate change could destabilise 'struggling and poor'

11 See further Donohue, L.K., 'Terrorism and the Counter-Terrorist Discourse' in Ramraj, V.V., Hor, M., and Roach, K., *Global Anti-terrorism Law and Policy* (Cambridge University Press, Cambridge, 2005).

12 See Report of the Secretary General, Protection of Human Rights and Fundamental Freedoms while Countering Terrorism (A/58/266 of 8 August 2003); Secretary-General, In Larger Freedom: towards development, security and human rights for all (A/59/2005).

countries, prompting migration pressures and conflict.[13] Equally, the United Kingdom government has subsumed issues ranging from climate change to poverty all within the rubric of its national security strategy.[14]

Second, the new priority of counter-terrorism has been reflected in legal reaction and international enforcement of it much more so than in the pre-9/11 era. For example, before 9/11, only four states (including the United Kingdom) had ratified the International Convention for the Suppression of the Financing of Terrorism,[15] a pattern reflected with other anti-terrorism international conventions. Within a couple of years after 9/11, almost all states had ratified. Many did so out of the conviction that they were contributing to collective security, but even recalcitrant jurisdictions which might not see themselves in the direct firing-line or might lack political sympathies with Western interests have been forced into reaction. This global reaction has been enforced through two sets of important mechanisms.

One set again consists of UN instruments, including Security Council Resolutions 1267 (regarding sanctions against the Taliban and al-Qa'ida), 1373 (condemning international terrorism in general and demanding action against it), and 1624 (calling upon action against incitement to terrorism). Resolution 1373 is especially broad and forceful as it is expressed in mandatory terms and so amounts to a claim by the Security Council to legislate for international and national jurisdictions, including the obligatory recognition of the Terrorism Finance Convention.[16] Resolution 1373 also embodies within article 6 the more general enforcement mechanism of the Counter-Terrorism Committee.[17] As a result, new criminal law offences and policing powers have been put in place. Prominent examples can be found in the United Kingdom with the Anti-terrorism, Crime and Security Act 2001, which further enhanced the enforcement of terrorism finance measures and restrictions on weapons of mass destruction. It has been followed by the Terrorism Act 2006, Part I of which responds through a neat hegemonic symmetry to the call in Resolution 1624 (sponsored by Tony Blair) for laws against the glorification of terrorism.[18] One might suppose that the United Kingdom would have passed much of this legislation in any event,

---

13 Thomas Fingar, evidence to the House Select Committee on Energy Independence and Global Warming, http://globalwarming.house.gov/tools/2q08materials/files/0069.pdf, 25 June 2008, p. 13.

14 Cabinet Office, The National Security Strategy of the United Kingdom (Cm.7291, London, 2008).

15 See http://www.un.org/law/cod/finterr.htm

16 See Szasz, P., 'The Security Council Starts Legislating' (2002) *American Journal of International Law*, 96: 901.

17 See http://www.un.org/sc/ctc/; Rosand, E., 'Security Council Resolution 1373, The Counter Terrorism Committee and the Fight Against Terrorism' (2003) *American Journal of International Law*, 97: 333.

18 See Walker, C., 'The Legal Definition of "Terrorism" in United Kingdom Law and Beyond' [2007] *Public Law*: 331.

whether demanded by the United Nations or not. But to return to the core point about the globalisation of the reaction to threat, the events of 9/11 have become a watershed since all other jurisdictions, many of which have not been affected by any actual terrorist attack or activity, must equally embody counter-terrorism laws in their codes, many for the first time. If one examines the CTC country reports,[19] then many examples of activity are repeated as each jurisdiction reports variants upon compliance with Resolution 1373. Even the chaotic state of Afghanistan reports the commitment of its military forces as a practical step in the combating of terrorism,[20] and, in the next instalment, reports changes to its Penal Code.[21] Nearly at the other end of the alphabet, Yemen, whose citizens have comprised a significant proportion of detainees at Guantánamo Bay,[22] has reported substantial changes in its Penal Code on money laundering with further implementation of international conventions still pending, the setting up of a General Directorate on Combating Terrorism and Crime within the Ministry of the Interior, and the shutting down of informal *madrassas*.[23]

The other enforcement mechanism concerns the regulation of global networks such capital markets. These are regulated through the Financial Action Task Force's Nine Special recommendations.[24] Use is also made for terrorist purposes of the internal records of other global networks, such as SWIFT (the Society for Worldwide Interbank Financial Telecommunication, dealing with the exchange of standardised financial transaction data) based in Brussels,[25] and the airlines' Passenger Name Records.[26] These control mechanisms are primarily in the

19 http://www.un.org/en/sc/ctc/resources/countryreports.html.

20 S/2002/668.

21 S/2003/353.

22 A figure of 108 Yemenis out of around 776 prisoners is quoted at http://www.humansecuritygateway.com/documents/BROOKINGS_DetaineePop_Guantanamo.pdf, p 7.

23 S/2006/329.

24 http://www.fatf-gafi.org/document/9/0,3343,en_32250379_32236920_34032073_1_1_1_1,00.html. See Zagaris, B., 'The Merging Of The Anti-Money Laundering And Counter-Terrorism Financial Enforcement Regimes After September 11, 2001' (2004) *Berkeley Journal of International Law*, 22: 123 at p. 141; Levi, M., and Reuter, P., 'Money Laundering' (2006) *Crime & Justice*, 34: 289 at p. 306; Wessel, J., 'The Financial Action Task Force' (2006) *Widener L. Rev.*, 13: 169; Shaw, C.J., 'Worldwide War on Terrorist Finance' (2007) *Journal of International Banking Law and Regulation*, 22: 469; Thony, J-F., and Png, C-A., 'FATF Special Recommendations and UN Resolutions on the Financing of Terrorism' (2007) *Journal of Financial Crime*, 14: 150.

25 See Connorton, P.M., 'Tracking Terrorist Financing through SWIFT' (2007) 76 *Fordham L. Rev.* 283; Fuster, G.G., De Hert, P., and Gutwirth, S., 'SWIFT and the Vulnerability of Transatlantic Data Transfers' (2008) *International Review of Law Computers & Technology*, 22: 191.

26 See Council Directive 2004/82/EC on the obligation of carriers to communicate passenger data; ECJ in *European Parliament v Council of the European Union and European Parliament v Commission of the European Communities*, C-317/04 and C-318/04, 2006;

hands of Western states or corporate bodies under their jurisdiction and so are amendable to subversion towards security purposes which are applied against all jurisdictions.

In short, after 9/11, terrorism is depicted as a global concern, as a threat to international peace and security which cannot be disputed or ignored by any state. What are the implications for criminal justice and police enforcement? Here begins the paradox addressed by this chapter, for the global threat does not necessarily produce global courts, global police or even national police. This claim to paradox goes even further and suggests not just the absence of global security policing but the growing localism of security policing.

The Growing Localism of Security Policing

National Security Policing Seems Alive and Well

The second leg of the paradox, concerning the growing localism of security policing, does not seek to oversell the overall thesis of this chapter by denying that the traditional modes of political policing might still be characterised as intelligence-led and politically sensitive.[27] These features have tended to produce structures which are remote from locality, secretive, specialist, and national. In particular, the seriousness of the threat of terrorism and its specialist nature has long shaped policing and security organisational stances in the United Kingdom. Within the Metropolitan Police, a Special Branch was formed in 1883 as one of the earliest detective public police units, in response to the then Irish bombing campaign. Nearly a century later, it was joined in the field by the Anti-Terror Branch, which offered an operational counterpart. This unit began life in 1970 in response to bombings by The Angry Brigade. It became the Anti-Terrorist Branch in March 1976. In later years, the Commander of the Anti-Terrorist Branch was appointed by the Association of Chief Police Officers (ACPO) as the national coordinator for the investigation of acts of terrorism and cases involving animal rights extremism.

As for the secret service organisations, the configuration has been especially secretive and remote. The very existence of the Security Service was not officially

---

Draft Framework Decision on the Use of Passenger Name Records for Law Enforcement Purposes (MEMO/07/449, 2007); Ravich, T.M., 'Is Airline Passenger Profiling Necessary?' (2007) *University of Miami Law Review*, 62: 1; Ntouvas, I., 'Air Passenger Data Transfer to the USA: The decision of the ECJ and latest developments' (2008) *International Journal of Law & Information Technology*, 16: 73.

27 See Walker, C., 'Intelligence and Anti-Terrorism Legislation in the United Kingdom' (2006) *Crime, Law and Social Change*, 44: 387.

acknowledged until the Security Service Act 1989, while its prime goals until the past two decades related to foreign espionage rather than terrorism.[28]

Many national elements of security policing persist today. Within the Metropolitan Police, the pressures of terrorism have sparked the merger of the latter versions of the Metropolitan Special Branch (SO12) and Anti Terror branch (SO13) into the Counter Terrorist Command (SO15) with 1,500 staff and headed by a National Coordinator of Counter Terrorism Investigations who will normally take charge of major terrorist investigations anywhere in the country.[29] For non-Irish and non-international terrorism, there is the National Extremism Tactical Coordination Unit (NETCU) – for tactical advice and guidance.[30] Other specialist units are the National Public Order Intelligence Unit and the National Domestic Extremism Team which are headed by the National Coordinator for Domestic Extremism.[31]

In 2002 a Police International Counter Terror Unit (PICTU) was founded within the Metropolitan Police. PICTU provided 'an advisory and interpretive conduit between the Security Services and police forces on matters relating to international terrorism.' This function has now been taken up by the ACPO TAM (Terrorism and Allied Matters) committee which is a forum of police, security and defence, and performs coordination, policy setting and prioritisation functions for the various organisations.[32] For international police liaison, there are Counter-Terrorism and Extremism Liaison Officers based in foreign police HQs. These are run through the National Terrorism and Extremism Liaison Section (NTELS) based at New Scotland Yard.[33]

Within the secret services field, the relevant organisations have expanded their roles, and their size and cost have grown accordingly. One might argue that national rather than local influence has prevailed. The principal overt step in allowing secret agents into the world of terrorism policing was taken in 1992,[34] when, by fiat of the Home Secretary, the Security Service took over the Metropolitan Police Special Branch's role as the lead Irish Republican terrorism intelligence-gathering agency. Its march into policing fields was extended in 1996 when it was expressly given a role in dealing with organised crime: Security Service Act 1996. The Security Service has grown by around 150 per cent since 2001. The growing importance of this national body entails some troubling debates. One is that the growing

28 See Lustgarten, L., and Leigh, I., *In From the Cold* (Oxford University Press, Oxford, 1994).

29 http://www.met.police.uk/so/counter_terrorism.htm.

30 http://www.netcu.org.uk/default.jsp.

31 http://www.netcu.org.uk/about/nationalresponse.jsp.

32 http://www.acpo.police.uk/ACPOBusinessAreas/TerrorismandAlliedMatters.aspx.

33 See Select Committee on European Union, After Madrid: the EU's response to terrorism, Minutes of Evidence, Memorandum by Association of Chief Police Officers – Terrorism and Allied Matters (ACPO-TAM) (2004-05 HL 53).

34 House of Commons Debates, vol. 207, col. 297, 8 May 1992.

prominence of the Security Service exacerbates underlying concerns about the subjection of these structures to public scrutiny or accountability.[35] For instance, the Director General of the Security Service has declined to give evidence to the Joint Committee on Human Rights to explain his stance on 42 days.[36] The other is that the growing cost highlights concerns about the quality of intelligence and its production across several agencies. As regards quality, problems were uncovered by the Butler Report.[37] The issue of liaison was addressed by the setting up in 2003 of the Joint Terrorism Analysis Centre (JTAC) which is meant to overcome the tensions and rivalries which have existed between different agencies for decades.[38] There remains unwillingness, however, to subject these features to any effective scrutiny. Even the government admits, in its papers, The Governance of Britain, that the Intelligence and Security Committee performs inadequately.[39]

So far, the line of evidence seems to have argued convincingly against the contention of looming localism in security policing. Security policing often does not involve locality or community. Even as late as 2003, the HMIC could issue a report about ports policing called 'Need to Know', which was silent about the community's need to know.[40] But that traditional position is now subject to increasing paradoxes tending in another direction.

Yet International Security Policing Is Neither Alive Nor Well

One is the paradox of the absence of international policing developments. So the features which have traditionally conduced toward national structures continue to conduce against international structures.

The first such factor is the tendency to mistrust the competence of foreign policing organisations. As far as the British police (and possibly the British press) are concerned, nobody does it better, and so foreigners cannot be trusted with sharing in our investigations or intelligence. Witness the often derogatory treatment of the Portuguese police over their handling of the alleged kidnapping of Madeleine

---

35 Even after the clear failure of intelligence represented by the London bombings of July 2005, the government has conceded at most a 'narrative' to set out the incidents. Report of the Official Account of the Bombings in London on the 7th July 2005 (2005-06 HC 1087). See also Intelligence and Security Committee, Report on the London Terrorist Attacks on 7 July 2005 (Cm.6785, London, 2005).

36 See Joint Committee on Human Rights, Counter-Terrorism Policy and Human Rights (Eleventh Report): 42 Days and Public Emergencies (2007-08 HL 116/HC 635) para 8.

37 Committee of Privy Counsellors, Review of Intelligence on Weapons of Mass Destruction (2003-04 HC 898).

38 https://www.mi5.gov.uk/output/joint-terrorism-analysis-centre.html.

39 See The Governance of Britain (Cm 7170, London, 2007) paras 89–96; The Governance of Britain: Constitutional Renewal (Cm 7342, London, 2008) paras 235–44.

40 HM Inspectorate of Constabulary Report, A Need to Know: HMIC's Thematic Inspection of Special Branch and Ports Policing (Home Office, London, 2003).

McCann.[41] In the terrorism field, this mistrust of foreign competence may be exacerbated by the suspicion of sympathy by the overseas police with the cause of the insurgents. Such accusations of collusion often arose against the Irish Gardai[42] in connection with the IRA.

Second, there is the strong tendency of national sovereigns to covet control over national security, including the freedoms to make political choices as to who are the nation's friends or foes. Therefore, there has been resistance to the pooling of sovereignty over terrorism, so that the designation of terrorist groups at a European level[43] requires unanimous consent.

In the light of these two factors, international security policing is stunted, and there is localism in that sense. This tendency to the national and local may be especially marked in powerful and geographically isolated jurisdictions such as the United Kingdom and the United States, where hegemonic power can be exercised more effectively. In the case of the United Kingdom, there is the additional factor of the fundamental contestation of the European vision in terms of it being the opposite to a Federal or integrative project. However, the results are clear enough at the level of international institutions. For example, Europol's involvement in the terrorism field seems to achieve little beyond facile TE-SAT situation and trend reports with their sweeping claims and muddy definitions.[44] It certainly does not act as a supranational force, and information exchange remains voluntary.[45]

The Trend of Local and Community Security Policing Is Born

The principal point of this chapter is that an apparently paradoxical facet of the impact of global terrorism is an emergent trend of returning political policing to localities and communities or, more accurately still, placing it there for the first time in the era of modernity. This trend is at least evident in the United Kingdom which has witnessed the emergence of structures and operational policies which

---

41 See Foster, P., 'Original Madeleine Theory may be Right, Says Portuguese Chief', *The Times*, 23 October 2007, p. 5.

42 See Cory Collusion Inquiry Report, Chief Superintendent Breen and Superintendent Buchanan (http://cain.ulst.ac.uk/issues/collusion/cory/cory03breenbuchanan.pdf, 2003); Cory Collusion Inquiry Report, Lord Justice Gibson and Lady Gibson (http://cain.ulst.ac.uk/issues/collusion/cory/cory03gibson.pdf, 2003). The former allegations are still being investigated by the Smithwick Tribunal of Inquiry (http://www.smithwicktribunal.ie/smithwick/HOMEPAGE.html).

43 See Regulations (EC) 881/2002 and (EC) 2580/2001, as amended.

44 See http://www.europol.europa.eu/index.asp?page=publications&language=.

45 See Douglas-Scott, S., 'The Rule of Law in the European Union – Putting the security into the area of freedom, security and justice' (2004) *European Law Review* 29: 219; Gerspacher, N., 'The Roles of International Police Cooperation Organizations' (2005) *European Journal of Crime, Criminal Law and Criminal Justice*, 13: 413; Muller-Wille, B., 'The Effect of International Terrorism on EU Intelligence Co-operation' (2008) *Journal of Common Market Studies*, 46: 49.

are more sensitive to the localities in which they operate and upon which they impact. The trend takes several forms.

Within the uniformed police, the most notable change is the establishment of, so far, four police regional Counter Terrorism Units in 2006.[46] The locations are West Midlands, West Yorkshire, Greater Manchester, and Strathclyde. Each CTU has around 350 staff, not all police but also interpreters, lawyers and accountants, who are involved in the gathering of intelligence and also operational investigations. They liaise closely with the Security Service and other security services, with the initiation of investigations being both directed and self-generating. But a significant part of their work, distinct from the old Special Branches which they incorporate, is 'community engagement' and 'consequence management' after operations such as arrests. More generally, CTU officers need to liaise with basic command units down to neighbourhood policing and community leaders. The need to engage in local community policing at this level is now recognised since the CTU require information to flow upwards. The terrorists are in the community, and it is the community which has most information about them. In addition, they must manage the public appearance of security policing. When the security services were chasing isolated Russian spies, and when there was no referent local community (except perhaps Cambridge University), the public were not affected and did not even need to know, since the public could not help with the chase. When chasing British Muslim men, the situation is transformed.

Beyond the CTUs, there are 16 Regional Intelligence Cells which have involved the Special Branches being been formed into regional clusters, along with a National Coordinator of Special Branches.[47]

The result of these institutional police changes signals a much more public and localised interface. This stance has begun to be reflected in operational policy documents. One of the most sensitive concerns the powers to stop and search under section 44 of the Terrorism Act 2000.[48] This provision is notorious for the fact that, having been authorised on application by senior police officer in a given police district, it does not require any element of reasonable suspicion as a basis for exercise by the operational officer. Inevitably, the allegation is often made that it is used in a racially patterned way in its outcome or even that racial profiling is consciously used in determining its exercise. Published statistics

46 Cabinet Office, The National Security Strategy of the United Kingdom (Cm.7291, London, 2008) para 4.11.

47 H.M. Inspectorate of Constabulary, *A Need to Know: HMIC's Thematic Inspection of Special Branch and Ports Policing* (London, 2003); Government Response to the Intelligence and Security Committee's Report into the London Terrorist Attacks on 7 July 2005 (Cm 6786, London, 2006) p. 6.

48 See Walker, C., *The Anti-Terrorism Legislation* (Oxford University Press, Oxford, 2002) chap. 5.

Table 11.1: Usage of Section 44[49]

Year	Stops *(n)*			Terrorism/other arrests *(n)*			Ethnicity *(n)*[50]			Location %		
	s 44(1)	s 44(2)	Total	s 44(1)	s 44(2)	Totals	White	Black	Asian	Metropolitan Police	City (London)	Other
2001/2	7,604	946	8,550	20/149	0/20	20/169	6,629	529	744	49	32	19
2002/3	16,761	4,774	21,577	11/280	7/79	18/359	14,429	1,745	2,989	61	21	18
2003/4	21,287	8,120	29,407	14/358	5/112	19/470	20,637	2,704	3,668	53	25	23
2004/5	21,121	10,941	32062	35/240	24/153	59/393	23,389	2,511	3,485	40	20	40
2005/6	25,479	19064	44543	46/246	59/212	105/458	30,837	4,155	6,805	51	15	35

49 Jones, A., and Singer, L., Statistics on Race and the Criminal Justice System – 2006 (Ministry of Justice, London, 2007).
50 Some are not recorded.

relating to the usage of s 44 are far from complete,[51] but they do reveal that, since 2000, five manifest patterns have occurred: a sustained increase in the use of this power, a low rate of consequent terrorist arrests, a higher rate of non-terrorist arrests, a disproportionate impact on Asian ethnic minorities and an uneven geographical delivery.[52]

The potential for causing community disharmony is evident, and the House of Commons Home Affairs Committee has picked up on this danger by finding 'a clear perception among all our Muslim witnesses that Muslims are being stigmatised by the operation of the Terrorism Act: this is harmful to community relations.'[53] As a result, the Association of Chief Police Officers, and latterly the National Police Improvement Agency (NPIA), have sought to allay concerns by issuing guidance which departs from the old, secretive, cloak-and-dagger approach to security policing. Instead, the NPIA's *Practice Advice on Stop and Search Powers*, issued in 2006,[54] states that in the exercise of these powers, the police are instructed that ethnicity should not be used alone as the basis for exercise on the grounds that '[a]ctions define a terrorist not ethnicity, race or religion.'[55] It again emphasises community involvement under s 44, since it will increase confidence, reassure the public, and encourage the flow of intelligence.[56] However, this general rule is subject to some reflection on whether it is safe to pass on information about the location and extent of section 44 activity. Operational reasons might also rule out prior consultation, but the Advice does consolidate the previous version and demands such consultation as soon as possible, so that communities are made to feel 'valued and respected'.[57] This advice should also be interpreted in light of the report from Her Majesty's Inspectorate of Constabulary, *A Need to Know: HMIC's Thematic Inspection of Special Branch and Ports Policing*, which emphasises 'the vital importance of extending the reach of the national security agencies by further utilising the close links between local police and the communities in which they

---

51 See Sir William Macpherson, *The Stephen Lawrence Inquiry*, Cm 4262-I (1999), recommendations 61–2; Home Office, Police and Criminal Evidence Act 1984: Code A (2008) 12–13.

52 See further Walker, C., 'Know Thine Enemy as Thyself' (2008) *Melbourne Law Review*, 32: 275.

53 Home Affairs Committee, Terrorism and Community Relations (2005-06) HC 165-I para 153. See further Brown, B., 'Community Policing in Post-September 11 America' (2007) *Police Practice & Research* 239.

54 The publisher is the National Centre for Policing Excellence (now the National Policing Improvement Agency), and the document covers all common statutory powers and not just the Terrorism Act (see http://www.npia.police.uk/en/6664.htm). The author thanks Charlie Hedges for the supply of a copy. See also Liberty, Response to Consultation (http://www.liberty-human-rights.org.uk/pdfs/policy06/ncpe-stop-and-search-practice.pdf, 2006).

55 National Centre for Policing Excellence, Practice Advice on Stop and Search, *loc. cit.* p. 27.

56 Ibid., p. 12.

57 Ibid., p. 14.

work.'[58] These messages are reinforced by the *Stop & Search Manual* which was published in 2005 by the Stop and Search Action Team in the Home Office,[59] though its statements on community involvement primarily relate to other powers.[60]

As one might expect, the localisation of the secret security services has been more hesitant, but there is again clear evidence both of decentralisation and a more public-friendly outlook. Decentralisation is not yet tantamount to community spying. So, the Security Service's increasing reach, previously very much confined to London and Northern Ireland, is evidenced by the setting up in 2006 and onwards of eight regional offices[61] (including in West Yorkshire). Yet, this physical diaspora is not yet accompanied by the express mandate to go out and network with the local populace in any systematic or overt manner, and even the location and activities of these offices remains secret. Nevertheless, the very establishment of regional offices must represent some kind of aspiration for more local contact. As for the more public-friendly outlook, aside from a more ambitious website, this trend is best evidenced by the hosting of the National Counter Terrorism Security Office (NaCTSO) within the National Security Advice Centre (NSAC) to handle liaison with the nationwide network of specialist police advisors known as Counter Terrorist Security Advisors (CTSAs) who can offer to the public (especially big businesses) help on counter terrorism security.[62] NaCTSO has since 2007 been located within the Centre for the Protection of National Infrastructure, which is within the Security Service and also incorporates the National Infrastructure Security Co-ordination Centre (NISCC) and MI5's National Security Advice Centre (NSAC).[63]

The third aspect of localism in security responses concerns the Civil Contingency Act 2004.[64] Part I deals with the phases of planning and resilience building, and it is notable that the Act's prime institutional mechanism is the Local Resilience Forum (LRF). This is the forum in which what are called 'Category 1 responders' have to cooperate under section 2 and to meet on a regular basis and plan how they will avoid the catastrophes of floods, plagues, and pestilence, as well as terrorism. The Minister of State for the Cabinet Office emphasised that 'The local response capability is the foundation of our response to all emergencies.'[65] The Cabinet

58 Her Majesty's Inspectorate of Constabulary, A Need to Know: HMIC's Thematic Inspection of Special Branch and Ports Policing (Home Office, London, 2003) para 2.3.

59 Stop and Search Team, Stop & Search Manual (http://police.homeoffice.gov.uk/news-and-publications/publication/operational-policing/stopandsearch-intermanual1.pdf?view=Binary, 2005).

60 Ibid., 18, 21.

61 House of Commons Debates, vol. 418, col. 303, 25 February 2004, David Blunkett.

62 http://www.nactso.gov.uk/.

63 http://www.cpni.gov.uk/. See further Walker, C., 'The governance of the Critical National Infrastructure' [2008] *Public Law* 323.

64 See Walker, C. and Broderick, J., *The Civil Contingencies Act 2004: Risk, Resilience and the Law in the United Kingdom* (Oxford University Press, Oxford, 2006) chap 4.

65 HC Debs. vol. 416, col. 1105, 19 January 2004, Douglas Alexander.

Office goes on to say that 'Category 1 responders will take the lead in the business of these forums, which may meet every six months, with Category 2 organisations required to attend or to be represented as appropriate.'[66] The LRFs are established on the basis of police force areas, but the chairing of the body is usually located within local authority bodies rather than the police. In this way, they follow the precedent set for multi-agency working in crime prevention under the Crime and Disorder Act 1998. The fact that the relations are statutory is thought to be helpful to encourage the sharing of sensitive information, though the laws or practices relating to official secrecy or security clearance have not been changed. LRFs do not have a role in the response phase – the lead agency identified within the plans will at that point take charge, and at a local level, it is often the police. In this way, LRFs are planning teams not action teams (the exception being Scotland, where the functions coalesce). When an emergency arises, the response and recovery phases will be dealt with by Strategic Coordinating Groups – these will strongly overlap in terms of membership, but are constituted differently and form a part of a different chain of command.[67]

LRFs are further elaborated in Regulation 4 of the Civil Contingencies Act 2004 (Contingency Planning) Regulations 2005,[68] which establishes that there must be a forum and confers its title. A few other substantive working rules are there specified. One is that Category 1 responders in a particular local resilience area must hold a meeting at least once every six months. Next, every Category 1 responder must, so far as reasonably practicable, attend such a meeting or arrange for representation at that meeting. Category 2 responders have the same level of duty of attendance whenever specifically invited to a specific meeting, but in the case of other meetings simply have to consider whether it is 'appropriate' to attend the meeting or to be represented. This weaker level of commitment may address the concerns of those national bodies, such as utilities, who might otherwise have to attend many LRFs. Central government departments or agencies (unless specified in the Act) are not present at LRFs, but one notable exception is the recognition of the need to maintain a link with the armed forces through the Regional Brigade, though military attendance is not formally required.

The extent of localism which is represented by the LRFs is a departure from the previous regime under the Civil Defence Act 1948. Whilst it likewise predominantly concentrated on the powers and duties of localities, section 1 did regulate the role of Ministers and made it 'part of the functions of the designated Minister to take such steps as appear to him from time to time to be necessary

66 Cabinet Office, The Draft Civil Contingencies Bill: Explanatory Notes etc., (London, 2003) para 24. See further ibid., para 31; Defence Committee, Draft Civil Contingencies Bill (2002-03 HC 557) para 35.

67 See Walker, C. and Broderick, J., *The Civil Contingencies Act 2004: Risk, Resilience and the Law in the United Kingdom* (Oxford University Press, Oxford, 2006) chap. 8.

68 SI No. 2042.

or expedient for civil defence purposes', followed by an enumeration of more specific duties. By contrast, the 2004 Act places no front-line statutory duties on ministers.[69]

The trend of growing localism and community engagement is paradoxical to many 'old hands' who struggle to make sense of security policing in the new setting which does not grant absolute operational secrecy. Old habits die hard with some of them, and so many of the initiatives which here described are far from perfect in their execution because of restrictions in the flow of information. Only after much deliberation has the Cabinet Office circulated to responders an annual National Risk Register as to the types and strength of various risks which responders should reflect in their planning processes.[70] At the same time, community-based policing has itself a long tradition, and so some police officers have found more aggressive preventative approaches to be equally uncomfortable.[71] In any event, there is change in the air, and this raises the question as to why it is happening. In terms of explanations, the trend might be attributed to four factors. Since these provide on reflection sound reasons for the trend of localism, it may only be a matter of time before the perception of paradox is dissipated in the minds of practitioners.

The first concerns the development of counter-terrorism strategy – made public in 2006 under the acronym of 'CONTEST'.[72] The four elements are suitably comprehensive and are certainly not confined to covert policing in the shadows or even the more overt processes of arrest and prosecution.

> The strategy is divided into four principal strands: PREVENT, PURSUE, PROTECT, and PREPARE. … Preventing terrorism by tackling the radicalisation of individuals … Pursuing terrorists and those that sponsor them … Protecting the public, key national services, and UK interests overseas … Preparing for the consequences.

There are a number of points to be picked up here. One is to reiterate just made about contingency planning and the Act of 2004 which is evidently very relevant to 'prepare' and 'protect'. The police and security services alone cannot alone 'prepare' and 'protect' in these wide senses. Hence the need for Local Resilience

---

69 See Cabinet Office, The Government's Response to the Report of the Joint Committee on the Draft Civil Contingencies Bill (Incorporating the Government's Response to the Report of the House of Commons Defence Committee on the Draft Civil Contingencies Bill) (Cm.6078, London, 2004), para 50.

70 http://www.cabinetoffice.gov.uk/resource-library/national-risk-register.

71 See Ortiz, C., 'Policing Terrorism' (2007) *Criminal Justice Studies*, 20: 91.

72 Home Office, Countering International Terrorism (Cm.6888, London, 2006). See further Gregory, F., 'National Governance Structures to Manage the Response to Terrorist Threats and Attacks' in Wilkinson, P., (ed.), *Homeland Security in the UK* (Routledge, London, 2007).

Forums, which are multi-agency, and resilience also requires locally based responses rather than centrally based responses.

The emphasis upon 'Prevent' is not so new. After all, prevention through detention without trial or through other executive-based policies like exclusion or control has been around for a while.[73] But, once again, 'prevent' is being conceived in broad terms. In previous eras, it might have been described as a campaign for 'hearts and minds', a term coined in the Malaya Emergency in 1952.[74] Nowadays, in the aftermath of the bombings in London in 2005, the United Kingdom has increased substantially its efforts to address the processes by which extremists become extreme enough to be prepared to kills others, especially seeking to interdict that process in young Muslim men and its end result in suicide bombings. There are several strands to this response, including a broad policy initiative which was called Preventing Extremism Together in 2005.[75] A number of proposals emerged from this work in reports in November 2005. A document in 2007 from the Department for Communities and Local Government, rationalised the responses around four approaches: promoting shared values; supporting local solutions; building civic capacity and leadership; and strengthening faith institutions and leadership.[76] Unfortunately, the causes of extremism are difficult to identify with any certainty and controversial and difficult to address,[77] nor, if dangerous consequences for rights to thought and expression are to be avoided, should they be unthinkingly depicted as synonymous with extremism.[78] In its Report of the

73 See Walker, C., 'Constitutional Governance and Special Powers Against Terrorism' (1997) *Columbia Journal of Transnational Law*, 35: 1; Walker, C., 'Keeping Control of Terrorists without Losing Control of Constitutionalism' (2007) *Stanford Law Review*, 59: 1395.

74 The phrase came from General Templer, Director of Operations and High Commissioner for Malaya, in 1952: 'The answer lies not in pouring more troops into the jungle, but in the hearts and minds of the Malayan People'. See Kitson, F., *Low-Intensity Operations* (Faber and Faber, London, 1971); Stubbs, R., *Hearts and Minds in Guerrilla Warfare* (Oxford University Press, Singapore, 1989); Ramakrishna, K., *Emergency Propaganda* (RoutledgeCurzon, Richmond, 2001); Lennon, A.T.J., *The Battle for Hearts and Minds* (MIT, Cambridge, MA, 2003).

75 See Preventing Extremism Together' Working Groups Aug–Oct 2005 (Home Office, London, 2005). See McGhee, D., *The End of Multiculturalism* (Open University Press, Maidenhead, 2008) chap. 3.

76 Department for Communities and Local Government, Preventing Violent Extremism – Winning Hearts and Minds (http://www.communities.gov.uk/publications/communities/preventingviolentextremism, 2007) para 10. See the further elaborations in Prevent Strategy – A Guide for Local Partners (http://www.communities.gov.uk/publications/communities/preventstrategy, 2008) and Preventing Violent Extremism: Next Steps for Communities (http://www.communities.gov.uk/publications/communities/preventingviolentextremismnext, 2008).

77 See further Abbas, T. (ed.), *Islamic Political Radicalism: A European Perspective* (Edinburgh University Press, Edinburgh, 2007).

78 See McGhee, D., *The End of Multiculturalism* (Open University Press, Maidenhead, 2008) p. 30.

Official Account of the Bombings in London on 7th July, the government sought to place 'Radicalisation in context'.[79] It concluded that a variety of factors could be important: attendance at a mosque linked to extremists; the influence of an extreme spiritual leader; the internet; the role of personal mentors; and then bonding with a group of fellow extremists. A more comprehensive version offered by Jacqui Smith in 2008 still pointed to 'ideologues' and vulnerable young people, which still is too much oriented to external influence and ignores self-generation.[80] But she did also include ideology, communities which are ill-equipped to challenge extremism, and grievances which may be domestic and foreign. Contrast these manifold and vague indicia with the ludicrous comments of the Home Secretary in which he urged Muslim families to 'watch for signs of brainwashing in their children by radicals grooming them to kill themselves in order to murder others. ... Look for the tell-tale signs now and talk to them before their hatred grows and you risk losing them for ever'.[81] The complex picture of 'neighbour' terrorism arising within the United Kingdom is not easily depicted as simply psychotic behaviour or the religious fervour of Muslims[82] but is sometimes more suggestive of theories of social anomie than theories of radicalisation, with minorities[83] of young Muslim men caught between the conservative and unreplicable culture of their parents and the unappealing culture of the West – 'torn between two cultures' as Ed Hussein would say – both to be rejected in favour of a pure and strong identity based on Islamism.[84] The modal setting of the small group of action-oriented friends certainly makes life more difficult for security services that cannot follow formal chains of command and must distinguish social from operational contacts and group affinity from radical rejection.[85] But there is no certain relationship between radicalisation and violence.

A further and more straightforward policy strand of 'prevent' related specifically to mosques and imams in the light of the activities of notorious foreign preachers such as Abu Hamza, Abu Qatada, and Omar Bakri Muhammed should be curbed; policy responses included tighter immigration and asylum rules, as well

79 (2005-06 HC 1087) Annex B. See also Home Office, Countering International Terrorism (Cm.6888, London, 2006) para 48.

80 Smith, J., 'Our Shared Values – A shared responsibility' (International Centre for the Study of Radicalisation and Political Violence, First International Conference, 2008).

81 McGrory, D., and Tendler, S., 'Reid's Message to Muslims is Drowned Out by Radicals', *The Times*, 21 September 2006, p. 6.

82 Sen, A., *Identity and Violence* (Allen Lane, London, 2006) p. 14.

83 Of course, the majority adapt and mix divergent cultures: Jacobson, J., *Islam in Transition* (Routledge, London, 1998) p. 80.

84 See Siedler, V.J., *Urban Fears and Global Terrors* (Routledge, 2007) p. 98.

85 See Post, J.M., 'The Socio-Cultural Underpinnings of Terrorist Psychology' in Bjørgo, T., (ed.), *Root Causes of Terrorism* (Routledge, London, 2005); Atran, S., 'Who Becomes a Terrorist Today?' (2008) II 5 Perspectives on Terrorism; Nasiri, O., *Inside the Global Jihad* (Hurst & Co, London, 2006); Sageman, M., *Leaderless Jihad* (University of Pennsylvannia Press, Philadeplphia, 2007).

as the application of criminal law offences of solicitation of murder, glorification of terrorism, and the possession of information for terrorist purposes.[86] A more positive, albeit somewhat fumbling initiative concerns attempts by the government to define and propagate 'Britishness', leading into wider debates about citizenship rights and responsibilities.[87] In the New Labour world order, Britishness turns out to mean rather universal values.[88] Many people would define Britishness in terms of cultural features, such as history or even food and football, and indeed diversity.[89] Seeking to impose a 'good' or 'mainstream' cultural identity risks further distaste amongst the disenchanted.[90] 'Britishness' and other 'identities cannot be confected in this way' from the shelf but are lived, generational experiences,[91] some of which make us proud and some of which should make us ashamed.

A second, related reason why there is a more local and public trend in anti-terrorism policing is that strategies which impact on the whole population in terms of their pockets and in terms of them their daily lives being affected by identity checks or CCTV[92] and in terms of them seeing the impact on a wide range of others must be handled in different ways to the days of espionage when there was no real need for transparency. If the police wish to undertake armed exercises in the centre of town, then they would be wise to let people know what they are doing.[93] If they wish to devise new policies about shooting to kill, then they can hardly expect the community to be sympathetic rather than shocked at their seemingly

86 See Walker, C., 'The Treatment of Foreign Terror Suspects' (2007) *Modern Law Review*, 70: 427.

87 See Home Office, Strength in Diversity (http://www.homeoffice.gov.uk/documents/cons-strength-in-diverse-170904/, 2004) chap.2; Lord Goldsmith, Citizenship: Our Common Bond (Ministry of Justice, http://www.justice.gov.uk/docs/citizenship-report-full.pdf, 2008). Following an initiative by the Home Secretary in 2002, a 'Life in the UK' test for would-be citizens comprises questions about British history, customs and values. See http://www.lifeintheuktest.gov.uk/. Citizenship was added in 2000 to the National Curriculum for schools. See Advisory Group on Education for Citizenship and the Teaching of Democracy in Schools (http://www.teachingcitizenship.org.uk/page?p=13).

88 Gordon Brown, 'Liberty and the Role of the State' (Chatham House, http://www.guardian.co.uk/politics/2005/dec/13/labour.uk, 13 December 2005).

89 See, for example, Commission for Racial Equality, Britishness (http://www.cre.gov.uk/downloads/what_is_britishness.pdf, 2005).

90 Siddiqui, H., 'Muslim-Bashing Dilutes our Democratic Values', *The Toronto Star*, 11 June 2006, p. A17. See further Brighton, S., 'British Muslims, Multiculturalism and UK Foreign Policy' (2007) *International Affairs*, 83: 1.

91 Nairn, T. (ed.), *Gordon Brown: Bard of Britishness* (Institute of Welsh Affairs, Cardiff, 2006) p. 13.

92 See Surveillance Study Network, A Report on the Surveillance Society (Information Commissioner, Wilmslow, 2006); House of Commons Home Affairs Committee, A Surveillance Society? (2007–08 HC 58).

93 See Carter, C., 'PC was Killed by Gas Cartridge', *The Guardian*, 11 June 2008 p. 9.

cavalier planning when they shoot dead a passing Brazilian.[94] Thus, there is now too much at stake in terms of impact on politics, social living, human rights, and public finances to leave these issues to the securitocracy.

A third related explanation is that the expanded remit of countering terrorism has resulted in new and expanded institutional formations, especially the Counter Terrorism Units. Though their cultural life has hardly started, it is arguable that the professional culture is likely to differ from the professional cultures of the old Special Branches and the like. The many extra officers who have been recruited are younger and have been transferred from ordinary community-based policing rather than being steeped in detection or special branches.

The fourth explanation concerns the dynamics of 'neighbour terrorism' which became evident in 2004 and 2005.[95] The bombings in London of 7 July 2005 rightly gave pause for official reflection upon anti-terrorism laws and community relations. The Prime Minister, Tony Blair, issued a stark warning on the 5 August 2005 of future amendments: 'Let no one be in any doubt, the rules of the game are changing.'[96] What was so remarkable about the London bombings of the 7 July 2005 was that they were perpetrated by British citizens – they were 'neighbour terrorists' like Mohammad Sidique Khan. There are now regular warnings from the security officials that the numbers of extremists is growing exponentially. The head of MI5, Dame Eliza Manningham-Buller, revealed in November 2006 that there were 1,600 waiting in the wings in the ranks of the 'enemy within'.[97] The head of the security service MI5 has revealed a dramatic rise in the number of terrorists believed to be operating in Britain to about 4,000. Speaking in central Manchester in late 2007, Jonathan Evans, said the service was aware of more than 2,000 specific people who now pose a direct threat to national security – and he said there may be as many who have not been identified.'[98] These people are amidst us – they are not barbarians at the gate or strange aliens who live in caves in the Tora Bora mountains.[99] So, while Tony Blair had in mind foreign terrorist suspects such as Abu Hamza, Abu Qatada, and Omar Bakri Muhammed,

94 See Independent Police Complaints Commission, Stockwell One: Investigation into the shooting of Jean Charles de Menezes at Stockwell underground station on 22 July 2005 (London, 2007), Stockwell Two: An investigation into complaints about the Metropolitan Police Service's handling of public statements following the shooting of Jean Charles de Menezes on 22 July 2005 (London, 2007).

95 See Walker, C., '"Neighbour Terrorism" and the "All Risks" Policing of Terrorism' (2009) *Journal of National Security Law & Policy*, 3: 121. This switch in emphasis has not been noticed by all; compare McGhee, D., *The End of Multiculturalism* (Open University Press, Maidenhead, 2008) pp. 11, 15, 44.

96 Ford, R., and Bennett, R., 'Row Over Tougher Rules on Preachers of Hate', *The Times*, 6 August 2005, p. 1.

97 'The Al-Qaeda Challenge', *The Times*, 10 November 2006, p. 19.

98 'We'll Beat Terrorists', *Manchester Evening News*, 6 November 2007, p. 4.

99 President Bush referred to bin Laden as 'a guy who, three months ago, was in control of a county. Now he's maybe in control of a cave': President, General Franks Discuss War

and either locked them up or sent them packing, the radical changes of approach related to neighbours.

This switch in emphasis from exotic foreign cave-dweller to nondescript neighbour causes us to reassess policies and to engage more with the communities from which our errant neighbours emerge. This change is fundamental in the field of terrorism and security. In the past, terrorism policing was marked by features such as secrecy and unaccountability. The relevant agencies have refused for operational reasons to engage with local communities, inform them what is going on, or even account to them afterwards. Now, the National Policing Plan 2005–2008 requires the police to build and increase trust and confidence within minority faith communities as part of their counter-terrorist strategy.[100] The police emphasise that they need to work with the community and that terrorism policing is for all the police and all the public, in line with the mainstream view that 'the public are the most important weapon in tackling crime'.[101] One might offer the example of the bomb manufacturing activity by the 7/7 bombers, whose activities caused leaves to fall from the trees outside their flat in Alexandra Grove because of the hydrogen peroxide. Why did no one report this, ask the police?[102] As a result, there are developing more general policing projects which seek to foster the idea that counter-terrorism policing is for all police ranks and also for communities. Communities in turn may need help to deal with the preoccupation of a minority with extremism, both by being tough on extremism and also on the causes of extremism. So this dynamic requires much more backing from the locality not only in identifying today's terrorists but also in preventing the birth of tomorrow's terrorists. To be tough on terrorism and on the causes of terrorism is a much more ambitious undertaking and has inevitably embroiled security policing bodies in community work.

The Future of Security Policing

Given the prognosis of the successive Directors-General of the Security Service and given the fatal attraction to political leaders of presenting to the public a strong and hard face against terrorism, it is difficult to see the trends involved in the mainstreaming of counter-terrorism policy and action being reversed, nor should they be. Those trends in many ways parallel 'normal' policing and can be expected

Effort <http://georgewbush-whitehouse.archives.gov/news/releases/2001/12/20011228-1.html> (28 December 2001).

100 (Home Office, 2004) para 3.60.

101 Casey, L., 'Engaging Communities in Fighting Crime' (Cabinet Office, London, 2008) p. 7. See further Brown, B., 'Community Policing in Post-September 11 America' (2007) *Police Practice & Research*, 8: 239.

102 Speech by Andrew Staniforth, Conference on Crime and Disorder Act 1998: Ten Years On – Community Safety, Leeds University, May 2008.

to include concepts such as community involvement, multi-agency working and public assurance. Elements are already present – especially public assurance, albeit that it is bizarrely sought through the passage of ever more repressive legislation. Those specialist policing units which have sought to distance themselves from communities, notably the Serious Organised Crime Agency, have not yet proven themselves to be all the better for their detachment and may suffer from confused perceptions as to priorities and accountability within and without that body.[103]

What perhaps remains to be taken from the mainstream policing vocabulary is the language of managerialism,[104] which might actually be a useful antidote to some of the wilder claims about threat and response. Thus, in the area of security policing, there is a dearth of research-based policy. Indeed, it is not even revealed what are the targets in terms of gains which are to result from the vastly increased budgets of the police and security services. On this score, the relevant Public Service Agreement 26, which seeks to emulate contractual language and to claim that the government has 'no higher duty' than combating terrorism, is not of course a binding obligation nor are there, because of claims to national security, even any published indications as to accountability or governance.[105] It is possible that politicians will eventually tire of expending so many resources for so few discernible results and will not be able to continue to frighten the public into quiescence.[106] However, there are few signs that there is any consensus upon a truly alternative approach.

103 Harfield, C., 'SOCA: A Paradigm Shift in British policing' (2006) *British Journal of Criminology* 46: 743; O'Neill, S., 'It Was Meant to Make Life Hell for Criminals but is Soca Just Too Soft?', *The Times*, 13 May 2008, p. 4.

104 See Raine, J.W. and Willson, M.J., 'Beyond Managerialism in Criminal Justice' (1996) *Howard Journal of Criminal Justice*, 36: 20.

105 HM Treasury, PSA Delivery Agreement 26: reducing the risk to the UK and its interests overseas from international terrorism (http://www.hm-treasury.gov.uk/d/pbr_csr07_annexc_92.pdf, 2007).

106 See Furedi, F., *Invitation to Terror* (Continuum Books, London, 2007).

Index

Page numbers in *italics* refer to tables.

www.ingramcontent.com/pod-product-compliance
Ingram Content Group UK Ltd.
Pitfield, Milton Keynes, MK11 3LW, UK
UKHW010955180926
475701UK00004B/377
9781138254022